RECOGNIZED IN FLIGHT

Recognized in Flight

A MEMOIR

Maya M. Porter

SYCAMORE HILL PRESS

Produced in the United States of America
ISBN-978-1-7329873-1-9
Cover design by Garin Chad Wiggins
Cover photo and background painting by Leslie Coston
Text design by Allshouse Graphic Design
Copyediting by Susanna Brinnan
Published by Sycamore Hill Press
sycamorehillpress@gmail.com

Excerpt from Three Dreams by Willis Harman on p. 301 used by
permission from Berrett-Koehler Publishers.
Photo of Willis Harman on p. 300 used by permission from
Berrett-Koehler Publishers.
Photo of Lou Mohley and Kate McKeown on p. 244 used by
permission from Kate McKeown.
Photo of Maya Porter on p. 302 by Kimberly L. Pilot.

Recognized in Flight

We stared, unblinking,
Not ten feet apart.
Such an odd-looking bird,
Strangely out of place
Perched atop my sun-warmed car
That cool October morning.
I wondered what it was.

Then suddenly it launched itself,
And soaring above my littleness
I saw its white-barred wings
And smiled.
Of course—
It was a nighthawk.

And something in me quieted.
I, too,
Will someday
Be recognized
In flight.

Maya Porter
[Betty Jean Leas]
1971

Contents

Part 2 – On the Move

Part 3 – Coming Home

Preface

When my last sibling died, I commented wistfully to my daughter, "Now there's no one else alive who remembers my childhood."

"Well," she replied, smiling, "Now you can have any childhood you want."

As I look back on my life today, in my eighties, I wonder how I got here. What shaped me all these years? Who influenced me? What pushed me or pulled me to develop in the direction I did? This book explores those questions. It also provides a brief family history, told from my point of view. Of course it is biased and incomplete, as all histories are.

But a memoir is not really a history—it's what I remember. I've written my memories as best I can, knowing they may not match other people's. That is to be expected, and does not mean any of us are wrong. All memory is subjective, and any discrepancies between my words and the reader's experience are not intentional.

Every memoirist has to decide what to include and what to leave out, and I have struggled with that decision. I've tried to balance honesty with discretion; I've omitted some events because telling them would not only embarrass me but would invade other people's privacy. As much as I could, I've avoided revealing events in other people's lives that were not directly involved in my life, which explains why my children do not have more prominent roles here. They will tell their own stories when they are ready.

As for the facts, I have checked their accuracy as much as I reasonably could. My niece Barbara gave me letters she found in her late father's effects that were extremely helpful—and in some cases, surprising. They included letters I wrote to her father, my brother Frank, when I was in my late teens and early twenties, letters I don't remember writing and

"

that include material about events I had completely forgotten. I have contacted relatives I haven't talked to in years; consulted old letters, school records, telegrams, WWII rationing books, and photo albums; and of course searched the Internet many times. I've changed some people's names, just to play it safe. They will know who they are, and they will know why.

Looking back over so many years, I've gained valuable insights about myself. Recounting some periods was difficult but instructive. May the result help my children and grandchildren understand and appreciate their history as well as mine.

Acknowledgments

I am deeply grateful to the Life Writing Group sponsored by the Fayetteville Quakers. Starting in 2015, they encouraged me throughout the writing process with their insightful, kind, and honest comments on every chapter. The group membership has changed over the years, but I especially want to thank Jim Adams, Mary Cochran, Seajay Crosson, Sarah Daniels, Debbie Graff, Jay Johnson, Bettina Lehovec, Dolores Mead, Jane Purtle, and Garin Wiggins. The resulting hours of revisions improved the book enormously.

I also thank my niece Barbara Moyer for the large cache of letters from her late father's file cabinets and for consulting with me on several family events.

Thank you to genealogist cousin Valerie LaRobardier, who supplied extensive information on our fathers' family history, including a 23-page genealogy going back nine generations.

I appreciate the various friends and family who read the earliest drafts and gave me feedback that guided me as I developed the manuscript.

Thanks also go to Susanna Brinnon for copy editing, to Shaun Allshouse for the book design, and to Garin Wiggins for designing the cover.

PART 1

Growing Up

1 The Early Days

My parents were among the few courageous or unlucky couples who had babies during the depth of the Great Depression; they actually produced three between 1929 and 1933. I made my appearance on April 6, 1933, in Washington, DC, the third child. My mother named me Betty Jean—Betty after her mother and Jean after her sister.

I have scattered memories of my early childhood. There is no connecting thread between the isolated pictures that come to mind, so a series of vignettes will have to be enough for a record of those years.

One of those few memories is of an incident when I was about ten years old. I was standing on the playground, close to the concrete-block building that served as our two-room schoolhouse, with my ten-year-old cousin, Ché-Ché. We sobbed on each other's shoulders, consoling ourselves that the death the night before of our elderly aunt, the sister of our grandmother's second husband, was timely and beneficent. "It's for the best," we declared knowingly to ourselves, echoing what our relatives had been saying to each other. The fact that we barely knew the woman and would miss her not at all was irrelevant; we were doing what we thought was expected of us. Death does not occur often in the life of a ten-year-old, at least not the kind that can be celebrated melodramatically but without real pain.

School was a joy for me in those days, before the years of adolescent agonies. We lived in Berwyn Heights, a small town (pop. 600) on the east coast, in what was then "out in the country," but would eventually become engulfed by metropolitan Washington, DC. There were 40 students in my

Berwyn Heights elementary school, in the 1940s.

school, filling grades one through seven, split between two large rooms with one teacher for each. With so little competition, I shone as a student and garnered the appreciation and attention of my teachers, as well as the admiration and respect of my peers. I thought of myself as competent, and with the confidence of one who is favored, I developed into a leader.

At school I was a happy, cheerful child, having learned early how to charm people into liking me—a talent that has served me well for many years. I remember feeling secure, well-liked, and happy in the days in that old school.

The cousin who shared my crocodile tears was my constant playmate throughout my early childhood, more out of necessity than choice, since she was the only child near my own age nearby, besides my older brothers. We had a love-hate relationship throughout our childhood. We fought regularly, and made up just as regularly. We were both bright, good students, but I remember her as an odd child, often contentious and complaining.

Ché-Ché and I were about eight or nine when we set the woods on fire. There was some kind of family picnic going on in the back yard, and one of us took a box of matches from the picnic table. Neither of us had a

Berwyn Heights elementary school, grade 5. Betty Jean is in the front row, third from the left. Fifth from the left is Peggy and sixth is Ché Ché.

clear idea of what we wanted to do, but we wandered off into the woods that bordered our property. We went deep enough to be out of sight and sound of the crowd, and decided to pretend to have our own picnic. For some reason this meant a fire, so we gathered up a small pile of leaves and set them burning. There was a deep layer of dead leaves everywhere, but in our childish ignorance we thought that the fire would burn only the ones in our little pile. As the fire rapidly spread to the surrounding leaves, we panicked and ran home. We feared punishment more than anything, so we simply joined the picnic and said nothing. Fortunately, a passing motorist saw the flames and called the volunteer fire department. Most of the men at the picnic belonged to the fire department in our little town, so the picnic was interrupted to put out the fire. It burned only a half acre or so, and no one got particularly upset. I realized later, whenever the fire was mentioned and my father looked at me with a grin, that we were suspected as the culprits, but we were never directly accused or punished.

In those days, the milkman delivered milk to our house every other day in glass quart bottles and left them in a metal box on the front porch. It was my job to carry them in to the refrigerator. It took me several trips,

The Porter siblings, Bobby, Frank, and Betty Jean, ca. 1943.

carrying a quart bottle in each hand, as we drank a lot of milk. I was bored with this little chore, and would swing the bottles, alternately, one arm at a time, in a complete vertical circle from the shoulder to make it more interesting. I've always been one to experiment, and one day I wondered if it might be fun to swing both arms at the same time. So I tried

Betty Jean, left, and cousin Ché Ché, tap dancing, age 9 or 10, in 1942.

it, swinging both arms overhead at once, with a bottle in each hand. Of course the bottles collided over my head, smashing them both, sending two quarts of milk and shards of broken glass cascading all over me and onto the porch floor. Mother came running, and I tried to explain what had happened. It made no sense to her at all, and she scolded me for my foolishness as she helped me clean up the mess.

In even earlier days, the milkman brought our milk to the door and handed it to Mother. On hot days, on those rare occasions when no one was home, he would bring it in and put it in the refrigerator. I assume he did that for all of his customers in our quiet little town.

I played with my two older brothers and cousins, but my closest and favorite friend was my dog, Doc. He was a little brown beagle who appeared on our doorstep as a stray puppy when I was about four, and lived with us for eleven years. As I got older, he went everywhere with me, and I considered him my dog, although I suppose my brothers would have disagreed. When I was especially lonely, I told him my troubles and imagined that he understood. Perhaps he did. The summer that I was fifteen, he disappeared for almost two weeks. We never knew where he went or how he survived, but when he returned, he seemed to be sick. He lay around listlessly for several days. Then late one evening, after I had gone for a walk with him following along, as he always did, we returned, but he would not come back into the yard with me. We stood in the middle of the gravel road, looking at each other. He had a wistful, sad look on his face, and I knew that he was saying goodbye. I whispered, "Goodbye, Doc," and watched him slowly turn away and walk off into the barnyard in the dusk. In the morning, we found his stiffened body on the front porch. I missed him terribly for a long time.

It seems I should remember Pearl Harbor, given the enormity of the event. I was old enough, at eight, and there must have been a fuss around the house. But I don't remember it, so the awareness that we were at war gradually crept up on me. I did learn to hate the Japs and the Germans, not really having any idea who they were. To this day, I wince at the sound of the name "Jap," remembering how easy it was to hate people because they looked different.

The major effect of the war on me was rationing. We were not accustomed to traveling more than a few miles from home anyway, so the lack of gasoline did not seem to me to be a hardship. The lack of sugar, however, was. My brother Frank, being three years older than I, was just old enough to have begun to learn to bake before the war began. He made cookies and cakes and sweet rolls. Once sugar and shortening were in short supply, only he was allowed to make these wondrous goodies, and only infrequently. By the time the war was over and we could afford the luxury of wasted ingredients on failed attempts, I had lost interest. I have always blamed World War II for my inability to make a decent cake.

I remember the end of the war vividly. It was early August, 1945. When the news came over the radio, we children all grabbed anything we could find to bang and raced into the back yard, making as much noise as possible. I had taken a large pot from the kitchen and pounded on it with a wooden spoon; my brothers found an old oil drum lying in the weeds and beat it with an iron pipe. There were sirens howling and horns blowing everywhere. My father said, "Come on, into the car!" and the whole family piled into the old '36 Chevy and drove all the way into the city.

I will never forget that drive. Everyone else had the same idea, and the streets were jammed with cars and pedestrians. There was something primordial about the urge to race out to the streets, to yell and cry together with complete strangers—who were that day not strangers, but family—to celebrate the end of a long, hard struggle for survival. At one point, somewhere around 13th and G Streets, I think, where we had come to a complete stop in a traffic jam, a woman stuck her head in the driver's window of our car and kissed my father. I was shocked and rather pleased. Mother frowned.

I don't know anyone else who grew up playing in coffins. The previous tenant had tried his hand at manufacturing coffins, the large concrete boxes that hold caskets when they are buried in the ground. The coffin-maker had moved on, leaving behind a dozen or so of his product, scattered about in the woods beside our house. Some of the coffins were still intact, with the huge concrete lids securely in place, but most were separated, so that the coffins held murky water. The lids that were lying about were only about a foot deep, while the coffins themselves were about three feet deep. They made marvelous playthings. We played in them, on them, and around them. Those that held water also held tadpoles and water bugs that we spent hours catching; the coffins that were still covered made deep thunderous sounds when pounded. My father moved an open one to the front yard, set it deep in the ground, and used it for a lily pond, with huge goldfish swimming about in it. It never occurred to me that there was anything unusual about our macabre playground.

The house that my father bought for $1,000 in 1934 nestled in a grove of huge oak trees on a triple lot. It sat on a gravel road that saw so little traffic that when a car came by, we all ran to the window to see who it might be. The property was mostly wooded, situated on the side of a steep, mile-long hill.

On the other side of the dusty road was an open field that we always referred to as "the barnyard," although the barn had disappeared long before we arrived. We could stand on our front porch and look out over the barnyard and beyond to the campus of the University of Maryland, five miles distant, and when the leaves were off the trees, we could see the Washington Monument all the way in the city. I can still see the sunsets of sweeping swatches of gold and orange and purple that we watched from that porch.

In the beginning, the house had no furnace and no plumbing, except for one faucet in the corner of the kitchen. It had a wood-burning stove for both heat and cooking, until my father installed a coal-burning furnace in the dirt-walled hole that served as a basement. The furnace had only one vent for the heat, located in the archway between the living

The Porter house in Berwyn Heights in 1955, after many renovations.

room and the dining room. We children used to race to see who could get to the register first to dress over the heat on cold winter mornings. I usually won, and would stand over the rising heat, letting it billow out my skirt. I still remember the smell of wet wool when we dried our woolen gloves and leggings over that hot air register.

I must have been about three years old when Daddy installed an indoor toilet. The earliest snapshot I have of myself is that of a two-year-old, playing with my two older brothers, with the outhouse in the background. I don't remember using the outhouse, but I suppose I did. Perhaps I was not toilet trained until the bathroom was installed. I assume Mother must have used it, and I often think of how hard it must have been for her to adjust to that primitive house. I suspect that using an outhouse may have been the hardest adjustment.

The previous owners had kept chickens in a room that stretched across the end of the house. My father cleaned it out, rebuilt the interior, cut a door into the living room, and it became our children's bedroom. It always amazes me, when I think of it, that the room never smelled. As

Betty Jean, age 2, in back yard of the house in
Berwyn Heights, with her father's Model T Ford.

we got older, Daddy divided the one room into two, so that I had my own
room—and the boys had to share a room until they left home years later.
As the years went by, that private room became my refuge from a world I
could hardly stand. It also got me into trouble, since the original outside
door was left intact, giving me access to the outdoors unobserved when
I became a teenager.

There was no indoor stairway to the basement, and when Dad installed
the coal furnace, tending the fire meant going outside to the garage door
under the house. So he cut a hole in the dining room floor and installed
a trap door with a ladder descending to the dark hole below. We children soon became adept at scooting up and down this ladder, learning
to hold the trap door so that it did not fall down on our heads. One of
our favorite tricks was to surprise guests, what few we had, by popping
up suddenly from the floor. Of course, we had to be careful that no one
placed a chair over the door unknowingly.

My father was a mechanic during my early childhood, working on cars
at a garage in the city. Most of the customers were federal government

employees. No matter how bad the Depression got, the government continued to function, and the employees had to get their cars fixed. We were poor, but even during the worst of the Depression, Daddy was never out of work, and we never went hungry.

At heart, however, he was a carpenter and general handyman. Eventually, while I was still a child, he became a union carpenter. He also spent much of his spare time renovating our house. I can hardly remember a time that something was not under construction. I think there is only one wall in the entire house that is original.

We lost the piano to one of the major revisions. We had bought the piano when the front porch was still in the center of the house, with the original, extra-wide front door. The renovation at one time involved moving the porch to the side and replacing the front wall of the house, with the installation of a modern, standard-size front door. The piano had to go now or never, as it would no longer fit through any of doors in the house. We had a family conference, and decided it was time for the piano to go. I was glad, as it meant I no longer had to listen to my brother Bobby practice. He was determined to learn to play, and would practice the same few bars over and over and over until I wanted to scream. He had a maddeningly mechanical style, and unfortunately never got any better. I had quit taking lessons some time before, having never learned to play well either. I don't remember what was done with the piano, only that it was carried out the front of the house while the wall was gone.

One summer, we remodeled the kitchen, at the back of the house. The lot was on such a steep hill that it was possible for a tall person to stand in the backyard and look over the roof. While this construction was going on, we were without complete walls, with blankets draped between studs. It happened that one night we had a particularly hard rain, a real gulley-washer. Because of the steepness of the hill, the water came gushing through the wall and ran right into the kitchen and across the floor, into the dining room. Daddy took one look at the flood, grabbed a broom, opened the trap door in the dining room, and swept the water straight down to the basement, where it ran out the garage door and continued on its way down the driveway. We kids took our turns with the broom, laughing uproariously, until the rain stopped. Mother fretted.

We never locked our doors. In fact, in the heat of summer we left them standing wide open, including that one in my bedroom that led directly outdoors, to catch the night breezes. That door was a remnant of the days of the chicken coop. Late one summer night when I was eleven, as I lay trying to sleep in the stifling heat, I was suddenly aware that the screen door was opening, and someone was entering my room. It was Uncle Hallie, who lived next door, and I could tell he was drunk. He played a flashlight around the room. As the light landed on me, instinct told me, "Freeze. Don't move. Pretend you're asleep." I lay still as death, terrified, not knowing what he would do. He stood next to my bed for a long, long time, looking down at me. Eventually, he clicked off the flashlight, turned, and left, closing the screen door gently behind him. I lay there, still afraid to move, both bewildered and relieved, vaguely aware that I had been spared something awful. I never told anyone.

Sometime in this period—age ten to twelve—I had an odd leap of consciousness. Probably psychologists have a term for this as a certain stage in child development, but I have preferred to think of it as something peculiarly mine. I was standing in my front yard, looking out over the barnyard, out to the horizon in the distance, when I suddenly had an utterly astounding thought: my house, my yard, my room, was *not* the center of the universe! This was a totally new concept, and it overwhelmed me. My whole world shifted. Does everyone experience this sudden realization, or does it usually happen gradually, or happen so young that it goes unnoticed? Or do some people never experience it at all? I could not have articulated it at the time, but I know that I have seen the world differently ever since.

I was the apple of my father's eye, and it was easy to be a tomboy to please him. I could run faster than anyone else in the fifth grade, I could hit the most home runs, I could climb the highest trees. I learned years later from a college friend who lived in the next small town that I had a reputation for being able to beat up every boy in school—a revelation that shocked me. The only fight I ever took part in resulted in a classmate's bloody nose when I accidentally hit him with my lunchbox as I turned to run away. Reputations come easily in grade school.

My way of escaping my mother's frequent angry moods was to stay out of the house as much as possible. I lived in the woods and the fields. I dug in the dirt, built tree houses, played in the ponds in the nearby gravel pit. Ah, the gravel pit! I often wonder what city children do for play. We not only had the wondrous coffins, we had a gravel quarry, as big as a city block, that had been abandoned some years before. It had sloping sandy banks, a little winding road, and many small ponds where shallow holes had filled with water. I spent many an hour there with my brothers and cousins, catching frogs, climbing and sliding down the banks, playing hide and seek, discovering mosquito larva and frog eggs in their mysterious milky goo, and an occasional harmless snake. In the winter, we skated

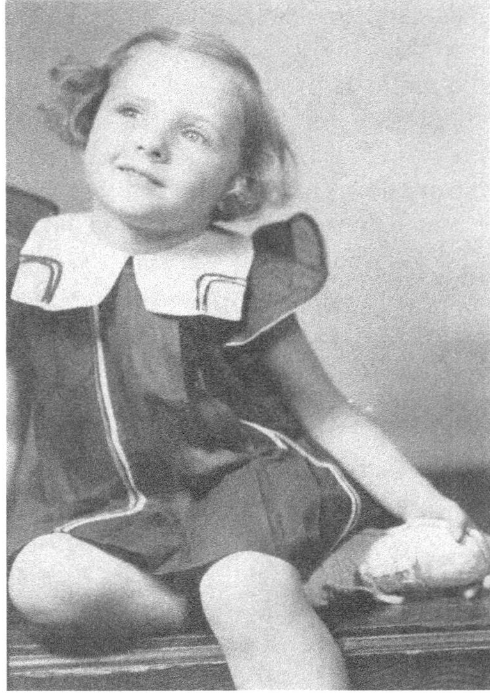

Betty Jean, age 5.

on the little ponds and rode our sleds down the bumpy banks. There was no end to the wonders to explore there.

My favorite activity, however, was climbing trees. Our house was surrounded by huge trees, mostly oaks. At night I could lie in bed and listen to the acorns plunking on the low roof above my head, then rolling plinkety-plinkety-plink to land on the ground. In the summer, I would sleep on an Army surplus cot under the trees, outside my room, swatting mosquitoes and half-listening for rain. I loved those trees, and to this day, I am not really happy unless there are trees within sight of my window.

When the occasional thunderstorm came up in the summertime, I loved to climb the highest tree beside my house. I would see the sky cloud over, hear the thunder, feel the wind pick up until it was fierce—and I would scramble up that old oak just as fast and as high as I could go. Being small, I could reach the very highest branches, at the point where it was no longer a branch, but was the very topmost point of the tree. I would get to that point where my weight was just enough to bend it, but not enough to break it. I would hang on and let the wind blow me back and forth, around and around, holding on for dear life, loving the excitement and danger. By the time the rain would start, my mother would discover what I was doing, and come running out the back door screaming at me to come down.

One of my regular chores was feeding the chickens. Daddy built a chicken house up the hill behind our house, and it fell to each of us kids to be their caretakers, as we got old enough for the responsibility. Every day, from the time I was about ten, I trudged up the hill to toss out grain, pour mash into the trough, and fill up the water buckets. There is nothing like the smell of chickens. I don't know if it was their droppings, the feed, the feathers, or what, but I still remember bracing myself against the odor when I opened the door.

It was also my job to get the eggs out from under the hens. Some of them were mean, and I often got pecked as I reached under their feathery breasts to see who was hiding eggs. Sometimes a hen would start "setting," meaning she was planning to hatch a brood of chicks. This happened only when we had roosters, which we usually did, to provide occasional fried chicken for Sunday dinner. Eventually I learned to hold the hens' heads aside with one hand while I reached deftly under to grab the eggs, feeling like a thief. After all, they were their eggs.

The chickens attracted rats. Lots of them. They dug intricate tunnels under the trees nearby, and I would often see them when I entered the chicken house. On winter evenings, after dark, I would stand with my eyes closed as I pulled on the light cord, to give them time to scurry away before I saw them. But sometimes they became so numerous that we could no longer ignore them, and we would have a rat hunt.

I have always abhorred violence so much that I have trouble stepping on cockroaches, so the rat hunts troubled me. I did not participate, but was fascinated enough to stand nearby, trying not to watch. First, my brothers and Daddy gathered up baseball bats or large sticks or rake handles, to have ready. They would search the area for all exits to the rat burrows, stuffing them with rags or anything handy to block the rats' escape, but leaving two of them free. Then Daddy would hook up the garden hose, shove the nozzle down one hole, and turn the water on full force. The rats would dash frantically out of the hole that was still open, and whoever was closest would club them. Of course some escaped, and there were always a few holes that had gone undetected and unstopped, so there was much confusion and yelling and chasing around, scrambling to smash the ones that were running away. After a few minutes of bedlam, there would be bloody rats, dead or wounded, littering the place. I can't remember how the carcasses were disposed of. Probably by that point I had retreated to my room and so never witnessed it.

I think I was thirteen when I killed my first chicken. One of the rites of passage in our family was being allowed to butcher the chickens that we ate. When a hen got too old to produce eggs, or when the young roosters reached frying age, it was time to get out the hatchet.

The first chore was to catch the chicken. When they were confined to the henhouse, it was matter of gradually walking the chicken into a corner and being able to grab faster than it could run, but when they were outside, it often took at least two of us to catch one. Then, dangling the squawking chicken by its legs, the executioner walked to the chopping block, hatchet in the other hand. It took some dexterity to hold the chicken with its legs higher than its head, draping it so that its neck lay over the chopping block (an old tree stump left in place for just this purpose), with the hatchet held high overhead in the other hand. When the chicken lay still for a second, down came the hatchet with enough force to chop off the head. Blood spurted out in all directions, so it was preferable to toss it aside by the legs immediately and let the headless torso thrash about on the ground. The expression "running around like a chicken with its head cut off" has real meaning to me, having witnessed the spectacle many times. It was not at all unusual for the bird to have enough life left in its nerves to flop about crazily, flapping and running in circles for a minute or so—soundlessly, of course.

The worst part was yet to come, however. Once the chicken settled down, it had to be plucked and cleaned. The feathers came off in handfuls when I pulled in the opposite direction from which they grew, and when all the feathers were gone, I twisted a brown paper bag into a long torch and set it afire, holding the chicken over it, just close enough to singe off all the fine, downy feathers that were left. (It had to be a brown paper bag—newspapers would not do. I don't know why.)

Then I slit the bird from leg to leg, beneath the breast. Reaching into the cavity to pull out the "innards" was the part I hated most. They were warm and smelly and gooey. Most of the blood would have drained out by now, but the entrails were full of all kinds of partly digested food and strange fluids. Sometimes in the hens I found eggs that had not yet been encased in their shells, and occasionally even a soft-shelled one that was due to be laid that day or the next. Daddy taught me to identify the parts that were to be saved—the heart, liver, and gizzard—and to be sure to remove the kidneys that were hidden deep in the crevices of the back. When everything was removed, I rinsed the carcass under the outside spigot and carried it triumphantly to Mother, to be served up as Sunday dinner.

2 Grammie

One major influence on my childhood, albeit indirectly, was my grandmother, Daddy's mother. Grammie was a strong, feisty, independent woman. I think I'm more like her than like anyone else in the family.

The last memory I have of Grammie is of her squatting in a flower bed in front of our house, trowel in hand, wearing shorts and a white shirt, with a short scarf tied on her head. She lived next door to us and kept flowers blooming in both our yards most of the year. It was 1948, and I was 15 years old. We were leaving on a rare vacation, driving from Maryland to Maine to visit my father's childhood home, where relatives still lived.

As we turned out of the driveway, I looked back to see Grammie at the flower bed, waving us goodbye. She died in her sleep that night, of a heart attack. She was only 62 years old.

When we arrived at my cousin's house in Maine, my aunt took Daddy aside after dinner and told him that his mother had died. The next day we all got back in the car and drove home again, another two-day drive. Only later did I think about what a hard trip that must have been for my father. He was very close to his mother. When Grammie left O.B., her husband, Daddy became the "man of the family" as the oldest child. He and my mother not only lived with Grammie after they were married, he kept his mother close by later building a house for her next door to us. Grammie was the glue that held the family together, and now that role would fall on my father. It was a somber trip home.

I wonder if Grammie had a premonition of dying. She lived alone in her house next door to us, and when we were leaving for two weeks,

Emily Robinson, 1886–1948, mother of Than O. Porter.

she arranged to stay with her daughter in the next small town while we were gone. Did she suspect she was going to die, and her body might not be found for some time? As far as we knew, she was in excellent health. However, when we cleaned out her house, we found heart medicine in her bathroom cabinet.

She also had held a "giveaway" just a couple of months before she died. She set up tables in her living room and put out all of the things people had given her over the years for them to take back if they wanted them. I took a set of drinking glasses I had given her for Christmas one year. She said she was just cleaning out closets, but we realized later that she was cleaning things out to make it easier on the family when she was gone. Everything—the giving away, the heart medicine, and staying with my

Oscar Byron Porter (O.B.), 1885–1955, father of Than O. Porter.

aunt when we left—points to her believing she would not live long. The Porter sense of independence would have kept her from telling anyone.

One night several weeks after the funeral, Grammie suddenly appeared to me when I was in bed and sat down next to me. I could smell the soap she used. It was not bad, just a particular smell, and I have never smelled it anywhere else but on her. She leaned toward me, and said in her gravelly voice, "Don't worry about me. I'm fine." Then she smiled and disappeared. That puzzled me, as it hadn't occurred to me to worry about her. Her appearance didn't seem especially strange or frightening. I just accepted it, and didn't tell anyone about it. It seemed too private to talk about, so I just filed it away in my mind as one of those things that would make sense to me some day.

Grammie, whose full name eventually was Inez Emily Robinson Porter Blair but was called Emily, was born in 1886 in Sherman Mills, Maine, and lived in Maine until she was 40 years old. When she divorced her husband, O.B., in 1924, she packed up her five kids and moved to Washington, DC. Her sister Alice had already moved there. At one time Grammie worked in a U.S. Representative's office near the Capitol. She later used some of his leftover stationery for paper to type a novel. She also sold insurance, and married a second husband, Paddy Blair, in 1930. I barely remember him, even though they lived next door. I heard that he was a heavy drinker but gave every paycheck to his wife, and I never heard complaints about him. My brother Frank mentioned once that we would go through their trash for targets to practice throwing rocks, because there were always lots of bottles.

After Grammie moved the family to Washington, her children had very little contact with their father, and I never knew him. Since Mother's father had died long before I was born, I effectively never had a grandfather. I wish I had. Many people have described how they cherish having a grandfather to talk to and look up to as a model. I had only a grandmother, and did not have her for long, only until I was fifteen. I was denied the kind of guidance that only grandparents can give.

My father's family was an impressive clan, and Grammie was its matriarch. Over the years, various aunts and uncles and cousins moved into the houses that Daddy built on our property. In addition to the two houses, a trailer had been towed up the hill behind one of the houses and a ramshackle extension had been built around it. First Uncle Hallie and his family lived there, and when they moved away, Aunt Saidee and her family moved in. Before Uncle Hallie moved away, Aunt Saidee's family had moved into Grammie's first house when she moved into the second one. At one point, after World War II, when Uncle Larry was discharged from the Army, he and his wife Gerry and their baby moved in with Grammie in the second house, before they moved to Wyoming. I was surrounded by Daddy's relatives throughout my childhood.

Grammie was an amateur painter, I am told, and a poet. I never saw her paintings, but I have read her poems that were printed in the local newspaper in the small town in Maine where the family had lived.

She wrote more than poems. She and her son Hallie wrote a murder mystery, *Three Saw the Murder,* which was published in 1938. I

Edwina Leavitt Robinson, 1875–1955, mother of Emily Robinson Porter.

have a copy and have read it several times over the years. Some of the characters are apparently based on family members. The narrator is probably Hallie, and his father in the story is like his real father, O.B., who is portrayed rather unfavorably, but not as much as he might have been. Grammie introduced me to bird watching, helping me to reach my life list of 60-some varieties by the time I was 15. Our houses were nestled in a grove of huge trees, mostly white oaks, that harbored many birds. Every spring and fall, the migrating birds like warblers and cedar waxwings came through in flocks. Grammie would come running over to our house, saying, "Come quick, the yellow-throated warblers are here!" and I would follow her to the right tree and peer

Cyrus Elmer Robinson, 1854–1921, father of Emily
Robinson Porter.

up, looking for the tiny colorful birds. We had no binoculars, so our
eyes had to be sharp. She also taught me about all the plants she
tended in our flower beds.

My grandmother was a surprisingly strong personality, considering
how little she was. She was tiny, only 4 feet 11 inches tall, and slim. She
wore her dark hair in a man's cut, very short, which was more unusual in
the 1940s than today. She had a gruff voice, and an abrupt manner. She
was always busy, her eyes twinkling with abundant energy.

After she died, we found a new suit in her closet with the price tag
still hanging on the sleeve, and it was given to me. It was a light blue-
gray, with a tailored jacket and a straight skirt. I wore it occasionally,
although it was hardly appropriate for a teenager, even though it fit
me perfectly. It seems strange now that she bought that suit and never

wore it. I don't recall ever seeing her wearing anything but her "work" clothes, pants and old shirts. She must have gone out at times and needed dressier clothes, and I don't know what else was in her closet. I have fantasized that she had a premonition of dying and bought the suit to be buried in.

Grammie and her sisters were very strong women, and I grew up in a setting dominated by them, creating a strong family ethic that still influences my life today. That ethic actually came from the Robinsons, Grammie's family of birth, but I experienced them in my own family of Porters.

There were many components of that family ethic, much of it predictable, considering our New England forebears. I've been told that my father's ancestors came over not on the Mayflower, but on the boat that immediately followed. At any rate, we had many of the typical Puritanical beliefs: hard work, thriftiness, honesty, productivity. Laziness was the only thing worse than lying or cheating. Function was far more important than esthetics. Getting the job done always took priority over having fun. And being true to oneself was more important than what anybody else thought; hence we were encouraged to be unconventional. And it was assumed that of course we were all highly intelligent, whether we actually were or not. In my teens I coined the word "Porterian," referring to that family culture.

Trustworthiness was something I took so much for granted that it still shocks me when I encounter dishonesty or lying. For instance, when we were teenagers, all three of us siblings had paper routes. On Christmas morning, we would have to get up as usual to deliver the papers. Santa Claus would have come during the night and left our presents, unwrapped, under the tree in the living room. My brothers and I had to pass through the living room to get out of the house, and we always averted our eyes as we passed through so as not to see the presents before our parents woke up. It never occurred to us to peek—that would have been cheating and therefore unthinkable.

Another Porter trait was a sense of humor. Wittiness was highly valued, and wisecracks flew back and forth frequently. Unfortunately, the humor was often barbed. We poked fun at each other constantly, in a way that was hurtful but was said with a smile so that the recipient had to pretend it was okay. Sarcasm was used as a weapon, as a way of establishing superiority. I became very good at it, but when I got out in the world I learned that it was not appreciated by other people. I saw how damaging it was, and made an effort over the years to stop doing it. I still enjoy a sense of humor, and remind myself constantly not to jab people with it.

It surprises me to realize that although Grammie lived next door from the time I was about seven years old until she died when I was fifteen, I really did not know her well. I suspect her influence on me was so pronounced because her attitudes about life permeated everything our family did, through her, her sisters, and my father and his brothers and sister. It was a powerful family, and I absorbed far more of their values than those of my mother. I was fascinated by Grammie, with all that she knew about everything and was eager to teach me. My Uncle Larry is quoted as having said about Grammie, "My mother knew everything and she always answered my questions." I did not understand until many years later that Mother had subtly discouraged me from spending hours and hours with my grandmother.

Being nonconformists was another important piece of the Porter culture, and I don't know if it came directly from her or from our father. It was certainly not from Mother, as her first thought was always, "What will people think!" I believe that one of the reasons we had so few guests in our house was because Mother could not bear to have people see how we lived. We could never measure up to her family's former circumstances, and while we had what we needed, our working-class house and furnishings never came up to her standards.

But the rest of the family prided ourselves on not conforming to "what other people think," so that I grew up being comfortable being different. I still am acutely aware of "group think," and always resist it. The more I think about it, I realize that the aunts and uncles were that way, too, and so it must have come from Grammie. In fact, her sisters were nonconformists also, so it is a trait that goes back several generations.

I loved and admired my grandmother. I wish I had paid more attention to her, as she was a smart, talented woman. There is so much I don't know about her, and can't ask anyone, as none of the cousins who are still alive lived nearby in those days and therefore knew her even less well than I did. For instance, I don't remember her driving a car, but surely she must have. She must not have stayed home all the time, but I don't know what she did, besides gardening and bird watching.

Grammie is still somewhat of a mystery to me. The coolness between her and Mother was a barrier that kept me from getting close to her. Considering how little time I actually spent with her, it is surprising that she had such a strong influence on me, but I credit my most positive traits, the ones I happily claim, largely to her.

3 Daddy

It's not surprising that the people who probably influenced me the most in my early childhood were my parents. They both tried to mold me in their own image, and while they both failed, I am grateful that Daddy came closer to succeeding than Mother did. (I still call him "Daddy," and always will.) I'm far more like him than my mother.

Killing and dressing a chicken was only one of the many things I learned from Daddy. He taught me how to swing a hammer, and the importance of taking care of tools. His tools were his livelihood, and he knew that if they were not abused they would last a long time. The only time I left a screwdriver out all night, I got a severe scolding.

My father, Than Oscar Porter, was born June 29, 1906, in Ft. Fairfield, Maine. He was the oldest of five children, four boys and one girl. The earliest pictures I have of him show a young man with a mischievous gleam in his eyes and a big grin. He was always cheerful, even when times were hard. He was a handsome man, short but well built, with sandy brown hair and the bluest eyes I've ever seen. Unfortunately, none of his children got those beautiful blue eyes. I don't know how tall he was, but I estimate about 5' 7", at most. In his old age, I think he shrank several inches. Perhaps it just seemed so because he stooped.

Daddy's father, Oscar Byron Porter, called O.B., began his working life as a pharmacist, but soon became a photographer, opening his own studio in 1913, in Houlton, Maine, where the family had moved. I heard that once he was so determined to get something, I don't know what, that he "walked to Canada." That really impressed me until one day I looked up

Ft. Fairfield and discovered that it is right on the border between Maine and Canada. He may not have walked very far.

I didn't know O.B. at all, as we had nothing to do with him while I was growing up. The family story is that Grammie caught him once too often with another woman, and she divorced him. He married that woman and had another family with her, including a daughter who is my age and who apparently looks much like me. When our family visited Maine in 1948, O.B. took photos of me and displayed them in the window of his studio. Passersby commented on the nice pictures of his daughter.

Daddy had already finished high school in Houlton when Grammie divorced O.B. and moved the family to Washington. He soon started to work in construction and left home for a job in Louisiana. In 1928, he made a visit home in Washington, and met my mother. I wish I knew more about their courtship. At some point, Mother went back home to Charlotte, North Carolina, and I think they were engaged by then. I have a telegram Daddy sent to Mother in Charlotte, asking her if she was okay, because he hadn't heard from her for three days! He must have been working in Louisiana still, as they were married there on February 23, 1929. I have a delicate, pale peach rayon robe, with ecru lace down the front, that was part of her trousseau. I wish I could wear it, but it's too fragile. It has hung in the back of my closet for many years.

After the wedding they moved in with Grammie and her younger children in Washington. I don't know anything about their life there, except that there were lots of relatives around, both in their house and in Grammie's sister Alice's house. My brother Frank was born on December 19th of that year, and brother Bobby on December 9th the next December. When I arrived in April 1933, that must have been one person too many in the house, so Daddy moved the family into a house in a Virginia suburb while Mother and I were in the hospital.

When I was a year and a half old, in 1934, Daddy bought that house in Berwyn Heights, far outside of Washington in Maryland. It took ten years to pay off the $1,000 mortgage.

At some point Daddy became a mechanic, instead of a carpenter. He worked for Call Carl, a garage in Washington that repaired cars. He always left the house early in the morning and returned late in the evening, as it was a long drive into the city and back. In winter, I used to wake up in the morning to the smell of coffee and bacon. He cooked himself a hearty breakfast and left before the rest of us were up. My bedroom was not heated so in the winter it was really cold, and I would lie there under several blankets, working up the nerve to get out of bed, smelling that breakfast and hearing the sounds of a train a mile away. They still used steam engines in those days, and in the winter I could hear the whistle blowing and the engine puffing as it started up at the station. Those smells and sounds remind me of childhood still.

Daddy's main interest in life was his lodge. He became a 32nd degree Mason, and held the highest office in the lodge several times. He and Mother were also active in Eastern Star, the branch of the Masons that admitted women, and he became the highest officer there also, something like High Worthy Patron. It seemed to me that the lodge was to Daddy what church was to many people. He and Mother never went to church, so this served the same purpose. There was much ritual to learn and recite, and I remember Daddy studying at the dining room table.

Mother and Daddy always expected that their children would follow in their Masonic footsteps, and were deeply disappointed that none of us had any interest in it. They insisted that my brothers join the DeMolay, the boys' organization, and that I join the Rainbow Girls. We all went to meetings a few times, but soon dropped out. It just didn't take for any of us. The Rainbow Girls seemed empty-headed and the rituals silly. But I think the Masons gave meaning to my father's life.

Daddy was also a volunteer fireman. Our little town of 600 people could not afford a paid force, so the fire department consisted of as many of the able-bodied men as could be recruited. Many times Daddy would be eating dinner or reading the paper when he would hear the fire siren and he would pull on his boots and coat, jump in the car, and race to the station, about half a mile away. We never knew what time he would come home.

Daddy always worked. He had his regular job and usually had one or two side jobs on weekends. When he wasn't working, he was at meetings. He was very active in the community, serving on several boards and for a while was town commissioner, something like a mayor. He was well known and respected in our town. For instance, once when I went to collect for my newspaper route, the woman who answered the door questioned how much she owed. She didn't know me, so asked my name, and when I told her, she said, "Well, if you're Than Porter's daughter, you must be honest," and paid the bill.

Children never really know what their parents' relationship is like, so I can only surmise what mine was like from what I saw. It seemed to me that they tolerated each other, but just barely. My theory was that Daddy found many reasons to be away from the house so he could avoid being around Mother. That may be projection, of course, because that is what I did. I took every excuse I could find to stay out of the house.

They seemed poorly suited to each other. Mother had a two-year college education and came from a well-to-do southern family, although the money was gone by the time she married. Daddy was intelligent and caring, but had only a high school diploma and surprisingly poor manners. For instance, he picked his teeth at the dinner table and would frequently spit on the sidewalk. His humor was rather juvenile, constantly reciting witticisms that had been stale for decades and expecting everyone to laugh. Mother seemed to be always frowning at him in disapproval.

Daddy was not drafted in World War II, although he was only thirty-five years old when the United States entered the war in 1941. His age alone would not have kept him out of the service, but I believe he was exempted because his work was considered essential. For a while he drove to Cedar Point, Maryland, and helped build the new naval air station that our country needed for the war. He stayed at Cedar Point during the week and came home weekends. One benefit of the exemption was that he received extra rationing coupons for gasoline so he could drive to work.

Daddy was first a mechanic, then a carpenter, and when he was in his late 40s, he changed again. The carpenters' union went on strike about once a year, and would be out for weeks, sometimes months. They always struck for higher pay, and they would eventually get it and go back to work. But one day Daddy did the math, and realized that counting the pay they lost when they were on strike, if they had continued working at the old pay without striking and received no raise, they would have come out the with the same amount of money. He said, "This is stupid," and quit the union. He cashed in an insurance policy and bought a gas station and managed it. I remember family members saying he was foolish to make a change so late in life, but I admired him for it. He ran the gas station for many years.

As Daddy got older, he gained weight, developing a pot belly. His sandy hair turned gray, but he didn't go bald, and his eyes stayed that gorgeous blue. He sometimes bragged about still having all of his teeth. When he was in his sixties, he had a serious heart attack. When he was in the hospital, Mother received a call from the doctor that Daddy had died. But minutes later, she got another call, saying that no, he was alive! Years later I heard Daddy refer to having a near death experience, but we

Than O. Porter, ca. 1956.

didn't talk about what it was like. I wish we had. I suppose it seemed too personal to ask him and he didn't volunteer any information.

Mother died of cancer in October of 1977, at home, in the bed she had brought from her parents' house almost fifty years before. She had been sick for a long time, but she got suddenly worse and needed to go to the hospital. Daddy knew there wasn't enough gas in the car to get there, so raced as fast as he could to the gas station and back, but Mother died in the short time he was gone.

Four months later, in February of 1978, at age seventy-one, he married Ruth, who had been my parents' friend for all their adult lives. Her husband, Mac, who had been a high school friend of Daddy's, had died many years earlier. Ruth had been like a member of the family, and did a lot of caregiving for my mother. In fact, she was staying there and was with Mother when she died.

Daddy was very popular with his Masonic friends, especially the women, largely because he was one of the few who continued to drive into his eighties. He became everyone's chauffeur. It was a little scary, because I thought he was a terrible driver. He was so short he could barely see over the steering wheel, and he always drove fast. But I never heard of any accidents, so maybe he was better than he seemed or he was just lucky.

I don't know when he gave up the gas station, but it was long past the usual retirement age.

When Daddy turned eighty, in 1986, my brother Frank and his wife Jean threw a big party for him at the family home, where Daddy had lived since 1934. About 200 people came, many old friends and neighbors and other relatives. I saw people I remembered from childhood, including my high school classmates.

When he was 81, Daddy had surgery for prostate cancer. I was living in the area then, and when he was ready to be discharged, he asked me to come to the hospital and take him home. As we walked slowly to the car, he gripped my arm tightly and leaned on me. He seemed diminished. This was the only time my father showed any dependence on me. He had never been dependent on anyone. I had a mixture of feelings—sad and protective, but uncomfortable in the unfamiliar role.

One Sunday evening in October 1988, when Daddy and Ruth had finished dinner, he sat down in his favorite recliner, took off his shoes, leaned back with a contented sigh, and died. He was eighty-two.

I got the call about 9 o'clock that night. Frank asked if I wanted them to keep his body there until I could get to the hospital. Daddy had arranged to donate his body to a university hospital for research, and they needed to get it quickly. I said no, I didn't need to see him.

Two weeks later we held a memorial service for him, with a full Masonic ritual. Many people said nice things about him. As with the 80th birthday party, people came whom I hadn't seen for many years.

Later I remembered that Daddy had called me one evening a few days before he died. We chatted a bit, and I kept waiting to find out what he

Than O. Porter and second wife Ruth MacKenzie. Married February 1979.

had called for. When I hung up the phone, I realized he called just to say hello. This had never happened before. We seldom called each other at all, and when we did, it was to ask something or tell something, never just to talk. I think on some level he knew he was about to die, and wanted to make that connection that we had not had since I was a little girl. I'm glad he did.

4 Mother

Unfortunately, my mother's influence was largely as a negative example—I grew up determined never to be anything like her.

Mother was born in 1901, the baby of her family, with an older brother and sister. Her father was a successful businessman in Charlotte, North Carolina. She was named Frankie Parks McGinn, after her father, Frank. I always wondered why they didn't give the father's name to the first born, the boy.

They were a prosperous family, with a winter home in the city and a summer home in the mountains. They had servants, presumably African American, as one snapshot of the family shows a black woman off to the side and a little black child playing nearby. They kept a stable of horses, and I have a photo of Frank McGinn sitting proudly in a racing sulky, reins in hand, a beautiful black horse standing in the traces. They were prominent enough in the Charlotte social scene that the local newspaper's society pages noted that the invitations to their daughter Jean's wedding had been mailed. I have another clipping reporting on a party, with my mother and her sister listed among those attending.

As a young woman, Mother was slim, with jet black hair and blue eyes, and fairly tall, although I don't know her actual height. In adulthood she put on a lot of weight, and all my memories of her are when she was overweight. Her hair did not turn gray until she was well into her seventies.

One day when Mother was a teenager, her mother was sweeping up and threw the contents of the dustpan into the fireplace. A glass shard flew out from the fire and hit my mother, blinding her in one eye. There was only a brown glass eye available at the time, so she spent most of her life with one brown eye and one blue one. When my brother Bobby was a teenager, he saved up his money and bought her a new blue eye. The old eye lay around in a dresser drawer for years and we kids use to take it out occasionally to impress visiting friends.

I don't know exactly when she lost her eye, but it had to be before she was fifteen, because that is when her mother died. The family story is that her mother had bone cancer. She was only in her early forties.

The sisters went to Peace Institute, a two-year girls' college in Raleigh. In Mother's scrapbook are many snapshots of her and her friends and classmates. It was the 1920s, the flapper era. She obviously had many friends and many social activities. She wore her black hair in a short bob. I have a picture of her standing by her house, wearing stylish jodhpur-type pants and a long shirt. She is not smoking in this picture, although she later became a chain smoker.

After college, Mother went back home and became her widowed father's hostess and managed the household. She was then about twenty years old and her sister and brother were gone from the home. She settled comfortably into a well-to-do life style, with all her needs met. I didn't learn until many years later how suddenly and drastically it all changed.

Since my father grew up in Maine and then lived in the DC area the rest of his life, I wondered how he and Mother met. One day it occurred to me to ask him. He chuckled, and said, "She was living in my mother's house!"

I don't know why I didn't ask him what she was doing there, but I didn't. I let it go. I don't know what he would have said. Did he even know why she was there? He didn't act embarrassed or evasive about it.

Years later I learned the story of how they met from my cousin, Mother's sister's daughter. She had learned it from her father, Willard, shortly before he died. The story broke my heart.

The initial connection with Washington was through my mother's sister, Jean. Jean had worked in Washington in a government job for a short while after college, sometime about 1918. While there, she met Nina McLaughlin, one of my father's cousins. They became friends, and after Jean decided to go back home to Charlotte, they stayed in touch.

Sometime in 1927, the event occurred that changed the course of Mother's life—she got pregnant. In her circle, this was scandalous, and she couldn't let anyone know. Her sister arranged for her to go to Washington and

Frank Parks McGinn, father of Frankie McGinn Porter. Died 1928, birth date unknown.

stay with Nina's aunt, my father's mother, to have the baby. Apparently no one at home except Jean and her husband Willard knew about the pregnancy. I have often wondered about the circumstances. Was the father a boyfriend, who wouldn't marry her? Did she want to marry him? Was it a "one-night stand"? How much of a party girl was she? Did the father know of the pregnancy?

I have not been able to learn exactly when the baby was born, but it had to be after March of 1928, because her father died that March, and Willard said that she was upset that she couldn't go to his funeral because she was pregnant. Willard said the baby was a boy, and was immediately given up for adoption. It had to have been before February of 1929, when she married my father. I have a picture of them soon after the wedding, and she is not visibly pregnant. I tried to find a birth certificate for the baby, but the adoption records in Washington are sealed for 100 years.

As mentioned earlier, Daddy was a carpenter, and had gone to Louisiana to work in construction, so he was not home when my mother was there during the pregnancy. At some point he returned on a visit, and they met. The courtship was brief, and they married in Louisiana on Feb. 23, 1929. Mother was twenty-seven and Daddy was twenty-two.

Elizabeth Flenigan McGinn, mother of Frankie McGinn. Dates unknown.

Did Daddy know about the baby? It seems that he should have, but possibly not. And if he knew, how did it affect his desire to marry her? My father was a deeply compassionate man, and perhaps he felt sorry for her and wanted to protect her. Maybe he was so much in love that he didn't care.

Frankie McGinn, 1901–1977. Age early 20s.

I wonder if Mother knew what kind of life she was entering, if she loved Daddy and didn't mind, or if she grabbed at a chance for someone to provide for her and give her respectability. Her chances at marriage must have been slim at twenty-seven, and she had little family support, with both her parents gone. She had no marketable skills and no way of supporting herself. Daddy was a good man and a hard worker, so perhaps she saw him as a rescuer. Or maybe she simply loved him.

After they married, they moved in with Daddy's mother and his siblings in Washington. One family story happened while they were living with Grammie in the city. One of Mother's friends came to visit and wanted to go shopping, but Mother couldn't back the car out of the narrow alley behind the house, so they had to stay home. Daddy had bought a motorcycle to drive to work, and one day on his way home, he hit an oil patch. The bike tipped over and dragged him along the road. He was

Than and Frankie, soon after their wedding in February1929.

badly bruised and bloody, but not seriously hurt and managed to drive the bike home. When he got home, Mother looked at him and said, "We're going to the hospital!" Without a thought, she backed the car out of that alley and drove to the hospital. The next day Daddy sold the motorcycle, but Mother was never able to back the car out again.

Mother was soon pregnant, and my oldest brother was born that December. The next December my other brother was born, and two years later I was born. So she had given birth to four babies within five years. When she learned that she would have to have a hysterectomy after the next pregnancy, she prayed that this one would be the girl she had always wanted. When I arrived, she was thrilled.

When I was eighteen months old, Daddy bought the property in Maryland, in a rural area about 20 miles outside of Washington. The house, hardly more than a shack, sat on a gravel road with no close neighbors. It had four rooms, with a porch across the front and a chicken coop across one end.

The only water in the house was a spigot in the corner of the kitchen. There was a wood-burning stove for cooking, and no bathroom. Over the years, Daddy steadily improved the house, so that it was under constant renovation during my entire childhood and beyond. When I was about twelve there was a celebration around the dinner table when he announced that the mortgage was paid. It had taken ten years to pay off the $1,000.

Frankie Porter, ca. 1945, shopping in Washington, DC.

I often think of what it must have been like for Mother. She was stuck in that awful house, with three children, ages four, three, and one, no indoor plumbing, a wood stove for heat and cooking, no friends and few neighbors, and Daddy gone to work in the city from early morning to late evening. I remember Daddy joking once about how Mother never learned to light a fire in the cook stove, so dinner could not even be started until he came home and built the fire.

That stove could have been the end of all of us. I was too little to remember this incident, but heard about it when I was a child. Mother always had a chenille bathrobe and often wore it around the house. One winter day she was tending a pot on the stove when the sleeve of her robe caught fire. She screamed, and Daddy came running. He grabbed her, dashed out the kitchen door, pushed her down, and rolled her around in the snow, smothering the flames. If he had not been home, I don't know what would have happened. It is very likely that she would have been seriously burned, perhaps died, and the house burned down. Surely she must have been burned some, but I don't remember hearing that. I think about how vulnerable she was, in that nearly primitive house with little children and Daddy gone most of the time.

What did she think when Daddy brought her there? Was she angry? Sad? Frightened? Accepting? Grateful, anything to get away from the in-laws? I'll never know, but it must have been traumatic for her, having grown up in a prosperous home with servants.

Her misery was soon compounded when my father's mother moved in next door. My father put up a house (a four-bedroom, two-story prefab ordered from Montgomery Ward for $300) on the southern side of our big lot, and Grammie moved in with her husband Paddy and Paddy's sister Eva.

A few years later, Daddy built another house on the property for his mother, and Daddy's sister Saidee and her family moved into the first house. Now Mother was again surrounded by her husband's family. She was outnumbered, and I became the bone to fight over, or so it seemed to me. Daddy and his family were determined to turn me into a tomboy; Mother was equally determined that I should become the dainty, feminine little lady that she had been. Fortunately, Daddy won.

I always sensed tension between Mother and her in-laws, although it was never overt. I wondered why, and now I think it might have been because of the way Mother entered the family, and their knowledge of her secret. Did they disapprove, and hold it against her? I doubt that, being the liberal people they were. But Mother was a bit of a snob, and I expect she never let them forget that she came from a higher level of society, no matter how reduced her situation had become.

Unfortunately, while she had that upper-class disdain for those beneath her, she herself had poor taste and no inclination toward the finer things in life. I not only learned almost nothing useful from her, I also learned nothing aesthetic. We had no music, no art, no literature in our house. We never went to movies or the theatre or concerts and never ate out. I was in my late teens before I ever ordered a meal in a restaurant, when I was with a group of young people. I watched them carefully to see how to do it. We had plenty to eat, clothes to wear, a roof over our heads, good health and security, and in our family, in the Great Depression, that was enough. But I have never understood why Mother had not been exposed to anything cultural, or if she had, why she so readily left it all behind.

She also never told me about menstruation. I had been told a few cryptic comments about it by my aunt, but I did not understand what it was—something about getting rid of bad blood, she had said, and I knew that at some point I would start to bleed. When one day I discovered fresh blood running down my leg, I ran into the bathroom in panic and hid. Eventually in desperation I yelled for Mother, who opened the door a crack and handed me a sanitary belt and a napkin. She was embarrassed and apologetic, stammering, "I always meant to say something." She never explained, never mentioned it again. I remember being horrified when I learned the following month that it was not a one-time event, but would go on month after month for many years. It was ghastly. I was eleven years old.

I remember Mother always with a stern, cold look on her face that to me meant she was angry. I never knew why she was angry, but, as children usually do, I assumed it was my fault. I realize now that she was probably just angry with life, but I grew up believing that I was continually guilty of something awful and did not know what. To this day, my habitual response to other people's anger is to feel guilty. I'm sure that if I had ever been able to talk to Mother about this, she would have been aghast to know what she had done to me. As time passed and I became more and more of a tomboy, I avoided her anger by staying out of the house as much as possible.

Only much later in my life did I think about another reason for Mother's angst. That hysterectomy in her early thirties, in about 1936, probably included removing her ovaries, and in those days I doubt that she would have been given replacement hormones. The resulting lack of hormones alone could have made her irritable and quick to anger. I wish I had understood this fifty years earlier.

I think I was a sad disappointment to my mother. She had a fantasy that her daughter would be a repeat of herself, only better. She expected me to be a pretty, gracious, dainty, feminine southern belle, waltzing about and curtsying in flouncy dresses. She may not have actually believed that, given the absurdity of such a vision in our circumstances, but the dream was there, and she never gave it up. She had that frequent southern attitude about what was correct and acceptable, meaning that appearance was everything. While my father's people were determined nonconformists, Mother's background made her painfully aware of what the neighbors thought. She was always ashamed of our house, of our clothes, of her reduced circumstances, of her husband's rough ways.

For most of my childhood, Daddy was a carpenter, and when you build something, the job is eventually finished. But he belonged to the union, and whenever one job ended he was sent on another. Every time he came home from a job on a Friday, saying he was out of work, Mother would fret and worry that we would go hungry. But on Monday he would go to the union hall and go off on another job. There was always work, but Mother never got over the precariousness of it.

I ask myself so many questions. How did she feel about her lost baby? How often did she think about him, and wish she could talk about him? What did she feel about the baby's father? Did she regret marrying Daddy? She always seemed to disapprove of him, which I could understand, as although he was a good man, he was coarse, with frequently rude manners.

Somehow, Mother got through those years, but I don't know if she ever got over the change in her circumstances. She must have grown up assuming that she would always be well off, would have a comfortable life in the South with a husband and children and servants, with her friends and her sister, enjoying bridge clubs and society luncheons. She could not have imagined how different it would be. We were not as poor as many people during those lean years, but it must have been devastating for Mother. I ask myself over and over again, how did she manage? No wonder she always seemed to be angry and resentful.

They were married in February of 1929, and the stock market crash occurred in October of that year. I don't know how much the resulting Depression affected them. At one point I asked Mother what happened to the family money after her father died, and she said, wistfully, "I never knew… It just disappeared." Years later I asked my father the same question, and he said, disgustedly, "Her brother made some foolish investments and lost it all!" I suppose this was a result of the crash.

We were not a happy family. I wonder if many families are, or is there something about life that causes us all to remember only the pain, not the joy? Or just my life? I remember one happy incident with my mother, and only one. I was too young for school, and on this sunny morning Mother was cooking French toast, for just the two of us. She was in good spirits, rare for her, and she swung me around in a circle in the kitchen and we sang "A Tisket, a Tasket," until we collapsed on the floor, laughing. I wish I had more memories of her laughing.

As a result of all this angst with my mother, I grew up feeling distant and resentful toward her. She became my negative example, and I couldn't wait to get away from her. As a result, I was estranged from my parents for many years. It took me fifty years to come to terms with my resentment.

Frankie Porter, ca. 1956.

Mother was always in poor health, and at the end of her life had been mostly bedridden for years. Once when I came to visit, we decided to go out so she needed to get dressed. As she sat on the edge of the bed and raised up her arms, I pulled her dress down over her head, and saw myself dressing my daughter when she was little. I felt sad.

Mother died of cancer when she was seventy-six years old and I was forty-four. We had never had a meaningful conversation.

5 Adventures with Peggy

When I was old enough to venture out of my immediate neighborhood alone on my bicycle, I developed a close friendship with my classmate Peggy.

Peggy lived in a tiny shabby three-room cabin about half a mile down our gravel road, on a small pond with ducks and colorful bantam chickens roaming about. On the other side of the pond were several small outbuildings—a chicken coop, a stable, and a log cabin with a dirt floor where Peggy slept in the summer. Her place always smelled of sweat and cabbage.

Peggy reached puberty sooner than I did. She had started her periods when she was ten, and by thirteen had fully developed breasts and heavy-lidded "bedroom eyes." She had wispy blond hair and was slightly overweight, with the extra pounds distributed in becoming places. I was somewhat awed by her. I was astonished and disturbed at the change that would come over Daddy when Peggy came to visit. He would linger in the living room, grinning self-consciously, his eyes gleaming. I always felt uncomfortable at this, and since Mother clearly did not like Peggy, we spent most of our time at her house. She had become my sole playmate by the time I was thirteen and the cousins had moved away.

I was forbidden to have comic books—too trashy, Mother said—but Peggy had them all. We pored over them for hours. They were peopled by absurdly voluptuous women being alternately threatened by dark, sinister villains and then rescued by costumed, square-jawed heroes. Smash! bam! zap! went Captain Marvel and Superman and all the others. Mother was right, they were trashy. Actually, I didn't really enjoy them, but lying on the floor with Peggy, talking confidentially, doing something forbidden, was delicious.

Peggy's mother was close to forty and trying hard to be twenty. Her eyelashes were always heavy with mascara, and she wore her red-dyed hair very long and curly. Her clothes were always too tight on her surprisingly trim body. She gave the impression of a middle-aged Kewpie doll. She was pleasant to me, and I felt a little guilty since I knew that I wasn't supposed to like her.

I never met Peggy's father, although I saw a picture of him once. The man who lived in the house was her mother's boyfriend, an arrangement that was far less common in 1946 than today. Actually, it was *more* common, in the sense that only really "common" people did it—and I'm sure this was the major reason my mother disapproved of Peggy. They were "poor white trash."

Paul, the boyfriend, was a taxi driver who drank too much and fortunately was not around often. When he worked at night he would sleep during the day, closed off in the bedroom. I'm pretty sure he beat Peggy's mother occasionally, and perhaps Peggy as well, although she never said so. I was afraid of Paul, and would not stay around when he was there.

I was both intrigued and frightened by the tawdry sexuality in that household. Sex did not exist in my house. It was not so much frowned upon or forbidden as it was eliminated, as many things are in the adult world, simply by never being acknowledged. Consequently, seeing no movies, reading no books, having few friends and no other adult confidants, I got my early sex education from Peggy.

When Peggy and I exchanged whispered adolescent intimacies, she would tell me of the shocking sexual activities that took place in her house. I didn't understand, and to conceal my ignorance, I would listen in dumbfounded silence. I was never sure whether these things really happened, and to whom and by whom, or if it was all Peggy's imagination fueled by those lurid comic books, but I suspect that she was sexually molested by Paul. If so, she seemed to take an odd sort of pride in it.

By far the major attraction at Peggy's was her brown and white pinto pony, Rex. He was big enough to be a real horse and small enough for young teenaged girls to handle. We rode him everywhere, both of us at once, bareback. We had one glorious summer when we were thirteen, hiking through the woods across from Peggy's house or riding Rex there, our dogs nipping at his heels. We would pack a lunch and spend the entire day in the woods. From Peggy I learned how to ride, how to care for horses, how to handle them—and how to maneuver on crutches.

I spent six weeks of the seventh grade on crutches as a result of showing off. We had returned from riding, and instead of sliding off the side of the horse, as usual, I thought I would be clever and push myself off over his rump. Actually, I had a vision of making a graceful flying jump backwards, landing lightly on my feet, waving goodbye and racing off to my house. I misjudged something, and fell heavily by Rex's hind feet instead, landing with my left leg twisted under me. It hurt, but I thought it was merely sprained and walked the half mile home. By the time I arrived, I was crying from the pain and could barely stand. Mother took me to the doctor who x-rayed my ankle, pronounced it broken, and smothered it in a cast.

The crutches did not slow me down much. I became quite agile on them, even hauling myself up and down the gravel pit banks with them, but it entitled me to a ride from Mother to school every day, and the teachers assigned another student from each class to carry my books for me. I rather enjoyed the attention.

The year I turned thirteen was the year school stopped being fun. I had to leave my little two-room school and enter the seventh grade in the big consolidated junior and senior high school with 600 students. It was total culture shock.

Fortunately, about a dozen of my classmates from the little school went, too, or I would have been totally lost. Most of the students came from two larger grade schools, and they all knew each other and rode the school buses together. That left the handful of us from my little town who walked or rode our bikes and knew no one but our own little bunch. There was no school bus service for us, since there were so few students in our town. We were on our own, and we were outsiders.

I started seventh grade with great enthusiasm. I had always been a successful student, a favorite with students and teachers alike. It took a while for me to realize that this was different, that I couldn't pull it off here.

The first year wasn't too bad. Alliances were not firm yet, everyone was feeling their way, and my social ineptitude was not yet obvious. Sheer energy and gall carried me most of that year. I was confident and loud, wisecracking and playing tomboyish games. But chasing the boys at recess does not play for long in junior high, and I soon learned that

Betty Jean, age 13 in front yard of house in Berwyn Heights.

this was not acceptable—something else was required, but I didn't know what. Thus began my excruciating adolescence.

I withdrew. I withdrew at school and I withdrew at home. My inability to socialize with my classmates coincided with my increasing dislike of my parents and feeling of rejection at home. At ages twelve and thirteen, I learned the ability to withdraw and to disappear into myself while appearing to be present, a technique I have used ever since to get through unpleasant but unchangeable situations. I could carry on a conversation, physically participate in any activity, laugh, work, anything that was required, while being closed off inside myself and merely observing, feeling nothing. (I have since learned that the psychologists' term for this is "dissociation.") I developed a shell around myself that kept the hurt and rejection away. I perfected the technique so well that I began really not to care that I was a social outcast. I had my nonconformist pride from my family to carry me through, and I had my friend Peggy. I shut out the other kids, the social life, my family.

I remember very little of the rest of junior high. I walked to school every day, attended classes, did my class work, walked home. I never saw my classmates outside of school, never talked to them on the phone, knew nothing of their activities, their lives—except for Peggy and occasionally one or two others.

I was still smart, however, and made good grades easily. I was elected to the Junior Honor Society—"elected" meaning that the teachers thought I deserved it, based on good grades and good behavior. It would have been hard for me to do anything else.

The year I turned fourteen turned out to be a traumatic turning point, the most painful year of my childhood.

I like to blame the horses. Near Peggy's house, far back in the woods on that gravel road, was a riding stable. There was a long, low barn that housed about twenty horses, with a tack room in the center, and wide sliding doors in both sides of the center section where the horses were led out. It had a large wood-fenced corral in front, and beyond that, nearer the long driveway, was a small white house where the stable manager sometimes stayed. Beyond the barn were miles of trails that wound through the woods across the road from Peggy's house. That whole area was bordered at one end by a Boy Scout camp and at the other by a Girl Scout camp, and the stable shared the trails with the scouts. This was the same woods where Peggy and I had spent so much time hiking, wading the streams, and riding Rex.

I would often take my allowance to rent a horse so that Peggy and I did not have to share Rex. We did this often enough that we became regulars and got to know the people who ran the stables, helping to feed the horses and let them out for exercise. They always let me ride much longer than the hour I paid for. We had free run of the place.

I don't remember just how I got started doing this, but that summer I started sneaking out of my room late at night, after the rest of the family had gone to bed, using that door that allowed me access outside, unseen and unheard. It was easy. I would slip off, run barefoot through the woods, avoiding the road, and meet Peggy in her little log hut where she slept in the summer.

I loved being out alone after midnight on a summer night. I always loved to run, and running at night was glorious. Night air seems to have more oxygen, and I felt light and powerful. My eyes adapted well to the night light, and I knew every stick and stone on the way by heart, since I had run that route barefoot for years. It never occurred to me to be afraid. There were no dangerous animals about, and if I had encountered a person, I would simply have slipped into the bushes and hidden. But I never saw anyone.

At first, we simply lay in Peggy's cabin and talked. That soon got boring, however, and we started taking short walks, enjoying the strange feeling of being out in middle of the night, when the world is a different place. It was Peggy, I'm sure, who eventually suggested we pay a visit to the riding stable.

The first time we merely lurked around the barn for awhile, feeling peculiar and daring. We weren't sure who might be around, or where they might be, and did not want to get caught. The next time, we were more confident. We scrambled quietly up onto the barn roof from the back and looked around. We looked down at the front of the building and were astonished to see a cot set up close under the eaves, and on it was a man, asleep.

It was Buck, the stable manager, a man of about thirty-five, good-looking in a rough way, always wearing a cowboy hat and giving the impression that he had just come in off the range. He was nice to us, and we liked him. And there he was, sound asleep, oblivious to our presence on the roof. It must have been about one o'clock in the morning.

We couldn't resist—we scraped up a few pine cones from the roof and tossed them down on him. After the second volley he turned over, and muttered. After the third cone hit him, he sat bolt upright, reached under his pillow, and jumped off his cot. We made startled sounds, and he saw us. He was shocked and bewildered to see us perched on his barn roof. After a few moments of surprised silence, we started to giggle. He told us to come down and explain what we were doing there. He also explained how close we had come to getting killed. He had pulled a loaded pistol out from under his pillow as he was waking up, and came very close to shooting before asking questions.

Of course we had no explanation, but he didn't seem to care. He invited us to join him on his narrow cot, and we all snuggled together to talk. It felt cozy and fun and a little wicked.

We had not been snuggling there long, all twisted up together, when I began to feel Buck's hand stroking my thigh, moving higher and higher. He began to slide his hand up and down inside my leg. I did not attempt to stop him, but let it go on for a long time, pretending nothing was

Betty Jean, age 15. Photo taken by grandfather O.B. in Houlton, Maine, on family vacation.

happening. At some point I realized that he was doing the same thing to Peggy with the other hand. Eventually, Buck suggested that we had better be getting home. We got up, mumbled some niceties, and casually left, about three a.m. As we walked down the woods path to Peggy's house, neither of us mentioned what had taken place. But we both knew we would go back.

And we did. Many times that summer. The stroking progressed to heavy petting, and Buck managed to find a double-width sleeping bag to lay on a blanket on the ground to give us all more room. It was scary, exciting, and lovely. Buck never seriously tried to have intercourse, at least not with me. I had hints that Peggy sometimes made night visits to the stable without me, but I never knew for sure.

6 Running Away

Near the end of the summer, Peggy and I had returned from our visit to the stables, and were lying in her hut, talking. It was about midnight. Suddenly, I heard my name being called. My name was being shouted—screamed, actually—by my brother Bobby, out somewhere on the road from my house. Instantly we realized what had happened. I had been discovered missing from my bed, and the search was on. My brother was yelling for me hysterically, running down the road. I will never forget the sound of the terror in his voice.

We panicked. Later it occurred to me that we could have simply emerged from Peggy's cabin, and explained that I had decided to go there for the night. I would have been punished, but it would not have been nearly as bad as what did happen. But our minds were clouded with guilt, knowing what we had been doing all summer, and I ran. I ran home, thinking frantically of what I would say when I got there.

As I approached the house, I saw that all of the outside lights were on at my house as well as at Grammie's next door, and my aunt was standing on our front porch, watching. I could not get in unseen. I marched up the steps, brushed past Aunt Gerry, went inside, and waited. There was no one else in the house—they were all out looking for me.

My aunt called the fire department, and the siren sounded with two blasts—the signal that I had been found. Shortly my father's pickup truck raced into the driveway, and he got out, followed by my mother. They were both crying; my mother was still wearing her nightgown under her old chenille robe. They hurried up the steps, and accosted me. It was obvious that I was alive, and after asking, "Are you okay?" and determining that I was fine, the questioning immediately shifted to demands. "Where were you? What were you doing?" The only answer I could think of was that I had gone for a walk, that I had been playing in the gravel pit. No one believed me, but they could get nothing else out of me.

The relief that I was not harmed quickly gave way to fury that I had been bad. Half of the town had been out looking for me, worried about me. For the first time that I can remember, my father raised his voice to me in anger. My mother grabbed me by my shoulders and shook me hard, saying over and over, "What will people think? What will they say?" When she let me go, I ran to my room, locked the door, and threw myself on my bed, realizing clearly that Mother cared much more about what people would think than she did about me. It occurred to me that she would rather I had been kidnapped, or murdered—there might have been less embarrassment and shame.

My ability to distance myself, to seal myself off from feelings, served me well. I lay on my bed, saying to myself that I didn't care, that it didn't matter, that I wasn't really there, I would never really be there. I didn't cry. I felt cold inside, and began to plot how I would get away.

The next morning, Dad came into my room with a hammer and, without a word, nailed shut that outside door. It was never opened again.

If there was gossip, it never reached me. Life went on as usual. The episode was never talked about, never questioned, never explained, as if it had not happened. That was the way we dealt with difficult situations in my house—with a conspiracy of silence. If we didn't talk about it, it didn't exist.

Thus ended my nightly wanderings, but not my visits to Buck. Since Peggy was not implicated in my shameful escapade, I was not forbidden to see her, and spending time at her house made it easy to continue going to the stables during the daytime, at least.

School started, and the days got cool and crisp. I took to riding my bicycle to school instead of walking, since it was much faster, and no one noticed that I left earlier than usual. I would ride off as if going to school, turn right instead of left at the top of the hill, and ride to the stable. Buck would be waiting for me, in the little white house. We would have a few minutes of secret time together, and off I would go to school.

I suppose there are people who would say that what we did was disgraceful, that Buck took terrible advantage of me, that I was scarred for life by this pseudo affair. Not I. I have always been grateful to him—grateful that we never actually had sex—but mostly grateful to be introduced to the idea of sex as a sensuous gratification, and to learn delightful ways to obtain pleasure that stopped short of intercourse.

I did not fall in love with Buck. It was very clear that while what we were doing was fun, and there was a certain caring and fondness for each other, there was never any question of a romantic relationship between us. Even a naïve fourteen-year-old knew that. And when he left in the late fall, moving on to another job, I did not grieve.

I am also grateful to have learned that it was lovely to be female—just in the nick of time, I suspect. I had not been at all sure up to that point. I had been raised as one of the boys, had been a total tomboy, and was not convinced that there was any advantage in being female. As I reached my mid-teens, it would have been easy to have continued on in that mold. I have known women who kept that mantle of masculinity into adulthood, and while they may or may not be lesbian, they at least seem to have renounced any femininity in their manner and conduct. I don't criticize them, but neither would I want to be like them. I came to glory in my femaleness. I like to think that I managed to keep the best of both aspects.

At any rate, I discovered the opposite sex. I did not date any of my classmates, but somehow I met the older brother of one of them, and we began to date. Benny was eighteen, a high school dropout. Our dates consisted mostly of rides in his car. He was very short and slight of build, and it was easy to believe him when he told me he was a jockey at a nearby racetrack. I found out later that he was only an exercise boy. He was not very smart, not attractive at all, and I think the only reason I went with him was that he was the only one who asked me. And he had a car that ran most of the time. He always smelled of car grease.

Peggy began to date Larry, a classmate, at the same time, so the four of us began spending time together. We never had any money, and I was not supposed to be dating anyway, so usually Benny would pick up the three of us at school and we would ride around until dinner time. Sometimes we would hang out at Peggy's house. I can't imagine what we talked about, but I'm sure we complained a lot about our parents.

Winter came, and with it Christmas. That was the year I received one of my strangest presents from Santa Claus. I don't recall why I wanted this so desperately, but somehow I persuaded my father to get me a gun—a single-shot, .22 calibre rifle. Mother objected, of course, but on Christmas morning, there it was, in all its lethal splendor, with its softly gleaming wooden stock, the long, dull black muzzle, cleaning supplies,

Betty Jean on senior day trip to beach, age 17

and a box of .22 shorts. This was no BB gun, no harmless plaything for an irresponsible fourteen-year-old. But it was mine, and I loved it.

Peggy and I often took the rifle to the gravel pit for target shooting, setting up old tin cans on the banks and taking turns trying to hit them. My aim was never good, and I actually enjoyed cleaning the rifle more than shooting it. I loved the feel of the barrel, the smell of the cleaning oil, the taking apart and putting together.

For many years when I became an adult, that rifle languished in my bedroom closet, traveling with me all in all my moves, usually dismantled and hidden in a box of linens or in a suitcase. In all those years I had no ammunition for it, since I could not bring myself to register anywhere as a gun owner and therefore could not buy bullets. That would have been too great an admission of this contradiction in my character, this weird fascination with the feel of power, of potential death in my hands.

My guardian angels worked overtime to keep me from serious harm again that year. Peggy and I spent hours complaining to each other about our parents, as I think many teenagers do. Sometimes our bitching sessions included our boyfriends, Larry and Bennie. Larry was a schoolmate of ours.

One day our complaining culminated in a plan to run away from home. The scheme was ridiculous, but that was not apparent to our adolescent brains. We decided that Bennie would pick up Peggy, Larry, and me as we walked to school one morning, and we would drive south. We could be many miles away before anyone discovered that we were

Betty Jean's high school graduation picture, 1951, age 18.

gone. We had no plans beyond that point. What we would do next, and what would happen, apparently didn't occur to us, and how we would get our suitcases out of the house undetected on our way to school was unclear. As it happened, it was my suitcase that sabotaged the whole scheme.

A couple of days before we were to leave, I packed an old brown suitcase and slid it under my bed. My mother never cleaned my room, so I was sure it was safe there. For some reason that escapes me now, I included my rifle in the suitcase. I have no idea whether I was thinking in terms of offense or defense, and I don't recall packing any bullets.

With the increasing alienation between Mother and me, she had given up ever going in my room. But for some unknown reason, that day before we were to run away, she decided to push the dust mop around under my bed. Of course she found my packed suitcase hidden there. I went to school that day as usual, but when I returned home, Mother was waiting for me in the kitchen. The suitcase was on the table. She glared at me, and demanded to know what *that* was all about.

I was dumbfounded, and didn't know what to say. Finally I blurted out that I hated her and was going to run away. She was furious, and sent me to my room. When Daddy got home, the two of them confronted me. I cried and cried, and tried to explain how unhappy I was. Finally I exploded in rage, yelling that I was running away because I hated them, and that if they stopped me I would try again and again until I succeeded.

They were shocked and deeply hurt. None of it made any sense to them. After much shouting and crying, a sort of truce was arrived at. They were terrified that I would carry out my threat, and were willing to make almost any concession to keep me home. Eventually, we made a bargain: I agreed not to run away if they would do two things: buy me a horse, and leave me completely alone to run my own life. No supervision, no questions, no advice. I can't imagine any responsible parent agreeing to such terms, but they—especially Mother— were so afraid of the consequences if I were to leave, that they agreed.

So they would buy me a horse, and leave me alone to run my own life, at age fourteen. And I stayed. Physically. Mentally I was long gone already, but at least now there was no pretense of communication or parenting.

For years, I had been riding other people's horses, and I had craved one of my own. When they agreed to buy one, they stipulated that I had to pay for its upkeep. I already had a paper route, which would bring me just enough money for feed, so I agreed to this arrangement, and the subject of what I had done was never mentioned again.

Family on vacation in Maine, 1948.

Peggy and Larry, however, were not so lucky. When I didn't appear, Bennie drove away, and that was that. But Peggy and Larry decided to go anyway, and disappeared. No one knew where they were. They were gone for three days, until they were discovered at a friend's house. In those days, for a teenaged girl and boy to be away together like that was scandalous, and there was much salacious gossip about what they were doing. When they were found, both Peggy and Larry were expelled from school, and neither of them ever went back. No one knew that I had been involved in the plan, and I suffered no ill effects. Again, I had escaped what could have been disastrous consequences.

The lack of parental supervision served me well as I got through my teen years. I lived at home, but I was on my own as far as decisions and choices. That suited me fine.

7 Domino and Muley Bates

To fulfill our bargain after the abortive running away episode, my parents needed to provide me with a horse, which meant we had to find one to buy. Daddy and I looked in the newspaper ads, but unfortunately, neither of us really knew anything about horses. The one we found that we could afford, at $300, was a 16-hand Tennessee Walker gelding, which we didn't realize was much too big and spirited for this 5-ft, 110-pound girl. He was so tall I couldn't see over his back. He came with a very old Army saddle, the leather cracked and brittle. We didn't understand the significance of any of this.

To pay for the horse's upkeep, named Domino because he was black with a white star on his nose, I delivered newspapers on my bicycle in the morning. This meant I arose at 6 a.m., folded sixty newspapers, loaded up my bag, and rode all over our small town on my bike, throwing papers into driveways. When I returned, I had to feed and water Domino, then bathe, dress, and ride my bike or walk a mile to school. Often, by the time I got home from school, I was too tired to ride. And when I did ride, it was a constant battle to control Domino. He was too big and headstrong for me. All he wanted to do was turn around and go home. Once we turned toward home, I could barely keep him from running away with me. It was exhausting, and not much fun. Sometimes I wondered if it was worth it. Riding him alone was not nearly as much fun as riding Rex with Peggy.

The defining event happened one day when I rode farther than usual from home, to visit a classmate in a nearby town. I had a good visit with

Frances, and as I was mounting to leave, putting all my weight in the stirrup to throw my other leg over, the stirrup strap broke. I fell, and Domino took off for home. The way home was down highway Rt.1. At the time, in 1947, this was the only direct route between Washington and Baltimore, and it was heavily traveled.

I called my father from Frances's house, and fortunately, he was home. He jumped in his pickup and headed as fast as he could toward us. Meanwhile, Fran's mother drove us down Rt. 1 toward my house. Domino was running mostly at the side of the road, but several times something spooked him and he dashed across the highway, cars careening this way and that, horns blaring. I could hardly watch, expecting him to be hit any minute.

Eventually, Daddy reached us, and he somehow managed to get hold of Domino's bridle. He repaired the saddle strap well enough for me to remount, and I rode Domino home, with Daddy driving the truck slowly beside us. The saddle was past repairing well enough to use. We still couldn't afford to buy one, and it was senseless to keep a horse as a pet, especially since he seemed to hate me, so we sold him for $200. He had been mine for a year.

On my sixteenth birthday I got my driver's license. My brother Frank had taught me to drive, using our 1936 Chevy. Once I had my license, I could go wherever I wanted. My father, being a mechanic as well as

Betty Jean with Domino, in backyard corral in Berwyn Heights, age 15.

a carpenter, always had at least three old cars—one for him to drive to work, one for my brothers or me to drive, and one being repaired. We could always count on at least one of them being available. The driveway was long but narrow, so the cars had to be parked one behind the other. We just took whichever car was closest to the street. Soon, both of my brothers had their own cars, so there was always one for me.

Whatever car was running was usually dependable, but one time it wasn't. I was seventeen, and had driven into Washington on a summer evening to attend an event. As I was coming home, on a county road, the car suddenly stopped and wouldn't start again. As I was sitting there, considering what to do, a car pulled up beside me with two men in it. One man called out the window, "Hey, need a ride?"

I said, "No, thanks. I called my father and he's coming to get me. He'll be here in just a few minutes." To my relief, they drove away. As soon as they were out of sight, I started walking. I was about a mile from home, and it was a warm, clear night, about 11 o'clock.

After I turned onto a side road, the same car pulled up alongside me and slowed down. The man called out to me, "Sure you don't want a ride?"

I said, "No, Dad will be here any minute." They drove slowly alongside me for a while, as I walked as briskly and purposefully as I could, staring straight ahead. I sensed that if I looked at them, they would interpret it as an invitation.

Again, they drove away. I made one more turn, still about six blocks from home, when I heard them driving up behind me. This time I knew I had to do something, so I immediately turned into the front walk of a house. I knew the people who lived there slightly, and I was sure they would help me, even though it was nearly midnight and the house was dark. I strode up their sidewalk as if I lived there, and as I was about to step up to the door, the car sped away really fast. I waited a long time to be sure they were gone, and ran the rest of the way home. The next day Daddy got the car started and we drove it home. I didn't tell him about the men in the car.

My memories of junior and senior high school are not pleasant. Most of those six years is a blur, with a general feeling of unhappiness. I never fit in, although I wasn't bullied or ostracized. I just hung around the margins, getting good grades and minding my own business. But one experience stands out in my mind. Every year we were required to enter a

Betty Jean astride Muley Bates at high school, age 15

project in the school's science fair. In my sophomore year I decided to do something a bit outrageous.

My classmate Frances lived on a farm out of town, and at some point years earlier a mule had died and been buried on their property. I had the idea to dig up the skeleton, clean it, identify all the bones, mount it, and enter it in the fair. I didn't know what a big project this would be.

My brother Bobby drove me to the farm in Daddy's old pickup truck. We found the grave, and began digging. Several feet down we began finding bones. As we lifted them out, I brushed off as much dirt as I could and wrapped them in old rags. The carcass had been buried along with some trash, and tin cans had rusted on some of the bones. Once we had recovered all of the bones we could find, we loaded them up in the back of my father's little pickup truck and carried them home.

We had a huge, two-story garage behind our house where Daddy worked on his cars. The second floor was mostly vacant, and I cleared a space to lay out the bones. But first they had to be cleaned. I set up a big tub of water outside, and with a bandana wrapped around my face to stifle the stink, scrubbed every bone with a wire brush—a messy, smelly job that took hours and hours over several days after school.

Once the bones were cleaned, I needed to identify and label each one. My brother Frank, who was a student at the University of Maryland, knew where there was a human skeleton hanging in one of the labs. He took me there, and when I figured out what bones corresponded to the ones in the mule skeleton, I sketched them and wrote down their names. An encyclopedia helped with the other bones. I discovered that I had all the bones except a few little ones.

Since the bones were discolored with rust, I decided to paint them white. Once the paint dried, I painted numbers on the bones and assembled them on the floor. At this point I named my mule Muley Bates. I have no idea where that came from.

The hardest part, after cleaning the bones, was to build a frame to hold them up. For this I enlisted my carpenter father. He showed me how to build the supporting frame, and a friend of his bent an iron bar in the right shape for the backbone. But I did all the construction myself. I drilled holes in the ends of the bones and wired them together.

Assembling it on the frame was a huge job, but eventually I got it done. The result was a full mule skeleton, standing upright as if it were alive. I wrote a story describing what I had done, and made a chart showing the names of the bones as they were labeled with numbers. The whole project had taken me about fifty hours after school and on weekends over about six weeks and cost about $15 (in 1947 money).

We loaded it into the pickup and took it to the school for the fair. It won a prize, so the next step was to go to the state fair, which was held some place in Washington, I don't remember where. But I do remember getting the skeleton there. Again, it went in the pickup, and I rode with it in the back of the truck, all the way into the city. It was great fun riding down Constitution Avenue in the nation's capital, my hand on the skeleton's back, waving at people as we went. People stared, and I enjoyed every minute of it.

The judging was heartbreaking. The judges gave it an honorable mention. One of them told me that it would have taken a bigger prize, but they didn't believe I did it myself. They were sure my brothers or my father must have done it. "No little fifteen-year-old girl could have done that!" My prize was a string of fake pearls. I lost it the first time I wore it.

I learned my lesson. The next year, I faked a project and got a second prize. I demonstrated how baking soda worked to make muffins rise. I just baked a bunch of muffins, picked out the ones that rose a lot and the ones that rose only a little, and labeled them as with baking soda and without, wrote up a poster, and submitted it. I was angry about the whole thing and took satisfaction in putting something over on the judges. I'm not proud of that now, but it felt good then.

After the fair, Muley Bates found a home in the biology room at my high school. Years later I went back for a visit and saw that he was gone. I learned that he had begun to smell, so he was removed. I don't know what was done with him. It would have been fitting if he had been taken back to Frances' farm and reburied.

True to our bargain, my parents made no effort to supervise me. So from age fifteen, I made all my decisions, such as what classes to take, and told them only after the decisions were made. If I needed a note for school, I wrote it and simply handed it to Mother to sign. I continued to earn money from my paper route, and spent it as I pleased. I also had a few hours of clerical work for some neighbors in their home business. I continued to do well in school, making mostly A's. School work always came easily to me.

In high school I was inducted into the Senior Honor Society, and was elected its president. I was also the editor of the school paper and thus wrote editorials. One of them made me very unpopular. Like most high schools, we had a rival school, Bladensburg High. On the day before we were to play their football team, someone from my school painted derogatory comments on the front wall of Bladensburg High. Naturally, the rival school was outraged. In response, I wrote an editorial deploring school spirit. I said something to the effect that believing our school was better just because we attended it was dumb. My fellow students were then outraged! I received many angry comments from them as I walked the halls, but I didn't care. I was convinced I was right. I still am.

Editing the school paper was a good experience. In those days, it was all written on a typewriter and after sending it out to be printed in galleys, we literally cut and pasted the text to arrange it in columns on the pages. Then the galleys were sent out to a printer. We stayed after school to work on it, and I enjoyed it. I also wrote a gossip column for the Prince George's county weekly newspaper as the representative for our little town of Berwyn Heights. I wrote about who had hosted the card club, who had visitors from out of town, who had had a baby, that kind of thing. I was paid a little bit, something like 25 cents per column inch, and I never had more than 6 or 8 inches. I had no idea then that I would eventually make my living with the printed word.

When I was a senior our school newspaper earned an award from the National Scholastic Press Association for the best newspaper in our size category. As a result, three of us on the staff went to New York to receive the award at a banquet at the Waldorf Astoria hotel. This was a big deal. Fortunately, our faculty sponsor who accompanied us had once lived in New York, so we were assured that we would be well taken care of. However, she couldn't protect us from everything. On our first day there, we took the subway to get to the hotel. We were standing in the aisle of the subway car, and when the doors opened we thought we heard our teacher say to get off at that stop. So we did. To our horror, we looked back to see the car gliding away, our teacher standing in the aisle looking shocked, saying "Stay there!" At least we thought that was what she was saying; we couldn't actually hear her. There we were, three young white girls standing on the platform in the middle of Harlem. We just waited, not knowing what else to do. Our teacher rode to the next stop, got off, and took the first car coming back to us. She was as relieved as we were when she ran up to us on the platform and saw us still huddled together there, terrified.

The event was nice, although there were so many people I felt overwhelmed. All I remember clearly is that part of our dinner was a Waldorf salad, which I had never eaten before. It was good.

The lack of parental control could have been disastrous for a teenager, but again, I was lucky. I was inclined to be a "good girl" anyway, and I had very little opportunity to be a "bad girl" if I had wanted to. We were isolated geographically and socially, and I had virtually no contact outside of classes with other students at high school, so getting in with a bad crowd there was highly unlikely. There really was no crowd available to me, good or bad.

8 Discovering Religion

But it was probably religion that saved me, no pun intended.

My parents were not churchgoers. Mother was raised Presbyterian, and Daddy was Unitarian. When they were first married, in about 1929, one Sunday they attended the big Unitarian church in Washington. Mother said the people there were well-to-do, the women in pearls and fur coats, and no one even spoke to them. They never went back. I guess that turned them off from church altogether.

Consequently, we had not been raised in any religion at all. I don't recall any conversation concerning any religious subject throughout my childhood. If it happened, it made no impression on me. As I mention in the chapter about my father, the Masons, including the Eastern Star, served as my parents' church.

My brothers were older than I, Frank by four years and Bobby by three. I didn't get along well with Bobby, but Frank and I were very close. Both of the boys had started attending a Baptist Church in another town, and when I was sixteen, I started going with them. It was an American Baptist church, which is very different from the Southern Baptists. It was not a fundamentalist church, although it was Bible-based. Until Bobby dropped out, we all went to Sunday School and worship service Sunday morning, worship Sunday night, and prayer meeting on Wednesday nights.

Eventually I decided to be baptized and join the church. I did not have a conversion experience, but it seemed like the right thing to do. Every Sunday there was an altar call, and one day I found myself walking down the aisle. The baptism itself was rather scary. It was by total immersion.

The baptismal font was kept hidden behind the pulpit, with a curtain in front of it. During baptisms, the curtain was drawn back and the minister and the person being baptized emerged from a little side door and walked into the water together. I think the water was about chest high for me. Both the minister and I had put on white robes, and after he said some solemn words, he held one of his hands behind my back and with the other put a small cloth over my nose, and then pushed me back and lowered me all the way under the water. He quickly pulled me back up, my hair streaming behind me. I didn't feeling anything other than relief that it was over. I've always been a little envious of people who speak glowingly of their conversion and baptism.

Surprisingly, our parents disapproved of our church going. As I said earlier, they had no church affiliation and had never suggested that we should. When we three became so caught up in church activities, they tried to discourage us. In retrospect, I think a couple of things were going on. Perhaps they felt chastised because we were the religious ones and they weren't, a reversal of the usual situation. Maybe they felt that it was a criticism of them that they had not taught us religion. But I suspect it really was that our church involvement happened in those teen years when we would have pulled away from them anyway, but suddenly, all three of us were putting our attention into something that took us away from home even more than school did. It was obvious that our loyalty was to another group, not to the family. I felt the disapproval more from Mother than from Daddy. He wasn't around often enough or long enough to notice much, but I think Mother felt abandoned.

As a consequence of our church attendance, when Frank started going to the nearby University of Maryland, he discovered the Baptist Student Union, called BSU. This was a student group nominally affiliated with the American Baptists, but was a highly eclectic group. It was led by a man named Howard Rees. I don't think he was an ordained minister. Everyone called him simply "Rees."

Rees was a charismatic man, probably about thirty-five, married, with a small son. He had had an accident when he was younger that had injured his hip severely. He walked haltingly, leaning heavily on two canes, and although we were told that he was in constant pain, he was the most cheerful, upbeat person I have ever known.

I started attending BSU meetings with Frank when I was sixteen and still in high school. I was the youngest person there, and while we were supposed to be college students, there were a couple of older people who were working full time. We were Baptist, Presbyterian, Methodist, and I suspect there was a Buddhist or two there, and perhaps even an occasional Catholic. I wouldn't have known, because we rarely discussed theology. The group had a strong culture that expected us to live a certain way, and our beliefs about God were irrelevant. We were expected to live a clean life, and perhaps more importantly, to be continually upbeat. There was a pervasive belief that life was good, everything worked out for the best, and no matter what happened, we would be optimistic. We had a slogan: "Maintain the glow!" with our thumb turned up. Somehow we were supposed to always maintain a kind of glow that came from our belief system, whatever that was. I suppose it must have been some version of Christianity, but I don't recall ever being taught any religious beliefs there. Probably it was taken for granted that we had beliefs in common and did not need to be taught them. Or perhaps I've just forgotten.

BSU became my adoptive family. All of my energy, when not in class or studying, was invested in the group. No one seemed to mind that I was so much younger than they. Almost all of the students in the group were "day dodgers" who lived at home and went to campus just to attend classes. Some of the students who brought their lunches to campus held noon meetings every weekday. Since I was still in high school, one of the BSU students would pick me up at school, take me to attend the lunch meetings, and return me in time for my next class. Sometimes I couldn't get back in time before class started, but my grades were so good the teachers looked the other way. This group was much more important to me than any of my high school classmates, who seemed juvenile.

The lunch group met without Rees, and we did our own programming. There would be six or seven of us, and we would eat our lunches and pray and have some kind of discussion. I don't remember any of the discussions, but they were always interesting and relevant to our daily lives. These meetings anchored my day.

When you think of a religious student group, you probably don't think of something like BSU. This was a loose-knit group of about fifty funny, lively, kind, interesting, and talented young people. Music was important, with lots of singing. It included three sisters who were especially talented and often performed for groups, singing a cappella in three-part harmony. We could always count on them to spring spontaneously into song, anytime, anywhere, and we would all join in.

It's hard to know what held this group together, except for Rees's charisma. We met all winter, we met weekly during the summer, we held weekend retreats, we cared about each other. No one smoked or drank or swore. It was an extremely witty group, with lots of laughter and good cheer.

I stayed in BSU for six years, until my senior year of college when I married and moved away. I credit this group with keeping me safe during my later teen years.

At the end of my senior year in high school, I wanted to go to an event somewhere, I can't remember where now, that took place just before graduation. I had no interest in attending the graduation ceremony, and signed up for the trip. When my principal heard that I was skipping graduation, he called me into the office and told me that if I didn't attend the ceremony, I couldn't get my diploma. I didn't know then that he couldn't do that, so I bargained with him that I would miss Baccalaureate but would return just in time for the graduation ceremony itself. So after the trip, I took a taxi directly from Union Station to the University of Maryland Armory for the ceremony. I stashed my suitcase under the bleachers and put on my robe that my parents had brought to me there. After the ceremony, I marveled at the girls who were tearfully saying goodbye to each other, sad at leaving high school. I was just relieved to be escaping and leaving it behind me.

My first summer job after high school was waitressing at a local Hot Shoppe, but after my freshman year at the university, I decided I wanted to attend a Baptist youth camp that met in Wisconsin right after classes ended. When I returned two weeks later, it was too late to find a summer job. I looked hard, riding the streetcar into the city, walking the hot pavements, answering want ads. No one had any openings. In desperation I signed up for a job selling encyclopedias door to door. It wasn't until the training ended that I discovered I was to be sent off to some remote area of the country with a team of kids and a supervisor. I wasn't willing to do that, so they assigned me to an area in Washington.

The first person I talked to not only refused to buy but lectured me that I needed to learn my pitch better, and I drove straight home, humiliated. Through tears, I explained to Mother that I just couldn't do it. That's the only time I remember ever being vulnerable with her, and she responded sympathetically. She assured me that I didn't have to do it, that they would pay for my next year of school. That is the only summer I had a real vacation. I enjoyed doing odd jobs around the house for three months.

For some reason I don't quite understand, perhaps because of my vulnerability, Mother and I got along surprisingly well that summer. Frank was gone, working at the Baptist Green Lake camp in Wisconsin, and Bobby was building a house by himself and was living in a tent onsite in nearby Virginia while he worked on it, so I was the only kid at home for the summer. In a letter I wrote to Frank, I commented on how well we were doing, and explained that I was making more of an effort than I ever had. I said,

> *The new policy here is really a very simple one. I have merely assumed that there is no gulf between the folks and me, and have attempted to take them into my confidence as much as is feasible, and try to keep nothing from them. I have just gone ahead and ignored the strangeness that has always existed, and lo! it isn't there anymore. It's hard to explain.… Mother hasn't said so, but I know that she is really enjoying having me around all day. Daddy is a little pleased because I can do some of the things he has always wanted done and doesn't have the time (or inclination) to do—painting screens and other trim, cutting down weeds, etc. As far as improving family relations is concerned, I feel that being unemployed is the best thing that could have happened.*

In another letter to Frank that summer, I said,

> *…believe it or not, I have at least realized that we, as our parents' children, have a responsibility to our home—a responsibility that was not incurred by us and over which we have no control. It is an integral part of being in the human race and we are being something less than human to attempt to avoid it. Why has it taken me so long to discover this? To think of all the years of unhappiness because I, in particular, have tried to avoid paying a debt simply because I didn't ask to owe it! … At any rate, I now live in a reasonably happy home where I thought pleasantness was impossible.*

Unfortunately, the pleasantness didn't last. I went back to college in the fall and spent very little time at home, and we settled back into the old rut.

The next summer, I was dating a young man named George. I was hired at a Kodak film processing plant, where George's uncle was the plant manager. We both worked there, that summer and the next. It paid well enough for us to easily earn our school tuition.

George's uncle saved my job when I screwed up badly the second summer. I ran a machine called a splitter. In those days, home movies were shot on 16-mm film, which then had to be split lengthwise and spliced together to make it 8mm. My job was to run the film through the splitting machine, splice the two pieces together, roll it all up on the machine, and put it back in the box it came in from the customer. Each box had a number perforated on the flap, and the same number was perforated on the end of the film. A critical part of my job was to match the numbers on the film to the numbers on the box, to be sure the film went to the right customer. The box and film had been separated during processing, and had been put back together just before coming to me. I was the last one to ensure that the right film went in each box. Each operation took about one minute. I was paid on the incentive system, which meant the faster I worked, the more money I made.

The temptation to skip checking the numbers was too great, and I often just skipped that part of the process. Eventually film started coming back from irate customers who had received the wrong film. I should have been fired, but George's uncle took pity on me and transferred me to another job in the plant, to finish out the summer. He knew I needed the money to go back to college.

During my first year at college I worked ten hours a week in the campus post office to earn spending money. It was there that I experienced sexual harassment on the job. The postmaster, a middle-aged man, would walk up behind me and press himself against me when I was standing at the counter. In those days we "girls" were expected to just endure whatever the boss did. To protect myself, I managed to maneuver so that I was never alone with him or was not in a position that he could get close to me. If he had become more aggressive about it, I don't know what I would have done. I couldn't afford to quit, and there was no supervisor I could appeal to.

The summer jobs paid for all my college expenses. In those days, at the University of Maryland in-state tuition and fees came to about $250 for the two-semester year. It didn't pay for books, however. I bought used books and then resold them at the end of each semester, but for some classes I didn't have a textbook. I was worried about Bacteriology 101, because the book was very expensive and I just couldn't buy it. But I took very detailed notes during lectures, and aced the class.

I remember very little of my college years, I suppose because other than BSU, it was rather unremarkable. Since I was a "day dodger," it wasn't that much different from high school. I was a liberal arts major until my junior year, when I chose childhood education, expecting to become a preschool/kindergarten teacher. Since I knew so little about children, I thought it would be good to learn something about that age group in preparation for having my own family someday. However, after one semester of practice teaching, I realized I would be anything, even a waitress, before I would teach little kids for a living. I was intolerably bored.

One incident in college does stay in my mind. Somehow I had made friends with Caroline, a student from Georgia who obviously came from a well-to-do family. She wore expensive clothes and gold jewelry, and drove a red sports car. One day I invited her for a visit at my house on a Saturday afternoon. We sat at the dining room table, drinking lemonade and talking. I noticed that she seemed a bit subdued, but didn't think much of it.

As I have mentioned earlier, my father was constantly remodeling our house. At this time the project was the dining room. He had torn out the walls to put up new sheetrock, so the studs were exposed, along with the insulation and wiring. Because removing the walls was a dusty job, we had strung up an old blanket in a doorway to keep the dust out of the kitchen. A stack of lumber was piled against one wall, and tools were lying around. This was a normal situation for us, but it must have looked pretty awful.

When Caroline left, I walked with her to her car to say goodbye. She got in the car, shut the door, looked at me, and with a slow shake of her head, said, "I had no idea." She rolled up the window and drove away. I never saw her again.

9 Marriage

One of the students in BSU was Bruce, a giant of a man, as sweet and gentle as he was big. He attended one of our weekend retreats, and brought a friend with him. I was attracted to the good-looking stranger, with his dark hair and brown eyes and quiet manner. We talked a lot over the weekend, and later began dating. His name was George Leas, and he was studying chemical engineering at the University of Maryland where I was also a student.

We didn't do much traditional dating, as neither of us had money or time for going out to dinner or movies. But we spent a lot time together at BSU meetings, or studying, or just talking somewhere. A year later we were engaged. He didn't actually propose; it just slipped into our awareness that we would marry. One night at the dinner table, I said casually that George and I were going to get married. My mother said, "That's nice," and the conversation resumed as if I had not spoken.

At some point, I pondered whether I really wanted to marry George. My decision was ultimately based on the flimsiest of reasons. I distinctly recall where I was and what I was doing when I decided to go ahead with it. I was driving up the street near my house, and said to myself, "Well, I don't really love him, but I surely will eventually, and if I'm not married by the time I'm twenty-one, I'll be an old maid." That sounds absurd now, but it in 1953 it almost made sense.

George was a handsome young man, and being a chemical engineering student, he was likely to be a good provider. He was steady, a nondrinker like me, and seemed dependable and considerate. My only

Betty Jean and George Leas leaving church after their wedding, June 4, 1954. Westminster Presbyterian Church, Bladensburg, Maryland.

previous boyfriend had left the university and gone back to Georgia, but we hadn't been serious before he left anyway. George was the only likely prospect of saving me from oldmaidhood.

We were married on June 4, 1954, the day after the last final exam of my junior year. I wish I could go back and handle the wedding differently. A daughter's wedding is a big occasion in a mother's life, and mine was the only one my mother would have. However, I shut her out of it completely. It seemed right at the time, given that we were so emotionally distant, but in retrospect I cringe at how much it must have hurt her.

I made all the arrangements myself, while studying for finals. It was not an elaborate ceremony, since my parents couldn't afford much, but it did take some planning. It was held in the Presbyterian church that George attended, conducted by his minister. It was small, with just two bridesmaids and a matron of honor. The reception was held in the church fellowship hall, and was catered by the women of the church at no cost to us—just finger foods and punch. I rented a couple of palms and bought my bouquet, but I created the other decorations myself. I rented a white lattice arch and placed it at the front where we would stand, flanked by the two palms. I cut all the blossoms from my grandmother's big white rose bush and wove them through the openings in the latticework. That was it. Simple but effective.

I found my dress on the rack in a bridal shop, on sale for $50. When I was looking through the racks, a saleswoman approached me to help. She showed me a few, and then asked, hesitantly, "Um… is this for your sister?"

Puzzled, I said that no, it was for me.

She looked surprised, and said, "Well, you look like you're about fourteen!" I was twenty-one. I had always looked young for my age, but I didn't know I looked *that* young.

My Uncle Quentin was a professional photographer and gave us a wedding album as a present. The whole wedding cost my parents $500, about $4,700 in 2018 money. I learned years later from my brother that my father sold one of the houses he had built for his mother to get the money for my wedding. Until then I had never thought about how it was paid for, as Daddy had never said anything about it. He was a resourceful man. I suppose if he had another daughter to marry off, he would have sold the other house.

Both George and I were still in college when we married, and we lived that summer in an apartment. I knew very little about housekeeping. The

Betty Jean and George's wedding reception, June 4, 1954. (l-r) Nancy Leas, Eleanor Bancroft, Jennie Hodgson, George Leas, Sammy Racette (ringbearer), Betty Jean Leas, Lois Leas, George Leas Sr., Frankie Porter, Than O. Porter.

most I had ever done was dusting, and I hated that. One day about a week after we moved in, I swept and dusted and picked up everything. A week later I noticed it needed it again, and I was appalled. I thought, "But I already cleaned in here!" It hadn't occurred to me that cleaning had to be done over and over. I thought once I did it, that was that! I also didn't know how to cook. I don't remember what we ate, but it must have been very simple.

Early in marriage I began to realize how unprepared I was for adult life. In a letter I wrote to my brother Frank on July 2, 1958, I complained about how little our parents had done to prepare me for what I needed to know to navigate in the world of grownups. Again, my bitterness shows:

... I have been embarrassed by the utter neglect from Mother as I was growing up.... She taught me nothing at all—and I mean nothing of the things a child, especially a girl, is supposed to learn at home. Do

you know that I did not know how to make a bed, or to scrub a floor? I know brides are supposed to be inexperienced, but my difficulty lay not in a lack of experience as much as in a lack of an example. I can't remember Mother ever scrubbing a floor. … And aside from house-keeping, there are so many other areas in which Mother and Daddy neglected me—and you and Bobby too, I guess, such as religion and sex. Mother never said a word to me about sex, not even about menstrua-tion.. They never even told me there is a God. It seems incredible to me now that a child can reach the age of 16 and not know that there is an Old Testament and New Testament, or who Jesus Christ was.

I started establishing a house being completely ignorant of almost every subject that a woman should be familiar with—house furnish-ings, for example. The differences in the different periods, and how to tell good quality, and how to arrange them. And flowers—until a year ago I didn't know the difference between a philodendron and an African violet—Mother still doesn't. Or antiques. Or entertaining. Or music or art or literature or even good grooming. … We never went to a library. There isn't a single thing that Mother passed on to me.

I realized as time went by that the isolation of our childhood had prevented me from learning the social graces that other people take for granted. I did not know how to order a meal in a restaurant, how to min-gle at a party, how to have girlfriends. I had no sisters, and never attended a slumber party or even spent the night at a girlfriend's house except those nights in Peggy's cabin.

So I watched. I watched what other people did, and imitated them. I managed never to be the first in line anywhere, so I could see what the people in front of me did. It took a long time for me to become comfort-able in many everyday situations. But I learned the basics, and faked the rest for many years.

Marriage was a wonderful relief from the cold, unemotional family I had been raised in. It was a joy to be in a relationship where we could express our feelings, where we were comfortable with casual touching. I grew up in a family who never touched each other. If I accidently brushed against someone in the house, I would say, "Oh, excuse me." George and I were affectionate, often expressing our love for each other. I never heard either of my parents say, "I love you." What a joy to be warm and loving with another person! We were happy.

After the summer by ourselves in the apartment, when school started in the fall we moved in with George's parents, along with his younger siblings, David and Nancy. In general I got along very well with them. I was close to Lois, my mother-in-law, closer than to my own parents. The wedding pictures unintentionally reveal the dynamics. In the receiving line, Lois and George Sr. are standing close to George and me, and my parents are standing a couple feet away from the four of us. That closeness with Lois changed in later years.

That fall my thyroid gland went berserk. Usually an overactive thyroid causes a person to lose weight, but I gained weight because I was ravenously hungry all the time. I also was burning up with heat, as if I had a fever. It soon became clear that something was wrong, and I saw a doctor. In 1954, the standard treatment for hyperthyroidism was to remove the thyroid gland. So in December, during Christmas break, I had surgery. I was in the hospital for about a week, and on Christmas day George brought me a tiny artificial tree, with multicolored lights and ornaments. It was about 18 inches tall. He found a place to plug it in on the table by my bed. I was touched by his thoughtfulness.

Then in mid-January, at the end of the semester, I began feeling sick. One day I came down the stairs complaining of nausea, and Lois just looked at me and smiled. She knew—I was pregnant. I was in the middle of my senior year, but George was a half year ahead of me and finished that semester. He had accepted a job in Schenectady, New York, and we expected that I would stay with his parents, finish school, and join him in June. We had not factored in a pregnancy, especially one that made me extremely sick, not just mornings, but constantly, day and night. I couldn't keep anything down.

I refused to stay there without him, as sick as I was, and dropped out of school. The dean of students called me into his office and implored me not to quit. I had almost an A average. To his credit, he insisted that I was making a big mistake. "Only one more semester," he said, "and you will have that degree the rest of your life." But I was determined. So in January of 1955 we packed up what little belongings we had and moved to upstate New York.

We found an apartment in an old farmhouse in Burnt Hills, a suburb of Schenectady. It had been a dairy farm, and the house was surrounded by pastures for Holstein cows. The landlord was a veterinarian whose hospital was on the property, near the house and a barn. The house was divided into three apartments, two on the ground floor and one upstairs. We were on the ground floor. The vet and his family lived in a big new

The farm house in Burnt Hills , New York, near Schenectady, 1955.
Betty Jean and George's apartment was on the ground floor.

house across the pasture, with a pond between us. We arrived in early February, with snow deep on the ground and only two trees in sight, their bare branches stark against the gray sky.

George worked as a chemical engineer in a plant that had weird working hours. The engineers worked for 14 days straight on one shift, then had four days off, then worked another 14 days on a different shift. This meant George was constantly adjusting to different sleeping hours, and could never really get a good rest. It was hard on him, but he endured it until after a few months he found a job with another company with normal hours.

He also had to endure my being constantly sick for seven months. The only food I could keep down was sweets, and consequently I gained 45 pounds. That winter was difficult for me, sick and alone a lot in that drafty old house with George gone at work so much and no friends or neighbors. I had never been away from home for more than a few days, so it was a big adjustment.

But the time was made easier for me when the vet, Stan, asked me if I wanted to help in the animal surgery. I was delighted. I became expert at assisting him with operations on dogs and cats, and then often rode with him to farms where he treated sick cows and horses. One time I went with him to a farm where a cow was having difficulty delivering a calf. I was shocked when he inserted his hand into the cow's vagina and pushed it in all the way up to his elbow. He felt around in the uterus, moved the calf around, and pronounced everything would be okay. I was impressed that he could go into a barn when the farmer was away, look around at the animals, determine which one was sick, decide what the problem was, and then treat it. He said it was actually easier when the owner wasn't there and he could deal with just the animals. I realized when working with Stan that a good veterinarian needs to get along well not only with the animals but also with their people.

I had many memorable experiences with Stan. For instance, he got calls to treat the animals in the circus when it came to town. He was called to see a lion that had an infection and needed an antibiotic. Giving a shot to a huge, unhappy lion is not easy. Stan managed to slip a thick rope around one paw that he could reach through the bars. He then tied the rope to a another cage nearby. He gradually pulled on the rope until the lion's paw was close to the bar. He reached in and put a needle containing a sedative into the leg near the paw. When the lion was asleep, he could proceed to treat it. At one point, one of the young men who worked at the circus was watching closely, leaning down near the lion's leg. Stan, always the joker, suddenly slammed his fist down on the rope so that the lion's leg jerked wildly. The young man screamed and ran, as we all laughed.

Stan had a big hayfield for his cows, and in late summer, when the hay had to be brought in, George and I helped with the harvest. My job was to drive the tractor. I wish I had a picture of me, eight months pregnant, perched on the tractor seat in the hot sun, my belly barely fitting under the steering wheel, driving up and down the field while the men threw hay bales on the wagon behind me. I loved it.

Soon after we arrived in Burnt Hills we registered to vote. When we reached the counter in the court house and said we wanted to register, the clerk asked, "Which party?'

George answered quickly, "Republican." I just nodded. I had not given a thought to what party I should belong to. My parents joked about how they cancelled each other's vote every election—Daddy was a New England Republican and Mother was a southern Democrat. But we never discussed politics at home, and I paid no attention, so I had no idea what I believed politically. Republican sounded as good as any.

10 Motherhood

In late August, our son Howie was born. I knew almost nothing about childbirth, although I did have prenatal visits with a doctor. When I began to have contractions, George took me to the hospital about 20 minutes away in Schenectady.

I was scared. I didn't know what to expect during the delivery and wasn't prepared for how much the contractions hurt. As they were rolling my gurney down the hall to the delivery room, I began to sob. I didn't know why, and George, who was walking beside me, was bewildered. "What's wrong?" he asked. I couldn't tell him. I just cried harder.

It was a Saturday, and George had planned to play golf. Labor was going slowly, and the doctor assured George it would be hours yet, that he should go ahead and play a round of golf. Soon after George left, Howie appeared. George felt bad that he wasn't there, although it wasn't his fault. In those days the father was not allowed anywhere near the delivery room anyway, so it wouldn't have made any difference to me if he had been there.

The arrival of our first child exacerbated my poor relationship with my mother. I did not want her to come see us when the baby came, and did not want her to have any opportunity to get close to our child. In one of the letters I wrote to my brother Frank just before Howie was born, I poured out my bitterness and determination that she have as little contact with him as possible. Apparently Mother and Daddy wanted to visit right away to see their first grandchild, and I had refused to have them come. Frank was asking me to reconsider. I don't remember now how bitter I was, and am surprised at how clearly it comes out in the letter. In a long passage, I say,

> *I cannot emphasize enough how <u>intensely</u> I do not want her to have anything to do with my children or my married life. ... To me there is something contaminating about her. When she touches something that is meaningful to me, it is ruined. I don't think you realize, Frank, what Mother has done to her family—all three of us have been more or less handicapped for life by living with her. And I resent it—although I'm not as bitter as I used to be. . . . I just wish I were heartless and cruel enough to break with them and disown them, but I can't, so I will go on pretending to keep from hurting them as long as they live.*
>
> *I agree with the advice Rees in BSU gave me years ago—to move away from home, reject my parents and get out of their sphere of influence before it was too late. ... I'm happier now than I have ever been or had any idea it was possible to be. And I think my children have a chance to grow into happy, psychologically normal, stable people—which Mother's children did not.*

Later in that letter I relented and agreed that my parents could come for a visit soon after the baby arrived. Apparently not only my parents but also at least George's mother came at the same time, although I have no memory of the visit. In a letter to Frank and Jean dated November 23, 1956, I say,

> *That episode when Howie was born was positively the last time I shall give in "to keep from hurting Mother's feelings." ... Every time I think about how much trouble I had getting started nursing Howie I kick myself for letting that crowd descend on us. It was the worst possible thing I could have done and no one will ever be able to tell just how much damage it did. Both Mother and Lois should have known better.*

Once we were home with the baby, we were awkward about taking care of him. Neither George nor I really knew anything about babies. I had years of experience babysitting, but only with older children. I had read books, which helped. Books have often been my tutors throughout life.

Howie was a difficult baby. He cried all the time. I wonder how much his crying was related to my reluctance to be a mother. I bonded with him instantly, and I never blamed him for being there, but deep down I resented having to take care of someone. I missed my life of independence. I knew I had no choice and did my best to be a good mother, but it was a hard adjustment. Now I recognize a deeply rooted selfishness. Not until much later in life was I able to see how selfish I had been in my early years.

One day we decided to go somewhere and got into the car as usual. As George reached to turn the key in the ignition, we suddenly looked at each other and said at the same time, "The baby!" We had both forgotten about Howie. We never did that again.

To make matters worse, George was drafted into the Army. Being a father in peacetime, he should not have been called, but he had registered when he was a teenager in Wisconsin, and our theory is that they needed to meet a quota and did not want to call up any of their locals. So in October of 1955, when Howie was seven weeks old, his father left for basic training at Ft. McClellan in Anniston, Alabama. It was six months before we managed to live together again.

That winter was the worst of my life. I was alone in that creaky old house in snowy upstate New York with a crying baby and not enough money. I was lonely and scared with no one to help. Shirley, the vet's wife and our neighbor, was some help, but not a lot. She had her own life and family and she was too away far to walk to in the winter cold and snow.

This was the only time in my life when my naturally cheerful nature deserted me. I realize now that I was close to a breakdown. At one point I thought I wanted to die. I had read that freezing to death is a relatively painless way to go, so one day in desperation I went outside and lay down in the snow. I thought I would just lie there and die. But then I heard Howie crying, and I thought, "Oh darn, I can't do it now, the baby's crying," and got up and went back inside. Fortunately, the urge passed, and I never thought about it again.

Money was a constant problem. A private's pay was not enough to live on. George sent me as much as he could, but after I paid the rent, there was not much left. I was nursing Howie, and I had to eat enough to keep my milk coming. That fall my neighbor Shirley and I had canned many pints of applesauce. Chicken wings were cheap, and that and the applesauce and ice cream sustained me all winter. Fortunately, I managed to lose some of those thirty-five extra pounds I had gained while pregnant. Several times I borrowed money from Stan and Shirley to get through the month.

The house in Anniston, Alabama, 1956. The Leas's apartment was on the ground floor.

It was hard for George, too, but somehow we got through it. He was living in the barracks, but eventually he got more pay, and found an apartment for us where Howie and I joined him in March of 1956.

Our apartment in Anniston was part of the first floor of an old two-story Victorian house in a nice part of town, complete with gingerbread trim, a sweeping front porch with rocking chairs, and a grape arbor in the back yard. The 75-year-old landlady lived in the other half of the first floor. What had been the front parlor was our bedroom, and what probably had been the dining room was our living room. We also had a small kitchen and bath, and more than our share of cockroaches and mice. We learned to live with them. George developed a game of waiting for a mouse to emerge and trying to hit it by throwing a golf ball. I don't think he ever hit one. It soon became a habit to keep my eyes closed for a few seconds after I turned on the light in the kitchen to give the roaches time to disappear.

Life in Anniston wasn't too bad for me. I got to play little housewife, wearing dresses and aprons. Occasionally I actually wore high heels and lipstick around the house, not unusual for a housewife in the Fifties.

Money was still tight, but George had found an ingenious way to make extra money. Ft. McClellan was where soldiers were sent for the

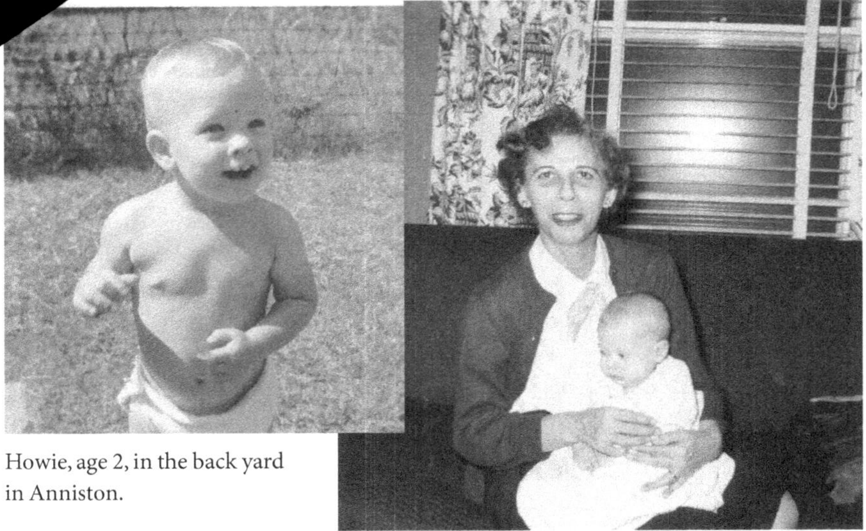

Howie, age 2, in the back yard
in Anniston.

Lois Leas, George's mother, holding Howie, 1955.

first six weeks of basic training. George had been kept there because he could type and they needed a clerk. All of the men coming through every six weeks for training had to have patches sewn on their uniforms, and the patches were thick and stiff and very difficult to sew by hand. While he was living in the barracks, George had bought a used portable sewing machine and offered to sew on patches for a fee. Most of the men were happy to have him do it, and he made a considerable amount of money. When I arrived, he brought the sewing machine home, and I began sewing patches and also making alterations for the soldiers, mostly shortening pants. George would mark what needed to be done, bring the uniforms home, I would do the work, and he would take them back and get the money. Every six weeks we got a new batch of soldiers. It was a nice little cottage business. We would have been hard pressed to survive without that money.

In Anniston, I was occupied with being a housewife, but mostly I was taking care of Howie. He was still a very unhappy baby. He cried and cried. He always woke up with a piercing cry, and the slightest noise would wake him. Eventually we began sleeping in the living room on the foldout couch, letting him have the bedroom, the biggest and nicest room in the house. He was two years old before he stopped

Betty Jean playing in the yard with Howie, Anniston. Note the dress and high heels!

George with Howie, Anniston, 1956.

crying so much. Probably not coincidentally, that is the same time I stopped resenting having to be a mother. I realized one day that the resentment was gone and I was at peace with it. I have no idea why. It never came back. I proceeded to love being a mother for the rest of my life.

George and Betty Jean with Howie, Anniston, 1956.

George hated the Army. His job was mindless clerical work, and for a very bright chemical engineer, it was maddening. He desperately wanted out of there. At the time, his father was a civilian working for the Army in Washington, DC, and he managed to pull some strings through his boss to get George transferred to Ft. Detrick in Frederick, Maryland. So in December of 1956 we packed up and moved again.

11 Becoming Homeowners

George's job at Ft. Detrick dealt with bacterial weapons. It was classified, so he couldn't tell me what he was doing, but he insisted he was not in any danger. The one disease he mentioned was touleremia, a disease of rabbits that can be fatal to humans. To this day I don't know whether he developed weapons or perhaps worked on how to counteract them. He still hated the Army, but at least he had challenging work in his field.

We found another old farmhouse to live in. We had the whole ground floor, and another young couple lived upstairs. Again we were surrounded by Holstein cows. The landlord was a dairy farmer who lived with his family across the road, at the end of a long driveway. He was a real farmer, making his living from his cows and crops. The only drawback was the constant influx of flies from the cow manure that was deposited not far from the house.

That house was one of my favorites of all the places we have lived. I have a snapshot of Howie as a toddler, sitting on a tractor gripping the steering wheel, pretending to drive it, and another of him in his blue snowsuit surrounded by a flock of white chickens in the backyard. Unfortunately, we didn't stay long, enjoying just one nice long summer there.

We moved again because George was discharged from the Army in October of 1957. He had found a job as a chemical engineer with Pfizer, the pharmaceutical company, in Groton, Connecticut. We rented a small Cape Cod bungalow in Mystic, a quaint little historical town. When I rocked Howie in the living room, I could look out the picture window over the Mystic Harbor and watch seagoing ships cross the

House in Frederick, Maryland, 1957. George and Betty Jean had the whole first floor.

horizon on Montauk Sound. It was a pleasant place, but we didn't stay there long either.

I was pregnant, and we decided it was time to buy a house. The rental house was quaint, but a disaster to live in. It was prohibitively expensive to heat, and the landlord was unresponsive when everything kept breaking down. He actually went to Florida for the winter and left no one for us to turn to for repairs. We had to get out. We found a small, three-bedroom ranch in a new subdivision about a half-hour drive from George's job at a price of $14,000. We didn't have enough cash for the down payment, so we asked my brother Frank for a $1,200 loan, at 6% interest. Frank was always the one in the family with money. He didn't make a huge salary, but he and his wife were extremely frugal and he invested wisely in the stock market. I have a letter I wrote to Frank requesting the loan, and in it I detail our income and expenditures, to demonstrate that we could afford the house and could repay the loan. The numbers seem astounding now, compared with today's expenses.

In 1958, $100 would be about $870 in 2018. Adding a zero to the numbers below gives a rough comparison with today. I'm puzzled at the proportions. For instance, we spent as much on food as we did on rent, and I can't imagine having a $550 monthly car payment today. Here is what I sent him for our monthly expenses in the rental house.

rent $95
heat 30
elect, phone 15
food 95
car payment 55
Sears payment 11
Stan's loan 50
car insur 30
car operation 20
clothes 10
savings 25
misc (incl. church) 30
Total $466

George's monthly take-home pay was $475 (about $4,100 in 2018). Even for the times, that was pretty good pay for a new engineer, four years out of school with two years of it in the Army.

Note the item "Stan's loan." This is money we borrowed from our then-landlord when George was drafted, I think to pay for the move to Alabama. That loan was the beginning of a pattern of borrowing that we

The first house the Leases owned, in Aljen Heights, Connecticut, 1958.

maintained throughout our marriage, a symptom of the way we viewed money. I was never really comfortable with our borrowing, but it didn't occur to me to object. In my mind, the breadwinner had the right to determine how the family's money would be spent. It is hard to realize now how subservient I was in this arrangement, but I was a product of the times, and that is the way it worked. George earned the money; he decided our finances, and I went along.

This pattern was repeated in our relationship for years to come. It seems incredible now how I accepted the mind-set that I was powerless, and that powerlessness was the normal way to be. Assertiveness simply didn't occur to me at that point in my life.

Frank and Jean agreed to lend us the money, and we bought the house. We moved in on February 8, 1958, one week before our second son was born.

Gary arrived in the midst of a blizzard. George drove me and Howie to the hospital, 30 minutes away, in blinding snow just before midnight. I was holding my breath in fear that we wouldn't make it in time. George had to just leave me there and go home, since we had no one to take care of Howie. They rushed me right to the delivery room for a labor of only five hours. My doctor couldn't get there because of the snow storm, so a resident delivered the baby. Fortunately, this labor was uneventful, much less stressful than the first one. The doctor joked, "All I had to do was catch him!"

George's mother came right away and stayed for two weeks. In those days, mothers and newborns stayed in the hospital for five days, or even longer if it was a boy who was to be circumcised. I got a good rest.

Now that we were permanently settled, we started going to a small Methodist church. I remember taking Howie to the children's room and having baby Gary lying on the pew beside us when he was only a few weeks old.

Thus began our long practice of church-going. In the future, wherever we lived, we always connected as quickly as possible with a church. It didn't matter what denomination it was, it just had to be Protestant, not too far away, and have friendly people. This provided us with instant community, and since we moved frequently for many years, we needed to make friends and establish connections quickly.

George was the typically reserved engineer, but with my gregariousness, we made friends easily, and we soon had a group of about five young couples who socialized together. One of our friends was the town

Gary and the family dog Sabre, 1959.

selectman, Connecticut's version of a mayor, and through him I got involved in politics, an interest that would stay with me for many years. At one point I was actually asked by some of the local political figures to run for state legislator. I considered it, but I was pregnant for the third time, and with two little ones already, it just wasn't feasible.

Our house was one of the first built in the subdivision, so there was constant construction going on around us. One day I noticed a huge, interesting rock across the road in a field. I asked the bulldozer operator to move it into our yard. He said, "Lady, you're nuts! You don't bring rocks *into* the yard in Connecticut!" But he moved it. I planted daisies and petunias around it and it looked great, much better than a plain grass lawn.

The memory of one terrifying experience still makes me shudder. Gary was about eight months old and had begun crawling. One day I left him and Howie playing contentedly on the kitchen floor while I took a load of laundry downstairs to the basement. I pulled the door shut at the top of the stairs, but didn't notice that it didn't latch. As I was putting clothes in the washing machine, I heard a thump, thump, thump, and turned to see Gary rolling down the stairs at the far end of the basement, one step at a time. The stairs were open, with no risers or railing. I dashed frantically the length of the basement, but before I could get to him, he reached the concrete floor and rolled up against the wall and back again. I picked him up, bracing myself for the worst, but quickly discovered that he was unhurt. Gary soon stopped crying, but I cried for an hour.

In September 1960, our daughter Christina was born (years later she changed her name to Grace). I was so hopeful that this one would be a girl, and was delighted when she appeared. Hers was the quickest and easiest labor. I was disappointed that I couldn't manage to nurse her for more than a few weeks. I had nursed Howie for seven months and Gary

Howie, Gary, and Christie in Aljen Heights, 1960.

for three months, but I didn't have enough milk this time, and with two other little ones in the house, I just couldn't devote the time to it. At least she got the benefit of those few weeks.

Now with three children, we needed more room, so we decided to build a bigger house in another new development, called Christy Hills. The project went pretty well, although as the job progressed the contractor discovered that the edge of the roof in the front of the house was going to bump into the trunk of a big tree in the front yard that leaned toward the house. We were unwilling to cut the tree down so persuaded him to design a notch into the roof edge to accommodate the tree trunk. I've wondered since if the tree eventually grew big enough to necessitate cutting further into the roof or if it was finally cut down.

But before we moved, George's mother came for a visit, with two other little grandchildren. This situation requires some explanation. George's younger sister gave birth to two babies as a teenager and had neither the means nor the desire to take care of them, so they were living with Lois and George, Sr. They were both very needy children, presumably as a result of their traumatic early days of neglect with their mother, and required constant attention. When Lois came to visit, leaving her husband at home, we had five children in the house, ranging in age from eight months to four years. Lois was exhausted when she arrived, and the care of all five children fell mostly on me. Lois had a strange habit of suddenly leaving her husband and going to visit various relatives for long periods of time. Sometimes she would arrive unannounced, and just settle in. She had a job at home, and I don't know how she managed being away so much. Perhaps she changed jobs often.

We had sold our house and moved into a rental while the new house was being built, but the owners of the rental house decided to return earlier than expected, and we had to move out. Lois and the children arrived while we were still in the rental house. The contractor assured us the new house would be ready when we needed to move, but of course it wasn't. We moved in anyway, with no functioning plumbing. For one weekend, we had three adults and five small children in a house with no plumbing. The contractor was dismayed that we actually moved in, and hastily hooked up the plumbing on Monday morning. When we said, "We *told* you we were moving in," he replied, "I didn't think you meant it!"

So all of us were living in our new house. It was a difficult time. Lois and I shared some of the care of the children, but I did all the housework. The kids did not get along at all. Shannon, the older of the visiting children, cried all the time and fought with Howie, and Donnie, the boy, fought with Gary. Our Christie was a baby and of course needed a lot of attention. Most often at dinner, I would help all of the children with their food, and when everyone got up from the table, I realized I had not eaten. I nibbled on leftovers while I cleared the table. I lost ten pounds that summer.

After a few weeks, to my astonishment, one day Lois announced, happily, "I found a job! I start Monday!" I was flabbergasted. I was not aware that she had been looking, and don't know how she did it. I expected George to question her, to find out what she had in mind by doing this, but he said nothing. George's usual way of dealing with difficult situations was to pretend they didn't exist. His attitude was that if you ignored a problem long enough it would go away, so he just nodded okay, and that was that. The two of them went off to work in the mornings and I was left with five children, the oldest still four years old. I was glad to get Lois out of the house, but it was hard work taking care of all of the children and doing all the housework as well.

Eventually my patience ran out and I demanded that George tell his mother that she had to leave. It was one of the most difficult conversations of my life. I felt sorry for Lois; she had a hard life, but I was exhausted and couldn't do it anymore. She had been with us for three months.

After I put my foot down, George told Lois she had to go home, and she soon packed up and left. But before she went, she said to George, "I thought that if I stayed long enough you would get so attached to Shannon and Donnie that I could leave them with you to raise." I was shocked. I suddenly realized how manipulative Lois was. She had a gentle way of getting everyone to do what she wanted without realizing that they really didn't want to.

Once they were gone, we settled into a comfortable suburban life. The area where we were living was near New London, where the Navy's nuclear submarines were built. The Blue Star bridge crossed over the Thames River, and occasionally when crossing the bridge, I could see a long, black submarine silently gliding out to Montauk Sound, with just the upper part of the ship visible. It appeared vaguely sinister.

Our first neighborhood was filled with Navy enlisted men and their families, but in the second, almost all of our neighbors were Navy officers. The man next door was promoted to commander of a submarine. We were invited to the ceremony when he assumed command, and I was allowed to climb down into the sub, while it was in the water—not

Howie and Sabre, Aljen Heights, 1960.

submerged, of course. I was amazed at how cramped everything was. I don't know how a crew could live there for three months at a time.

In 1960 several of our neighbors bought a vacant lot across the street from us and built an underground bomb shelter. This was during the Cold War when people worried about Russia dropping atomic bombs on us. George and I thought the shelter was silly. Everyone seemed to think that after a bomb fell, they would just emerge into the sunshine and go on with life.

It was in the years we lived in this town that we began our intense involvement in both church and civic life. In the church, we both sang in the choir (George was always more in demand than I, as tenors are scarce), taught adult Sunday School, took care of the nursery, and assumed various other jobs as they arose. George began singing in a barbershop quartet, which he did for many years, and he played on the church softball team.

We also took on many responsibilities in this little town. I served on a committee to investigate adopting zoning regulations, and was appointed to a regional water committee. We both worked on political campaigns, especially for our friend the town selectman. That is one of the few campaigns I have ever worked on when my candidate won.

One accomplishment I'm rather proud of was making a presentation to the school board that convinced them they had to reroute the school buses to serve our housing development, which they had refused to do because if they came into our development, they had to go into all of them, and that meant buying more buses and hiring more drivers. I had taken a photo of the dangerous curve where our son had to wait in the dark on winter mornings to get the bus, and took the plat map from the developer's office wall to show them where they could route the bus instead. They reluctantly agreed that the time had come that they had to accommodate the new housing developments. The day after the school board meeting, the superintendent called me and asked me, "Where do you want your bus stop?"

Gradually, I became more involved in civic activities than George did, mainly because he had a job to go to all day and I didn't. I needed to get out of the house and into stimulating activity. I don't know how much George minded spending so many evenings with the kids, but he never complained. Of course I always had to be sure to bathe the children and put them to bed before I left the house for the evening, so all George had to do was be there.

It isn't hard to become a big frog in a little pond for someone with my energy and drive. At one point I couldn't just run into the local grocery store for something in a hurry; I had to plan on being there for some time, because I would be recognized by several people who would keep me in conversation longer than I wanted.

In one of my letters to Frank, in December of 1959, I describe one of my activities.

> *I'm typing this for practice so I can do the correspondence as sec'y of this zoning planning committee I'm on. [I go on to describe the committee.] ... This business of town planning is very complex around here. The town has experienced a sudden rapid growth which makes some sort of regulation necessary but the old, diehard Yankees will have none of zoning or anything that smells of it. It is almost impossible to convince them that they will wish they had it in another ten years. ... You wonder how I have the time. I wonder why other people <u>don't.</u> I got into this specifically because I was bored and had time on my hands and didn't know what to do with it. Of course if I had just wanted to keep busy*

doing <u>something</u> I could keep the house cleaner and iron sheets and read magazines but I need to be with people more.

I was heavily involved in several organizations that had public meetings in the evening, sometimes on the same night. One time when I thought it was important that I make an appearance at all of them, I purposely arrived at one meeting early and mingled in the front of the room, greeting people as they arrived, and then sat down in the back row. When the meeting was underway, I slipped out the back and drove to the next meeting. There I came in the back door, sat down and made a point of asking a question so everyone would see that I was there. Then I slipped out again and drove to the next meeting and again came in the back. As the meeting ended, I lingered, chatting with people, who did not notice that I had not been there the whole time. I later learned that politicians do this all the time.

We lived there only two and a half years, but when we left, I counted fourteen volunteer positions that had to be filled to replace either George or me.

I loved living there. But in 1962, Pfizer transferred George to their Indiana plant, so we moved again. In the eight years after we married in 1954, we moved nine times.

12 Terre Haute

Terre Haute, Indiana, is the only place I have ever lived that smelled terrible all the time, primarily from chemical plants. People who lived there jokingly referred to it as "the armpit of America." George worked for Pfizer, the pharmaceutical company, which may have added its own aroma to the mix. We got used to it.

When we arrived in town, in the summer of 1963, we first found a rental house that would be our base while we explored the city to discover where we wanted to live permanently. While George was at work, I had a realtor drive me around to look at what was available. One day we drove up to a big, two-story gray house with white trim with huge oaks in the front yard, and before we even got out of the car, I knew it was mine. When we stepped onto the front porch, I reached into my purse, pulled out my wallet, and said, "I want this house. I will give you all my cash as a deposit right now."

The realtor sputtered, "But you haven't seen it yet!"

I replied, "I don't need to. I know it's my house."

Of course I did look inside, and it definitely was what we wanted. I loved that house. It was just old enough to have character but not old enough to need major repairs, with a living room that extended all the way across the front of the house. It had a huge dining room, an eat-in kitchen, and four bedrooms upstairs. It even had front and back staircases, one from the living room and another from the kitchen. It also had a full basement and a full finished attic. The previous owners left a big cedar chest in the attic that was filled with old clothes, and our two-year-old daughter spent hours and hours playing dress-up with them.

The house on Washington St., in Terre Haute, Indiana, 1962–1965.

For many years after we moved away from there I had frequent dreams about that house. It got larger and more grand with every dream, until in the last dream it was a mansion, almost a palace, with huge rooms and a turret, and gold everywhere. Eventually the dreams stopped; I don't know why.

A few days after we moved into the house, I scouted around for a grocery store to restock the kitchen. After shopping, I loaded the bags in the car, settled into the driver's seat, turned the key in the ignition, and then realized I did not know where I was or how to get home. My mind was a complete blank. I just sat there and ran through a mental checklist of places where we had lived, until I came to the present one. Then it fell into place—go down this way, turn left, and so on. It was a scary moment. I fervently hoped that this would be our permanent home at last.

Howie was not quite eight years old when we moved to Terre Haute. It was the first move that affected him very much, as he had to go to a new school. Our previous moves had occurred either when he was very young or had been within the same general area, so were not so disruptive. This one was different. I will never know exactly what happened, but I saw a change that never left him.

Before the move he had a sweet, vulnerable air about him, but when he came home from his first day at the new school, he was a different child. He developed a bravado, a slight swagger, a tough-guy veneer. He seemed to have adopted a persona to protect himself. It pained me, but I didn't know what I could do about it. He never complained about school, and made average grades. I have always wondered how different Howie's life might have been if we had stayed in that little town in Connecticut. Among the many choices George and I made as a couple, I regret that we moved so often. Not for myself, but for the children.

Howie and Gary walked to a grade school a few blocks from our house. One of my favorite memories is waiting for them on the front porch in the afternoons on sunny fall days, as they ran up the walk bursting to tell me about their day. Gary was in kindergarten and then first grade, and Howie was in the second and then the third grade. At this time I loved seeing them so wide-eyed and eager to learn, in that early stage of willingness to learn that young children have. Unfortunately, for both of them that eagerness faded to boredom about the fifth grade.

We didn't get involved in partisan politics as much there, but I became an activist with a group called Housewives' Effort for Local Progress, or HELP. It was organized by a woman named Jane Hazeldine, a powerhouse. She was about fifteen years older than I, and became my mentor. Terre Haute had been a hotbed of corruption and vice for years in the past, and although it had been pretty well cleaned up in some respects before we arrived, both gambling and prostitution were still openly rampant. HELP wanted to clean up the city. I joined with a group of women who drew up petitions, held press conferences, and demanded a conference with the mayor.

Our two boys were in school, but since I seldom had a baby sitter, I usually took Christie with me wherever I went during the day. When HELP eventually had our audience with the mayor, I took her along, and sat her down on the floor while we talked in his big, impressive office. Christie got hold of some red candies from a dish on the desk, and proceeded to smear them all over the carpet while we talked. We didn't get a satisfactory response from the mayor, so I felt secretly pleased that the carpet was a mess when we left.

Betty Jean with Christie on Easter, in Terre Haute, 1963.

I remember at one point we were trying to figure out how we could get some inside information on what bars were fronts for prostitution. One of us suggested that we go into one, sit down, and strike up a conversation with someone who looked like he might know what was going on in the back rooms. And then we burst out laughing. We knew it was absurd to think we proper middle-class housewives could blend in and gain the patrons' confidence in a hookers' bar.

I was so involved in this campaign that George eventually complained that I was neglecting the children. I didn't think it was true, but perhaps it was. One day I was being interviewed about HELP's campaign by a reporter from the *Indianapolis Star*, and while I was talking on the telephone, I suddenly heard Gary scream. He had caught his hand in the kitchen's swinging door. I quickly mumbled an apology to the reporter, slammed down the phone, and dashed to extricate him. I realized things had gotten out of control, and resigned from the organization.

About this time I began to realize that I was vaguely dissatisfied with my life. There was nothing obvious to complain about—I had a nice house, three beautiful, healthy children, and a husband who had a good job and was everything a husband was supposed to be. But something wasn't right. I became convinced that there must be something wrong with me, and if I could just figure out what it was and fix it, everything would be fine. This belief stayed with me for many years, despite my persistent failure to discover what that something was.

I remember sitting in the kitchen one day when the thought suddenly flitted through my mind, "Someday I will need to leave George." But it was so shocking, so unthinkable, that I pushed it away quickly. I immersed myself in being a better housewife and mother, thinking that would surely do the trick.

In most ways I enjoyed our Terre Haute experience. We became campers, spending our vacations in campgrounds with lakes where we could fish. At least George and the kids could fish, while I stayed in camp cleaning up and preparing meals. I was glad to do that, as fishing didn't interest me much, and it gave me some time alone in the woodsy campsites. We started out camping in a big tent, but soon graduated to a fold-out camper that we towed behind the station wagon.

One summer we went to upper Wisconsin to the Chippawa Flowage near Hayward and camped for two weeks. It was not an official campsite—it was just a fairly level space near the water's edge where we could pull up the camper, put in the bass boat, and create our own campsite. We arranged a circle of rocks for a fireplace, built a stand with sticks in a tree fork to hold a big water jug, and dug a latrine. We had to carry in water in five-gallon jugs. The nearest people were five miles away by road, although there were some people closer if we went downstream by boat. In the evenings we sat by the fire and watched deer come to the water to drink, just a few feet away from us. We loved it.

We learned about the place from George's Uncle Hugo, who was a fishing guide in the area. George wanted to spend one day with his uncle, fishing for muskie, a fish that lives only in the northern fresh waters and can grow as much as four feet long. If he went, it meant leaving me alone with three young children and no car in a remote area all day. I was reluctant, but I knew it was important to him to spend time with his uncle and it would probably be his only chance to catch a muskie, so I agreed. When he left with the car, I laid down strict rules for the kids—no fire, no knives, and no swimming. Howie, who was the oldest at 8, knew how to start the motor on our little boat, so in a real emergency we could go downstream to find help. I felt like a modern version of a pioneer woman, alone on the frontier while my man was off hunting. The day was uneventful, and a bit boring. Sadly, George did not catch a muskie.

We had a little propane camp stove, but I managed to cook all of our meals for two weeks on that rudimentary fireplace. I never once fired up the stove, and we ate good hot meals. It was fun. Day by day, we kept adding to our camp, making it more and more less primitive. I don't know if it was George's engineering traits or if everyone does this, but we could not resist building more little conveniences every day, like pounding nails into a tree trunk to hang clothes on. I could see how the early settlers gradually improved their homesteads.

For a vacation one year we drove to Arkansas with another family and rented a cabin on Bull Shoals Lake. George enjoyed that so much that he started talking about someday retiring to Arkansas. I rejected the idea out of hand, thinking it was just woods and there was nothing to do there. I had no inkling that Arkansas would someday become my home.

I began sewing in earnest, using that old Sears portable sewing machine that had brought us the extra money we needed in Alabama. I made some of my clothes, including a lined wool suit with bound buttonholes, which was quite an accomplishment. I made several lined wool skirts that I wore for many years, altering the hemlines up and down as fashions changed. I made dresses for Christie. When the boys wore holes in the knees of their jeans, I came up with a fun way to patch them—I went to Tandy's and bought a package of rabbit fur pieces, cut them to fit, and stitched them onto the jeans. The boys were the only kids in their school with fur patches. They lasted a long time!

As always, we immediately found a church. It was Presbyterian, and became the social engine of our life. We did the usual—choir, adult Sunday School, Bible study, various committees. We were the first to arrive on Sunday morning, and the last to leave after coffee hour. We dressed the boys in suits and ties, and Christie in pretty dresses and black Mary Janes. You could not have found a more proper, Presbyterian, middle-class family anywhere.

One Christmas, the church asked for someone to decorate the sanctuary. I volunteered, and decided it needed something proportional to the huge space. There had previously been a wreath of greens above the altar area, but it was only about two feet across, much too small for the vast wall. A couple of people helped me create a huge wreath of artificial greens, about six feet across. It filled the space beautifully. Then I wanted to put candles on the windowsills, but couldn't find any big enough. The sanctuary had four enormous stained glass windows, at least ten feet tall and four feet wide, and regular candles looked pitifully small.

I bought several big blocks of wax and melted them in a double boiler. I discovered that if I let the wax cool a bit and then beat it with the electric mixer, it would turn white and frothy. Then I took empty half-gallon milk cartons (we drank a lot of milk), stacked them three high, and covered them with the foamy wax, molding it like pie meringue, working quickly before it hardened. I learned that hot wax is hard to work with, burning my hands several times, but it was worth it. The result was four beautiful white candles, each about three feet tall and four inches square. Unfortunately, I couldn't find a way to put a functioning wick in them so we couldn't light them, but they looked spectacular on the sills, flanked with more greens. The church continued to use them for several more Christmases until the wax began falling off in chunks.

I had given up the civic organizing to devote more time to being a housewife and mother, but then Jane Hazeldine, the HELP organizer, recruited me into the Community Theater of Terre Haute. Jane was its founder and president, and naturally I heard about it from her. From then on, amateur theater was my hobby wherever we went for many years.

The theater was conveniently located just a few blocks from our house, so I could walk there and back. The first production I worked on was "The Little Foxes." Jane, a woman of many talents, directed the play and also starred as Regina Giddens, the female lead. I worked on props, the crew that gathers all of the various items that the actors need on stage and then scurries around the stage between acts putting it all in place. It is critical that everything the actors need to handle during the play be there when they need it. Being on the props crew is an easy way to break into amateur theater, working with the other members and getting to know them. On other plays I worked on costumes and makeup, and painting sets. Eventually I got a small part on the stage, and loved it. I discovered that I am a ham at heart. I was hooked.

The more involved I became, the more I was away from the house, spending many evenings at the theater, leaving George at home with the kids. I was just as involved as I had been with HELP, but this hobby did not require me to be out during the day when the children and the house needed my attention. As long as the kids were okay, and the house was clean and food was on the table, I was doing an acceptable job as wife and mother. I was able to immerse myself in housewifely activities and also in a hobby that allowed me an outside creative outlet as well.

As in Connecticut, George and I gathered a small group of couples around us for a satisfying social life. They were mostly from the church, but also included two couples from George's job at Pfizer. The group of church friends had lots of parties. Alcohol was never served at these parties, which suited us fine, as George and I had always been nondrinkers. (George often joked that he *stopped* drinking and smoking when he turned twenty-one.) One New Year's Eve we hosted a party for about twelve people, and it was a huge success. I made up pizzas ahead of time and spread them on big cookie sheets that fit exactly into the grooves of the stove where the racks were supposed to go. I was able to get enough to serve all of us on four cookie sheets and everyone sat down to hot pizza together at twelve o'clock. Guests stayed until well after midnight, and a few even came back for breakfast the next morning.

Over the years, our social life never included alcohol, no matter where we lived. Our friends were also nondrinkers, at least around us, and they were always exceptionally clever, witty people. Genuinely funny people are funny even when sober, and I enjoy their company more than people who need alcohol to loosen up.

Gary, Howie, Betty Jean, and Christie, in Terra Haute, 1964.

One day when I was grocery shopping I heard a song on the speaker system that was different from the usual music. It was rock, but not quite rock, an interesting sound. It was the Beatles! It was either 1964 or 1965, and they had just become known in the United States. I think the song was "I Want to Hold Your Hand," but I'm not sure. I'm not generally a rock music fan, but I liked the Beatles instantly. Whenever I hear any Beatles song, my mind goes right back to the cereal aisle in that grocery store.

In 1964, one day when we had returned from a camping trip, I was throwing a sleeping bag over the clothesline to air out and discovered I was so weak I could barely lift it. I had noticed that I was unusually tired most of the time, and had been gaining weight. I was eating less and less, trying to lose the extra pounds. Then one day I woke up one morning after George had gone to work and realized I had fallen asleep and two-year-old Christie was up and running around the house alone. I had been sleeping for at least two hours! I knew that something had to be drastically wrong and immediately made an appointment with my doctor.

Testing showed that I was seriously deficient in thyroid, and was anemic as well. I remembered that when I had most of my thyroid gland removed in 1954, the doctor said that eventually I would need to take replacement thyroid. It was now ten years since the surgery. I had the typical hypothyroidism symptoms of weight gain and sleepiness, and I had also become anemic as a result of eating so little. The solution was taking thyroid pills every day for the rest of my life. It worked, but it has been a bumpy ride of constantly testing and adjusting the dosage up and down ever since. I have become an amateur expert on the thyroid gland.

One memory of Christie, the two-year-old, stands out for me. In the backyard, between the kitchen and the garage, was a huge patch of prickly pear cactus. I can't imagine why anyone would plant such a large patch of cactus, but I didn't pay much attention to it until one summer day when Christie was playing just outside the kitchen window, I happened to look out just at the moment that she was reaching across the cactus to retrieve a toy, lost her balance, and fell right into the midst of the cactus patch. When I picked her up, she was screaming in pain. I rushed her into the house, put her in the bathtub, stripped off her clothes, and tried to wash off the thorns. She was covered with them, even under her underpants. It took a long time to remove them all.

George was a chemical engineer at Pfizer, manufacturing pharmaceuticals. He didn't seem to enjoy his job, although he didn't complain very much. He also may not have enjoyed our house as much as I did. Not only did we have a big yard, we also had a huge field behind the house that had to be mowed, and George spent every Saturday morning, from spring to fall, riding the mower. In addition, the house was all wood siding and trim, and the paint was peeling in places when we moved in. George began scraping and painting, and just managed to get the whole house finished in time to start over again where he had begun. With the full attic, it was effectively a three-story house. George was afraid of heights, but he managed to get up on a long ladder and paint even the top point under the eaves. Gary told me that one day he climbed a tree in the front yard and reached a point as high as the roof top where George was painting. He called out to his father, who looked over at him and nearly fell off the ladder.

One day in the summer of 1965, George came home from work and announced that he had been transferred back to Connecticut. Today, companies have become more enlightened, but in the middle of the twentieth century, they moved employees around like a child playing with toy soldiers, and if you valued your career, you didn't resist. So we immediately began getting ready to move. Since Pfizer was paying for it all, we just called a moving company and had them do all the packing. We had only a couple of weeks before George was to report for work in Groton, so we had to move fast. It suddenly occurred to us that the following weekend was the Fourth of July, and we didn't want to be on the road then, so we had to either leave in the next few days or wait another week. We couldn't wait, so we had three days to leave town. The movers packed one day, loaded the truck the next day, and the third day we left.

It was a whirlwind move. We had to stop all of the utilities, pack our personal belongings, tell friends we were leaving, return library books, and take care of everything else entailed in a sudden move. I was astonished that the movers packed the entire eight-room, three-story house in one day. They simply grabbed everything and threw it in boxes. I saw one man take the sugar bowl off the table with sugar still in it, wrap it up, and stuff it upside down in a box. They packed a cereal box with six flakes of cereal in it. They were like a horde of locusts devouring everything in their path. But they got it done, and very little was damaged in the move.

The Leas family portrait, 1965. (Betty Jean made her suit.)

We would have a place to live when we arrived in Connecticut because Pfizer owned several houses they rented to employees. The company bought our house in Terre Haute, so housing was handled without a hassle.

It seems strange now that I didn't question why this transfer happened so suddenly, but I accepted it as normal. In my world, a good wife didn't complain about her husband's career moves. But several years later I heard from another Pfizer wife that this was not a normal transfer. I have never asked George about it and it may not be true, but I suspect it is. The story I was told is that he made some very serious mistake, and his boss was about to fire him. It must have been George's fault and cost the company a lot of money. The plant manager said no, don't fire him, just get him out of here, so they quickly sent him back to headquarters in Groton. I have wondered if perhaps it wasn't George's fault at all, and the boss was covering up his own mistake. As far as I know, George never had any other problems with his work throughout his career.

Whatever the reason, our time in Terre Haute was over. We packed our three kids and the dog into the station wagon and headed east. It had been a good two years.

13 Connecticut and New York

The trip to Connecticut was leisurely and pleasant. We took our time, to allow the movers to arrive ahead of us. We did some sightseeing and visited friends along the way. By this time the children were good travelers, and George and I both enjoyed driving.

We arrived in Ledyard in midsummer of 1965, to a beautiful, spacious house. It was a split level, with four bedrooms and several extra rooms. It was in a small development of about five houses along a wooded country road. The developer had built this house for his family to live in while he built the others, and consequently, it was huge, very well built, of luxurious materials. For instance, there was a large foyer with a slate floor and a built-in planter and an elaborate chandelier. We would not have been able to afford that house if it had not been owned by Pfizer.

However, we soon learned why the company owned it, and it was not good news. For many years, the company had disposed of toxic chemicals by dumping them in the woods across the street. This area was many miles away from the plant and at the time must have seemed like wilderness. But when people began building houses there, they discovered that their wells were contaminated and sued the company. As part of the settlement, Pfizer bought the houses, rented them to employees at a low rent, and provided free bottled water for the tenants. In the lawsuit, Pfizer insisted that the water was not harmful to people, but they lost the suit, and provided bottled water as a result. We never knew whether it would have hurt us to drink it, and we were glad not to take the chance.

We could shower in the water from the faucet and wash clothes in it, but not drink it or cook with it. Several five-gallon jugs of water were delivered to us each week. It took a while, but we got used to it.

The movers had arrived, unpacked our belongings, and taken away the boxes. We had to rearrange things, such as moving the drinking glasses from where they had inexplicably put them in the cabinet above the refrigerator, but that didn't take very long. It actually was the easiest move we ever made, since other people were paid to do all the work and it happened so fast we didn't have time to stew over decisions.

George went to work at the plant where he had been before, but it soon became apparent that it was not a good career move. They had no real job for him, which reinforces the thought that it was an unplanned and unwelcome transfer on the company's side as well as ours. George was given an office but few responsibilities, and of course he immediately started sending out résumés.

Meanwhile, we did our usual thing of finding a church. We had become Presbyterians since we left there, so we didn't go back to the little Methodist church we had joined earlier. We found a church in Groton, about 30 minutes away, and joined the choir. We didn't attend as often or get as involved as we had in previous churches, and I'm not sure why. Perhaps it was just too far to go, or being a bigger church made it harder to get engaged. But I made one contact there that proved to be hugely important for me.

At coffee hour one Sunday I struck up a conversation with a woman named Alayne Van Deusen, a tall woman about my age, with a softly modulated voice. We hit it off immediately. Somehow the subject of theater came up, and she told me she had graduated from a drama school in New York City. The more we talked over coffee cups, the more excited we got, and the idea grew on us to start our own amateur theater.

We put an advertisement in the local paper to find other people in the area who wanted to join us. Several people responded and met with us to organize. Before long we had assembled about thirty people and founded a community theater.

We incorporated and organized in the typical hierarchical style, with the usual officers. Alayne was far more experienced than I, but I had more time, and became President. Since we were near Montauk Sound, we called ourselves the Shore Theater. We had no building, so we met in homes and performed in school auditoriums. We recruited about a dozen sponsors and patrons who donated funds and materials.

The Leas house in Ledyard, Connecticut, 1966.

Our first play, in January of 1966, was "Hay Fever," a comedy by Noel Coward. Alayne directed and I was assistant director. It went well, although at one point we were not sure it would go on at all. The woman who was to play Judith Bliss, a major part, was hospitalized with pneumonia five days before opening night. In desperation we decided that I would take the part if she did not recover in time. I was her size so could wear her costumes and was about her age at thirty-two, and I had been present for every rehearsal and did much of the directing, so I knew the script well. But I did not actually know the dialogue, and had to memorize it quickly. Alayne came to my house and we "ran lines," over and over and over. I was both terrified and elated to think I might have to play the part. However, the actress recovered in time for dress rehearsal and did a great job. I was both relieved and disappointed.

The next play, four months later, was "Mary, Mary," a comedy by Jean Kerr. I was the producer of this one, and one of our recruits directed. In this play I witnessed one of the most amazing recoveries I've ever seen on stage. One actress missed her entrance cue, and two actors were left on stage with no dialogue, not knowing what was happening back stage.

They were both complete amateurs, having never been on a stage before. But they both stayed in character and went on with lines of dialogue that were to follow later. When the actress finally rushed on stage, the other two picked up the dialogue that she was supposed to have started, and when they reached the later part, they worked it in seamlessly. The audience never knew anything was wrong. It was an incredible instance of professionalism by amateurs.

The theater consumed me. The children were all in school, and we had acquired a second car, so I could spend my days in theater business. There was so much to do, so much to organize. I made sets and costumes, rehearsed actors, designed programs, raised money, did publicity, anything that needed doing. I was on a local radio call-in show, to tell the public about the theater. I loved it all.

I did have a life outside the theater. The two Pfizer couples that we knew in Terre Haute also were transferred to Groton, and we resumed our friendship. Our children thrived in their schools. They went to three different schools, all within walking distance, cutting through a small woods and a field to their schools. One day they said they had seen a rattlesnake on the way home.

Behind our house was a small cliff that the kids liked to climb, rising perhaps 20 feet, with woods and more houses above us. One day Christie scrambled up and then when coming down, slipped and fell. She was wearing a swimsuit, and slid down the bank on her back. I rushed her into the house, laid her down on a couch, and pulled off her swim suit so I could see where she was hurt. She had a scrape down her spine, but otherwise seemed okay, but she kept crying and crying. A woman who lived next door happened to be there, and together we tried to find out why she was crying so hard. When Christie eventually calmed down, she told me that she wasn't in pain but was terribly embarrassed that I had taken off her clothes in front of the neighbor. I had no idea that she was so modest at age four. She still remembers that incident and being embarrassed.

That same neighbor was pregnant with her fifth child. When her water broke, her husband was out playing golf and couldn't be reached, so she asked me to drive her to the hospital. It was a 30-minute drive, the same one George and I had made seven years earlier when Gary was born, and her contractions were coming faster and faster. I was very nervous that we were going to deliver the baby in the car. We made it, with only minutes to spare.

During the summer of 1966, we took a camping trip to the White Mountains in New Hampshire. We were set up in a comfortable campsite, and in the late afternoon the kids and I decided we would go for a hike. I saw a sign for a trail to Hanging Rock, and thought that would be a nice walk. We set off, Howie, not quite eleven, Gary, eight, and Christie, five, expecting to be back in a couple of hours at most. We walked and walked, going farther and farther up the mountain, expecting to see the hanging rock around each next turn. After a long time, it occurred to me that we were not on the right trail. I didn't have a watch with me, but I knew it was getting late, and we were still going up.

I began to worry a little, and decided we needed to go back, but it was too far to retrace our steps. So I steered us down the next trail that branched off downhill. It would soon be dark, and I had no idea where we were or where this trail would take us. I kept up a cheerful patter, hoping the children would not sense my increasing concern. At one point the trail was hemmed in by tall brambles, and we could barely make our way through. The branches were taller than Christie, so Howie picked her up and carried her through. Suddenly we came to a steep drop-off; we had to jump down, and I realized that if we did that, we could not possibly get back up even if we wanted to. We were committed to going forward, wherever the trail took us. Sometime later, just as it was getting dusk, to my great relief, I glimpsed a blue tent through the trees. When we reached the tent I realized we were at the edge of our campground. We hurried gratefully to the camper, to be met by George, who said angrily, "What took you so long?" Apparently it had not occurred to him to worry about us. I never found out how far it was to Hanging Rock, or why we never got there.

Knowing that we would be moving away from that area any time, I deliberately groomed my successor in the theater. I had suggested a vice president who I knew would make a good president, and gave her a lot of responsibility. The secretary would be a good vice president, and one of the other volunteers could take her place. I wanted everything to be in place so when I left, the organization would continue to run smoothly without me. And it did. It continued for years, eventually merging with a larger theater in the next city.

George sent out many résumés, looking for a job. We could not tell anyone that he was job hunting, as he didn't want Pfizer to know. I realize now that surely they assumed he was searching and would not have objected if he told them, but it would have been bad form, and we couldn't risk his getting fired.

It took a year, but in the summer of 1966, George found a job with Bristol-Myers, another pharmaceutical company, in Syracuse, New York. We didn't have a house to sell, so we could pick up stakes and move relatively easily. I don't remember much about the actual move. I do remember packing, so the new company must not have paid for all of the relocation costs, but we hadn't been there long enough to accumulate much stuff. Leaving Connecticut was not hard emotionally, as we had avoided making any close friends, knowing that we were there temporarily. It was also easy to leave that bottled water behind.

We bought a house in Manlius, a small town just outside of Syracuse. It was another old farmhouse, on a main road with no other houses around except a new subdivision nearby, across the highway. It had several large trees and a two-story garage in the back yard. The driveway was long and slightly crooked, so that backing out to the street required some skill.

I was unprepared for the intense cold in Syracuse that winter. I hated it. I was not used to living where the weather was a real threat, with snow on the ground most of the time. It got so cold, a woman fell in the snow on her way from her barn to her house and froze to death.

Howie was eleven, and starting the sixth grade. Gary was eight, in the fourth grade, and Christie was six, in the first grade. Since we moved there in the early summer, the kids had a hard time, not knowing any other children and having no way to meet any until school started. They played with each other until they got bored, and I did everything I could think of to entertain them, such as taking them to museums and on picnics. George hung a rope swing on one of the big trees, and stretched another rope between that tree and the garage and hooked a ring over it so they could ride it down. That entertained them for hours.

At this time Howie and Gary began to fight a lot. Perhaps they always had but they hadn't been together as much as they were that summer. More than once I had to break up a vicious fight. Howie was older and bigger, but Gary was quicker and more agile, so neither of them got the best of the other. Sometimes they fought so hard they scared me. It was a huge relief when school started.

The first day of school, Howie's bus did not bring him home when I thought it would. I wasn't sure what time it should come, so wasn't too concerned at first. But when it got really late, I called the school and was told that he should have been home hours ago. As I was hanging up the phone, he walked in. He had gotten on the wrong bus, and the driver had taken him all the way to the end of his route and put him out at the

The house in Manlius, New York, 1967.

side of the road about five miles from home. Fortunately, in our drives around the area all summer, he had learned the roads and knew where he was and how to get home. So he walked. He didn't seem especially upset at the experience, but I was furious. How could the driver do that? We complained to the school, but nothing was done about it. I was proud of Howie that he knew how to get home. Obviously, we had no cell phones in 1966.

I soon began having a series of little accidents, like running the car into a culvert that I didn't see, burning my hand on the oven, and slamming a window down on my fingers. This was unusual for me, and I wondered what was going on. It occurred to me that maybe I was unconsciously looking for attention. I needed something to do, something that would bring me some adult company and some recognition.

We had joined a big Presbyterian church, but weren't very involved. I couldn't think of what I might do with myself until one day I saw a notice in the newspaper that the local community theater was holding auditions for their next play, "The Diary of Anne Frank." Aha! I went to the audition and was given the part of Anne's mother.

This group drew from a larger metropolitan area than any I had joined previously, and was larger and more almost at the professional level. They performed in a huge high school auditorium, and I was challenged more than I had been before. To my dismay, I discovered that I could not project my voice well enough to reach the whole auditorium. For some reason, I just couldn't get sufficient volume. Halfway through rehearsals the director decided we would do the whole play with German accents. I recalled the sound of my German professor in college and imitated him. The astonishing result was that with the accent I acquired a whole new voice! I could project; I could really get into the character. The play went well, and I had acquired a new community.

The next play was the musical "Carousel." I was the assistant drama director, which meant I rehearsed the minor actors, the ones who did not sing or dance. It is important for the quality of the whole production for all of the actors to be equally good, even the ones who don't get the spotlight. I met with them in a separate room and worked with them on blocking and speaking their lines. It required that I be there almost every evening for six weeks straight.

George went with me to opening night. He saw my name on the playbill, but in watching the show, it was not apparent that I had done anything at all. He wondered out loud what I had been doing all those evenings, as if it was wasted time. I couldn't explain it to his satisfaction.

George was becoming more and more dissatisfied with my outside activities. He seldom criticized me openly, but his resentment was obvious. I was not neglecting either him or the children, and was not willing to give up the theater. I needed it, and he just had to accept it. He had no activities of his own, but he could have if he had made the effort.

I realized later that I didn't know exactly what George was thinking. I guess I never did. He did not show or express his feelings, and we didn't talk about what was going on with him. Our relationship was rather superficial, so that we dealt with the day-to-day details of life but not with our innermost lives. We talked about the children, the house, his job, everything except what either of us was really thinking or feeling.

Our love life was active and satisfactory, but we were never genuinely intimate. That's a hard thing to explain. It's possible to have good, satisfying sex and never deeply connect with your partner. Without that intimacy, I was driven to have deeper contact and connection with other people. The stage did that for me. Connecting with an audience is intoxicating and deeply satisfying. It isn't actually a personal connection, of course, but when you are on that stage and you know the audience is with you, it *seems* totally personal. And a strong camaraderie develops between stage people.

During this time I became friendly with our pastor and his wife Julie, and I talked about George's criticism one day with her. Julie suggested that George might be jealous, which was a startling thought. He may have been jealous that I was getting so much attention from other people, including men, and I was enjoying my activities so much, while he didn't have any activities other than his job. It may have been true, but I didn't see what I could do about it.

That winter the minister and his family took a vacation trip to California, and came home with a new practice called "meditation." This was in 1967, and meditation had not yet spread into the mainstream. They approached me and a few other people they thought would be open to this new idea and invited us to meet in their living room to meditate. They held the sessions discreetly, knowing that the congregation would not approve of this "far-out" practice. I took to it immediately.

Thanksgiving at the Porter grandparents in Berwyn Heights. (l-r) Gary, Howie, Christie (front), and Frank and Jean's son Christopher and daughter Barbara, ca. 1965.

This was the beginning of my awareness of spirituality, as opposed to religion. I will be forever grateful to them for this introduction.

They also lent me books, such as *The Gift of Healing* by Ambrose and Olga Worrall, and many other books on spirituality and healing. In those days, the more esoteric spiritual books were hard to find. They were not on the bookstore shelves or lying around on anyone's coffee table. You had to be aware of who had them and let them know you were open to reading them. It's hard to realize now how unacceptable "New Age" material was to the general public at that time. The whole subject was highly suspect in the mainstream churches.

This experience of meditating opened a whole new world for me. Ever since my teen years, I had always been involved in one church or another, but this was different. Meditation did not mean believing a theology or dogma, and did not require following rules. I learned that the physical world is only one aspect of life. I was eager to experience all I could of this unseen world, and learned to meld meditation with the kind of prayer I was familiar with. I continued to attend church with George and the kids, but my time alone and in the meditation group became more meaningful than Sunday morning.

The children seemed to be happy, doing well in school. The boys were never more than average students, but made acceptable grades, and we always heard positive comments at teacher conferences. Christie was a better student. She made excellent grades and received frequent praise from her teachers. They sometimes indicated that she was a bit bossy, telling the other students what to do. She always finished her work first, and then helped the other kids with theirs. In the second grade, she wrote, directed, and starred in a play about the Erie canal.

We had one close call with tragedy. We had all been out for the evening, and when we returned, an awful acrid, chemical smell met us as we opened the door. We dashed about the house looking for the source, and discovered it upstairs in the boy's bedroom. Their beds had foam mattresses, and earlier in the day, while horsing around, they had knocked over a lighted lamp onto one of the beds and the shade had fallen off. It had been lying there for hours, and the light bulb had melted a deep hole in the foam, scorching it, creating the awful smell. I shudder to think of what could have happened if it had not been a foam mattress.

The second year we decided that we needed to remodel the house. I can't remember exactly why we did this, and I wonder if George came up

Gary and Howie at the Manlius house, after helping George tear out the chimney for remodeling.

with it as a project for himself. We didn't do it half-way—we gutted most of the downstairs, changing the use of rooms and the traffic pattern. We moved the kitchen to what had been the dining room, and vice versa. Consequently, we lived in a constant mess for months, reminiscent of the house I grew up in. I enjoyed the whole process, going with the contractor to pick out light fixtures, tiles, appliances, and so forth. It was all very creative. And expensive.

As time went by, for some reason George became less and less happy with his job, and started another job search. In the spring of 1968, he found one with a corn processing company in Clinton, Iowa. I don't remember the name of the company, but I know that they made laundry detergent, among other things. Detergent was a new product at the time. As a chemical engineer, George could work in just about any plant that used chemical reactions. We finished the house remodeling just as he found the new job. In fact, he nailed down the new carpet on the stairs the day he received the job offer from the new company.

George, Betty Jean, and Christie fishing on vacation in upstate New York.

The children did not accept this move easily. They had settled in to their schools and had made friends, and Iowa seemed like the end of the world. When we told them we were moving, Gary said incredulously, "Mom—*no* one moves to *Iowa!*"

This time, we had a house to sell, so George went to work in Iowa, coming home on weekends, while I stayed home with the children to make the sale. This was the period when I began to really understand just how unsatisfactory our relationship was. During the week everything went well, but when he came home on the weekends, we slipped into an uncomfortable dynamic. I suppose that dynamic had been there before, but the contrast with his being away made it more apparent. I realized that George expected me to relate to him as if I were taking care of him, emotionally as well as physically. He wanted more of my attention than

I was comfortable giving. I knew that it was hard on him to be separated from us, but at the same time it was clear to me that I enjoyed life more when he was gone. One day I had the startling revelation that I had *four* children, and *one of them was never going to grow up.*

During this time George's mother died in Texas where she and George Sr. were living. George flew to the funeral straight from Clinton, but I stayed home in Manlius with the kids. We had not been close to Lois for years, and although I felt sad, it was not emotionally difficult for me. George seemed to accept it easily, although, as with everything else, surely he must have had more feelings about it than he showed.

The house did not sell as soon as we expected. We had to reduce the price twice, the second time to the same price that we paid for it. When it finally sold, we lost the $5,000 we had spent on the renovations. That is the only time we ever lost money on a house. When the end of the summer was near, we decided we had to pack up the family and move to Clinton so the children could get started in school, leaving the house with a Realtor to sell.

For the first time, I had to manage the move by myself. George was able to spend some time at home to help with packing, but not much, as being new in the job, he couldn't get many days off.

This move took place in the summer of 1968, when I was thirty-five. I remember the date because of the assassination of Robert Kennedy. In early June, we thought the house would sell soon, and we needed to investigate housing in Clinton. I flew out there to look the area over with George, and then took a Greyhound bus home. The shooting happened while I was on the bus, and in those days, there was no way for us to get information while we were on the highway. At each stop, when someone got on, we all called out, "How is he?" The concern created a strong sense of community among the passengers. Kennedy died the next night.

We still had the pop-up camper and wanted to take it with us. It was up to me to get us all out there, towing the camper behind the station wagon. I realized that I needed to learn to back up with the camper, in case I had to do it on the road. A friend of George's went with me to a shopping center parking lot to practice backing. I got good enough so I could easily back the camper out of our crooked driveway, but I never once had to back up on the two-day drive.

When everything was loaded up and the movers' truck left, it was too late for us to start on the road, so we stayed in a motel that night. I had never rented a motel room before. We had stayed in them many times, but I had always stayed in the car with the children while George went to the office and rented the room. It felt strange doing this by myself!

Early the next morning I packed the three kids and the dog into the station wagon and we took off for Iowa.

14 Clinton, Iowa

We arrived in Clinton in late summer of 1968. We didn't have a place to live yet, so we set up our camper in a small park on the edge of town. The first night we were all shocked awake by the sound of a train apparently barreling into our beds. We had not noticed that we had parked the camper only a few feet from a set of train tracks. The train came through only in the middle of the night, and after a couple of nights I was surprised that we all slept through the noise. We stayed in the campsite for a couple of weeks.

We bought a big two-story house in a good section of town. Not upscale, but comfortable. The previous owners had lived there a very long time. The wife had been born in the house, lived there all her life, and died there in her eighties. In the attic we discovered a small diary with handwritten entries from the late 1800s. Most of the entries detailed all the chores she had done that day, like ironing and beating rugs, and almost every entry ended with "I'm tired." We tracked down the woman's relatives through the real estate agent and mailed the diary to them.

It was fun in the spring to see what plants emerged in the yard. Since the previous owners had lived there so long, there were established plantings everywhere, including a big asparagus garden that produced copiously, and many tulips of all colors. Unfortunately, the tulips had been planted in rows straight across the middle of the side yard, right where the children played ball. The tulips were regretfully sacrificed to ball games after the first spring.

The Leas house on Kennilworth Ct. in Clinton, Iowa, 1968–1973.

A large patch of another plant that we didn't recognize grew up next to the asparagus. One day one of our young friends was visiting, and as he went out the back door, he happened to look over that way and grinned. I saw where he was looking, and asked him if he knew what those plants were.

He laughed and said, "I wondered if you knew. I was surprised you were growing that here. It's pot, and it looks mighty healthy!"

I was astounded. I had no idea we had 6-foot marijuana plants growing in our back yard. I can't imagine that the previous owners planted pot on purpose, or knew what it was. We never found out what it was doing there, but we knew we had to get rid of it. How do you dispose of a big garden of pot? Legally?

George cut the plants down with a scythe, and burned them. It seemed like a waste, but there was no way we could let them stay there, especially with teenagers in the house. I wondered if any of the neighbors got high on the fumes.

This house had a two-story garage, in addition to the big yard. And like the house in Terre Haute, it had two staircases, the front stairs from the living room and the back stairs from the kitchen. The back stairs were not carpeted, and I could tell where the kids were by hearing the clattering of their feet on the stairs as they raced up or down.

It was during our time in Clinton that the relationship between George and Howie became really difficult. George had always been hard on his older son, but it wasn't so apparent until Howie started having serious problems with math in the eighth grade. I especially remember George trying to help him with his homework and getting angry with him, yelling at him in disgust when he didn't get it right. Of course the more George belittled him, the more mistakes Howie made.

I cringe now to realize how much I failed Howie. I could have intervened, pointing out to George what damage he was doing, and he might have stopped. But I didn't. For some reason it's hard for me to fathom now, I just didn't know that I could. How could I have been so passive? This was a pattern in our relationship, my seeing behavior I didn't like but not being aware that it was possible for me to do anything about it. It wasn't really a case of passivity as much as it was ignorance. I just didn't know. Seeing that mind-set now, I can empathize with people who stay in abusive relationships. It isn't as simple as it seems from the outside.

When Howie turned fifteen, adolescence hit him hard. He changed almost overnight to a sullen, rebellious teenager. He refused to participate in family activities, resisted bathing, and was generally uncommunicative. I now recognize it as fairly typical teenaged behavior, but didn't know what was going on at the time. We were just upset, and the more obnoxious he became, the worse George treated him. By the time Howie was sixteen and driving, we rarely saw him anymore. He set up a cot in the upstairs of the garage and basically lived there. He strung a line from the garage window to the back door and when he got a phone call, I tugged on the line so it would ring a little bell in his room upstairs. He took his meals there, and kept his clothes there. In some ways his isolation disturbed me, but it didn't seem to be harmful, and if it made life easier for him, it was okay with me.

Howie went through a huge growth spurt at this time, eventually reaching 6 feet 4 inches. He was good looking, slim, with dark hair and grey eyes, and kept his hair short, unlike his little brother. As far as we could tell, he was not involved in drugs, although from what his siblings told me years later, he was probably drinking, but it was not apparent at

Howie relaxing in the TV room in Clinton, 1971, age 16.

the time. He did satisfactorily in school and had a few friends. However, I was not pleased with these friends. They were nice enough, not bad kids, but were clearly not very bright. I asked him one day why he didn't chose smarter friends, and he said, "I like to feel superior."

Gary went through a rebellious period then also, at age thirteen. He insisted on wearing loud, flowered bellbottom pants, and let his beautiful curly red hair grow very long, flowing down over his shoulders. He was never obnoxious, just determined to be his own person. His basic good nature kept him from getting much disapproval from adults. George didn't like these new "hippie" ways, but I thought it was charming and we didn't argue about it much. We did have a problem with his wearing the loud bellbottoms to church, but we relented, to avoid fights. Fighting with Howie was all we could handle.

Christie adapted well to her new school and made friends, including a couple of girls her age who lived on our block. As usual, she made good grades. In the third grade, at nine years old, she was the narrator for a Sunday School skit that was performed in the church sanctuary. She stood in the pulpit, poised and self-assured in a simple dark green dress with a white collar. The minister commented to me what a remarkable girl she was. I was delighted to see that she had an amazing stage presence.

Gary with his new bike in Clinton, 1971, age 13.

Christie (rt.) and neighbor Kim, in Clinton, 1972.

Unfortunately, the stage was not an outlet for me in Clinton. I tried, but the local group was not welcoming to newcomers. I did some backstage work, but got no acting parts, and did not feel at home with the people. Some small-town theaters are like that, and I was lucky I never encountered more of them. However, I did get to know a man named

David, who remained a close friend for more than forty years. We stayed in touch throughout the many ups and downs of our lives.

So the church was my major outlet. We joined a Presbyterian church, in an old Gothic stone building, like the cathedrals in Europe. I loved that building. The all-stone sanctuary had a high ceiling with huge wooden beams crisscrossing it and wrought iron chandeliers hanging throughout. Often when I sat in the choir loft, I watched an angel perched on one of the crossbeams. Even though the angel wasn't a physical being, I could sense its presence clearly. It was comforting and at times it seemed even a bit mischievous. Since I couldn't actually see it, I don't know what it was doing, but the impression was clear.

George and I were both deeply involved in the church, taking part in almost every possible activity. As always, we sang in the choir and taught Sunday school. And as in Connecticut, I met a woman at coffee hour who had a huge impact on my life.

Her name was Carol, and she had the sweetest smile I have ever seen. She radiated an inner presence, that kind of peace and serenity that transcends everything. I was drawn to her immediately and we became friends. Her husband was a hospital administrator, and they had two children a few years younger than ours.

Carol had been exposed to spirituality at a level that I didn't know existed. She took it for granted that there were forces at work that could be accessed and drawn on for help and sustenance. We talked at length about healing and intercessory prayer, and together decided that we wanted a spiritual healing group. We discreetly put the word out in the congregation that we would be meeting to pray for healing for anyone who wanted it. In 1969, in a small Midwestern city, this was daring. We were very quiet about it, not knowing how it would be received.

Three other people joined us, and we struggled to find a time that we could meet. Most of us were mothers of young children and could not find a time during the day, as some of the children were not in school, or even during the evening when our husbands could babysit. We settled on meeting at 10 o'clock on Tuesday nights in a corner of that stone sanctuary. Because I was so active in the church, I had a key, and we could come and go when we pleased. Wanting to be unnoticeable, we turned on only one light, so it was almost dark with deep shadows surrounding us. We felt like early disciples in the catacombs.

The Leas family with an exchange student from Ghana, in Clinton, 1972.

An amazing experience in that group helped shape my belief system for the rest of my life. One of the participants was a woman named Charlotte. She was a bit older than the rest of us, who were in our thirties. She had been a concert pianist, but had developed severe arthritis in her hands and in her knees, so could not play the piano anymore and walked with two canes. We could hear her approaching the meeting by the sound of her canes tap, tapping down the hall.

She confided in us that she wanted help in overcoming the sounds that she heard in her head. She explained that all of her life, she had been able to hear what other people were thinking. For example, one day when she was on a bus, a man sitting next to her wondered what time it was. She glanced at her watch, turned to him, and said, "It's 2 o'clock."

He stared at her and said, "I didn't ask you. I was just thinking it."

She realized that she had heard his thoughts. She had never dared tell anyone about this strange ability, other than her mother.

She also heard music all the time. She would reach to turn off the radio and realize that it wasn't on; the music she was hearing was in her head. When she played in concerts, she would sometimes improvise, playing the music she heard. People would ask her what that beautiful piece was, and she didn't know what to say.

Sadly, she saw this ability as a curse. When she was a child, her mother had scolded her about it, telling her she had to stop it, that it was from the devil. She felt guilty, and wanted us to pray to make it stop.

When Carol heard her story, she was ecstatic. "Do you know what a gift that is?" she asked. "It's called clairaudience, and it's a beautiful gift. You are *blessed!*"

Charlotte was shocked. No one had ever told her this ability was a *good* thing. It even had a name! It was a great relief to understand she had nothing to feel guilty about.

A week later, Charlotte surprised us by appearing quietly, with no tapping down the hall. As soon as we opened the meeting, she gave each of us a small strip of cloth, carefully embroidered with "Shalom" and a descending dove, with tassels on each end. "Those are bookmarks," she explained, "my gift for what you have done for me. I made them. Not only can I play the piano now, I can do needle work, too. And notice—no canes!" Her arthritis was completely gone, and she was beaming.

Charlotte's husband took a job in another city soon after that, and they moved away. I don't know if her arthritis was gone for good or if it returned, but even if it was only temporary, her healing made a lasting impression on me. At the time, I saw the experience as an example of the power of prayer. I still think so, but I also understand it as the power of the psyche to affect the physical. Charlotte had been literally crippled by intense, lifelong feelings of guilt. When the guilt was removed, her body was no longer crippled. To me, that is as much a miracle as prayer, and I have combined prayer with psychological work ever since.

The experience with Charlotte is related to one with my lttle nephew about the same time. George's younger brother, who was in the Air Force, was sent to Vietnam, and his wife and their three young children came to Clinton to live while he was gone. She rented a house across the street from us, and enrolled in school to become a practical nurse. She could get her diploma in the year that her husband was gone.

Their son was five years old. He often seemed out of control, and could sometimes be hard to be around. There was something wild in his eyes that bothered me, something not quite right. He went to kindergarten at the school nearby, and after his morning session, he would stay with me until his mother got home from class. My experiences with Carol and spiritual healing led me to wonder if he was possessed. I know this sounds really weird, but it didn't seem so outrageous to me at the time.

One day I decided to see what I could do about it. When he had settled down next to me on the couch for his nap after lunch, I lay my hands on his head and said quietly but firmly, "In the name of the Holy Spirit, I command the evil spirit living in this child to depart. Go to the outer regions where you can do no harm and do not return." The child was asleep.

A couple days later, when his mother came to pick him up, she said, "I don't know what has come over my little boy. He's been so sweet lately! It's like he's a different kid!"

I never told anyone what I had done. He continued to be a rambunctious child, but the wildness was gone, and didn't come back. Did my "exorcism" have an effect? Was it coincidence, that he was just maturing? I am still convinced that whatever was disturbing him responded to my command. If Charlotte's crippling guilt could be removed by prayer, so could a little child's demons.

I continued with the healing prayer group, and with my own version of meditation. As I was meditating one day, lying on the living room couch, I suddenly was aware that I was sitting up, without intending to. I was seeing the room from an upright angle, but I looked back and saw myself still lying down. I realized I was leaving my body, and then felt a gentle tug and went back. It was a brief but illuminating experience, and has never happened again. Years later I took a course on how to leave the body but did not succeed in doing so.

My religious interests expanded when someone told me about a local group of Pentecostal Catholics. I hadn't known such a thing existed, and when I heard about it, I couldn't resist checking it out.

The group met one night a week in a small house in a town in Illinois just across the Mississippi River. I arrived somewhat apprehensively, not knowing anyone there. But they were very friendly and welcoming, and I discovered it was a potluck. They had plenty of food for the twenty or so people, including several little children. After we ate, we all settled down in the living room. People landed wherever they could find room, including on the floor and up the stairs. The children stayed with us, nestled at their parents' feet.

Someone stood up and read a chapter from the Bible, probably one of the gospels. Then after a short silence, another person began praying out loud. It was a sweet prayer, asking for healing for someone, and then something amazing happened. Someone else began speaking in tongues! And then another, and then another. Soon the room was filled with impassioned voices, all speaking reverently in a language that made no sense to me.

After some time, the tongues stopped, and a person started praying again in English. Different people stopped and started praying, some overlapping each other. Then the unknown tongues started again. I was unaware of how long this went on, and was astonished when I glanced at my watch and saw that it was almost twelve o'clock! It had seemed like an hour or two at most. The children had long since fallen asleep on the floor.

About midnight the praying gradually stopped, and the meeting was over. Everyone said goodnight, and I headed home.

I attended several more of these meetings, and never really figured out what was going on. But I was impressed by the intense energy in the room and the obvious compassion everyone felt for the people they were praying for. In comparison, my Presbyterian worship seemed so pathetically anemic!

Still not having enough to do, I volunteered once a week at the local Job Corps Center. I helped in the ceramics center, where the young men painted vases and plaques and had them fired. Another volunteer was an elderly nun, who needed a ride each way, so I picked her up at her church and took her back. One day, I had gone to the library first and taken out a book to read to Christie at night. The book was lying on the seat beside me (this was in the days of bench seats.) While the nun and I were riding to the Center, I wondered out loud if she had been nervous about getting into a car with a stranger. She replied, "Well, when I looked in and saw that book, I thought, 'Anybody who rides around with Winnie the Pooh on the front seat has to be okay!'"

After a few weeks of our rides together, she asked me one day, "You haven't been around nuns much, have you?"

Puzzled, I replied, "No, actually, none at all. But how can you tell?"

"Because," she said, "you treat me like I'm a real person!"

One of my church activities was sponsoring the youth group. We had about seven or eight senior high schoolers, including Howie. One time as we gathered for our meeting, I learned that one of the boys was missing because he needed a ride. I asked, "Where does he live?" and someone named the street. I said, "Oh, I know where that is, I'll go get him."

I rushed off and then realized when I was almost there that I didn't know his house number. How was I going to find his house? I just drove slowly down the street until I felt that a particular house was the right one. I parked, knocked on the door, and he came running out, ready to go. I just knew it was the right house. I had never been on that street before.

When it came to the end of their senior year, it was time for these kids to join the church. All of them did so, except Howie. He said that he really didn't believe "all that stuff," and he just couldn't do it. George and I were not pleased, but we accepted it as his right, and he alone of the group did not become a member. I was a little embarrassed, but was proud of him that he felt obligated to act on his conscience and was secure enough to defy everyone's expectations, including his parents and his minister. Some of the other kids later told me that they didn't believe it either, but they didn't dare not join.

Somehow, I think through the church youth group, I met a young couple I will call Greg and Jody. They were in their mid-twenties, I think, too old for the youth group, so I don't know what the connection was. They were into the hippie culture, and he wrote poetry. I don't know what he did for a living, if he worked at all.

About ten o'clock one night the phone rang, and when I answered, I heard Jody say, "Can you come over? Now? Quick! I'm scared! Greg's gone crazy! Please!" She sounded desperate. I said okay, told George I was going out to help a friend, and drove to their apartment.

She was waiting for me at the top of the steps. She let me in, sobbing, and when I went through the door I was shocked. Greg had trashed the place. He had broken a big mirror and glass shards were scattered on the floor, lamps had been knocked over, pictures were hanging crooked. Greg was pacing around the apartment, room to room, muttering and shaking his fists. He had taken some drug, I don't know what, and was having a very bad trip.

I tried to talk to him, but he didn't seem to hear me. At one point he rushed toward me, as if he were going to attack me. I retreated to another room, Jody right behind me. It was clear that I couldn't do anything, and I told Jody we had to call for help.

She pleaded, "Not the cops! We can't call the cops! They'll put him in jail and he can't stand that. Not the cops!"

I made my way to the telephone, thinking of who could help, and remembered the local Episcopal priest, Father Thompson. He was known to be sympathetic to young people and their problems with drugs. I called him, and he agreed to come over.

When he arrived, he simply walked up close behind Greg, reached his arms through under Greg's armpits, and locked his arms over Greg's chest so that he couldn't get away. Then, still standing behind him, he proceeded to march the young man around and around the room, moving their legs in tandem. Gradually, Greg calmed down. After about an hour of this nonstop walking, with Jody and me huddled in a corner, Father Thompson gently lowered Greg down into a chair, where he looked around, dazed, trying to figure out how he got there. We all began to breathe again.

The priest was exhausted. He put on his jacket, walked to the door, turned, and said to me calmly, "Next time, call the cops."

Fortunately, there was no next time. Greg and Jody moved away soon after that, and I don't know what became of them.

15 Later in Clinton

In 1972, our senior minister at the Presbyterian church left, and we needed to call a replacement. The search committee came back with a person for the congregation to decide whether to call. I did not like the man. He was arrogant and authoritative, and I thought it would be a disaster to call him to be our pastor. The method in the Presbyterian church was for the candidate to fill the pulpit one Sunday, and then after the service, the congregation would meet and be asked what we wanted to do. The vote was to be yes, to call him, or no, not to call him.

The moderator asked, "All those in favor of calling, say aye."

There was a resounding "Aye" from the two hundred or so in the sanctuary. In almost an aside, he then said, "All those opposed say no…" and paused, expecting silence.

I alone spoke up clearly, "No."

There was a shocked silence, and people turned around and looked at me, surprised. I wanted to slink down in the pew.

Traditionally, when the motion to call was not unanimous, the moderator would then ask the congregation in second vote to make it unanimous, for appearance's sake. He explained the procedure, and then said, "All those in favor of making the call unanimous, say aye."

Again, the reply was a clear "Aye."

"All those opposed, …..?"

And again I said, "No." This time there was a murmur of disapproval throughout the room.

That meant that the minister had to be told that the call was not unanimous. I learned later that he almost refused the call for that reason. However, he did come, and many members did not like him. After he had been there awhile, one person came up to me one Sunday and whispered, "We should have listened to you."

We had a young assistant minister, David Warren, whom George and I liked very much. David welcomed the newer ways of worship that were just taking hold. Vatican II had changed the Catholic church in many ways, such as saying the Mass in English instead of Latin, and many Protestant churches were instituting a less formal style of worship service. Our church had begun an early service that experimented with these new forms, including using guitar music. It was designed to appeal to the younger generation, and was attended mostly by people like George and me. As a result, there became almost two congregations, one of the younger people who attended the early service led by David, and the other of older, more conservative people, who came to the traditional service led by the new minister.

The term "conservative" has to be understood in context here. The most liberal of us would still be considered conservative in most circles. In a small mainstream church in a small Midwestern town in the early 1970s, our liberal was still pretty conservative. George and I were still Republicans.

About the time the new minister came, George and I began teaching an adult Sunday School class called Building Your Own Theology. We had no textbook, so created our own materials. The class of about twenty people, mostly couples, met for several months, reading the Catechism that states the basic beliefs of the church and discussing it item by item, attempting to adopt the ones that we could use as our own theology.

For example, the first question is "What is the chief end of man?" and the answer is "To glorify God and enjoy him forever." The second one is "What rule hath God given to direct us how we may glorify and enjoy him?" and the answer is "The Word of God, which is contained in the Scriptures of the Old and New Testaments, is the only rule to direct us how we may glorify and enjoy Him." We didn't have too much disagreement about the first answer, but we stumbled over that second one. We discovered that most of us did not have faith in the unerring scriptures, and believed that there were other ways to know God, if he existed, which some of us were not so sure about either. It went downhill from there, or uphill, depending on your point of view.

It soon became apparent that hardly any of us believed any of the basic tenets of Presbyterianism. This was deeply upsetting to some of the class. I received a couple of phone calls from class members in tears, disturbed to discover that they did not believe the basics of their faith. They had never admitted that fact to themselves, much less to anyone else. Being a heretic is an uncomfortable place to be.

This class helped me discover more than ever that traditional Christianity just didn't suit me. I had been paying lip service to those beliefs for many years, and it just didn't work anymore. The church had been such a refuge for me for so long that it took a group experience to coax me out of it.

This class increased the sense of a separate congregation of younger, more liberal people. The class members constituted a block that opposed most of what the rest of the congregation wanted, creating some animosity between the two groups. I was sorry to see this, but was not surprised.

Eventually, the schism became sharp enough that some of the more liberal people left. I forget now what the issue was at the time, but it was serious. Some of them tried attending the only other Presbyterian church in town, but it was located in the low-income neighborhood with a very different kind of congregation, and they didn't stay long. George and I hung in reluctantly for a couple more years.

In 1970, while still in Clinton, I received a letter from my friend Jennie. She had been the matron of honor at our wedding, and we had stayed friends with her and Skeef as a couple and as young parents. They lived in Ithaca, New York, where Skeef was doing research in agriculture at Cornell University.

The letter was brief and to the point. She said, "How I wish I could tell you why. I put off writing as long as I could, hoping I could tell you something meaningful about it. I can't." Enclosed was a newspaper clipping. It was Skeef's obituary. He had killed himself. He took a vial of cyanide from the lab, drove far into a dense woods, and drank it, dying instantly. He left no note, no explanation. He had not been obviously depressed or upset. He was forty-two years old. I wrote back to Jennie, knowing that nothing I could say would make it better. Jennie lived to be eighty-two, and never remarried.

We took one of our long camping trips to California one summer. All the way there and back we saw lots of motorcycles on the highway, and I kept thinking that looked like a lot of fun. As soon as we returned home, I started looking for a motorcycle for myself. I found one that was just right. It was little, a Honda 50 step-through, bright red, almost a scooter, but still a motorcycle. I practiced on a parking lot, took the test, and got my license. I was one of only two women with a motorcycle license in the whole county. The other woman was the one I bought it from.

I had fun zipping all over town on that bike. I often rode down the street where Gary's school was located, and he could see me out of the school windows. One day he pleaded, "Mom, please don't ride the bike down past my school where the other kids can see you. It's embarrassing!"

I was surprised and disappointed. I had thought he would be proud of his mother for doing something out of the ordinary. After we talked about it a while, he nodded, and said, "Yeah, I guess it's pretty special. It's okay!"

One day the doorbell rang and I found a city policeman standing there with Gary at his side. Gary had taken the bike out of the garage and had been caught driving it around town. He was 14 years old. I said that I would be sure he didn't do it again, and the policeman left, grinning. But Gary did it again, and I decided as much as I enjoyed the bike, it wasn't worth having Gary get in trouble. He just didn't get it that he couldn't ride it, and so I sold the bike. It was fun while it lasted. I bought two more motorcycles in later years.

At the same time all the turmoil was going on in the church, another outlet for my energy appeared. David, the friend I had made in the theater, told me about a class that was starting in Dubuque to study a new psychology theory called Transactional Analysis, to be taught by Doug Johnson, a psychiatrist. It was not very expensive, so I signed up. Several people from Clinton attended, and we carpooled.

Transactional Analysis, or TA, had a beneficial effect on my life for years to come. Most people have heard the expression "I'm okay, you're okay," but don't know where it came from. Thomas Harris wrote a book with that title in 1969 that explained TA as it had been developed by Eric Berne in the early 1960s, and it became very popular in the early 1970s. Doug was a tough teacher who made us examine ourselves and didn't let us get away with avoiding anything we discovered there.

I won't attempt to explain what TA is all about here, except to say that it describes the human psyche in terms of three aspects: the parent, the adult, and the child. All interactions between people act out the relationships between those parts of each person. Understanding which part in myself is acting with which part in another person enables me to choose how I want to interact consciously, instead of unconsciously. I began to see the basis of the interactions between the members of my family, which gave me some ability to stop behavior that wasn't helpful.

Another tenet of the theory is that we all play "games" and "pastimes" all the time, usually unconsciously. One pastime I began to recognize in myself is "If Only." If only I had nicer clothes, if only Howie would act better, if only spring would come, if only George would be X or Y, if only we had more money.... it went on and on. Life would be great if only those circumstances would change. I began to see how I was putting off enjoying life in the present, waiting for events that might never happen. I also saw how I was relating to Howie, giving him the power of a critical parent and wanting him to make me feel okay. And I saw how George was putting me in the role of nurturing parent or dependent child, depending on his needs at the moment. TA was a tool that served me well as I navigated the family dynamics, especially in later years.

One of my friends during those years was a woman named Norene. Her husband was also an engineer, like George, and they had two girls about the same age as Christie. Norene and I often commiserated over coffee about how vaguely unhappy we were. We both had comfortable lives, with no serious problems (Howie was just annoying, not really a problem), but neither of us could say that we were happy, and we couldn't understand why. We explored hobbies, thinking we just needed more interests. Norene and her husband actually learned potting and established a business making and selling pottery as a hobby. They dug their own clay and made their own glazes. I still have a vase Wayne made. I couldn't come up with a hobby besides sewing, which I had always done. Years later, I understood what we were going through when I read Betty Friedan's *The Feminine Mystique* and recognized what she called "the problem that has no name."

Attempting to deal with my boredom, one day I suggested to George that maybe I could get a job. I can still see us sitting at the kitchen table, and I can hear his reply over his shoulder as he walked out of the room: "Oh, don't be silly. You could never hold a job. It's a tough world out there." I dropped the subject.

It suited George to belittle my abilities, so much so that whenever I made a mistake, the children and I had a stock response, said with rolling of eyes: "Oh, no! Mommie goofed again." One day George could not find the checkbook and started berating me for misplacing it. He strode into the room where the children and I were watching television, and demanded, "What have you done with the checkbook? I can't find it." I knew I had not done anything with it, so I led him into the study, pulled out the desk drawer, and pointed to the checkbook, lying where it belonged. Then I demanded that he come back into the TV room and apologize to me in front of the kids. He did so, sheepishly. It felt really good to restore some of my self-esteem.

One of the sad experiences in Clinton was having to put our beloved dog to sleep. Sabre had come to us as a little puppy when we lived in Connecticut, about fourteen years before. He was a wonderful dog, a German shepherd mix. He looked like a German Shepherd but had the disposition of a golden retriever. He was extremely protective of the children when they were little. The house in Connecticut was situated on a corner lot, and there was a sandy area near the corner where the children liked to play. I could see them from the kitchen window. Sabre would plant himself between the children and the street, and stand guard over them as long as they played. With his German shepherd coloring and build, he gave an unmistakable message, "Don't mess with me." His bravery was never challenged, as far as I know, but I was confident that the children were safe under his watchful eye.

We all treasured Sabre. He had not a single bad habit. We never made any attempt to train him, but he was the best-behaved dog I've ever seen. He always came when called, didn't bark at people, didn't jump on people, never chewed on anything. But as he got older, he became more and more infirm, and eventually could no longer control his bladder. He began peeing around the house, on the carpet. At that point we knew we had to let him go. Howie did his best to talk us out of it, but he wasn't the one cleaning up the messes. Everyone else was either working or in school when the vet's office was open, so it fell on me to do the deed. I struggled to get him in the station wagon, and cried all the way to the vet's office. I loved that dog.

Christie wanted to take piano lessons, so we acquired an old upright piano from somewhere. I think someone gave it to us. But when a man came to tune it, he said,

"I can tune this, but it will never hold. The soundboard is cracked."

No wonder someone gave it away. We realized we didn't want it either, so we had to dispose of it somehow. How do you get rid of a huge, upright piano?

One of the kids said, "It would be easy if it wasn't so big."

"Well, we could take it apart," I suggested.

Gary said, "Yeah, we could smash it up!"

And we did. We dragged it onto the grass median in the street in front of our house and let everyone come and smash it to pieces. It was great fun. All the neighborhood kids and a few adults took swings at it with axes and hammers and anything else they could find. Once it was in pieces, it was easy to find someone to haul it away.

One winter day Howie went with his class on a skiing trip. He had never skied, and was excited about it. That evening George and I went to a concert at the high school. During the performance, a woman approached George and told him that we had a phone call in the office. We learned that Howie had been in an accident and was in the local hospital. We raced there, not knowing what we would find. He wasn't badly hurt, just had a severely sprained ankle. There was some confusion, as I thought the phone call had said that he had been in a *car* accident and I couldn't figure out what the car was doing on the ski slope! We had a bizarre conversation until that was cleared up. He used crutches for a while but soon recovered. It did not surprise me when I thought he had been in a car accident. Howie had had several accidents, none serious, putting scratches and dents in the little green Datsun we bought for him to drive.

One way I dealt with my general dissatisfaction with life was to take off on long drives alone. In spring of 1971, I took a two-week trip to the East coast by myself. First, I loaded up the freezer with casseroles and pies for the family to eat, and left detailed lists of who needed to do what while I was gone. I had visions of the family being helpless without me there to direct their lives.

I left on a sunny morning in May, the station wagon packed with everything I thought I would need for two weeks. I left George an itinerary, but told him I would not call him every day. Long distance calls were expensive, and although I would be staying with friends most of the time, I didn't want to run up their phone bills. Surprisingly, George was okay with this whole arrangement. It puzzles me that he didn't try to talk me out of the trip. I had made long-distance trips before, mostly to visit my parents near Washington, so he was used to my driving alone, but this was longer than usual.

Some of the trip is lost to memory, but I remember stopping in Ithaca, NY, to visit Jennie and the girls. This was less than a year after Skeef died, and we talked about how hard it was for her to come to terms with his suicide. She learned that he had taken out a large life insurance policy just two years before he died, suggesting that his death was planned well in advance. The policy left her with a significant amount of money. She also found cash stuffed in odd places throughout the house, such as in books and kitchen drawers.

I stayed there a few days, and then drove to Maryland to stay with my parents. It was now April, and Vietnam veterans were gathering to demonstrate in Washington to protest the Vietnam War. Many of the vets were hitchhiking on the highways, and I picked up a couple of them. Hitchhiking has pretty much died out now, but in those days it was common. It didn't feel risky at all.

When we approached DC, the vets got out to catch rides into the city. I went on to Berwyn Heights and stayed with the folks. I was getting along with them better at that time than when I was younger. I had made several weekend trips to see them, and if I didn't stay too long, it was not unpleasant.

One day we were watching the news on TV, and I saw the demonstrations going on in the city. The veterans were throwing their medals over the fence at the Capitol. I wanted so badly to join the demonstration, but didn't dare go. George would be furious if I got arrested, and would be angry if he even saw my face in the crowd on his TV. So I stayed put in my easy chair and squirmed.

When I left the folks' house in Maryland and headed home, there were still a lot of hitchhikers on the highway. I picked up a young man who was headed west. He didn't care where, just west. He was a high school history teacher, and for several years he had spent his summers hitchhiking around the country, just for the experience. He was intelligent and well read, and we had interesting conversation for miles and miles. When we reached Indiana, it was getting late and I was tired, so I decided to stop for the night. We found a motel, and stayed in separate rooms. In the morning, we stopped at a roadside diner for breakfast. It was an unusually elaborate meal, and inexpensive, too. When we got to the Indiana-Illinois border, he said that it was time for him to get out and find a ride going farther north. He was headed for Canada this summer. So we said goodbye, and I drove on home.

A week or so later, I received a postcard from him from somewhere in Canada, saying, "I remember that outrageous breakfast!" I had some explaining to do to George. I think he believed me, but I couldn't blame him if he didn't.

Those long trips alone away from home were my therapy. I think that was the first one, and I made several more in the next few years. It was good to know that I could take care of myself on the road, finding my way and making my own decisions as I went.

In early 1972, when we had been there four years, George realized that there was no future for him with the company in Clinton. He decided it was time to move on to something better and started sending out résumés. By summer he had been offered a job with a big company in Chicago. It was a good job, a promotion, with a good chance of advancement in management. He wanted to accept it, but I was extremely reluctant.

"I just don't want to move to a big city," I said.

"Well, that's not a problem," he explained. "The plant is in the middle of a cornfield miles south of the city. A pheasant flew over my car on the way in. You won't need to go near Chicago."

I still was not eager to leave, but had no more reasons to say no. However, Howie flatly refused to go. He would start his senior year in the fall, and he was simply not willing to transfer to another school for his last year.

"I'll go live with Dan's family," he said, referring to his best friend. "Or I can stay at the Y. But I'm not going."

After much discussion, we arrived at a compromise. George would accept the job, but the family would stay in Clinton and George would commute home on weekends until Howie graduated. It was less than a 3-hour drive, and he could leave home on Sunday night and return home Friday night. That seemed doable, so he took the job.

That was a good year for me. I had the week alone with the kids, and then it was good to see George on the weekends, when we could catch up on my week and his, and he was there to fix whatever needed, like repairing the broken dryer. He rented a room in a motel and ate his meals in restaurants. I hoped that this enforced time away would stimulate him to develop a life of his own, perhaps find some group to join or some hobby to take up. But it didn't work out that way. As far as I could tell, when he wasn't working, he stayed in his room watching television.

Even with George home only on weekends, his relationship with Howie did not improve, and they avoided each other as much as they could.

Howie and I were getting along better, but there was still a lot of tension. We just couldn't seem to get past his bad attitude and my impatience.

In late spring, as it came near to the time for him to graduate, Howie announced that he was going to enlist in the Navy. His buddy Dan was going, and they wanted to go in together. I was adamant that he not go. Fortunately, he was still only seventeen, and could not enlist without written permission from a parent, but to my horror, George agreed to sign for him. As usual, I seemed unable to do anything about it. Could I have stopped him? I don't know. I didn't try very hard. They both knew I didn't approve, but George signed the paper and Howie enlisted. If we had refused to sign, he still could have enlisted at the end of the summer when he turned eighteen, so it probably didn't make any real difference. He was to report for induction soon after graduation.

So one warm, sunny day we all piled into the station wagon and drove Howie to the bus station. He put on a brave face, and I did my best to keep from crying. We all said our goodbyes, and he and Dan boarded the bus. As soon as the bus pulled away, we walked to our car, tears rolling down my cheeks. No one spoke on the drive home.

My oldest child was out of the nest.

16 New Lenox, Illinois

With Howie away in the Navy, it was time to move to Illinois. George's plant was located in Park Forest, a suburb south of Chicago. George and I drove there to look for a house to buy. George was right; at that time it was definitely rural. We engaged a Realtor and specified the kind of house we wanted. As we drove around, I noticed a huge white box of a building sitting by itself in one of the cornfields and asked the Realtor what it was.

"That's Governors State University," she said. "It's new. It's kind of different, for nontraditional students. It's for after the community college's two years, so you can get a four-year degree there."

Hmmm, I thought. *Maybe I could finish my degree here. I'll have to look into that.*

We did not find a house we wanted in the immediate area, and expanded our search. That first trip was unsuccessful, so we returned, bringing Gary and Christie with us. This time we went as far afield as New Lenox, a small town about a 30-minute drive west of the plant.

The agent was getting as tired and frustrated as we were when nothing she showed us was suitable. At the end of the day she said, "Well, there's one more. It really isn't what you want at all, but it's a good price, and it's available now."

I replied, "It won't hurt to look at it."

So we drove to a small ranch house almost at the end of a quiet dead end street, nestled into the lot like it had grown there, surrounded by trees. It had only five rooms in an open floor plan—three bedrooms, a

The Leas house in New Lenox, Illinois, 2018.

living room, a kitchen, a bath and a half, and a dining area. It had a fireplace, and was situated at an angle on the lot so you couldn't see any of the neighbors. Its most attractive features were a cathedral ceiling and huge floor-to-ceiling windows in the dining area.

We stood around, looking and thinking. Suddenly Christie said, "This is it!" We all nodded, while the agent's mouth dropped open.

"But it isn't anything like what you said you wanted," she objected.

I said, "I know, but it feels right."

George immediately began planning an addition. We could add an extension with a basement, doubling the floor space, and the price was so low we could afford to do it. So it was decided—this would be our new home.

The next step was to sell the house in Clinton. We had hardly arrived back at the house when the doorbell rang. When I opened the door, a woman was standing there, and said, "We heard you're moving. I'd like to look at your house."

"Sure," I said, "come on in."

She looked around, asked some questions, and came back later with her husband. They bought the house at the asking price, and we were set to go.

New Lenox was a small, sleepy town, about 40 miles southwest of Chicago when we arrived in 1973. The nearest shopping was in Joliet, a small city about 10 miles west of us. (We later discovered that Joliet was most known for the state penitentiary located there.)

Howie's high school yearbook picture, Clinton High School, 1973.

As usual, George and I looked for a church. The nearest was a small Methodist congregation, in the center of New Lenox. We attended it for a while, but never felt at home there. I don't remember any of its activities or people. We soon gave up on it, and I thought for a while that I was finished with organized religion, until I discovered the Unitarians.

But first I discovered Governors State University. In the fall of 1973, I drove to that big white building in the cornfield that had caught my eye

George Leas, 1975, age 43.

before we moved there. I knew I wanted to finish the degree that I had abandoned twenty years earlier in the middle of my senior year at the University of Maryland, but I didn't know how I was going to do it.

I parked in the huge parking lot and found my way to what I guessed was the front entrance. It was hard to tell, as it didn't seem like a main door. Once inside, I looked in vain for a receptionist, or a sign, or something to tell me where to go. There was just a small entryway that led to a long hall. I started walking, and discovered that the building was laid out in a maze that went on and on with many small offices opening off the halls. I had no idea how I was going to register, and there was no one to ask. I was so frustrated and upset, I stood in the hall and felt tears start down my cheeks. I couldn't believe I was going to stand there and cry, but I couldn't help it.

Finally, a middle-aged woman in jeans approached and said, "You look upset. Can I help you with something?"

I wailed, "I want to register, but I can't figure out how!"

She asked me what I wanted to study. I said I didn't know. I was so bewildered by the whole place, I was at a loss to know what to tell her.

Gary's Lincolnway High School graduation picture, 1976.

Eventually she helped me find the right office, and I managed to register for classes. But it took me the whole first semester to figure out how the place worked. No one told me what courses to take, as their philosophy was that you designed your own degree. I signed up for some courses, went to classes, and waited for someone to tell me what to do next, but no one did. It finally dawned on me that my education was up to me. This university didn't even give grades—they granted "competencies." After you completed a course, the professor decided whether you had become competent in the skills you were supposed to acquire, and either gave you credit for those competencies or didn't.

Once I figured it out, I loved it. I majored in Behavioral Studies, which was basically psychology. The school accepted all of my credits from those many years before when I majored in Childhood Education, and I could finish my bachelor's degree in one year.

Christie's Lincolnway High School graduation picture, 1978.

Going back to school was a major turning point in my life. The education itself was important, of course, but not as important as the way it opened my eyes to a different life. I had spent all those years enclosed in a comfortable bubble as a conservative middle-class housewife. Suddenly I was immersed in a cauldron of ideas and lifestyles of liberal intellectual aging hippies, many Jewish. I had no idea that world existed, and I certainly didn't know that I belonged there. I soon realized I had found my people.

The classes were small and informal, often conducted sitting in a circle. The school was truly designed for nontraditional students. My fellow students were mostly older, relatively low income, attending part time while working real jobs, and included many blacks from Chicago. This was definitely not Ivy League. The class discussions were deep and relevant, since all of us had some maturity and life experience. I heard points of view I had never considered, and they all made sense.

But when I went home, these new viewpoints were not welcome. It became clear one evening at the dinner table. Something had been in the news involving a flag burning, and I said confidently that it was a valid protest and should not be against the law. I looked across the table to see George scowling, and heard him say something like, "We should lock them up and throw away the key!"

He probably did not say exactly that, but whatever he said, it was clear that there would be no more discussion on the subject. I learned very quickly to keep my new opinions to myself, and the gulf between my life at school and my life at home grew wider and wider. That 30-minute drive back and forth to school became a bridge between two worlds.

About this time, I began to paint. I had always been creative, but had never explored art. With the addition to the house we had extra rooms, and we designated one my studio. I enjoyed buying tubes of oil paints and various brushes and canvasses. I had no training and didn't know what I was doing, but it was fun. Some of my efforts were awful, some were okay, and one I still have hanging on my living room wall.

Painting coincided with another event that increased the liberating effect of the university: I stumbled on a copy of *Ms.* magazine. It had first appeared in 1972, but I had never heard of it. As I read, I realized that every word in it was aimed at me. I know this is a cliché, but like most clichés, it's true. *Ms.* opened my eyes to what my life was like and what it could be instead. It gave me courage to think of how I might change it.

Howie was stationed on a destroyer tender in Norfolk, Virginia. Whenever he came home on leave, he had no interest in staying with us. His life was back in Clinton, and as soon as we brought him home from O'Hare airport, he would take one of our cars and drive to Clinton, returning just in time to be taken back to the airport. I realized then what we had done—he had no room in the new house and there was no life for him with us. If we had been on good terms, we probably could have made better arrangements, but as it was, he was happy crashing on the couch for one night on his way back and forth.

For one trip home, he borrowed a car from a fellow sailor and drove to New Lenox from his base in Virginia. He stopped to see us, then went on to Clinton. He returned in two weeks, and had left us to return to the base. After a few hours, we received a phone call. He was calling from a rest stop restaurant; he had wrecked the car, and wanted us to come get him.

We found him slumped against the door in the entryway to the restaurant. He seemed dazed, but okay. He explained that as he had approached a high bridge, instead of driving onto the bridge he had somehow driven off the road and off an embankment into the creek below. We needed to report the accident so we located the nearest state police office and went there to make a report.

When we entered the troopers' station and started to explain why we were there, the officer looked up in amazement at Howie and said, "Are you the guy in that car?"

Howie replied, "Yeah, that was me."

The officer said, "Are you okay? How in hell did you survive that fall? We've been out there searching for bodies!"

We learned that Howie had driven off a 70-foot cliff into a creek. The water level was unusually low, but was just deep enough to cushion the fall. The car landed flat on its wheels, in about 2 feet of water. Howie had a slight bump on his head, but was otherwise fine. After filing a report, we drove home. We bought a plane ticket for him to get back to the base.

Howie told me later of an interesting part of that experience. After he landed in the creek, he climbed up the embankment and started walking along the highway. Suddenly he was aware that two young men were walking beside him, one on each side. He glanced at them, but felt somehow that they were not friendly, and ignored them, and eventually they faded away. A trucker picked him up and took him to the rest stop. With my understanding of unseen worlds, it was not hard for me to believe that such apparitions could appear. Perhaps two young men had been killed along that stretch of highway and their spirits were lingering in the area. They might have been attracted to Howie, recognizing that he had nearly become one of them. It surprised me that Howie did not seem to question their existence or why or how they had appeared, but we didn't talk about it anymore.

Gary did not adjust as well to the move as I hoped he would. We had bought him a motorcycle, a dirt bike, and as soon as he turned sixteen and got his driver's license he rode in the area behind the houses across the street. The high school was much more conservative than he was comfortable with and was not happy with his mildly hippie ways, and he hated it. He found a job at the gas station on the corner, and in his senior year in high school, he arranged a work-study program that allowed him to attend only part of the day at school and work the other hours. If not for this program, I doubt that he would have made it through high school.

However, he continued to be a generally happy kid, made acceptable grades, and was easy to get along with.

In the process of building the addition to our house, we had become friends with the contractor, Leroy Johnson. Gary began to work with him, and continued to do so after our house was finished. This experience served him well, as he has spent his working life ever since in some phase of construction.

Christie discovered acting. She made good grades, as usual, and joined the drama club, appearing in several plays in junior and senior high. She was extremely talented, and received an award as best actress three years in row. At age fifteen, she persuaded us to get her a horse. The family next door at the very end of the road had acreage and a horse barn. We bought a horse, and they allowed us to keep it on their property. To help pay for it, Christie found a job at a pizza place in New Lenox. I was reminded of my own teen years, with a horse that I had to work to pay for.

When I finished my year at Governors State in the spring of 1974, I graduated with a bachelor's degree in Behavioral Studies. I knew I needed to get at least a master's degree and probably a doctorate, but money was an issue, even though it was relatively inexpensive at the state university.

One day early that summer, I took my car into the dealership to get it serviced. In the waiting room, I overheard a conversation between two men sitting nearby. I heard one say, "Do you know any man who is looking for a job?"

Jokingly, I turned to him and asked, "Why does it have to be a man?"

"Well, no woman could do this job," he replied.

"Oh? What is it?" I asked.

He explained that he was the district manager of a company that made small fasteners, like screws and bolts and such. He was looking to hire a man to make the rounds to customers who bought their products, places like garages and companies with fleets of vehicles, and take orders.

"Why couldn't a woman do that?" I asked, seriously this time.

"Well, we've never hired a woman, but I suppose …. Are you interested?" he asked me.

On the spur of the moment, I said, "Sure. Tell me more."

His name was Jim, and he was intrigued. The more we talked, the more inclined he was to hire me. It sounded like something I could do; I had been around tools and car repair all my life and thought I could handle it.

A few days later he called and said that it took a lot of talking, but he persuaded his boss to hire me on a trial basis. I had a job!

I had no idea how to do this, but Jim insisted he would train me, going with me on calls for as long as it took. The day before we were to start, he gave me the book I would be ordering from. It was daunting—the size of an old Sears catalogue.

"You mean I need to learn all of those things?" I asked, aghast.

"No, not all of them, but you need to learn what most of them are and where they are in the book," he said. It was still a lot to learn. Perhaps this wasn't going to be as easy as I thought.

The next day we set out to see the first customer. It was a garage, with two bays, a dirty floor, the usual girly calendar on the wall, and an odor of axle grease and sweat.

As we walked in, a mechanic looked up and said, "Hey, Jim. Good to see you. Brought the girlfriend along, huh?"

Jim hastened to introduce me as the new hire. The mechanic looked me up and down, and said with a grin, "Well, she sure will pretty up the place!"

I thought with some concern, *Uh-oh! What have I gotten myself into?*

Jim showed me the bins where the nuts, bolts, screws, and various other little fasteners were kept. He showed me which bins were nearly empty and then where the items were listed in the catalogue. He filled out the order form while I watched. The mechanic had disappeared, so we left and headed to the next place. We repeated this at several more garages that day. Jim was good company, and we talked about a lot of subjects while driving around the countryside to customers. I saw why this is called "outside sales." At the end of the day, Jim added up the orders and pronounced the day a success. I had no idea what to compare it to, so assumed he was right, although it didn't seem like much to me.

We did the same thing the next day, and the day after that. I was basically following Jim around while he did the work. I wondered at what point I was expected to take over and do the job myself, but he seemed in no hurry to give it to me. The products were becoming more familiar, and I could find my way around in the catalogue. Eventually I started filling out the orders myself, while he watched over my shoulder.

One day I went alone to a big construction company that had a fleet of trucks, cars, and a helicopter. As I was assessing what needed ordering, the helicopter pilot approached me. He had been friendly before, and today he said, "I have to fly over to a construction site in the next county. Want to come along?"

It took me a nanosecond to reply, "Yeah!"

We climbed into the copter and took off. I had never ridden in one before and was surprised at how noisy it was. We couldn't really carry on a conversation, so I just looked at the scenery below. We landed at the site of a new shopping mall, and I hung back while he talked to the construction superintendent. It took only a few minutes, and we were off again, back to the main office. I went back to filling out an order form.

After a month or so, I told Jim I didn't think I was doing well. He replied, "Are you kidding? You're doing great!"

I couldn't tell, because I wouldn't get paid for some time. I had been enjoying myself, but as the weeks went by, I started getting bored with it. I was tired of dealing with macho mechanics and their thinly veiled flirtations, and knew that I didn't want to keep the job much longer. Finally, after the first month, I told Jim I wanted to quit. He was deeply disappointed.

"You don't know how well you're doing, do you?" he asked. "You're our top salesman in the district for the past month! How about you stay on a few more weeks?"

I was astounded. I had no idea I was doing that well. Jim was proud of me, but I felt like a fraud. It was mostly Jim's work, not mine. He was still going with me most of the time, and filling out the orders and sending them in. I just couldn't keep it up.

When I finally received a paycheck, it was for $2,500! For about six weeks' work! In 2018 money, that would be about $11,000. I couldn't believe it. Jim had been telling me I was doing well, but I couldn't understand that the markup in the fasteners business was so incredibly high. Soon after I quit, the industry changed; that huge markup was not allowed any more, and I would not have made nearly as much money if I had continued in the job.

Jim was so disappointed that I was quitting partly because he had gone to bat for me to get me hired, and his own standing with his boss was on the line. I felt bad for letting him down. It had been a good experience, but it wasn't the job for me.

The money from that job paid for me to go back to school at Governors State in the fall of 1974 and get my master's degree.

By now I understood how to function in that university. I knew that I wanted a degree in social work, but unfortunately, because the school was so new, it was not yet accredited to grant that degree. I had the choice of getting a different degree or going to a different school. I settled for a master's in Communication Science. I think at the time it was called Interpersonal Communications, but my diploma does not say so. Perhaps they changed the name before I graduated; the university was still being developed and kept changing. That degree required all of the same classes I would have taken for an accredited social work degree, and when I graduated I could take the state exam and become a licensed social worker. It would also be a good foundation for eventually getting a Ph.D. in psychology.

As with my bachelor's degree, I was expected to design my own curriculum. I met with my advisor and told him what I wanted to accomplish—I wanted to be able to work as a psychotherapist when I graduated. There were some required courses, but I had a lot of leeway. I took classes in psychology, including several therapy modalities.

I continued to make new friends and discover new ideas. I joined the Association of Humanistic Psychology. The group held annual conferences in Chicago, and I attended them all. This is where I really branched out into "New Age" thought and practices. The spiritual beliefs I had been exposed to through Carol, the woman who started our spiritual healing group in Clinton, served as a foundation for more advanced ideas. I learned about crystals, yoga, breathing techniques, different forms of meditation, past life regressions, reincarnation, Buddhism, Tarot, ... you name it, someone was teaching it. Most of the people were beautiful and inspiring. I felt like I was being transformed, and it was frustrating that I couldn't talk about it at home. The chasm between George and me widened still further.

I was thinking that it was time I had a serious conversation with George about a separation. I didn't know how we would accomplish it, since I had no income and no way to earn a living, and it didn't seem right to expect him to support me separately when it wasn't his idea. Divorce was a scary prospect, and being a single mother was even scarier, but I was feeling more all the time that I needed to get out. I just had to find the right time to bring up the subject. But the subject suddenly became overshadowed by something much more urgent.

17 Howie's Accident

At six o'clock one morning in April of 1975, we were awakened by the telephone. George answered it, and spoke softly, briefly. When he hung up the phone, he turned to me, and said, "Howie's been in an accident. He's in the hospital. He's in a coma. The doctor couldn't tell me much."

I was stunned, and didn't know what to think. What had happened? How serious was it? Where was he hurt? We didn't know.

Later that morning, the doctor called again. George asked more questions this time, and learned that Howie had been out bar-hopping the night before with a buddy. The friend was driving, and they came to a construction area where a barricade marked a hole in the street. The friend did not see it in time, swerved to miss the hole, and hit a pole at the side of the street. Howie, in the passenger seat, was pitched forward, and his head hit the pillar of the car by the windshield. The friend had a broken leg and was also in the hospital.

The doctor said that Howie had suffered head trauma, but they could not tell how bad it was or what the effect would be. His brain had been slammed against the skull and badly bruised, but that was all they knew. They were treating him as much as they could, but there wasn't much to do but wait and see.

I can't describe how frightened and helpless I felt. Howie was in Norfolk, Virginia, in a Navy hospital. We were in Illinois, about 800 miles away. We didn't know what to do. Should we drop everything and go there? The doctor said no, we should wait for him to wake up and see what the situation was. So we waited.

Every day we called and asked about his condition, but there was no change. I moved in a sort of trance, going through the motions of life but feeling numb. The not-knowing was terrible. We just didn't know what was the best thing to do. The doctors could not tell us if he would ever wake up, and if he did, what condition his brain would be in. Would he be paralyzed? Would he be brain damaged? Might he stay in a coma for years? No one knew.

I was torn between two opposite urges—to prepare myself for him to die, or to hold onto the thought that he would survive and be okay. I knew it was illogical that to prepare for his death would make it happen, but I couldn't help it. So I vacillated, and kept visualizing him alive and well, at the same time that I knew he might die.

In another two weeks, we couldn't wait any longer. We decided that George and I would drive to Norfolk in my car, find a cheap place for me to stay near the hospital, and then George would fly back. I would stay as long as it took. So we left early one morning. We arranged for Christie, who was fourteen, to stay with a friend's family for a few days until George got back. Gary was sixteen and could stay home by himself.

It was a long drive. We didn't talk much. We were both lost in our thoughts and couldn't share them, since we had become so distant from each other. We never did talk much about the situation, then or in the years to come.

When we reached Norfolk late that day, we went directly to the hospital. A nurse took us to Howie's room. I was shocked to see him lying there with tubes and wires and machines all around. He was lying on a kind of rack that allowed the nurses to turn him several times a day to prevent bed sores. He was not covered by a blanket or anything.

I asked the nurse, "Is it okay to touch him?"

"Of course," she replied, as if it was a dumb question.

I didn't know. I had never been around anyone in this condition. It looked like I might break something if I touched him. I leaned over and touched his face, stroked his forehead.

I asked, "Can I pull the blanket up over him?" I didn't like seeing him uncovered like that.

She replied, "No, we are trying to cool him down. The injury bruised his brain, and it has swollen. We need to cool him to bring down the swelling."

At that point I broke down. I turned to George and we held each other while I cried. It was so hard.

The nurse took us out of the room and found the doctor for us. We sat in an office and talked about Howie.

"As best we can tell, the impact pushed his brain against the back of the skull. It bruised the area where the hippocampus is, and that part of the brain controls the body's temperature. As a result, the brain's temperature has risen. If it rises too much, the brain has nowhere to go and it will press against the skull. So we are cooling him as much as possible, waiting for the swelling to go down."

The doctor did not say so, but it was clear to us that if his brain swelled too much, Howie would die. And even if it did not swell too much, there was no way to know the extent of the damage.

We thanked him, and went to find a motel for the night. When we had checked in, we called the hospital and told someone at the nurse's station where we were so they could reach us if there was any change during the night.

About 7:30 in the morning, the phone rang. I answered it this time. It was Howie's doctor. He said, "I'm so sorry. I have bad news. Your son died about 2:30 this morning."

I blurted out, "Why didn't you call us?"

He replied, "We didn't know where you were. We've been calling all the motels in the area."

"But we told the nurse! We called and gave her the number!"

"Well, then, it's our fault. I'm so sorry. No one told us you left a message."

We dressed quickly and drove to the hospital. The doctor took us to a room where we were to make arrangements. He told us that Howie had died from pneumonia that had developed so quickly they were unable to stop it.

We signed papers and made some arrangements that I don't remember. In fact, I don't remember much more about what happened then. I just know that we left the hospital and decided that I would fly home that day and George would drive the car home.

When I boarded the plane, I was relieved to find that my seat was in the front, behind the bulkhead, and no one sat next to me. I cried all the way home.

As soon as I arrived at the house, I drove to pick up Christie at her friend's house. I waited until we were alone to tell her that Howie had died, but as soon as we were in the car she blurted out, "He died, didn't he? He must have, or you wouldn't be here." I had to say yes, and we both started to cry.

Gary already knew, because he had called us at the motel that morning. When I answered Gary's call, he said simply, "He died. I know he died. Last night I decided I couldn't stand it and was going to drive out there, gassed up the car and everything, ready to leave early this morning, but in the night in a dream I could hear Howie saying, 'Help me! Help me! I'm dying!' so I knew." I told him yes, Howie had died, and we were coming home.

The Navy arranged for Howie's body to be shipped to a funeral home in New Lenox. As soon it arrived, we went there to see him. He was already embalmed, in a casket, ready to be buried. I reached out and stroked his forehead and was shocked to discover that it was hard and cold, like stone. That's when I understood why a body is referred to as "the remains"; that was not Howie, it was what remained after Howie was gone. I also reached into the casket to his feet, to check that he had his boots on. He always wore those boots, and we had specified that he be buried in them. He also had his bulky keychain on his belt, with many keys hanging on it. I never knew what all those keys were, but he wore them all the time. It seemed important that he be buried with what mattered to him. I couldn't help but notice that his knees were bent slightly, as at 6' 4", he was too tall for the casket.

We had to plan a funeral. We barely knew the minister at the local Methodist church that we had attended briefly and felt strongly that we wanted David Warren, our former Presbyterian minister in Clinton, to conduct the ceremony. He had left Clinton and was the pastor at a church in Maryland. We called him and asked him to come. He agreed, even though it was Memorial Day weekend.

We were grateful that David was there to help us. Neither George nor I had had any experience with death or funerals and we had no idea what to do. David made suggestions, and gently guided us with decisions. Cremation was not as common in 1975 as it is now, and it had never occurred to us to ask for it, so we had a traditional open casket funeral. It was held in the Methodist church, and we asked the minister there to assist David, as the polite thing to do, since it was his church.

About seventy-five people attended the service, which seems like a lot, considering that we had lived there only two years and Howie had not lived there at all. George's brother and his family came, and some friends from out of town. We had no place for people to stay in our house, and some of our neighbors offered to have people stay with them. I can't recall now who all the people were who attended and I don't have a registry book. I don't remember seeing one, but I was still somewhat in shock and don't remember much of the whole event. We buried him in a small cemetery in New Lenox.

A couple days after the funeral, all the visitors went home, George went back to work, and the kids went back to school. I was standing in the living room, feeling very alone, thinking *Now what?* when the phone rang. It was the postmistress at the New Lenox post office. A package had arrived, and she knew it contained Howe's effects from his locker on the ship. She asked if she should have it delivered then, and then asked something I would never have expected.

"Are you alone? Do you want someone with you when the package arrives?"

I was touched by her kindness, and assured her that I didn't need anyone with me, that I would be fine. When the box came, I opened it and found only ordinary things, like a pair of jeans, some shirts, and a book. I was surprised at the book; it was a hard copy of Arthur Koestler's *The Roots of Coincidence: An Excursion into Parapsychology.* I wish I knew why he was reading that book, what it said about his thinking. What conversations we might have had!

A death in the family requires paperwork, and it was all new to us. We did what we were told. Years later I wished that we had asked for a copy of the autopsy. We will never know whether Howie would have lived if he had not developed pneumonia, and if so, whether he would have ever come out of the coma and what his condition would have been. We received a nice letter from Howie's commanding officer, stating what a good man Howie was, how well-liked he was by his fellow sailors, and how much he would be missed on the ship.

Much to our surprise, we also received a check for $20,000, from insurance the Navy carried on its sailors. We opened the envelope together, and were so surprised to see the check that at first I didn't notice how it was made out. We soon saw only my name, because Howie had named me as the sole beneficiary and not George. George didn't show how he felt about that, but it must have hurt. It created a dilemma for me. I knew I would be leaving George at some point and that money would certainly help, but I couldn't bear to cut him out of it. It just seemed too cruel. We talked about it, and decided to give $5,000 each to Gary and Christie, and George would use the rest to start a business. He had been thinking he wanted a construction business, building houses on spec, and this was his chance.

Howie in the navy, 1974, age 18.

I rationalized my decision by thinking that Howie had made his statement, and it would make both of us happy for George to have a successful business. He had never been really satisfied in his career as an engineer, and this might allow him to do something else.

The construction business idea grew out of the experience of building the addition to our house. George pictured himself building houses and making a lot of money selling them. He had no construction experience, but our contractor had been doing it for years and was happy for George to put up the money. That $20,000 in 1975 would be roughly $90,000 in 2018, so even half of it was not a trifling amount. Together they started a company called Cedarwood Construction.

Meanwhile, we all went on with our lives. It puzzles me now to realize that with all I had learned in school, all the human potential movement had taught me about open communication and expressing feelings—I was a Communications major!—we didn't talk to each other about how we felt. I have no idea how George felt or how he dealt with his grief.

Howie's gravestone and flag.

I had been conducting a therapy group of six women as a requirement for my master's degree studies, and they became my support group for a short while to help me through my grief, in a kind of role reversal, as they counseled me. They listened when I cried, when I talked about how hard it was.

One day when Gary and I were alone in the house I tried to tell him how sad I was, but when I started to cry, Gary seemed to be very uncomfortable. I suddenly realized that it was important to him that his mother be strong. I had always been the emotional anchor of the household and for me to be vulnerable must have been frightening. I quickly changed the subject.

My main source of comfort was my spiritual beliefs. All those years of studying spirituality had given me a basis for understanding Howie's death in way that made it less difficult to bear—not easy, but less difficult. I hadn't yet totally accepted the concept of reincarnation, but I did believe that we all come into this lifetime with a plan about what we need to do. I don't mean accomplishing something in the world like finding a cure for cancer, but reaching the necessary stage in our own development to be ready for the next stage. I had already moved beyond any belief in heaven and hell, or any kind of divine judgment. The soul lives on, and continues on its journey toward final enlightenment, whatever that is. I believed that Howie had finished what he was to accomplish in his short life and it was time for him to move on. For him, dying was not a tragedy; it was the transition to the next step in his own journey, and therefore a good thing.

So I didn't grieve for Howie's sake. He didn't need any more of that lifetime. He was okay.

That didn't mean it was okay for me, of course, and grieving was hard. The grief was strangely unfocused, because on the surface, nothing changed. He had been gone out of our daily lives for two years and had never lived in that house so did not leave behind an empty room or any change in our family routine. But he was gone, and was never coming back. Like many mothers, I had a special feeling for my first-born child. There was a hole in my chest, a physical ache that was always there, every minute of every day. It felt like someone had reached into the middle of my chest and pulled out a big chunk. That aching hole remained with me for a long time. One day about two years later, I woke up one morning and realized the hole was gone, but to this day it seems to be always lurking somewhere, ready to reappear any time.

I found myself reading all the obituaries in the newspaper, paying special attention to the deaths of young men. It seemed like there was a rash of them, mostly from car crashes. I also kept seeing Howie in public places, walking down the street or in stores. I would see a young man who looked like him and catch my breath, thinking, *There he is! I knew it— it was all a mistake!* and then came the crushing realization that it wasn't him after all.

Howie's death erased all thoughts of leaving George. I could deal with only so much emotional stress at once, and my plate was full. The marriage was no better, it was just overshadowed, and seemed less important.

18 My First Job

The next session of school at Governors State soon started, and I went back to classes. The intensity of grief faded some, and I could get through what I needed to do at school and at home. That semester I had only a couple of classes and they met in the evening.

I was halfway through the master's requirements, and I was beginning to doubt my earlier decision to go on for a Ph.D. in psychology. The previous semester I had been required to serve an internship in a treatment center for mentally ill people, and I was assigned to Tinley Park State Mental Hospital in a nearby town. My placement was in a ward for psychotic patients. It was an open ward; the patients were locked inside a wing where they could roam freely. There was a counter with a room behind it where the professionals had their desks and records. I was to report there for three hours, two days a week, for eight weeks.

My first day on the ward was terrifying. I had never been around psychotic people and was afraid of them. At first I took refuge behind the counter, but after a couple of days I realized I was not going to learn anything that way and forced myself to go out into the ward and mingle with the patients. I knew intellectually that none of them were violent, just bizarre, and the threat was only in my mind.

The ward included a large room, with windows on one side, furnished with a television set, an old stained sofa, and plastic chairs scattered here and there. It was impossible to have a coherent conversation with any of the patients, but I kept trying. Our interactions usually went something like this:

Patient: "Can I have a cigarette?"

Me: "I'm sorry, I don't have any."

Same patient, two minutes later: "Can I have a cigarette?"

Me: "No, I don't have any."

This went on and on. They mostly stared at the TV screen, sitting numbly in the chairs. Every morning I attended their group therapy session. The therapist was way out of his depth, in my opinion, and the group sessions consisted mostly of just talking randomly. The patients also saw a psychiatrist regularly to get their medications adjusted. In 1974, keeping patients heavily medicated was the norm.

I was particularly upset over one patient, a young man named Greg. He was brought in soon after I arrived for my internship. He had been found wandering on the street, apparently behaving strangely, although I never learned exactly why he was admitted to the hospital. He seemed normal to me, showing none of the symptoms the other patients had. He arrived on a Thursday, and my next day on the ward was the following Tuesday. When I came in that day, I was disturbed at the change in him. His clothing was disheveled, his hair uncombed, and he was frightened. Over the next couple of weeks, he deteriorated severely. He began speaking gibberish, he lost a front tooth (I was told he had gotten into a fight with another patient), and he constantly glanced wildly around the room. If he was not psychotic when he came in, he was now. I still think about him, and wonder whether he was made crazy by being locked up in the ward, or if he really was mentally ill when he came in and I just didn't see it.

Another young man also stays in my mind. He was in his early twenties, physically healthy but clearly schizophrenic. He had been committed by his elderly parents, who could no longer take care of him. He had been a patient before on occasions when he became more than his parents could handle. The law said that he could be admitted without his consent for only two weeks and then had to be discharged unless he was "a danger to self or others." This young man was not dangerous, but no one would take him in. He had worn out his welcome with all of his relatives and friends. The social workers' solution was to put him on a bus with a ticket that would take him to the end of the line, where he would get off with no money and no place to go. We all knew that before long he would be picked up and brought back to the hospital, and the cycle would start over again. No one knew what else to do.

One patient was a middle-aged woman who was another "repeat customer." I don't know what her specific diagnosis was, but it came out in group therapy that apparently she was considered mentally ill by her husband because she was unwilling to perform her household duties. She failed to clean the house or cook meals, or do any other "wifely" chores. This was in the early days of the modern women's movement, when "housewife" was still considered the normal job for women and being a good wife meant doing the housework. (It wasn't until later that I realized how absurd this was.) There was more to her diagnosis, of course, and she did seem to be genuinely out of touch with reality. But one day she suddenly woke up as a normal, ordinary person. It was obvious looking at her that she had "recovered." She was discharged that day. The staff told me that she did this from time to time, becoming psychotic and then for no apparent reason becoming a sane person overnight. The staff knew that she would eventually come back.

I finished that internship thinking that every person should have to spend some time as an observer on the psych ward in a mental hospital, even for just a few days. It gave me a new perspective on what extreme mental illness is like, and the hopelessness of most treatment, at least in a facility like that. I left wondering if we would ever find a better way to understand and treat people who were diagnosed as psychotic, and whether this was where I wanted to spend my professional life. It was discouraging.

About this time I also discovered community theater again. Someone in the Unitarian group told me about the Joliet Drama Club. It was 1975, the year before our country's bicentennial, and some civic-minded people waged a campaign to build a park with a theater to commemorate the date. They succeeded, and the Bicentennial Theater was built, the Drama Guild moved in, and it became my home away from home for the next few years.

The first production in the new theater was Shakespeare's "A Midsummer Night's Dream," an ambitious undertaking. It was a huge success. I met some interesting, friendly people, and worked on all aspects of several plays. As it had done in other cities, the theater became my escape from the house. Between my life at the university and my life in the theater, I had less and less connection with my life in New Lenox.

That little Unitarian fellowship continued to help me in significant ways. One of the men in the group, Bob Lindberg, was the executive director of a sheltered workshop, a place for disabled people to work in Joliet. He had obtained a one-year grant for a pilot project for the workshop in conjunction with the Illinois Department of Vocational Rehabilitation, or DVR. The project was to take over the intake interviews for DVR, to lighten the paperwork load for their counselors. He needed to hire a project director and three interviewers.

One Sunday as we were leaving the worship service, he pulled me aside, told me about the project, and then said, "How about you be the project director?"

I replied dismissively, "Oh, no, I couldn't do that!"

"Sure you can," he said. "It won't be hard. I'll help you."

This was in July of 1975; I was forty-two years old and had never held a real job. I was still working on my master's degree, and I couldn't imagine going to work for an employer in a professional capacity. But Bob insisted, and persuaded me I could do it. It paid very little, something like $6,000, and was for eleven months, because one month of the grant period had already passed. I had time, since I had only a couple of classes and they met in the evening.

George was not enthusiastic about the job. He said that it really wasn't worth doing, since it paid so little. The thought occurred to me fleetingly that he might be reluctant because he realized it could be my ticket to leave him; if I had my own income and some work experience, I could possibly support myself on my own. But he didn't actually object, and I took the job. That $6,000 sounds trifling now, but in 2015 dollars it would be about $28,000. It did seem tiny compared with what George made. His salary then was somewhere around $70,000, which would be almost $320,000 today. So in his mind, my salary would be peanuts.

On August 1, I reported for work. Bob had hired the other staff, all young people right out of college, and a secretary. The first two weeks we spent in training in the DVR office, and then moved to the office space Bob had rented for the project.

Having a job was almost as life-changing for me as going back to school had been. When I recalled that years before George had said to me derisively, "You could never hold a job," I grinned. I was doing it! Fortunately, that particular job was the perfect way for me to ease into the working world. The work was interesting and not too challenging, the boss was accommodating and helpful, and my fellow workers were fun. The office was some distance across town from both the DVR office and the sheltered workshop; consequently, supervision was pretty lax. The grant was administered by both the DVR and the workshop, so I reported to both Bob and the director of the DVR office, a man named Jim. They both seemed to assume that the other was taking primary responsibility for the project, which gave us a lot of freedom. Bob actually signed the paychecks, so I interacted mostly with him, and I liked that, as I knew him and his family pretty well.

The job consisted of receiving DVR applications for assistance from disabled people who wanted help in finding a job and then interviewing them in their homes to determine whether they were eligible for services, and if so, what services would be appropriate. Every few days, as the director, I received a batch of paper applications, and I assigned them to each of the three interviewers. I also did some of the interviews. After each interview, we filled out the paperwork and sent it back to the DVR office. Some of the applicants clearly did not meet the eligibility requirements, and having us determine that saved the DVR counselors a lot of intake work.

I didn't have a system for who should get which client application, except that I soon realized that I didn't want to deal with people whose disability was the result of a head injury. The other interviewers understood.

Joliet at the time had a black ghetto, a community of extremely poor people, and some of our applicants lived there. It was called "The Hill," and it was literally up a steep hill on the south edge of town. I took a few of those applicants and was shocked at what I found when I went into their homes. I didn't know such squalor existed. I was nervous about going there, thinking it wasn't safe for a white person, and started assigning most of those applicants to Doris, the only black person in the office.

One day Doris planted herself in the chair across from my desk, her arms crossed defiantly over her chest. "It isn't fair," she said.

"What isn't?' I asked, puzzled.

"You give me all the black people on The Hill."

"Um… I guess I do. Isn't that a good idea?"

"*No!* You don't understand! It isn't safe for me. You can go in there and nobody will bother you because they think you're the welfare lady. I'm just a black girl who's fair game. It's dangerous for me."

Of course, that made sense. I realized how clueless I had been, and stopped giving her all of those applicants. I gave her a few, but chose those in the areas that seemed somewhat safer. I spread the applications over the other two interviewers, a white woman and a white man, thinking their race gave them the same protection it gave me, although maybe not so much for the man—he wouldn't have the cover of being mistaken for the "welfare lady."

I continued with my studies, preparing to graduate with an MA in June of 1976. Working full time, going to school part time, and being a wife and mother with two teenagers kept me busy, but it was doable. In fact, as soon as I started the job, I sat the family down and declared, "I've taken a job, but it's not an *additional* job. It has to replace something. Who wants to do what instead of me?" We discovered that George actually enjoyed grocery shopping. I had always hated it. He found he liked browsing the store, finding different foods to eat. A side benefit was that he learned how much everything cost. For years he had scolded me for spending so much on groceries; now he understood.

Meanwhile, George and his partner Leroy, the contractor, had bought a couple of lots on the edge of town and were building a house to sell, and he was happier than I had seen him in years. During this time he left the company in Chicago and became an engineering consultant instead of an employee, working for one of the clients of the old company. He liked being a consultant, enjoying the freedom of being his own boss. His income increased, as well. Things were going well for him.

When I received my master's degree, the next step was to take the state exam to get my social work license. The other interviewers in the project had already graduated the year before but had not taken the exam, so one day we all rode the train into Chicago to take it. The test took all day. It wasn't hard, and we all passed, but I decided not to apply for the license. The application fee was fairly high and I didn't think I would ever need a license, and so I let it go. I was right; I've never needed it, but I've sometimes wished I had it, just because that credential would beef up my resume.

My contract ran out in June of that year. The state government decided not to renew the project, so I was out of a job.

19 Leaving

George and I were still distant, and I felt more alienated than ever. Knowing that I could hold a job gave me the confidence to think seriously about a separation, probably leading to a divorce. I tried to talk to George about it, but he didn't seem to hear me. It was so hard to explain what was wrong! He didn't do anything "bad": he paid the bills, he didn't drink, didn't beat me, and didn't run around. He just couldn't understand that I was unhappy for no apparent reason.

It wasn't until years later that I realized just how strong the barrier was that kept us from being emotionally intimate. It's hard to know how much that barrier was maintained on George's side and how much on mine; surely it was both. George had such an uptight, critical, judgmental personality that it was hard for anyone to be close to him, but my defenses didn't help. Over the years I had come to recognize that I really didn't like George, and didn't *want* to be close to him. Consequently, I couldn't let down my guard enough to let myself be vulnerable, and without vulnerability, there can't be intimacy. We were virtually strangers. George didn't know who I really was, and he never would. I wanted to be able to be myself, to have encouraging support around me, to have a companion in the lifestyle I wanted. He couldn't understand that.

I gave up trying to explain myself, and set about finding another job.

In September I went to work for the Will County Mental Health Department in Joliet. The director had received a grant to develop a transitional living center to serve people with mental illness coming out of the mental health hospital, mostly psychiatric patients. Three of us were hired, and we quickly discovered that the director had given no thought as to what we would do or where or how we would do it. When we appeared at the department office, we had no office, no desks, and no telephones. We were handed forms with information about people who had been discharged from the hospital and were expected to contact them and invite them to participate in the program. However, there was no program. He had not yet hired a program director, either.

We three stumbled around for a few days, sitting at any vacant desk we could find, or using other employees' telephones, and waited for the director to get the program together. Before long, he found us some desks and arranged for a low-cost hotel downtown to be used as the halfway house. The hotel was shabby and smelly, and there was no meeting room, just the residents' individual rooms. We were expected to meet with the clients in their rooms or coffee shops, or whatever we could arrange. He hired a program director who looked great on paper, but was all bluster. He talked about doing a great deal, but never seemed to get anything done. He and the rest of us seemed to be working at cross purposes all the time.

The department director was less than a year away from retirement and was obviously just putting in time. He called staff meetings every morning, and used the time telling jokes. He spent the day in his office on the phone or reading magazines and the newspaper. He and several of the other staff were chain smokers, and since this was long before anyone heard of a no smoking policy, the whole office was blue with smoke all day.

I lasted three months. One day the program director called me into his office for my 90-day evaluation. I read the paper in front of me and saw that the only item marked satisfactory was "Comes to work on time." All the other items were marked unsatisfactory. I looked up at him and said, "If I gave someone an evaluation like this, I would expect them to resign."

He glared at me and said, "Well…?"

I replied, "You'll have my resignation in the morning."

I had mixed feelings about the experience; I felt bad about having to quit, but good about recognizing that it was an impossible situation and that I needed to leave. I knew how fortunate I was that I had a husband with a good job and I didn't have to support myself. I don't remember George's reaction. He probably was relieved that I would be a housewife again. We wouldn't miss the money. At least not then.

One day soon after, we were riding in the car, and I told George that I was going to start painting again and had bought a lot of art supplies that day. He winced.

I said, "What's wrong?"

He said, "I lost my job today."

George had never before been a consultant and did not realize that he needed to be marketing himself all the time, developing potential clients. He apparently thought he would have that one client forever. That client suddenly decided they didn't need him anymore and terminated his contract. All of a sudden he had no income, except for what Cedarwood Construction would bring in, which wasn't much.

I was collecting unemployment compensation, but George didn't want to apply for it. He probably assumed he would find another job quickly and wouldn't need it. However, he soon discovered that he was overqualified for every chemical engineering job that was open. He sent out many résumés with little result. An engineer with his experience, especially as a consultant, put him in the upper-level management positions, and they were scarce. Most employers would think that he was looking for an interim job and would leave as soon as he found more clients.

George had a friend who had a headhunting firm in Chicago, and the friend suggested that George come into his office every day and pretend to work there. He could have a desk and telephone, and could read all of the job openings that came in. If one looked right for him, he could apply for it. He had no other options, so he jumped at the opportunity, even though it didn't pay anything. He put on a suit and tie and drove into the city every day as if he were going to work, and looked at job openings.

Months went by with no results. We had my unemployment comp and that small income from the construction company, but nothing else. Soon there was no cash to put into materials or wages for the company, so they closed it. Money got very tight. We pinched pennies wherever we could. I found a store called Railroad Salvage that sold damaged goods gleaned from various sources, all of it good but in damaged or dirty packaging. I never knew what would be on the shelves, and bought whatever was available that we would eat. We did our best to keep the children from knowing how desperate the situation was.

All thoughts of leaving George were put on hold, again. I couldn't do it after Howie died, and now I couldn't do it while we were struggling to survive. Even if I could have figured out how to support myself, I couldn't do that to George while he was completely demoralized by being out of work.

After ten long scary months, when my unemployment had run out and we were down to our last few dollars, George finally found a job, an opening that had come across his desk at the headhunting firm. He started immediately, and we were soon back on our feet again.

One evening in October I received a phone call from my brother Frank.

"I have sad news," he said. "Mother died this morning."

Our mother had been sick for years, in and out of hospitals frequently. It was never clear to me just what was wrong with her. Once before, we were told that her condition was serious enough that I should come see her in the hospital, so I drove out there and stayed for a couple of days. She was in great pain, and I remember Daddy saying angrily, "The docs won't give her enough morphine. They don't want her to get addicted. Damn it, who cares if she's addicted at this point?" He insisted so vigorously that the doctors relented and gave Mother enough drugs to keep her relatively comfortable. She recovered from that episode and went home.

So it was not totally unexpected that she might die, but I was still taken by surprise. I had not heard that her condition had changed. We didn't communicate much, partly because of the high cost of long-distance phone calls, and partly because I was so immersed in my own life I hadn't given much thought to theirs. Our estrangement had lessened somewhat over the years, but we were still not close, and I felt that if I satisfied my basic obligation as a dutiful daughter, that was enough.

Of course we went to the funeral. Gary was working and couldn't get off, so Christie, George, and I drove out to Maryland. I remember very little of that visit. My only clear memory is of walking with Christie down the aisle in the funeral home to view Mother's body in the casket after the service. When I reached the casket and looked inside, I saw *myself* lying there! I knew that I looked a lot like Mother, but only when she was lying there with no personality molding her features did I see just how much alike we were. It was shocking to see myself lying dead in a casket, and I burst into tears. I couldn't stop sobbing as we walked back down the aisle. It must have appeared that I was grieving for the loss of my mother, but in fact I was grieving for myself. I still don't know exactly what that experience meant for me, but it was traumatic.

The funeral was an Eastern Star ritual, and most of the mourners were from the lodge. I was a bit surprised that so few people were there. Considering that our family had lived in the same house for 44 years, and my parents had held every office in the lodge and the Star, I thought many more people would attend.

Not until many years later did I really grieve for Mother. At the time I had very little sentimental feeling for her, and as little contact as we had had, I did not miss her.

Now that our family was in good shape again, with a good income and everyone doing well, I decided that it was time to start the separation process. First, I needed to be self-supporting. I found a job at Wescom, an electronic components company in Downers Grove, half an hour up the interstate, as an Employment Representative in the Personnel Department. I hired hourly employees and helped with employee relations. It was part time, with a good possibility of becoming full time.

I had always thought that I couldn't leave while the kids were still in school. Gary had graduated from high school in 1976, and had moved out to live with his girlfriend, Mary. They were staying on a farm with some friends, and he was still working for Leroy. Christie was finishing high school early, in December of 1977.

Once I had a job, I told George that I really wanted a separation. I knew that divorce was too drastic to think about yet, and even separating was hard for him to accept. I said that it would be a trial separation, although deep inside I knew I wouldn't come back. We talked and talked. I explained how unhappy I was, but he still didn't seem to understand. Eventually, I agreed that we would go for marriage counseling.

I found a marriage therapist in Chicago and set up an appointment. About ten minutes into the session, the therapist said, "How invested are you in this marriage?"

George replied fervently, "*A lot.*"

They both looked at me and I said honestly, "Not much."

The therapist asked me, "Then why are you here?"

I replied, "Well... it just seemed like we should."

The therapist shook his head and said, "I don't think there's much I can do for you." That ended our marriage counseling.

The more we talked about it, the more I realized there was no way I could stay in the marriage. The final straw came one day when I was again trying to explain myself to George, and I said something like, "I just want more freedom."

He replied, in exasperation, "But I give you all the freedom you want!"

At that point I knew he would never understand; he couldn't see that my freedom was not his to give. I couldn't find common ground to talk about it; it felt like we lived on different planets, were speaking different languages. I told him I was going to find an apartment and move out. After much discussion, we agreed that it would be temporary, a trial for six months, and he would help me get started. I couldn't live on that part-time job, so he would take over my car payment and help me more if I needed it. I was confident that the job would become full-time before long, and I would have enough income to live on. I think he really believed I would soon discover that I couldn't live alone and would come back.

It was December, and we postponed doing anything about the decision until after Christmas. We went through the motions as usual, acting like nothing had happened. But the time came to make the move, and I started apartment hunting.

We hadn't told the children anything, but now it was time, and I had to do it. I sat each of them down and said that I was moving out, temporarily. They seemed to accept it, and we didn't talk about it much. I remember Gary saying, calmly, "Well, do whatever you have to do, Mom."

It was all very civil. No raised voices, no tears, no arguing. We kind of tip-toed around each other. I found a one-bedroom apartment in a complex in Joliet, and started packing a few things. George agreed that I should use household money to buy a bed, and I picked out a few pieces of furniture from the house. I would take some plants, my art supplies and paintings, and my personal belongings. I went through our collection of family photographs and divided them, some for me, some for George. George and Christie would need to continue to function in the house, so I took only a few basics from the kitchen, thinking I could get what else I needed from yard sales. I wanted to make it as easy as possible for him. It wasn't his fault that I had changed so much. I felt both guilty and excited. George was glum.

The apartment was to be available the first week in January, but when the day came, it wasn't ready. I couldn't stand waiting any longer, so I asked a friend if I could stay with her for a few days, and she agreed. She lived in Joliet, not far from my new apartment. I packed a suitcase and stayed in her spare room.

Finally, moving day came, and I went back to the house to get my stuff. We made a couple of trips, using Gary's van. After we loaded some bags and boxes into my car for the last trip, George and I stood beside my car in the driveway, saying goodbye. We held each other, both of us in tears. I drove away, and didn't look back.

PART 2

On the Move

20 On My Own

My tears dried quickly as I sped down the highway in my silver Trans Am, the bright Firebird decal splayed across the hood. My new apartment was on the second floor in a complex on the west side of Joliet, in an inexpensive, relatively safe area. I had very little furniture, but I didn't mind, as the idea of living sparely appealed to me.

It was mine! All mine! I was alone, no one to tell me what to do, no one to get angry with me, no one to ask me for anything, no one frowning in disapproval.

I unpacked my few things and drove to a grocery store to stock up. It wasn't until I was back home that I realized that I had walked right past the meat counter. I didn't consciously stop eating meat; it just happened. I simply didn't want it. I'm still not sure how that figured into my new independence. No one had required me to eat meat before, although I was expected to serve it at every meal.

I set about putting things in place, hanging pictures, placing plants by the one big window in the living room. I had a bedroom, a kitchen, a living room with an el for a dining table, and a small bathroom. Compared with a ten-room ranch on a half-acre lot, it was tiny, but it was quite adequate for me.

I can't describe how thrilled I was with that apartment. I was forty-four years old and had never lived alone. It was glorious.

When night came, I put the new sheets on the new bed, and settled in to sleep. That night I had a dream that haunts me still. I dreamed I could hear bloodhounds baying in the distance—they were coming after me to take me back! I woke up terrified, but quickly realized no one was coming after me; no one could make me go back. Ever. I was free.

❖ ❖ ❖

The next day, George called to tell me how unhappy he was. I had urged him to start dating, to be looking around for someone, but he didn't know how to go about it. As with most couples of our generation, I had always been responsible for our social life, and he had no social skills, no idea how to meet people. It was clear he was miserable and was hoping I would come back.

One evening, he came over to visit me. We sat on the couch, his arm around my shoulders, trying to talk about what to do next. It was awkward! We had nothing to say to each other. I felt guilty. It seemed like I was punishing him for what was my fault. I wanted him to go on with a happy life, but he couldn't seem to picture one without me.

I started thinking of who I could set him up with. I thought of Joyce, the woman whose house I stayed in while my apartment was being readied. She was single, about our age, and it occurred to me that she and George might like each other, so I gave him her number and suggested he call her.

He did, and they hit it off immediately. Not long after, Joyce came to me and asked, "What would you think if George and I were dating? I really like him."

I said, "That would be great!"

She said, "Are you sure? You won't mind?"

I replied that it was fine with me. I was delighted! I felt a twinge of jealousy for an instant, but it quickly turned into hope that she might lift him out of his depression.

I had left the house in early January, and this exchange took place in February. In March, George called me and said he wanted a divorce. He and Joyce were getting married! Remembering that we agreed to a six-month separation, I asked, "What about our agreement?"

He replied, "What agreement?"

I said, "Never mind."

So we worked out how we would get a divorce. In Illinois in 1978, you could get a divorce based on physical abuse, abandonment, adultery, or mental cruelty. No-fault divorce had not yet become law. The only option that would work for us was mental cruelty. I thought George and Joyce were being a bit hasty, and told him that if he wanted a divorce that soon, he would have to be the one to get it. So he hired a lawyer and sued me for mental cruelty.

It was all very amicable. Everyone said I was being foolish, but I was okay with using his lawyer and trusting that he was being honest and forthright about our finances. I was confident that he did not wish me harm and would not take advantage of me. I also knew the lawyer and trusted him, as much as I would trust any lawyer.

The negotiations were pretty simple. George added up our assets and liabilities, and we split it down the middle. The exception was that he took over all of the debts. I was shocked to learn that we owed $10,000 on several credit cards! That would be about $38,000 in 2018 money. (There are several ways of calculating inflation values of money. I've used the most conservative one.) Other debts came to another $9,000. I had never known much about our finances, believing that it was his money to do with as he pleased. That part I regret now, but it was not an unusual attitude for couples who came of age in the Fifties.

Christie would continue to live in the house in New Lenox with George, and since she would soon be eighteen and no longer a minor, custody was not an issue. Technically, George would have custody of her for the next six months.

I didn't want the house, and George definitely did, so we figured what it would cost him to buy me out. With the debts set aside, George owed me money for half of our assets. He couldn't pay me outright, so I agreed to a payment of $15,000, to be spread over three years. As I had expected, my job had become full time and I had enough income to live on, but that $400+ a month made it easier.

April may not be the cruelest month, but mine certainly was eventful that year. In April of 1978 I had my forty-fifth birthday, bought a new car, moved into a new apartment, had surgery, and got divorced. And it didn't seem all that difficult, which testifies to the high energy level I had in those days. It all seemed quite doable.

Now that I had a full-time job, I bought a new car—a 1978 gold special edition Firebird. I was really into cars, and this was one wicked car. With a generous trade-in for the '76 Firebird, the new payment was only slightly more than the old one. The Firebird looked and felt like a sports car. It was an attention getter, and boosted my morale a lot.

Of course Gary was enamored of it too, and one day I let him borrow it. When he returned it, I looked at the gas gauge and saw that it had as much gas as when he took it.

Well, that's a surprise. He actually put gas in it! I thought, pleased.

The next day I drove to a night seminar that my work required me to attend in Chicago, and on the way home the car suddenly died and wouldn't start. I walked to a nearby house and used their phone to call a tow truck. At the gas station where they took me, I called Gary to come get me. It took him half an hour to get there.

Just before this I had I developed severe bleeding. I was just entering menopause, and my periods were erratic. The bleeding had continued, relentlessly, for days and days. When the car broke down, I was bleeding profusely and did not have any pads with me. So I stood in the gas station, waiting for Gary, with blood running down my leg. Fortunately, I had worn dark slacks.

The next day the gas station attendant called me.

"We found the problem," he said. "You were out of gas. The gas gauge is broken."

I should have known Gary didn't put gas in it. What 20-year-old kid puts gas in his mother's car voluntarily?

When the bleeding didn't stop, I saw my doctor, who said I needed a D&C. A few days later I drove to the hospital and checked myself in. I had to stay overnight, and the next day I drove home. I was greatly relieved when the bleeding stopped.

Meanwhile, George and I and the lawyer were working out the details of the divorce. I was determined that it be as painless as possible, both for our sake and the children's. I had known of too many acrimonious divorces that left all parties scarred for years and saw no need for that to happen with us. I didn't want anything from George; at the time I just wanted out, as quickly and easily as possible. I agreed with what the lawyer told me. Of course I read everything carefully and understood what it all meant, and if I had seen anything I didn't want, I would have objected.

I had to swear that I had been mentally cruel to George, enough to justify his divorcing me. That part was uncomfortable, I think for George as well as for me, but it was necessary, so I went along with it. The lawyer asked me several times if I understood that I was not getting any alimony. I had not asked for it and didn't feel that I needed or should get any. I had a master's degree and a job, and could support myself. If George had been at fault or if I had been unemployable, I would surely have seen it differently, but it was a matter of fairness and pride that I didn't expect him to support me.

Looking back after all these years, I realize it probably was not smart for me to handle the negotiations the way I did. I don't know how George figured the value of the house, and looking at the numbers now I wonder if he actually included everything in the assets. Perhaps he did, but it seems like even in 1978 dollars, my half of the house should have been worth more than $15,000. I don't know if he included any life insurance policies or pension funds or stock options. In the long run, it probably wouldn't have made a difference, but there were several years in the 1980s when I was nearly destitute, and a few more dollars in the bank would have been helpful. But I made my choices, and it all worked out okay eventually. According to what the children tell me, I'm actually in better financial shape today than he is.

My one real regret about the divorce is that I should have waited another couple of years for Christie's sake. I'm sure she would have been much better off if I had been in the house for her late teen years. I told myself that I couldn't wait, that I was suffocating, but I was surely influenced by the culture at the time. The divorce rate in the United States had been gradually increasing over the previous couple of decades and peaked in 1980, tapering off ever since. It seemed that the hippie rebellion in the late sixties and the human potential movement that grew in the mid-seventies gave us all permission to seek our own happiness, and it was more acceptable than ever to look for it with someone new. In my case I had no one in mind, but I was convinced that I would find happiness with a better match for a mate. I felt guilty then about leaving George; now I regret leaving Christie too soon.

The divorce took place on April 25 in the county courthouse in Joliet. For some reason I don't remember, I thought it was important that Christie and Gary be present for the event, so I insisted that they attend.

I took the stand, and the judge asked me if the charges in the suit were true.

"Yes, your honor," I said, knowing that I was lying. Everyone in the courtroom knew this was a charade, that we were going through a performance that was repugnant but necessary, as the law stood.

Then he asked, "Do you understand that you will receive no alimony? That this is final?"

"Yes, your honor, I understand."

I don't remember whether George testified, but if so, he had to swear to the lie also.

The whole process took about half an hour.

As we were leaving, I invited the kids to go out for breakfast with me. I made sure that George saw us leaving together. Later I regretted doing that, as it appeared that the children were somehow on my side, which wasn't true. They had succeeded in staying neutral throughout the whole process. But at the time it felt good to me. It was a statement that I was doing fine, that no one needed to feel sorry for me. I certainly didn't feel sorry for myself. I felt relieved that it was over and I could move on. It was also a relief that I didn't need to be concerned about George anymore—he had someone else to provide his emotional life.

The divorce decree granted me my old name back, so after being Betty Jean Leas for 23 years, I became Betty Jean Porter again.

21 A New Life

My new life depended on being able to support myself, unlike all those years when I had a husband who earned a good living. I was grateful to have a job with a regular paycheck.

My job at Wescom was as Employment Interviewer in what in those days was called the Personnel Department. The company made circuit boards for some kind of electronic equipment, I never understood exactly what. The plant consisted of a two-story office wing and a huge room as big as a high school gymnasium, filled with long tables with a moving conveyor belt along the front edge. The 100 employees, all women, sat at these tables, elbow to elbow, and soldered tiny components onto the boards, one after the other, for eight hours, five days a week. Each person had a small box of components in front of her, and as each board came down the assembly line, she grabbed it, soldered on the pieces she had, and put it back on the line for the next person to repeat the process with different components.

Most of my job was hiring the people for that assembly job. Those jobs were filled almost entirely with uneducated, middle-aged, low-income women who had done this kind of work for most of their adult lives. They often rotated from plant to plant, wherever they heard a rumor that the pay was a little better.

Each woman filled out an application that was brought to me before her interview. I was instructed to look first at the boxes where height and weight were written. If she was obviously overweight, I was not to hire her. I was never told why, but I assumed it was because the company thought she would have too many health problems. This was illegal even in 1978, so I could not let them know the reason for rejection. I would just say, "Thank you, we'll get back to you" and then toss the application in the no-hire pile.

I soon discovered that I was not good at this part of the job. All my instincts were wrong. I had about 20 minutes to interview each applicant, so I didn't have time to really get to know anyone and had to decide very quickly whether to hire her or not. The problem was that the ones I liked were the ones who would not stay on the job. I took an instant liking to those who were lively, verbal, and interesting, and hired them. But those people quickly found that sitting at an assembly line all day soldering little things onto boards was not for them, so they would work a few days or a week or two and not come back. I had to discipline myself to reject the ones I connected with and hire the ones less attractive. Once I figured that out, the turnover rate dropped considerably.

My previous jobs had been with small nonprofits, and I didn't know how to behave in an office in a big corporation. I didn't know how to relate to a boss or to colleagues who weren't social workers of some kind. The fact that my personal situation was so hectic and unstable at the time, in the midst of a divorce and moving, didn't help. I struggled for several months until I got comfortable with the company culture.

This job presented me with my first and only experience of vicious office politics. My immediate boss was a woman named Chris, and we got along pretty well. She was strict and not especially friendly, but she was patient with me while I learned the job and helped me when I needed it. But suddenly, a new manager was brought in over her. He was odd, kind of sleazy, but it didn't matter much to me, as I didn't deal with him directly. But then he brought in a buddy from his previous company and created a job for him that was identical to Chris's job. This maneuvering was way above my pay grade, so I wasn't privy to how it happened, but somehow Chris was demoted in practice but not in appearance. Her duties were taken away from her and given to the new man, and she was left with an office, a phone, a job title, a secretary, and no work. We all reported to the new man instead of to her. It was humiliating for her.

It was obviously an attempt to make her resign, to get rid of her without having to fire her, since there was no legitimate reason to do so. For several months she sat in her office, sending out résumés, looking for another job.

Meanwhile, the new man became very demanding and autocratic. One day he announced that we had additional work coming in and the assembly line was expanding; consequently, we needed many new hires quickly. He ordered me to find twenty new workers, immediately.

"How can I do that?" I asked him.

"I don't care how, just do it," he replied. "I want them working next week."

We always ran a standing ad in the newspaper for workers, but that was handled by someone else, and even if I could get the ad changed somehow, it would not result in that many new applicants that quickly. I couldn't just go out on the highway and flag down people.

I went back to him and said, "What you're asking me to do is impossible."

He looked up from his desk and said, "Are you telling me you don't want to work here anymore?"

Without a second thought, I answered, "I guess so. You'll have my resignation in the morning."

So I quit, effective December 29, 1978. I had been there fourteen months. I didn't have another job, and this time I didn't have a husband supporting me. But I didn't care. The job had become intolerable under the new bosses.

I thought I would be considerate and give more than the usual two weeks' notice, since no one had expected me to leave so suddenly, and they would need to start the hiring process from scratch, so I gave a month's notice. Much to my amazement, within a few days the boss had promoted his secretary into my position. I was delighted, as Sigrid was a highly competent woman and would otherwise never have been able to move up out of the secretarial ranks into a professional one. She deserved it and would do well in it. However, I needed that month's pay, so I stayed the month and spent the next four weeks training Sigrid. The boss gave me a positive letter of recommendation.

I had a few dollars in the bank and was sure I could find another job soon, so I wasn't very concerned. I immediately applied for unemployment compensation, which would provide enough money to cover most of my basic expenses for six months—all but the payment for that gold TransAm. So I sold the car. I found a buyer quickly, who paid me almost as much as I had paid for it a year earlier. An 18-year-old kid bought it and I heard he totaled it within a few weeks. With the money from the sale of the car I bought an old Ford station wagon and had several thousand dollars left over.

Betty Jean, 1978, age 43.

Being unemployed gave me more time to spend with a man I had been dating. I had met him when I took the Firebird into the Pontiac dealership where he was the service manager. Ray was not a man I would ever expect to be attracted to. He was tall, rangy, with sandy hair that flopped in his face, and a droopy mustache. He was uneducated, uncultured, a smoker, and a heavy drinker. But his most redeeming trait was the sparkle in his eyes. He rode a motorcycle, and he was fun. The fact that he was strongly attracted to me was a bonus. After all my years with George's anger and rigidity, Ray's freewheeling lifestyle felt exciting and just a little dangerous.

Having been a teetotaler my entire life, I had no idea how to drink alcohol, and Ray was eager to teach me. I learned that I didn't like red wine, but loved kahlúa and cream. I also learned that I don't tolerate alcohol well—I get drunk very easily. Fortunately, Ray held his liquor well and looked after me when I had too much.

Even with my inexperience with alcohol, I knew better than to drive when I'd been drinking, but one time I was distracted and forgot. One afternoon before I left my job, our sleazy department head asked me go have a drink with him after work. I wasn't sure how to respond, being new to office politics. I didn't know what he would think if I said no; perhaps he would be angry and make trouble for me at work, or maybe he had something to discuss with me privately. Not being naïve, I knew he might be up to no good, but I could just leave if he did something inappropriate.

We went to a nearby restaurant, a nice one, and I ordered wine. We had a superficial conversation, and I still have no idea why he asked me there. But I made the mistake of having a second glass of wine, and when I left, I realized I was tipsy and should not be driving. But I had to get home, and there was no other way to get there. I drove as carefully as I could, staying just below the speed limit and holding steady in my lane, watching for any possible problems. It was interstate highway all the way, so I didn't have to deal with city traffic. When I got home safely I vowed never to be so foolish again.

Being unemployed also gave me time to explore painting. I had always wondered if I could possibly be a real artist. My painting hobby had been satisfying, but I never took it seriously. My friend Valerie was a professional artist who had been supporting herself with her art for years, and I asked her if I could study with her. I didn't want to take her classes; I wanted individual attention. She agreed to mentor me for a while, to see how I developed. I had done only abstract painting, but she wanted me to do something representational. After I had worked on one painting for awhile, she told me that I had talent, that I could be a successful artist if I spent twenty years or so working at it. I was sure that at forty-five I did not want to spend twenty years learning the craft, and gave up the idea of being an artist. But it was gratifying to hear that she thought I had talent.

I still have the painting I was working on, put away in a closet, and sometimes I take it out and look at it to remind myself of who I was then and what that time was like for me. The picture is of me, seen from behind, standing at a big open window. The window is like the one in my living room, with a green upholstered chair beside me. I have no clothes on, and I've placed my hands on the top of a low curtain rod, looking out the window, my clothes strewn on the chair. The picture is clearly unfinished, but the sense of newness, of anticipation, of wonder, is there. Both the picture and I are unfinished.

22 Moving to Peoria

Finding another job was not as easy as I expected. I sent out résumés, but got no results. Meanwhile, I continued to date Ray, and we had many fun times together. He earned good money and enjoyed spending it. The winter was severe, with lots of snow and ice, and I was just as glad I didn't have to go out to a job every morning.

But as spring was coming on, I began to get concerned. My savings were running low, unemployment comp was about to run out, and still no job appeared. In addition, one evening Ray told me that he had been offered a job managing the service department at the Pontiac dealership in Peoria, about 90 miles away.

"Are you going to take it?" I asked, worried.

"Well, it's a good job, and pays better, and …. I want to."

Seeing the frown on my face, he added,

"Why don't you come with me? You need a job, and there's nothing for you here. Peoria is a bigger city and it's thriving. You can live with me and find a job there."

It didn't take me long to agree. It seemed like a good solution. We had been spending so much time with each other that living together seemed like a reasonable next step. My son Gary had a good job and was living with his girlfriend, and Christie had moved out of the house in New Lenox and was working in Chicago. With no job, there really was nothing keeping me in Joliet.

Ray moved first, and found an apartment in Peoria. I drove there for weekends for a while and got a feel for the place. It was a good city; I could see myself living there. It didn't take long to pack my few belongings and move.

I immediately started looking for a job. Someone told me about an office downtown that helped people find work, and I went there to apply. As I was waiting to talk to someone, I strolled around the waiting room and read the bulletin board. The first thing I saw was a notice of an opening in that very office, for a vocational counselor. I fit the qualifications perfectly. When the interviewer called me into her office, I took the notice with me and asked her about it. She looked at my résumé and raised her eyebrows.

"This is most unusual. Let me get my supervisor."

I was soon being interviewed by her boss.

They needed someone right away. "How soon could you start?" he asked me.

"Tomorrow," I answered.

It wasn't that fast, but I did start the next Monday, June 11, 1979. I had been in town for three weeks.

I soon learned that I had stumbled into the office of the Comprehensive Employment and Training Act, or CETA. It was a federal program, administered by the U.S. Department of Labor, through the city of Peoria. The program offered training and temporary jobs for the disadvantaged, a bureaucratic term for very poor people. The usual applicants did not have master's degrees.

I was hired as a vocational counselor, interviewing applicants who had low prospects of being hired because of their lack of either work skills or education or both. We would pay for them to take classes at the local community college, or get them short-term jobs with agencies or companies who had signed up with us and received financial help with the person's wages.

It was a discouraging job. Some of the enrollees finished their training and found jobs, and a few of the people we placed in the temporary jobs were eventually kept on permanently, but they were the exceptions. Most of the people I placed dropped out or were fired, or just disappeared. The exceptions kept me going.

I had been doing that job for about a year when a staff position as a contract specialist opened. I grabbed it. I was burned out from all those interviews with desperate people.

Meanwhile, I had heard of an apartment that was opening up in town, and took it. It was the whole first floor of an old house on a quiet city street. Ray had a monthly lease on the other place, so moving quickly was not a problem. We moved together into the new place.

I had taken the new apartment in only my name because I had a feeling that the relationship with Ray was not going to last much longer. My attraction to him was wearing off, and our lifestyle didn't seem like so much fun anymore. With a rewarding, challenging job, I had less need of a social life of dinner out every night with more drinks than were good for me.

We had taken many long rides on Ray's motorcycle in the Illinois countryside, including some weekend trips, and I began to yearn for a bike of my own. Remembering the little step-through I had in Clinton, I started looking in the ads for used bikes.

I soon found a little yellow and black, 90-cc motorcycle that I could afford. It was big enough to take on the Interstate and small enough that I could pick it up if I dumped it.

First I had to take driving lessons so I could be licensed for it, and get a helmet. Once that was done, I was good to go. I loved it, but Ray found he was not as happy with me having my own bike as he thought he would be.

"It was more fun with you riding behind me on my bike," he complained. "I liked having your arms around me, holding on, and we could talk to each other. Now it's like we're not really together."

But it suited me fine. I went out for rides alone sometimes, exploring the area around town. Wearing a helmet bothered me, because I couldn't hear sounds of the birds or feel the wind in my face, and occasionally I ventured out without one. I knew it was dangerous, and didn't do it often.

Those psychic experiences that I used to have had not occurred for some time, but one day I was sitting at my desk at work when I suddenly had a mental picture of Christie driving a car past in front of me, stopping at a stop sign, and then starting up again. Just that, nothing else. But the car was a red Volkswagon, a Beetle, and I knew that Christie drove a gray car, a Chevy or a Buick. A few minutes later the phone rang, and it was Christie.

"Guess what!" she said. "I just bought a car! It's a cute Beetle!" However, it was orange, not red. My vision was a bit off.

I often went back to Joliet to visit friends. One weekend as I was packing to leave, Ray said, "Why don't you take my car?" He had just been given a new one as a perk of his job. He had had it only a few days, and I was surprised that he would lend it to me.

"Are you sure?" I asked.

"Sure," he replied, "I'd feel better with you driving it out of town than that old beater of yours."

So I did. It was a nice car, one of the more expensive models, with all the bells and whistles that were available in 1979. But as I was leaving Joliet Sunday evening to go home, a light on the dashboard came on, and I noticed that the brakes were not working well. I drove into a gas station and asked the attendant to tell me what was wrong. He was not a mechanic, but he knew enough to tell me that the hydraulic fluid in the brake system was leaking fast. Somehow the cap, or whatever kept the fluid where it belonged, was missing. I would very soon have no brakes at all.

It was Sunday night and no place was open that could fix it. I had to get home and go to work the next day, and decided to leave anyway. There was little traffic, I was only a few blocks from the Interstate, and I figured I could drive slowly and get there all right.

It was actually not difficult at all. I could gauge my speed so that I could slow down and drift to a stop at the one traffic light I encountered, and do the same for making turns. It was clear sailing all the way down the highway, and when I got to Peoria, my house was only a few blocks from the exit. I did the same slowing to a stop at the stop signs, and drifted to a stop in front of the house. I had driven 90 miles, an hour and a half trip, with no brakes.

Later, someone asked me why I didn't just use the hand brake. It hadn't occurred to me. I'm not sure whether that brake would work anyway without brake fluid, and it might have been disastrous if I had tried it and it failed.

Since my job was stable and paid well, I traded in the Ford on a new Pontiac; not a Firebird this time, but an Esprit, the next model down. Silver, this time. It's astonishing to remember now that I paid only $8,000 for it, and I ordered it with the accessories I wanted. I was making $23,000 a year, which was good money then. It is the only time in my single life when I have had substantial discretionary money to spend as I pleased after the bills were paid.

By fall, I realized that the relationship with Ray was over, and I asked him to move out. He was reluctant, even angry. He just didn't want to believe it, and kept trying to persuade me to change my mind. But I was firm, and he finally agreed. However, he simply rented the apartment above me in the same house!

Peoria city employee ID photo, 1978

Consequently, I still saw him frequently, and heard him coming and going up the outside staircase that was near my bedroom window. I saw him and heard him in the driveway, and his car was in the other bay in the garage. He told me how unhappy he was, that he loved me and wanted us to get back together. We stayed friends, but I resisted his offers to do things together. I wasn't angry with him, and appreciated our good times together, but I was not going to get drawn back into the relationship. In some ways it was nice, having him so nearby, and eager to be helpful and supportive.

At this time I had one of the strangest experiences of my life.

23 Harassment

I was hurrying out one morning to drive to work at the CETA office when I saw that my car was listing to the left. Oh no, I had a flat tire. I called the corner gas station, and they sent someone over right away to change it. On the way home, when I stopped to get the repaired tire, the mechanic said, "I couldn't find anything wrong with it. It must've been a slow leak."

That's odd, I thought. *It wasn't low yesterday.*

The next morning the same tire was flat again. Again I called the gas station, annoyed that the mechanic hadn't fixed it. When I went to pick up the repaired tire a second time, the mechanic said, "Ma'am, there's nothing wrong with this tire. I checked it out and put in a new core, but I don't know why it went flat." I paid the five dollars and went home, thinking dark thoughts about mechanics and tires.

The next day I had a class in the evening, and when I came out to go home, a different tire was flat! *I don't believe this*, I thought. *Are all my tires wearing out at the same time?*

I went back into the classroom and used the office phone to call Ray.

"I'm sorry, but I have another flat tire. Would you come change it for me? I'm at class." Ray still hadn't gotten over our breakup and jumped at the chance to help me with anything I needed. As I expected, he came right over and changed the tire.

"This is getting pretty annoying," I said to the mechanic the next day.

"Lady, there is nothing wrong with this tire either. Somebody is letting the air out of your tires."

That's absurd," I said to myself. *Who on earth would do that?*

194

That evening as Ray and I sat on the porch talking, we puzzled about it. Ray was worried. "It's obvious someone is doing this to you. You must have made somebody mad. Have you had a fight at work?"

I thought about it. As far as I knew, I was in everyone's good graces. I wasn't overwhelmingly popular, but I got along well enough with everyone. There was that secretary who sat at the front desk when the receptionist was out… She was a bit odd, but she was always pleasant to me. And my co-worker Tom seemed a little jealous sometimes when I got the boss' praise and he didn't, but he was such a gentle, sweet fellow, I couldn't imaging him sneaking around in the night letting air out of tires.

Ray finished a cigarette and went upstairs to his apartment. He was having a hard time. He had lost his job and had trouble finding another, finally going to work at a dealership in Bloomington, forty-five minutes away. He complained a lot about how unhappy he was, and asked me often if we could get back together.

I went to my apartment and got ready for bed. I heard Ray's car going out the driveway, as he went out for a late night cup of coffee, as he often did. I thought it a strange habit, but we all have our quirks.

No more tires went flat, and I forgot about it. A week later, Ray knocked on my door and asked if we could talk. Expecting the usual conversation about getting back together, I said, "Oh, Okay," and we went out onto the porch.

"I had a strange phone call at work today," he explained. "A woman called and asked me if I knew that you're having an affair with someone at work. She wouldn't say who she was or how she knew, but it sounded like she must be a co-worker of yours."

"Well, that's just silly. I guess people at the office don't know that you and I have broken up. Somebody thinks it would matter to you if I were having an affair."

Ray frowned. "Well… are you?"

"No, of course not. Not that it's any of your business. But no, there's no one at work who interests me in the slightest. Does the call bother you?"

"Well…. there's more. She said that it's with a black man."

"That's even sillier. The only black man in the office is Marcel, and he's the head of the department. He's my boss's boss, and I would never get involved with the boss, no matter what race he was."

It wasn't until later that it occurred to me how strange it was that someone in my office would not know that Ray and I had broken up, but would know where he was working in Bloomington. It was all very odd.

The next week when I left the evening class, I had another flat tire. This time I called another friend to come change it, and the next day I bought four pressurized air cans with nozzles for putting air in flat tires. I figured I would be prepared.

The next day Ray received another phone call, this time saying that I had gone into Marcel's office and closed the door, and added, "What do you suppose they're doing in there?"

"I can't imagine who this is. Doesn't she give you any clues? Keep her in conversation and maybe she'll drop a hint."

I began to look at everyone in the office with suspicion. Who would want to cause me trouble? Why call Ray? Is it an attempt to make me do something? To frighten me, or just to hassle me? But again, why?

The pressurized air cans rattled around in the back of the car, but no more tires went flat. And then the phone calls started. Late at night, the phone would ring, and when I answered, no one was there. When I hung up, it rang again. I hung up, and ten minutes later it rang again, and on this went until midnight. After a couple evenings of this, I just left the phone off the hook for the night after the first call.

Then late one night, I answered, and a deep male voice said, "Tonight." Nothing else, just "Tonight," and hung up.

Up until this point, I had not really been frightened. It seemed that the person intended just to annoy me, not hurt me, even after this call. I was afraid for a few minutes, but then the strong gut feeling that I was not in danger returned, and it seemed vitally important that I not give in to being afraid.

The next day in a conversation with a lawyer friend in Chicago, I jokingly mentioned the harassment. "Betty Jean, *call the police*," he said. "You're being foolish. This could get you hurt. If something really bad happens, you have to have it on record. Please, call the cops now."

Reluctantly, I called the Peoria police station from work. I felt silly, as no real crime had been committed, and it all seemed so incredible. A Lt. Walker came and interviewed me in my office. He looked more like an accountant than a cop. He took down the information with little comment and few questions. I wondered if he was taking it seriously.

"Who do you think is doing this?" he asked.

"I have no idea. If I did, I would do something about it."

"Well, the only thing we can do is put a tracer on your phone. You'll have to keep precise records of what time the calls come, and then let me know the next day. We'll check the record at the phone company and see where the calls come from."

It wasn't much, but it might be enough.

Ray was glad when I told him that the calls would be traced. "Good," he said, "that ought to take care of it. I'll feel better."

There was only one call that night, at 10:33. The voice said, "You'd better be ready." I wrote down the exact time, confident that I would soon know who was making the calls.

"Not much help," the lieutenant said the next day. "It came from a phone booth on the north side of town. Could have been anybody."

The calls continued, each time from a different phone booth. A man's voice would make cryptic, threatening remarks. Once he said, "That big boyfriend of yours can't help you. I'll get him, too."

After that call, I lay in bed, determined not to call Ray. I practiced meditating, calming myself, picturing myself safe and protected. And then I realized that there was something peculiar about the calls. When I answered, there would be a pause, then the voice would start, making a statement, and then the phone would click off. There was no attempt at conversation, and there was a strange background noise. Then it dawned on me—it sounded like a recording! It sounded like someone was dialing the phone, waiting for me to answer, starting a tape recorder, playing a sentence or two, and then hanging up. Someone was playing a prerecorded tape! Was that possible?

Saturday I went to Radio Shack and bought a little device that attached to my phone to record phone calls. I knew it was illegal to do this without telling the other person, but in this case that didn't seem relevant. I did feel slightly criminal as I held the button against the receiver when I answered the phone that night. But I got him! I got his voice on my tape recorder!

The next day I told the lieutenant triumphantly what I had accomplished, ready to play the tape for him.

He was shocked and angry. "You can't do that," he said gruffly. "It's against the law. I'm going to forget you said that."

I was deflated. I kept listening to the tape myself, trying to identify the voice. I couldn't.

I still had occasional flat tires at night. The garage was an old dilapidated building with no door, so it couldn't be secured. I left my back light on all night, and one night Ray and I actually sat up in my kitchen, watching out the back window, but saw nothing. The phone calls to Ray continued, elaborating on the affair I was supposed to be having.

Then one day when I returned from work, the back door to my apartment was standing open. I was sure I had closed it and locked it when I left that morning. I stepped into the kitchen, listened, and walked slowly around the apartment. No one was there. Nothing was out of order, nothing appeared to be missing.

As I stood puzzling, I heard Ray drive in. I called him in, and told him what I had found. He looked intensely worried. "I have to tell you about the call I got today," he said. "A man called this time, and said, 'Tell Betty Jean that I just wanted to show her that I can get in.' I had no idea what he meant. Obviously he managed to get into your locked apartment."

I immediately called the police. "We'll be right there," I was told. "Don't touch a thing."

Two policemen in uniform arrived within minutes. They began dusting for fingerprints, and asked who had keys to the apartment. "It's obviously not a break-in. There's no sign of forced entry. Do any of your friends have a key?" he asked, with a knowing look at Ray.

No, no one had a key. It had been hard to persuade Ray to give his back, and I couldn't be absolutely sure that he hadn't had a copy made—for sentimental reasons or in the forlorn hope that he would be moving back in— but I did get it eventually, and had never given one to anyone else.

I told the cop about the call to Ray that day, and about the threatening phone calls at night. He frowned, and then made a surprising offer.

"Sounds like someone is really out to get you. We can bring an alarm in here if you'd like. It'll be activated by any movement in the apartment. You set it when you go to bed and when you leave. It'll detect the presence of anything that moves, and will set off an alarm at the station. A patrol car will be here in two minutes."

Greatly relieved, I said, "You bet. I had no idea such a thing existed."

Within hours, my apartment was wired. Two sensing devices were mounted at angles so that most of the small apartment was covered. There was a button on a long wire that I was to keep beside the bed, so that I could turn the alarm on when I went to bed and turn it off when I got up. "Remember," the officer said, "to turn it off when you get up during the night—or you'll set if off. And we don't like that—we scramble like hell when one of these things goes off, because it means someone's in real danger."

They put a control box on the counter by the back door, with instructions to push the button just as I was stepping out the door. I had ten seconds to get out before my own movement would set it off.

I felt secure for the first time in weeks. Remembering to turn the alarm off when I stumbled out of bed in the middle of the night took some getting used to, but I reminded myself it was worth it, and I was soon handling it automatically. The slim box with the little red light mounted at the top of the hallway wall became a friend, a presence almost human. I often glanced in its direction, smiled, and resisted the urge to talk to it.

My curiosity whether it really worked was satisfied one night when a friend and I decided to go to a movie. Becky, a large woman fortunately with a good sense of humor, met me at my apartment, and we left together to use my car. I was careful to push the button as usual as we went out the door, and we walked the 30 feet or so the garage. As I opened my car door, I turned to see two uniformed policemen advancing toward us around the corners of the house, guns drawn, intense concentration furrowing their faces.

Realizing instantly what had happened, Becky and I watched in fascination as more officers surrounded the house, and police vehicles began screeching into the driveway. In all, seven cars and vans with a dozen cops converged on my house within seconds. They saw quickly that it was a false alarm, and relaxed.

Smiling sheepishly, I apologized. "I don't understand it. I did exactly what I'm supposed to do," I explained.

"Did both of you go out the door after you set the alarm?" asked one of the officers, looking quickly back and forth between Becky and me.

"Yeah, sure," I replied, puzzled.

"That's probably what did it," he explained. "The combined weight and mass of both of you is more than it's set for. Next time, let your visitor leave before you push the button."

The cops were surprisingly good natured. I was embarrassed. Becky was excited. "This may never happen to me again," she said, grinning.

Two weeks had passed, with no threats and no intruders, when Lt. Walker called me. "Looks like they've quit. We have to take the alarm system out. We only have two of them, and we need that one somewhere else. Sorry."

I felt abandoned as the alarm was removed. However, the flat tires stopped and the calls, both to me and to Ray, had become fewer and fewer. They had not stopped altogether, but whoever was doing it seemed to be losing interest.

I had begun to sleep better.

Then late one night I woke up suddenly with the feeling that something was wrong. It took only few seconds to realize that I had been awakened by the sound of something large and solid hitting the side of the house, on the outside wall of my bedroom. I jumped out of bed, my breath coming in gasps, my mind racing to figure out what was happening. I looked out the window next to the bed, but could see nothing in the darkness. The clock by the bed said 3:30. Frantically, I called Ray.

He answered immediately. "Call the cops. I'll be right down."

It took him only seconds to pull on his pants and hurry down the outside stairwell. I let him in through the living room, and he wrapped his arms around me to comfort me. I was terrified and shaking.

When the police officer arrived, we went out with him to see what we could find. A hefty chunk of concrete was lying in the driveway, and there was a dent in the aluminum siding underneath the bedroom window. The street was empty.

"Good God, what next?" I asked. "It keeps escalating! What else can they do?"

After the officer left, Ray said, "Honey, would you like me to move back in? Just until this blows over? I really worry about you."

I was tempted, but said, "No, I'll be okay. It's enough that you're nearby. It means a lot to me that I can call on you. I still don't really think I'm going to be hurt."

Shaking his head, Ray went back upstairs.

The next day, I called Lt. Walker. "Isn't there anything else you can do? Do I have to be killed before you can do anything to stop this?"

"What would you have us do?" he asked. "It would help a lot if you could give us some idea of who it might be. There must be someone you can think of. No one does something like this out of the blue, for no reason at all."

I couldn't think of anyone.

It was a week before it happened again. This time when a brick hit the wall at 4 a.m., I knew what it was. I called the police again. When Ray heard the siren and saw the police lights outside, he came downstairs.

Together we watched the cop pick up a brick that lay next to the house. It was used brick, and could have come from anywhere. It was too rough to hold fingerprints. There was another dent in the siding, closer to the window this time. And of course there was no one on the deserted street.

The officer left, and we went to our respective beds.

I had planned to attend a conference in Chicago the next week, and was looking forward to getting away for a while. It would be a relief to get away from the stress and worry.

Late the night before I was to leave, I awoke to the sound of a brick crashing through my bedroom window. I screamed. It was all I could do the dial the police and control my voice enough to give them my address.

I waited, shivering, for them to arrive. I couldn't tell if the shaking was more out of fear or rage.

"How dare they do this to me?" I demanded, finally furious. I yelled at the police when they came, and I yelled at Ray when he came dashing downstairs. I came as close to losing control as I ever have in my life. I was livid.

There was nothing the police could do, as usual. They took the necessary information, and Ray tried to persuade me to stay with him the rest of the night.

"I think I'm safe here now. Surely they won't come back again tonight."

The next morning I left for Chicago, and was gone for a week.

I was never harassed again.

Months later, I was stopped for making an illegal left turn, by the same cop who had installed the alarm in my apartment. We recognized each other, and as we chatted about why I should or should not get a ticket, the young officer suddenly said, "Did your old man ever stop bothering you?"

I froze.

"What do you mean?"

"Oh, you know, the big guy who lived upstairs. It was him doing it, you know."

"Oh? What makes you think that?"

"Oh, I'm sure. A couple of us guys went to see him after that time the brick came through your window. We told him that if anything more happened, we were going to arrest him. It stopped, didn't it?"

24 A New Name

When the relationship with Ray ended, I looked around and realized I had no life. I had been so involved with him that I had not established any connections with other people.

How did I let that happen? I asked myself.

I remembered that all those years when we as a family had moved from state to state, we immediately found a church to create an instant community for ourselves, so I looked in Peoria for a church that would suit me. I soon found the Universalist Unitarians and became an active member. That church became the center of my life for the rest of my time in Peoria.

I also found a theater group. Peoria's Cornstock Theater staged excellent plays. In the summer, they performed theater in the round in a huge tent. The group welcomed newcomers and I soon felt at home with them. Over several years, I was involved in many productions, but the one that stays in my mind the most is *On Golden Pond*. I played the part of Chelsea, the daughter. The main characters were the elderly parents, and my part was relatively minor. It was the most difficult and the least satisfying part I ever played on stage, because Chelsea was so bland. She was mostly a foil for the two leads and was not an interesting character. It was pretty much a walk-through part. To get the part, I had to promise the director that I would not ride my motorcycle until after the last performance. I agreed reluctantly, as it meant most of the summer with no riding.

In the course of my activities at the UU church, I met two women who became an important part of my life. Barbara was from Tyler, Texas, and had a charming southern way about her. She was a social worker, divorced, with part custody of a young daughter. She was thirty-eight years old. Kate was twenty-eight, never married, and had a sales position with a big company whose headquarters was out of town. She traveled a lot.

I don't know why we hit it off so well, what it was that brought us together, especially considering our age differences—late forties, thirties, and twenties—but something did. At some point, I started talking about not wanting to live alone any more.

One day during coffee hour at church, I was whining about not liking living alone.

"I'm not lonely, exactly," I explained, "and I need my solitude, but it would be nice also to have people around sometimes. "

"I know what you mean," Barbara replied. "But having a roommate would be too much togetherness. Too much like being married!"

Kate chimed in. "I'd like to share the rent with someone. Maybe several someones!"

"Yes," I said. "How about a group house, where we each had our own rooms but could be together when we wanted to in the common area?"

Gradually the idea took hold, and the three of us decided to rent a house together. It seemed so right, we didn't have to do much planning. It all came together almost effortlessly. We were all living alone, except for Barbara having her daughter part of the time, and could get out of our current places easily.

Another woman in the congregation, Ruth, had just gone through an ugly divorce and was moving out of town. She got the house in the divorce, a big brick house in a good part of town. She offered to rent it to us and we jumped at the chance.

The first time we went to look at the house, I actually shuddered when we walked in. I could feel strong negative energy, an oppressiveness. The house had witnessed bitter fights and still harbored dark, angry feelings. I remembered that Carol, the woman who had started the healing prayer meetings in Clinton, had taught me a method to clear energy from a room. Clearing the energy in that house seemed like a good idea.

I found a time to visit the house alone and spent an hour going from room to room, basement to attic, chanting, dispelling the heavy, negative energy and replacing it with healing energy and light. I was pleased that the next time we all went to the house, Kate said, "Hmm. This place feels different." It did.

Gary visiting with Betty Jean in her first group home in Peoria, 1982.

The house had three bedrooms, a sunroom, and a finished basement. Being the oldest and having the highest income, I was allotted the master bedroom and bath and paid the most rent. Kate was unhappy in her job and soon quit, and took the smallest room and paid the least. Barbara's room was big enough for her to share with her daughter when she came to stay.

The sunroom was soon occupied by a young man I met at the theater. He was then working as a baker and needed a place to stay temporarily. We all liked him and liked having a man in the house. He was also an incredibly talented actor.

People often warned us we would have problems, and that we should have house meetings to establish house rules and enforce them, and while it seemed like a reasonable idea, we never got around to it. We had no rules, except be nice to each other and be responsible, and over several years, we never had a house meeting. We just didn't need any. We were so compatible we never had any conflicts that we couldn't resolve with talking to each other.

With all three of us extroverts so active in the UU church, it was not surprising that the house became a social hub. We started an event we called "salon," and invited everyone we knew to come for discussion and socializing. We soon had twenty to twenty-five people showing up every Tuesday night, gathering in the large living room and engaging in discussion on what we designated as "noble" topics. No politics, no football, and no arguments. It was dialogue, exploring each other's experiences and feelings. It was mostly UUs who attended, although people brought their other friends. We had only very loose guidelines, such as "speak from your own experience, no lecturing, no arguing, and be respectful of each other." We had no topic determined ahead of time. Instead, we would begin by asking if anyone had a subject they would like us to talk about. Several people would suggest something that was on their mind, and then the group would just move into talking about the one that appealed to them the most. We often had differences of opinion, but everyone respected other people's points of view. Anyone who attended and didn't fit into the culture felt uncomfortable and didn't come back.

About eight months after we moved in, Ruth sold the house. It was on the market when we rented it, so we weren't surprised, and set about finding another place. The new house was even bigger and better. It had three stories, with six bedrooms, a huge study/office on the first floor along with a large living room, kitchen, and dining room. It was only a few blocks from Bradley University, which meant there were sorority and

Betty Jean's 48th birthday party, Peoria, 1981.

Salon group at Parkside house , Peoria, 1982.

fraternity houses in the neighborhood. This worked to our advantage, as the neighbors were less likely to notice our multiple tenants or complain about them.

More people moved into the house, and salon continued as before. One of our salon attenders, a dentist, told us that he had been referred a patient who was a 19-year-old refugee from Poland, being sponsored in Peoria by Catholic Charities. This was 1982, before the Iron Curtain came down. Our friend said that this new patient needed a place to live and asked if we could take her. We said, yes, of course, and so Alina moved into one of the third-floor rooms. Alina spoke almost no English. The first of the month after she moved in, she came down to the dining room where the rest of us were eating, and waving her rent check in the air, asked,

"Who boss of house?"

We were perplexed by her question, and just stared at her. She looked around the table, and spying me, said, "You! *You* boss of house!" and handed me her check. I was dumbfounded.

Bob, a friend of Barbara's, moved into the other third-floor room, and Dennis, a friend of the house, moved into the fourth room on the second floor. Various people came and stayed with different house residents, and it was hard to keep track of who was where. Kate, Barbara, and I, were the constants.

We also had many wonderful parties. We partied for any occasion, or no occasion at all. With so many people coming to salon, someone was always having a birthday. The word would go out that we were having a party, and twenty-five to thirty people would show up. We would set out a few drinks and guests brought food. These were not rowdy parties, and no one got drunk or high. Some people may have smoked a joint or two on the porch, but if so, they were very discreet about it. But the parties went on late, and sometimes the three of us hosts just went to bed, telling the stragglers to turn off the lights and lock the door when they left.

One morning after a party, I came downstairs to the living room and noticed a young man asleep on the couch. He didn't look familiar, but I assumed he had been there the night before and just crashed rather than going home. As the morning went on, other people came downstairs and also saw him but said nothing. Later, as I was passing through the room I saw him get up, stretch, put on his shoes, and walk out the front door. We never knew who he was; everyone had assumed he was someone else's friend. He probably had been drinking at a fraternity party down the street and wandered into our house thinking he was someplace else. We joked about how lucky he was that he flopped in a house where the people were so casual about it. Some people would have called the police, at least. I like to think of the energy of the house reaching out to that young man, saying, "Come on in, you'll be safe here."

Another fun party was for my fortieth birthday. There was nothing special about that particular birthday, but it was another excuse for a party. We asked people to write something about me to share at the party. People were surprisingly creative, writing poems and songs. I was moved by the tributes, realizing that these people appreciated me and really cared about me. I have pictures taken at that party and look at them once in a while with nostalgia.

After two years, the salon came to an end in an unfortunate way. A woman began attending who was mentally disturbed, although we did not realize it for some time. That alone would not necessarily have been a problem, but she began giving detailed, graphic descriptions of her sexual experiences. The first time was not too disturbing, and we ignored it and went on. But she continued at every salon, and people began staying away as a result. The three of us hosts discussed what to do, and we were all reluctant to say anything to her or to ask her to leave, because we were committed to being inclusive of everyone. Consequently, the group wasted away. Perhaps it was time for it to end anyway, but I have always regretted that we didn't do something about it. She needed help, and just listening to her while the group disintegrated was not a good solution. In hindsight, I think we should have taken her aside and asked her to get help and not return to salon until she could contribute appropriately. I learned from this experience that it is sometimes necessary to exclude people for the good of a group.

An important part of the glue that held the house together was Kate's personality. She simply loved people, and welcomed everyone she met with open arms, often literally. She was Irish through and through, with black hair in soft curls around her shoulders, blue eyes, and a hearty laugh, and always battled extra pounds. She carried her weight well, with a large portion of it above her waist, and enjoyed the attention her chest received. She was charismatic as well as attractive. She was also extremely intelligent, with a quick wit. From her I learned a lot about generosity and acceptance of everyone, no matter what they were like.

Kate was voted the president of the board of directors of the church, which was unusual considering how young she was. She instituted the practice of using consensus at church meetings, such as at the annual meeting. She was able to keep a group of about a hundred contentious people in order and reach difficult decisions with a minimum of bad feelings. It was fascinating watching her in action. With her the president of the board, and so many congregants involved in salon, no one was surprised when the minister went on vacation and notified everyone that our house was the interim church office. The church secretary made a mistake in the church bulletin and referred to the house "saloon."

The salon had created a large community of loving, accepting people, who listened to each other and helped each other. It also provided an ideal environment for meeting people and developing a relationship, resulting in half a dozen weddings. Some lasted, some didn't. I enjoyed a romance of my own for about a year, until we both figured out it just wasn't working. Jack was twenty years younger than I. It was great fun while it lasted. After the breakup with Ray, I dated several younger men, none as young as Jack, however.

For me, the most memorable party was for my fiftieth birthday. Memorable not only because it was a great party, but because it was the occasion when I changed my name. I decided to do the second half century my way. I never liked the name Betty Jean; it was more fitting for that nice southern girl in my mother's fantasy. I chose "Maya" from a woman I had known years before who had taken it for a similar reason. I liked the name, and she was long gone from my life and surely wouldn't have minded that I appropriated it even if she had known.

I had discovered I had a talent for creating and leading ceremonies. The UU church was open to anything I wanted to do, so I wrote and led winter solstice observances, water ceremonies, and a New Year's Eve ceremony. The one for the new year was so popular I continued to conduct it for the rest of my years in Peoria and again in other places I lived later. People would gather at my house for the ceremony and then go on to their parties afterward. Some people who attended the ceremony took it with them when they moved to other areas.

So it followed that I would write a christening ceremony for the occasion of my fiftieth birthday. I wore a long, off-white dress that I found at a vintage store, and Kate wove some bright flowers into a crown that she placed on my head. We couldn't put fifty candles on a real cake, so someone covered a big flat box in pretty paper and stuck the candles in holes in it.

Maya' 50th birthday and name changing party at group house on Rebecca Place, Peoria 1983.

First we had a couple of readings, and I made a statement about changing my life. I made a statement about forgiveness, and we read a litany together. I'm reproducing the ceremony here. Unfortunately, I no longer have the poems or readings.

****

<u>Gathering music</u>
<u>Poem</u>: Linda
<u>Introduction</u>: Betty Jean

Next Wednesday I will be fifty years old. I have asked you to be here to help me observe the occasion because it is from my friends that I receive the affirmation, inspiration, courage, and comfort that I need as I look at what this birthday means.

Being fifty means having a history, a foundation; having roots, but also having enough time and energy left for a future, a future of being free to do whatever it is I want to accomplish. I like the line in one of Carolyn McDade's songs: "Roots that hold me close, Wings that set me free."

I look at this as a beginning—the beginning of my second half-century. And I identify with something Carolyn said when she was here: "I become more radical with every breath I breathe." I feel myself becoming more radical, more daring, more willing to take risks.

However, I think that I can't move forward into a new phase without getting rid of some of the baggage that I have accumulated over all those years. To do that, I feel the need to be forgiven. Forgiveness is a releasing mechanism, a freeing thing—and something we rarely do for each other, or even ask for. I'm asking you to do that for me, here, tonight. You can forgive me, if you will, symbolically, for everyone I have ever hurt or wronged.

Barbara will now lead us in a statement of forgiveness.

Barbara :
For being cold and distant when you needed me to be warm and close;
For being impatient when you needed me to listen;
For finding fault when you needed acceptance ;

Betty Jean: *I ask your forgiveness.*
Barbara:
> For being stubborn when you needed me to understand;
> For being so mired in my own stuff that I did not see your struggle;
> For protecting myself when you needed me to trust;

Betty Jean: *I ask your forgiveness.*

Barbara:
For sometimes being closed,
> Group: *You are forgiven.*
For sometimes failing,
> Group: *You are forgiven.*
For sometimes being less than a loving friend,
> Group: *You are forgiven.*

Press photo from TV interview for Peace Network, Peoria, 1983.

<u>Christening with the new name</u>: Kate
<u>Poem</u>: Christie
<u>Blessing</u>: Maya

As I go forth into the next fifty years, I would like to take your blessings with me. As the last part of this ceremony, I would like each of you, who feels so moved, to come up here, light a candle, and give me a blessing. It may be simply a statement, "I bless you," if you don't feel creative. I thought this would be a symbolic way of making a statement individually, but would also have a cumulative effect, after all the candles are burning.

<u>Everyone Sing Jubilate Deo</u>

✱✱✱✱✱✱✱✱✱✱✱✱✱✱✱

Changing one's first name is awkward. People are accustomed to women changing their last names, but not their first. Before I decided to do it, I asked my children if it was okay with them. They both, independently, responded with, "Can I still call you Mom?"

I said, "Of course."

They each shrugged and said, "Well, I don't care what your name is."

Most of my friends made the change with minimal fuss, but my boss simply refused. I don't know whether he couldn't remember or didn't like the idea. I just stopped responding when he called me by my old name, and eventually he adjusted grudgingly. The only person I didn't expect to make the change was my father, and he didn't.

I was also surprised at how much paper work was required. The IRS, the post office, Social Security, my bank, driver's license, car registration, doctor's office…. the list went on and on. But it was worth it.

I felt different. I felt more adult, more grown up. "Betty Jean" was gone, and "Maya" had taken her place.

Gary, Mary, and baby Matt, 1983.

25 Peace Work

I had no idea how much more than my name was changing.

In May of 1983, a friend invited me to go with her to a conference in Washington, DC, about the threat of nuclear weapons. I had not thought much about the subject, although I knew that testing of nuclear bombs was going on in the western part of our country.

That conference changed my life. My first grandchild was due to be born to my son Gary and his wife in late May, and of course I was thrilled to become a grandmother. However, at the conference I thought about what the use of nuclear weapons would mean, and it occurred to me, *What kind of a world will my grandchild grow up in?* Horrified, I went home inspired to do something about it.

Ronald Reagan had become president in 1981, and his administration proceeded to cut the federal social services budget drastically. One of the casualties was the CETA program. To cut expenses, over the next two years the guidelines for acceptable participants were tightened so that only the most likely to succeed could be helped. Consequently, those most in need were denied. Many of us in the CETA offices were upset by this change, because the real reason for the program was being eliminated.

The combination of the peace conference, my grandchild's birth, and the cut in services at CETA convinced me that I needed to leave my job and work full time to prevent nuclear war. Because of the cuts in the budget, someone had to be laid off in my department. The person in line to be laid off was Connie, a young single mother. It occurred to me that I could be laid off and she could take my job.

I went to Merril, my boss, and said, "How about you lay me off and give my job to Connie? She needs it more than I do. She already does some of my job, and I can train her on the rest in a couple of weeks."

He replied, "It's okay with me if it's okay with you."

He agreed to give me a voluntary layoff, which meant I could draw unemployment compensation. Connie, of course, was thrilled. Not only did she not lose her job, she was promoted into a higher position with better pay. I was able to quit my job and draw six months of unemployment while I figured out how to work for peace. I loved it that the Labor Department would pay me to counteract the Defense Department.

With four or five people paying the rent and utilities, living in the house was already cheap, allowing me to build up some savings. To cut expenses even further, I moved into the smallest bedroom (Dennis had moved out), which was barely big enough to hold my bed, my desk, and a chest of drawers. That was all the room I needed. My car was paid for, and unemployment comp with my savings would be enough to cover me for some time. As it turned out, I got a six-month extension on unemployment. I would not have been able to leave my job if I had not lived in a group house. Not only could I afford it, but my housemates approved completely of my decision and supported me in every way. I needed that support, especially emotionally, as it was a big leap of faith.

My last day of work at CETA was June 3, 1983. I decided I would volunteer in the peace movement for a year and then I would have to find a job.

At first I had no idea how I would go about working for peace. My UU church had a peace committee, and that seemed a good place to start. I soon discovered that other churches in town had similar committees, and began attending some of their meetings.

I visited about eight other church peace committees, and found that we were all concerned about nuclear war, but the different groups did not know that the others existed. Consequently, we each felt like we were the only people working on the issue. It occurred to me that it would be good for us to be connected, to share our efforts and resources. I invited the other groups to create a network, called the Peoria Peace Network. We met monthly, and I put out a newsletter.

I learned a surprising and counterintuitive lesson from this experience. I thought that gathering six or eight people from eight or so groups together would result in forty or fifty people attending the network meetings. Not so. We had about ten or fifteen people at our meetings. I found that people would attend the meeting in their own church because it was theirs and in their familiar space, but would not go to a larger meeting in a different place where they didn't know everyone. There is a sense of ownership in a smaller meeting that disappears in the larger group.

Undaunted, we invited various peace-related groups besides churches to join us, and after a few months the network consisted of thirteen different groups and had a mailing list of about 500 names. The group sponsored events and sent out press releases, and even though we had fewer people than I expected, we were a presence on the local level.

I learned something about how the news media works. Peoria was part of a larger media market that included Chicago and St. Louis, but the city wasn't big enough to have a constant stream of news to report. Consequently, they were always looking for news to fill the air time, and it wasn't hard to get coverage. I learned to cultivate the news reporters and to make sure to give all of them the information they needed in time to cover our events. On one occasion when we were planning an event, in response to our press release the local TV news asked to interview me. The TV crew came to our house, set up their lights and cameras in the living room, and a reporter asked me questions. I had never been on camera before and was nervous, but I was told it didn't show. The brief segment was shown on the five o'clock news and got us wide recognition. The Network was referred to in newspaper articles also, with headlines such as "*Peace network may seek vote on freeze issue.*"

This publicity brought us to the attention of the Illinois Nuclear Weapons Freeze Campaign, headquartered in Chicago, that was part of a national group promoting the end of nuclear bomb testing and development. The organization wanted more presence in "downstate" (which they called all of the state outside of Chicago), and one day Bernice Bild, the executive director of the Illinois Freeze, called me. "We want to hold the next annual conference in Peoria. Could your network host it?"

"Sure," I replied, confident that the rest of the network members would agree. Fortunately, they did, and we set about arranging for more than a hundred people to come to town for a weekend meeting.

The headquarters staff took care of all of the programming, but it was up to us to take care of the logistics. This meant primarily me, as most of the members of the Network were busy with regular jobs. I arranged to use the local high school, persuaded several motels to give us a block of rooms at a reduced rate, hired a caterer to provide meals, sent out publicity, set up some home hospitality, sent out maps and directions (this was long before the Internet or cell phones), determined what room each session would meet in, and arranged for audiovisual equipment. It was a huge task and I loved it.

The conference went very well, and as a result, I developed a good relationship with the Freeze Campaign headquarters staff in Chicago.

I also developed a close friendship with one of the Chicago Freeze board members. Ted was an interesting man, short and chubby, and highly intelligent. We didn't see each other much, with him living in Chicago, and communicated mostly by phone and letters. His sales job kept him on the road throughout the state most of the time, and when he was in central Illinois, we would get together. Our shared commitment to preventing nuclear war was the main glue that held our friendship together. We collaborated on the organization's efforts, and he supported my work in Peoria.

Meanwhile, life in the house changed. Bob, a salon attender, had moved into one of the third-floor rooms, and when he and Barbara developed a romantic relationship they moved out into an apartment of their own. We needed to replace at least one of them, and about that time a couple who had been coming to the salon divorced. We agreed to let Norman, the husband, move in with us. Big mistake. Norm was a former Marine sergeant, who presented himself as a feminist, but really wasn't. His wife's high-paying job had supported them, and Norm didn't work. He intended to live with us on a small income from an inheritance in a farm in Wisconsin.

On the surface, Norm was an agreeable guy, a big teddy-bear type, but we soon learned that he was lazy and highly passive aggressive. He spent his days sitting at the dining room table, reading the paper and working crossword puzzles. When approached about anything objectionable in his behavior, he would get angry and sulk. We soon regretted letting him move in, but didn't have the heart to ask him to move out, and didn't have anyone in mind to move in and share the rent in his place. As the culture of the house changed drastically, we realized how much the previous years of harmony had been the result of a combination of unusually compatible people.

That spring the Illinois Freeze decided it was time to hire a downstate organizer, and I applied for the position. Only one other person applied for the job. Since I had worked with the Chicago staff closely and they knew I did good work, they hired me over the other person. I found out later how much that choice would affect me.

I started work as the Downstate Organizer for the Illinois Freeze Campaign in early June of 1984, exactly one year after leaving CETA. The pay was much less than I had earned before, but it was enough to get by, and I was excited about the work. I would be paid to do the work I had been doing for nothing.

The job meant I had to move to Springfield, about an hour and a half south of Peoria. Before I left, the UU church held a going-away party for me. I have had many of these in my life of frequent moves, and it always makes me think of being present for my own funeral and listening to eulogies. It was very life-affirming to hear how much I was appreciated. The gifts were nice, too.

I didn't have to look for a place to live right away, because Tom, a young single man who was the pastor of the local Brethren church, was leaving for South America on a mission project for the summer, and offered me his apartment while he was gone. He had a cozy attic apartment with two windows that let in a breeze. His big plants added a kind of jungle atmosphere. I was grateful to have a place to crash while I got settled into the city.

The house in Springfield, Illinois. Maya's apartment was the whole second floor.

My job entailed traveling the state of Illinois to organize chapters of the Illinois Freeze Campaign. Originally the idea was that I would cover all of downstate from Chicago to Carbondale, which is southeast of St. Louis, but after one trip to Carbondale, it became obvious that I could not cover that much territory. I soon concentrated on a swath across the middle of the state, from Danville on the eastern border to Quincy on the west. It was still a huge territory, and meant that I spent most of my time on the road. I never actually unpacked my suitcase, just took my clothes out, washed them, and put them back. I enjoyed it.

I drove to Chicago once a month for staff meetings and stayed overnight in Joliet with friends. One day as I was walking down State Street to the office, wearing a dark business suit and swinging my leather briefcase, I remembered that years earlier I had pictured myself doing exactly that. I had finished my degree, moved out on my own, and had a professional job, going to a staff meeting in a big city. I had arrived!

However, I soon discovered what winning the job over the other applicant meant for me. The other applicant was an active member of the peace group in Springfield, and some of them felt strongly that he should have been hired instead of me. Those people resented me, and I was constantly dealing with an undercurrent of hostility. They already had resented the main office treating them like stepchildren, and hiring me over their own person added insult to injury. Fortunately, there were others in the group who supported me and were convinced, as the home office was, that John would not have done the job as well. But it made my work difficult. I worked around it as best I could.

I took my motorcycle with me to Springfield, and rode it out in the countryside when I had time. In the summer I sometimes rode my bike to the Y to swim after work. It was simpler to wear my swimsuit under my shirt and shorts and then just take off the wet suit and wear those clothes home for the short drive, with nothing under them. One day I was riding home when I suddenly realized that I was feeling an unusual breeze on my chest. I looked down and saw that the wind had come up under my shirt and had blown it up above my armpits. I was putting on quite a show. Fortunately, it was a one-way street, so no traffic was coming toward me. If there had been, I probably would have been aware of the situation sooner!

Three religious groups supported me in my work: the Church of the Brethren in Springfield, the Quakers in Urbana-Champaign, and the

Catholics in Danville. The Brethren donated space in their church for my office, and the church members were friendly and helpful. In Urbana-Champaign, a Quaker family let me stay in their guest room when I came to town, giving me a key to their house so I could stay there anytime.

The situation in Danville was unusual. My main support there was the Catholic priest, Father Bob. I stayed in the rectory where he lived. The house had been set up for two priests, so there were two separate wings off the main living area. He designated one wing as mine, and I could stay there whenever and as long as I wanted. I actually had a lovely accidental vacation there. One winter day when I had driven to Danville for a meeting, a fierce snowstorm came up and I was snowed in. I relaxed happily for four days. We watched movies, ate frozen dinners, and had long talks. He walked to the church to take care of business during the day, so I had the place to myself. It was lovely.

In one of our conversations, the subject of our different religions came up. I mentioned that I was not really a Christian, and Bob replied emphatically, "You're more of a Christian than many of my parishioners!" I didn't know how to explain that I meant I didn't believe in the traditional view of Jesus, so just let it go. I didn't need him to understand. His support of my work was enough.

One day a visiting nun joined us for lunch. When I explained what I was doing, she remarked, incredulous, "But you're doing it alone? We would *never* send anyone out on a mission alone! We always send two people together. They need each other's support."

She was right, I should not have been doing this job alone. It would have been so much easier with a companion in my travels, but I didn't have that luxury.

On Friday nights Bob had a longstanding tradition of meeting the priest from the neighboring town for dinner, and he declared that he wasn't going to miss it and I was going with him. I protested, but he insisted. The streets were still icy, but he was confident we could make it, so off we went. Naturally, the two priests talked through the entire dinner about parish business, which was all a foreign language to me. They both drank like the Irishmen they were, and as the evening went on I became more and more anxious about getting home safely. The streets were risky enough for sober drivers. But Bob got us home okay, very late, and I had one more laid-back day before the Interstate was clear enough for me to drive home.

On another trip to Danville I hit a deer. It was late on a winter night on the Interstate in the middle of nowhere. I saw the deer just as it ran into my headlights, and there was no way I could avoid hitting it. There was nothing I could do but drive on. I considered whether I should stop, but I couldn't have done anything for the deer if it was alive, and it wasn't safe for me to stop. I hope the deer either recovered or died quickly. It did $2,000 worth of damage to my car. Fortunately, my insurance covered it.

After a few months, the job became discouraging. I was supposed to visit different cities and persuade them to establish Freeze chapters, but it was a hard sell. They appreciated my visits, as it made them feel supported and they wanted the information and materials I brought, but there was no advantage in becoming a chapter. They would have to pay dues and would receive nothing in return. The advantage was all for the organization, not for the chapters, and I couldn't argue with that. I didn't establish one single chapter, but I did help the various groups get better organized and do more peace activities in their areas. They clearly wanted my visits, and the home office realized that what I was doing was valuable, even though not what they expected.

I was especially pleased with one activity in particular. To make a statement on the anniversary of the atomic bombings of Hiroshima and Nagasaki, we staged a covert action on the streets of two downstate Illinois cities. We wanted to emphasize the effect of the bombs on the people by painting outlines of people lying on the sidewalks as if they had been incinerated by the bombs. To do this, we made up buckets of a substance that looked like paint, but would wash away in the rain. It was something like whitewash, created by one of the artists in the group. We took turns lying on the floor while others drew life-sized stencils of our bodies lying in various poses, both adults and children.

Late on the night of August 6, at about three o'clock in the morning, several groups of us fanned out over the city with our buckets and brushes and stencils. As one person stood watch on the corner for the police, the others put down the stencils and painted around them with the whitewash. I was one of the lookouts, standing on a street corner that during the day had heavy traffic. I watched for any approaching cars, ready to tell my conspirators to run. Being out on the street in the middle of the night, acting like a criminal, was exciting. It really wasn't vandalism, as the "paint" would wash off. It was no worse than children drawing on the sidewalk with chalk, but it felt decidedly illegal—and fun. I never did anything like that when I was a teenager.

The next morning, as people walked the sidewalks to work, they stared at those outlines of people scattered around, some draped over benches

The shadow project commemorating Hiroshima/Nagasaki, in Springfield, 1983.

at the bus stops. It was eerie. Photos appeared in the next day's newspapers, with captions wondering where the ghostly figures came from. We congratulated ourselves privately, but never took public credit for them. That event is one of the most satisfying things I've ever done.

Maya at Freeze Voter organizing meeting with labor union official, Springfield, 1984.

As the summer was ending, Tom, the pastor, would soon be returning, and I needed to find a place to live. I asked around, and answered a couple of ads in the paper, but nothing suitable turned up. Then one day when I was talking with a group of people and mentioned I had to find a place, one of them said, "Oh, I'm moving to Seattle. I have a great apartment. Come look at it and see if you want it."

I did, and it was perfect. I arranged with Carole, the tenant, when I would move in, and I started packing my stuff, what little I had. A few days before I was to move, Carole called me.

"I'm really sorry to tell you this, but my job in Seattle fell through and I'm not moving."

I was stunned. Tom was returning in a few days and I had to move out.

"Carole, I don't know what I'm going to do. I was really counting on moving into your place and I have no place else to go."

She replied, "Well… I have two bedrooms. Why don't you just move in with me?"

When I hesitated, she added, "I'll move into the smaller bedroom and you can have the bigger one."

That settled it. I moved in two days later. We had the second floor of an old brick house on a nice residential street. Our entrance was up a wooden outside staircase, which was treacherous in icy weather, but I didn't mind. At that point, at fifty-one, I was still young and agile enough that it wasn't a problem. The rent was cheap, and it was warm and comfortable. It worked out really well. Carole was one of twelve children and her siblings all lived in town. They were a close-knit family, so she had a busy social life, and with my traveling, we didn't see much of each other.

A few months later, Carole sat down at the kitchen table and said, "I'm moving to Oregon to live with my boyfriend. You can have the place all to yourself!"

I liked Carole, but I really wouldn't miss her, as we saw each other so little, and it would be good to be alone there. The rent was affordable, even by myself.

Just before Christmas, I decided to give a party. I did a lot of cooking and cleaning the apartment. It was a last-minute decision, so people had only a few days' notice, and I didn't expect many people. But no one came. Actually, one woman came for a little while just because she knew no one else was coming and she felt sorry for me. She explained that many people were out of town or had company, but I knew that even those who were available didn't come because they still resented me. It hurt a bit, but I was able to laugh about it.

I did manage to have some social life in Springfield, even with my limited time. I attended the local Unitarian church on Sundays when I was in town, but didn't take on any responsibilities. I was friendly with a few single women, and we met for lunch occasionally and commiserated at the lack of men in our lives. One of the women, Jane, started a singles group that met for socializing one night a month. I didn't meet anyone interesting there, but after I left town I heard that Jane met a man there and married him. I was glad to know that it worked for someone. Between the people in the groups around the state, seeing the board members in Chicago once a month and staying with friends there, I had enough connections with people that I didn't feel lonely.

I was so passionate about the issue of preventing nuclear war that it became an obsession. It occupied my mind all day, from waking up to going to sleep, every day. I had little energy or time for anything else.

26 Freeze Voter

In 1983 the national Freeze Campaign established a political action committee, named Freeze Voter '84, to campaign for candidates for U.S. House and Senate seats around the country who would support nuclear weapons control. In Springfield, the local peace group campaigned for Paul Simon for the Senate and Dick Durbin for the House. Both won their races, and gave us credit for helping them. I still have a letter from Dick Durbin, thanking us for all we did in his campaign. He is now, in 2018, a Senator from Illinois, and has always impressed me as that rare person—a genuinely decent man in politics.

As a consequence of this involvement in the 1984 election races, I got to know the Freeze Voter staff in Washington, and thus began my serious involvement in party politics.

I became the director of the Freeze Voter chapter in Springfield, in addition to the downstate organizer for the Freeze, and recruited volunteers for the Senate and House candidates for phone banks. In those days, we used "telephone banks" with many phones hooked up in one big room where volunteers called the people listed on voter registration lists to urge them to vote for our candidates. Through Freeze Voter we supplied several full-time workers in the candidate's offices, freeing up some of their paid staff for other work. I also traveled to Washington, DC, to be trained in effective campaign tactics and lobbying. At some point in this period, I don't recall just when, I was elected to the national board of directors of the Nuclear Weapons Freeze Campaign. My friend Ted, who was on the national board also, was instrumental in my election to the board, as he knew of the work I had been doing in Illinois.

For these meetings, I drove to St. Louis from Springfield to get a flight to DC and then drive home again late at night when I returned. I was still driving around the state for organizing activities, so I spent even more time away from home than ever. Having no family or pets to look after made it easier.

Being on the national board was an eye-opener. It meant regular flights to Washington for board meetings and observing up close what happened there. Ironically, this "peace" group was most fractious group I've ever known. About twenty-five people attended the meetings, and most of our time was spent arguing about procedure. There seemed to be at least two major factions in the organization, those who were either task-oriented or process-oriented. The task people wanted to get things done quickly, and the process people wanted to take time to be sure everyone was heard thoroughly and that we understood why we were doing what we were doing. We frequently got bogged down in process and ended the meetings with bad feelings all around. At that point in my life I gravitated more toward the task-oriented group, and was always frustrated with the lack of action. Today, I probably would lean more towards the other group, and would be equally frustrated.

After the election of 1984, in which Freeze Voter was instrumental in several victories, activity slowed down somewhat and I started feeling restless. The job had become routine, and since I was not able to create any new chapters, it began to feel pointless. At the same time, the Illinois Freeze decided to hire a full-time staff member in the Chicago office, and I thought about applying for the job.

Living in Chicago would bring me nearer to my children and grandson, who all lived in the area, and my friends. I knew the executive director pretty well and knew we could work well together. The only drawback was the salary. It was set at $15,000 a year, which is what I was getting in Springfield as the downstate organizer. I could make that work in Springfield, but didn't see how I could live on it in Chicago, where living expenses were much higher.

It was a dilemma. Should I apply for the job, and if I got it, then negotiate more money, or should I say that I would apply if the salary was higher? I believed that in the corporate world, you got the job offer, then negotiated terms before accepting it, so I decided to do that.

I applied, and was offered the job. But when I said, "Okay, now let's talk about the salary," the director was shocked.

"But you knew what the pay was when you applied!" she said.

Maya with Christie at Christies' home in Indianapolis, Indiana, 1985

"Yes, but you know I can't live on that little money in the city," I replied.

"Well, you know we don't have enough money to pay any more. Why did you mislead us like this?" She was really angry. "That's what we pay the other staff person."

"But," I countered, "she's twenty-three, lives in a basement apartment with three other young people, and rides a bike to work. I'm fifty-one years old, and I can't live like that." The offer was withdrawn, and my relationship with the home office was strained, to say the least.

I immediately put the word out in Freeze circles that I was available for a job, and very soon received a phone call from the Freeze campaign in St. Louis.

"We'd like to consider you for the Executive Director position in the St. Louis Freeze," said Kathy, the president of the organization. "Can you come for an interview?"

I agreed, and drove to St. Louis the next week. My reputation had preceded me, and I was hired on the spot. I was both amused and puzzled by this, as my job had been to organize chapters, and I had failed completely. But somehow I had gotten a reputation of being a hotshot organizer. The salary was the same as in Springfield, but the cost of living was not as high as Chicago, so I accepted it.

I didn't know what a hornet's nest I was getting into.

When I drove to St. Louis to find a place to live, Kathy took me around and showed me the different neighborhoods. I found a two-bedroom apartment in an old brick two-story building in a section of town called Dogtown. It was near the zoo, and sometimes I could hear the lions roaring at night.

Soon after I arrived, in early December 1985, I attended my first board meeting and discovered just how poor the organization was. There was barely enough money in the bank to pay my first month's salary, so my first job was fundraising. One of the group's major supporters was a wealthy woman who was a Monsanto heir. I approached her first, and she pledged $5,000. This gave me some breathing room, for a while.

It didn't take long to learn that the board was composed of two groups who thought very differently. The line was drawn not so much along ideological lines but on personalities. When I was hired, the job title was actually Executive Director/Organizer, but everyone referred to the job as the director. One day when I was talking with Kathy, the president of the board, I asked her about the Organizer part of the title.

"Oh, you can ignore that. We just put that in there to keep a few people happy."

"That's good, because I came here to be the director," I replied, relieved.

She was wrong. It gradually became evident that they really wanted an organizer, not a director. There wasn't much to direct, except fundraising, and the group wanted lots of protests and demonstrations organized. I was not happy about that.

I was especially unhappy when the board wanted us to demonstrate in downtown St. Louis by blocking the main street during a weekday lunch hour. We were protesting a nuclear bomb test that was being conducted on that day out west.

Reluctantly, I organized about twenty people to go downtown and form a line, stretched across an intersection of one of the main streets at 12 o'clock noon. We walked across the intersection with the light, and then held hands and stayed there in a line, across the whole street. Traffic backed up in both directions, horns honking and angry people yelling at us. After about ten minutes, a policeman arrived and ordered us to leave. Kathy, as our leader, refused. The officer then said that we had to either move to the sidewalk or be arrested. We opted for moving to the sidewalk. We had made our point.

Maya at Freeze Voter board of directors meeting, Illinois, 1984.

It started to rain, and we were not sure what to do. Kathy suggested that we go into the lobby of the building behind us. I think it was a bank. We all congregated in the lobby, and then we realized we had not planned how to end the action. We didn't want to just wander away. Suddenly someone who had been listening to a radio, called out, "They cancelled the test!"

"Yaay!" we yelled, and used that as our excuse to leave, clapping and laughing. Of course the test had been cancelled because of bad weather, not because of our demonstration, but we felt vindicated anyway.

I returned to the office, disturbed. I couldn't see how actions like that served a good purpose. It got us publicity, but not the good kind. It made people mad at us, not supportive. I vowed not to do any more like it. That was the beginning of my real troubles with the board.

Although work was not going well, I had an enjoyable social life in St. Louis. I went to the Eliot Unitarian chapel in the suburb Kirkwood. One Sunday a young man (young to me, anyway, in his forties) approached me and suggested we meet for lunch to talk about my work with the Freeze. In the course of lunch, it became obvious that Ric was more interested in me than in my work. We began dating, and had many pleasant times. We spent more time at his apartment than mine, because it was nicer and was closer to the places we went for entertainment. We also connected with two other couples, and the six of us went out often for dinner and movies.

Eventually I became more aware of how much the other five people in our little group were drinking. I joined them in a drink or two, but not to the extent they did. After Ric stood me up a couple of times when he was supposed to come over after work, I discovered that he really had a drinking problem. Both times he had started drinking when he got home and fallen asleep on the couch. Soon after that, the wife of one of the couples was hospitalized from an alcohol overdose. Nevertheless, I stayed friends with them all until I left town. I liked St. Louis, in spite of the work problems. I still feel a twinge of nostalgia whenever I pass through the city and see the Gateway Arch.

At this time I decided I wanted to get on the national board of Freeze Voter. Looking back, I realize it was purely an ego thing and I had no real business being there as I had little to contribute, but I lobbied hard and was elected to the board. This meant more trips to DC for more meetings, but these meetings were enjoyable, as it was a smaller group, much more task-oriented and less contentious. Most of the board and the staff had a great sense of humor, which is always important to me. It also meant more occasions to see my friend Ted, who was on the board and was still my main contact in the both the Freeze and Freeze Voter. By this time he had moved to New York.

My situation with the Freeze in St. Louis got worse and worse. The difference in expectations of my job widened, and there was a serious split in the board with two factions on each side of several other issues as well, and I aligned myself with the wrong one. At least it turned out to be the least powerful one. They were determined that I was to be an organizer, not a director. The board and its president wanted to run the organization, and my job was to organize demonstrations, not to direct the group. I was not willing to do that, and eventually I was told I was no longer welcome as the director. It was not so much that they rejected me personally, although that was true for a few people, but they did not like how I did my job. Not everyone was opposed to me, but those who were opposed carried the most weight, and I just couldn't deal with it anymore.

I resigned rather than waiting to be fired. I could have stayed on as the director of the local Freeze Voter chapter, but that didn't make any sense to me, so I left both positions. My last day of work was July 4, 1986. I had been in St. Louis for not quite seven months.

The St. Louis experience is the worst I have ever had with a job. I've rarely been rejected or failed, especially in work. Being competent in my job has always been basic to my self-image, and to have my employers so unsatisfied with my performance was devastating.

It was so upsetting that I started crying and couldn't stop. I cried almost nonstop for a month. I knew I needed help, and started seeing a therapist. She was familiar with most of the people in the Freeze in St. Louis, and assured me that the situation was largely not my fault. She told me that the group had a reputation for being impossible to deal with, and I later heard the same thing from other Freeze groups around the country. She also helped me realize how I had contributed to the problem, and how I could avoid repeating the situation. I saw her five times in a month, and consider it money well spent.

With no job, in August I decided to take a break and go visit my son and family in Joliet. My grandson Matt was three years old, and I wanted some time with him. While I was there, I learned that a young man, Shawn Collins, was a Democrat running for U.S. Representative against an incumbent Republican. I went to Shawn's office to see if I could volunteer. I was immediately offered the job of volunteer coordinator and I accepted it.

Of course this was a temporary job that would end with the election in November, so I kept my apartment in St. Louis. The campaign found me a place to live in Joliet—an attic room in the home of one of Shawn's main supporters. It was a pleasant place, and the couple were nice. I wasn't there much, as I went to the campaign office early in the morning and stayed until late at night.

Shawn was new in politics, and ran a somewhat amateur campaign. His campaign manager had no experience in politics; most of his campaign workers had been involved in many previous campaigns, all of them unsuccessful. The Democrats had not won this Congressional seat since 1959. It would be an uphill battle.

My job was to recruit and manage volunteers. I got the voter registration lists, and started calling. We had yard signs and flyers printed. The district extended over a large area of the southern and southwestern suburbs of Chicago. We needed more support in the eastern part, so we opened another office there. The national Freeze Voter hired a young man to work in that office. I arranged for a bank of phones to be put in, and got a team started making calls. I recruited people to put up yard signs and go door to door with flyers. However, I concentrated more on phone calls and focused on areas where we were more likely to get voters out to the polls.

I went back to St. Louis a couple of times, and once to Washington for a board meeting. When I was about to drive to St. Louis, I realized that I was completely out of my thyroid medication. I was going to arrive in town late Saturday night and fly out Sunday morning. How could I get a refill? I called the drug store that had my prescription, and described my dilemma.

"No problem," he said. "I'll fill it and leave it at the bar next door. They stay open until midnight. If you can get there by then, they'll have it for you. You can pay me for it when you get back to town."

So that's what I did. It felt really strange to go into the neighborhood bar late at night and ask for a package.

"Sure, lady, here it is," the bartender said, and reaching under the counter, handed me a brown bag. I thought about how that must have looked to anybody watching.

Back in Joliet, I leaned heavily on Freeze Voter for help. They sent a consultant out to meet with us in the campaign office, and I was on the phone with him frequently. This did not sit well with the old-timers in the campaign. They resented having "out of town" people so involved, and argued with me about tactics. But I stood my ground. One day one of the biggest supporters, whose house I was living in, came to the office and confronted me.

"You and those hotshot consultants are going to cost us this election!" he yelled. He actually got right up into my face, so we were shouting toe to toe.

Maya with Shawn Collins at his Collins for U.S. Representative headquarters, Joliet, Illinois, 1986.

"They will help us win it!" I yelled back.

"We know what we're doing! We've run campaigns here for years!" he replied, getting red in the face.

"And how many have you won?" I asked. He stomped out, furious. He left me alone after that.

Between the Joliet office and the Chicago Heights office, we covered at least 300 precincts with literature, staffed about 50 phones with 200 people, and covered 40 precincts with get-out-the-vote teams going door to door on election day. I was pleased with my work, considering that we accomplished all this in just eight weeks.

Election night was a cliffhanger. We gathered at one of the larger bars in town to listen to the returns. The tension rose by the minute, with people getting more and more boisterous the later it got and the more drinks they consumed. The race was so close we couldn't call it. By 11 o'clock we knew the results: We had lost by 1 percentage point.

The next morning I packed up my stuff and drove home to my apartment in St. Louis. It had been a grueling two months, and I was exhausted.

27 *Beyond IBM*

I was also out of a job. I was content to rest for a while, but the job in the Collins campaign had paid barely enough to cover my expenses, and I would soon be broke.

After a few weeks of rest, I got a call from Kate, my former housemate in Peoria. She had moved to Washington, DC, about a year earlier.

"What're you doing these days?" she asked, after the usual pleasantries.

"Actually, not much," I replied. I explained that I had just finished the political job and was wondering what to do next.

"Come to Washington and help me write a book," she suggested. "I have a contract with McGraw Hill and have enough money to pay you. How about it?"

"Sure," I replied instantly. I had nothing better to do, and would be glad to go back to Washington. It was my home territory. I was born there and had relatives and friends there, in addition to the Freeze people. It was a no-brainer. Of course I would go help Kate write a book.

I had no idea how to write a book, and neither did Kate, but we were sure we could figure it out. When I arrived for a visit in early December, she filled me in on how she got the contract.

Kate had moved to Washington to develop a consulting company. She believed that her work experience gave her enough insights to be able to help struggling entrepreneurs, even at the young age of thirty-three. At a conference she met a man named Lou Mobley, who had retired after thirty-two years as an upper-level executive at IBM. They became close friends, and together they developed the idea of a book. With Lou's credentials and experience at IBM, they were able to get a contract with McGraw-Hill with a hefty advance.

Lou had the information and contacts, and I soon discovered that Kate was an excellent writer. Their agent said that the proposal was "one of the best I've ever seen." On the basis of just the proposal and Lou's name, there was so much interest in the book that their agent held an auction. McGraw-Hill won and gave Kate and Lou an advance of $57,000. In 2018 dollars, that would be about $125,000. In 1986, big advances were not that unusual.

It was good to be connected with Kate again. Her friend and co-author Lou was a delightful elderly man with a puckish sense of humor. The three of us got along well.

The basis of the book was a computer program that Lou developed when he worked at IBM. Called the Mobley Matrix, it was a financial management and planning tool that allowed a company to decide on the best planning numbers quickly and easily on a personal computer. All the numbers could be entered into the Matrix and everything else would be adjusted immediately, such as ROI, or return on investment. In the 1980s, this program was highly innovative. I never really understood it, but fortunately, I didn't need to, since the two of them did.

The book was titled *Beyond IBM: Leadership, Marketing and Finance for the 1990s*. Between Lou's many years in upper management at IBM and Kate's business and consulting experiences, they developed a theory of how companies could survive and thrive through the change from the industrial age to the information age. The finance section included the use of the Matrix and promoted the sale of the software.

Over the Christmas holidays at the end of 1986, I moved to Washington, living at first in Kate's apartment until the one I had rented was available. I had found an apartment in the Berkshire, a high-rise where Kate lived. We were both on the first floor, at opposite ends of a very long corridor. It was convenient to be so close by, because her living room became our office.

I liked that place. Even though the first floor of the building was on the ground level, the building was situated on a hill with a huge ravine behind it, and my windows looked out over the ravine, three floors up. The ravine was heavily forested with huge trees, and provided me a beautiful view.

We quickly worked out a system for writing. Lou, who lived far out beyond the suburbs, drove in to Kate's in the morning, and the two

On her way—Maya moving to Washington, DC, November 1987.

of them collaborated at the kitchen table, developing ideas of what to include in each chapter. Then Kate would write it all out in long hand. At that point we had no computer, so I found a woman who typed manuscripts for a fee. When a chapter was written, I took the pages to her and she typed them on her computer and printed them. We soon realized this would be too cumbersome and expensive, so Kate bought a computer. It was one of the so-called "portable" Compaq computers, which was actually the size of a suitcase with a handle on one side. It was so heavy I could barely pick it up. The screen was about 8 inches square. I was relieved when before long Kate bought a better one.

The computer came with WordPerfect and I had no idea how to use it, but it was my job to type in all of Kate's writing. I learned by trial and error—lots of error. We were both always afraid that I would accidentally delete everything we had written. Sometimes when I was typing away, suddenly something would go wrong and I would say, "Oops!" After I did this a couple of times, Kate said, "*Please* don't do that! It terrifies me every time!"

Kate would write out a few pages while sitting on the floor and hand them to me. I typed them, printed them out, gave them back to Kate, she made changes on them, gave them back to me, and I retyped them and printed them out. This went on all day.

I soon learned that Kate and I had very different internal clocks. I'm a morning person, and she's a night person. I would be ready to work long before she was, and she would still be writing at midnight, after my brain had shut down. I arrived in the mornings to find many pages ready for me to type.

I didn't work all the time. I joined the Washington Independent Writers, a now-defunct group that encouraged freelance writers. There I met Paula Hirschoff, a writer/photographer who is still a close friend after thirty-one years. I also started a salon, similar to the one in Peoria. My old friend David had moved to Washington with his new wife Barbara, and we found a few more people to join us. We met at the members' homes, twice a month. It was a pleasant group, but never evolved into the same kind of group we had in Peoria. Being in a big city probably made that more difficult to accomplish, as we were scattered around a wider area and didn't gather much except for the salon evenings, so didn't develop a close community.

I also looked for a church. I tried the Unitarian church on River Road, but wasn't satisfied. The service was okay, but the people were surprisingly unfriendly. One Sunday I tried an experiment: I stood in the middle of the room during coffee hour, coffee cup in hand, and waited. Not only did no one speak to me, no one even made eye contact. They actually walked around me as if I were a piece of furniture. I didn't go back.

I was feeling the lack of a romance in my life, and started attending the single's dances at the UU church on Friday nights, but the men who attended were not appealing to me, and I soon stopped going. I even put an ad in the "lonely hearts" section of a local magazine. I received many responses and went out for coffee with about a dozen of them. Two of them even rated a second date, but that was all. It was very discouraging.

I did develop a tentative relationship with a writer named Larry. I looked young for my age and he appeared old for his, so neither of us knew at first how different our ages were. He estimated I was about forty-five and I thought he was about forty. When we revealed that I was fifty-four and he was thirty-five, the romance cooled quickly. He said he didn't want to be a "cliché." We continued to hang out together, however, and remained friends for years.

Money was always an issue. Kate paid me as a contractor at $2,000 a month, but I had never freelanced before and didn't know that I had to pay my own taxes out of that. When tax time came, I was shocked at how much I owed. Kate gave me a bonus to cover the tax that year, and I saw that in the future I had to be more frugal to survive with Washington's high cost of living.

The apartment building we lived in was on Massachusetts Avenue. Down the hill about a block was the National Cathedral, the Episcopalians' national church, a magnificent Gothic stone structure, complete with gargoyles. I loved that building, and often slipped into its inspiring sanctuary to sit quietly. Whenever I go back to the city I still like to visit it.

Having given up on the River Road Unitarians, I looked around for something else. I saw a listing of a Unity church downtown and went there one Sunday. I should have realized that being in downtown Washington it would be a black church, but it didn't occur to me. I was surprised to walk in and see an almost totally black congregation; I was one of three white people among about 200 worshippers. It felt strange but interesting, and I stayed for the service. I don't recall the sermon, but the service was not that different from any other church I had attended. There were a few "Amen!" calls from the pews, but otherwise it was surprisingly sedate.

After the service, I followed the crowd upstairs for the coffee hour. The people were friendly and welcoming, and several of them engaged me in conversation. But as much as I appreciated their friendliness, I didn't go back. It just didn't feel like the place for me.

The Freeze movement was winding down. Negotiations on the START 1 treaty were ongoing and seemed promising, as President Reagan and Soviet President Gorbachev held a summit meeting in Washington and reached some tentative agreements. The treaty would reduce the number of nuclear weapons by both the United States and the Soviet Union. The Freeze Campaign merged with SANE that year to become Peace Action, and in 1988 Freeze Voter closed down and turned over its assets to the Professionals' Coalition for Nuclear Arms Control. I still attended a few meetings in 1988, but it had taken a back seat in my priorities.

The lack of involvement with the two Freeze groups meant my fellow activist Ted and I rarely saw each other, and our friendship faded, although we exchanged Christmas cards for many years. In about 2005, I received a note from his wife that he had died suddenly from a massive heart attack at age sixty-four. I was sad he was gone. He had been an important influence in my life during those activist years.

One day in 1988, while walking down a sidewalk in Washington, I had a distinct feeling that a little switch in my chest, like a light switch, had flipped to "off," and I knew it was time to move on from the peace movement. It felt like my work was done, and I could let it go. I had the impression that my effort, while tiny in the overall scheme of things, had been crucial, but it was finished.

My full-time commitment now was writing the book. We had to write a 250-page book from scratch with all of the content coming out of Lou and Kate's minds. Having never written a book, we didn't know what a daunting task we had taken on.

We were all passionate about the book. We were totally committed to it; when we weren't actually putting words on paper, we were thinking about it or talking about it or planning for it. It was all-consuming, especially for Kate and me. Lou's son Chris joined the team and helped us both with my computer skills and also with sales materials for the Matrix software. In his early twenties, he was skilled in the emerging field of computer science and was a huge help to us.

It soon became apparent that selling the Mobley Matrix would be our major income producer, so we began putting more effort into developing that business in addition to writing. We set up a corporation for that purpose, in addition to McKeown & Company, the corporation that Kate already had for her consulting business. The Mobley Matrix, the book, and Kate's speeches were all interrelated, making it easy for each product to support the others. Kate was paying all of our salaries and our expenses out of the book advance, but we also had some income from the Matrix sales and Kate's speaking engagements. We had to make the advance last throughout the whole writing process. It was my job to keep the books, not because I knew how but because no one else would do it. Surprisingly, we discovered I was good at it. I actually did the taxes for both of the corporations, including an additional company we set up later.

Our agent sold the book rights to several foreign countries, adding about another $50,000 to our bank account, although the money didn't come in all at once. It was my job to manage those contracts, in addition to dealing with McGraw-Hill in New York. Kate and Lou were the visionaries while I did the grunt work, and this division of labor suited us all well.

We also had some additional money, because back in 1986, an investor in California who was an old friend of Lou's had invested a large sum in the Mobley Matrix for part ownership. He also advised us from time to time with marketing strategy. He was an enormous help to us during this time.

Kate was a genius at getting well-known people to write blurbs for the book jacket. She would say to me something like, "Maya, get me Lee Iacocca's direct line" and I would set about finding it. I dialed the number, and once she got the people on the line, she worked her magic, and they would write glowing statements of praise for the book. I don't think she was ever turned down. The back flap of the jacket is crowded with sixteen of these endorsements, such as William Simon, former U.S. Secretary of

Beyond IBM, book Maya and Kate published in 1987.

Kate McKeown, 1987.

the Treasury; John Valenti, president of Motion Picture Association of America; Norman Cousins, author ; Paul Rizzo, Dean of UNC Business School; Debbie Fields, President of Mrs. Fields Cookies; and Theodore Levitt, Editor of *Harvard Business Review*.

In the fall of 1987, the apartment owners had to renovate the apartments to remove asbestos, and all of the tenants had to move out, in stages, for about a month during the construction. They worked on one section at a time, and whenever they could, they moved tenants into vacant apartments on other floors for the month. Kate was moved to the eighth floor, while I was still on the first floor.

We worked night and day to get the book written. Lou sometimes stayed late to work with Kate in her apartment upstairs. About nine o'clock one evening I got a frantic call from her.

"Get up here quick!" she screamed, and hung up. I raced to the elevator and commanded it to fly up the eight floors. When I got to Kate's door, it was locked, and I banged and banged until she came to let me in. We dashed into the living room where Lou lay on the floor.

"Push on his chest!" she said. She began holding his mouth open and breathing into it. We kept that up for a few minutes when suddenly I felt his body go slack. All his muscles had let go. I knew that Lou's spirit had just left his body.

Kate had called 911 before she called me, and the EMTs arrived, two young men who acted casually, as if they had come to move a piece of furniture, in no hurry. The way they threw Lou on the gurney, it was obvious they knew he was gone.

"I'll go with them in the ambulance, and you come to the hospital in your car," I told Kate. As I started to get into the elevator with the two men and the gurney, one of them stopped me, saying, "You can't come with us, unless you're family."

"I'm his *daughter*," I said, and they let me in. It's one of the few times I've ever felt justified in telling a blatant lie.

The next couple of hours at the hospital were surreal. Kate was dazed, barely comprehending what was going on. She looked bizarre; while attempting CPR on Lou she had bitten her lip, and there was blood smeared on her face and all down the front of her white blouse.

I gave the nurse Lou's home number, and we waited for the family to arrive. The hospital had that spooky, silent late-night feel. When Lou's wife and son arrived an hour later, Kate and I went back to her apartment, still numb with shock. It had happened so fast. Lou had simply collapsed with a massive heart attack. He was seventy-two years old.

I didn't know what we would do with Lou gone.

28 Enter Publishing, Inc.

Kate grieved hard at the sudden loss of her friend and business partner, and I wondered if I would ever see the old effervescent Kate again. It was weeks before she was able to work on the manuscript, but the book's concepts were all in place, and she was confident we could complete it in time to send to the publisher.

Finally, in early 1988, we sent a final draft to McGraw-Hill. They were pleased with it, and printed a run of 10,000 books, which were all immediately ordered by bookstores. We were just beginning to relax when one day Kate took a phone call that changed everything. She answered the phone, and said, "WHAT?" After a few more sentences, she hung up and turned to me, stunned.

"They dropped our book!" she said.

Unknown to us, McGraw-Hill had been withdrawing from the trade books business for a year or so; they had just spun off that division, and our book was among those that did not go to the new company. McGraw-Hill still owned the book, but no resources were allocated to promote or sell it. There would be no advertising campaign, no book tour, no more books printed, no sales, and no royalties. *Beyond IBM* was going nowhere.

We stared at each other. What now? All this, and no book?

"Oh no, they don't!" Kate exclaimed. "We'll just sell the damn book ourselves!"

"How can we do that?" I asked, dumbfounded.

"We'll just create our own publishing company. How hard can it be?"

Lou Mobley and Kate, from the jacket of Beyond IBM.

McGraw-Hill still owned the rights to the book. Kate got on the phone and began negotiating to get them back. She bargained them down to $10,000. Her mother paid it, and the book was ours.

Before we could create a legal entity, we had to decide on a name. We tried out names for hours, over days. Finally Kate said, "Well, we're entering the publishing business, let's call it Enter Publishing."

So that was it. It was also a riff on the stage directions "enter laughing." That seemed appropriate, since keeping our sense of humor was going to be critical in the months to come. Enter Publishing became our third corporation, in addition to McKeown Consulting, Inc., and Mobley Matrix, Inc.

Kate had an ally at McGraw-Hill, and he helped us get started. In those days, it was impossible to market a book without a national distributor. The biggest distributor was Ingram in Tennessee, and our friend at McGraw-Hill put Kate in touch with the right people there. She negotiated a deal with Ingram, and we were set to sell our book.

I flew to Chicago and negotiated a deal with R.R. Donnelly & Sons, a book printer, to print 5,000 copies. It was just like the McGraw-Hill version, except with Enter Publishing on the copyright page and the spine. We rented a U-Haul unit to store the 125 boxes of 40 books each.

We had to get an advertising campaign in place. To our dismay, we discovered that an ad in the *New York Times* would cost thousands of dollars. Other outlets were also out of our range. This was in the days before the Internet or social media, so our options were far more limited than they would be today.

To help us develop a marketing strategy for both the book and the software, we hired Adrian, a tall, distinguished-looking Englishman, with a clipped British accent. We turned a corner of Kate's bedroom into an office for him and paid him $3,000 a month. I never understood exactly what he did or why we paid him so much, but he was pleasant to have around. He was by far the highest-paid person on the staff.

Kate came up with many schemes for publicizing the book. One was to copy the executive summaries from each chapter and send them out as a package to various people in business with an order form. I found names and addresses of many business people, put together numerous packets, and FedExed them out. We sent various "tchotchkes" to anyone who might buy or publicize the book. For instance, we attended the American Booksellers Association convention that was held in Washington that year and talked to everyone we could buttonhole. Kate used copies of the book as calling cards, giving them out freely at appointments and meetings. We used many other creative techniques, some wilder than others.

Someone in Kate's business network knew of a man in a foreign country who was interested in investing in Enter Publishing. I'm going to call him Matt. We had to be very secretive about him, because taking money out of his country into the United States was strictly illegal, and if they caught him he could be sent to prison.

We were bleeding money, so a potential investor was welcome news. Kate's friend brought Matt to Washington and Kate went out to dinner with the two of them. Surprisingly, based on that dinner conversation alone, Matt gave us $100,000. I don't recall what return he expected on that investment, but it was pure speculation. Kate fully expected *Beyond IBM* to be a best seller, with sales of a million books, and her confidence was contagious. I can't overstate her charisma and charm. As far as I could tell, no one ever said no to Kate.

Because of the illegality of the investment, we couldn't talk to Matt openly on the telephone about it. Given the political climate in his country and his frequent international travel, he was sure that his phone was tapped. He and Kate devised a code system so that when he called, we could carry on what sounded like a chatty conversation but would really be an inquiry about sales or something. Kate drilled into me that if Matt called while she was out, I had to be very careful about what I said. A conversation would go something like "How's my cousin doing?" and the reply would be "She's fine, the surgery was successful and cost about $5,000." The calling was complicated by the time difference. The other country is seven hours ahead of Washington, so the times that we could reach each other were limited. I was petrified that I would have to take a call from him and I would mess it up and he would be arrested. To my great relief, he never called while Kate was out.

Gregarious Kate had a way of gathering people wherever she went, and consequently there was a constant flow of people through the apartment. One of them was Adam, a young chubby man with red hair and talent with both computers and music. He helped develop some of the software promotional materials. Some evenings a group of us would gather in the living room and sing along with him while he played the guitar. Our favorite song was "*The Mary Ellen Carter*."

That song is about a ship that goes down in a storm and the heroic efforts to raise it from the ocean floor. The final stanza is

> "And you, to whom adversity has dealt the final blow
> With smiling bastards lying to you everywhere you go
> Turn to, and put out all your strength of arm and heart and brain
> And like the *Mary Ellen Carter*, rise again.
> Rise again, rise again—though your heart it be broken
> And life about to end,
> No matter what you've lost, be it a home, a love, a friend,
> Like the *Mary Ellen Carter*, rise again."

The lyrics were especially meaningful to us as we struggled to make a success of our businesses without Lou.

Kate also had a habit of "adopting" strays—stray people, that is, and Adam was one of them. He told us stories of his life adventures, some amazing and all entertaining. He lived in New York, and when he came to town on business he would stay at Kate's.

Eventually Adam told Kate that he had been hired to write a regular column for *PC Computing*, a popular computing magazine at the time. But he said he wouldn't be paid for a month, and he would be evicted from his apartment if he didn't pay his rent in the next week. Kate felt sorry for him and lent him $2,000. He went back to New York and disappeared. When Kate couldn't reach him, she contacted the magazine

Christie and her grandfather Than in Maya's apartment in Washington, 1987.

and was told that he didn't work there, they didn't know him. With more inquiries, we learned that he was a pathological liar, that he told everyone wild stories, and none of them were true. We never heard from him again. Years later we learned that he told one too many lies, and someone shot him to death. Very sad. He was such a charming person.

With the new investment money, the bookkeeping became too complex and time-consuming for me, so we hired a part-time accountant. I was glad to be rid of keeping the books, but I was still responsible for filing the taxes. With the companies' products and services so interrelated, the income and expenses could be allocated to whichever company needed it at the time. When the software company was losing money, I could take Kate's consulting fee and count it as income for that company. Expenses for the book could be accounted to the consulting company. Since most of our money was capital, with this careful maneuvering of income and expenses, at tax time we owed only a few hundred dollars in taxes for all three corporations. At that time, tax law allowed for the first $25,000 in profit to be tax-free, and I could almost manage to keep each company's profit below that.

The difficulty in promoting the book was compounded by Lou's absence. He was the major draw for the book, being the creator of the Mobley Matrix and the author with many years in management at IBM. I don't know for sure, but I suspect that one reason McGraw-Hill let the book die was because they knew they couldn't promote it successfully without Lou. They had planned a national book tour with Lou as the star, and without him they didn't think Kate could carry it. She was only thirty-five years old and had no real business management experience. The people at McGraw-Hill did not know what an accomplished public speaker Kate was, or how much business acumen she had learned on her own, and could not envision her as a sufficient draw for publicity.

Since McGraw-Hill would not be sending Kate out on tour, we decided we had to do it ourselves. We hired Larissa, a public relations professional, to take over the marketing. She set up a book tour in about a dozen states, and scheduled radio and press interviews. This cost more money, but we thought it was necessary to save the book.

We hired an additional staff person to help with the paper work, a young woman named Susan. She was a fun person, very lively and bright. As we hired all those people and sent out more and more material, and Kate traveled on the tour and went more and more conventions, the expenses continued to mount.

In late 1987, when we were still with McGraw-Hill, as we approached finishing the book, we knew it needed to be copyedited before we sent it to the publisher. Kate found Walter, a freelance editor who was retired from one of the big news magazines. We hired him, and he came to the apartment in the mornings and edited the manuscript onsite. I typed in his edits, and as I saw what he had done, I thought, "I could do this." I asked him how I could get started as an editor.

"George Washington University has a course in copyediting you could take. I think the one course would be enough," he replied. I filed that information away for when I might need it. Now, months later, as I saw how we were losing money, I decided it was time to look into finding other work I could do, and maybe copyediting would be it.

I took the course at GW. It met on Saturday mornings for 16 weeks. I found it was easy for me, and I enjoyed it. When I finished the course, I asked Walt how I could find clients.

"Well, I have one I'll give you. This guy is writing a book and he's a terrible writer. I can't make sense out of what he's doing. I'll be glad to refer him to you if you want him. He's writing about New Agey stuff, like channeled material, things like that."

"Sounds good to me," I replied. "How much should I charge him?"

"Charge him the same as I'm charging, $30 an hour. He won't know the difference." Thus began my copyediting career, in 1987. It has supported me for many years.

We began to realize we couldn't stay afloat much longer. Kate persuaded Matt that more money would save his investment, and suggested he send us more. When he flew to Washington we sat down with him and projected how much money he would make when we sold a million copies in several years. He wrote us a check for another $100,000!

However, when his Washington contact heard about this, she was furious. Matt was her friend and business associate, and she felt an obligation to him. She knew how precarious our financial situation was and couldn't let him throw away more money. So she intervened, and Matt asked for the second $100,000 back. Some of it had already been spent, but we returned most of it. The friend's relationship with Kate cooled after that.

As it became apparent that we weren't going to sell a thousand copies of *Beyond IBM*, much less a million, a low-level panic began to set in. Tensions rose, and relationships between all of us were strained. Kate had a way of inspiring loyalty in everyone who knew her, and I was no exception. I wanted to leave, but I felt I needed to stay with her until the last dime was spent, not only out of loyalty but because it seemed to me she was so fragile that if I left she would feel abandoned and it might push her over the edge. All of her dreams were collapsing, first with Lou dying, then Matt taking his second funding back, then the gradual realization that the book was not going to sell, and tepid sales of the Mobley Matrix. She had such grandiose visions, and as they crumbled, I could see signs of despair increasing every day.

I had been more than an assistant for Kate. I had been the rock, the one who kept the wheels running, kept everything grounded, and I suspected that without me she would not be able to keep it all together. So I stayed.

To save money, Kate looked around for a cheaper place to live. The cost of housing in Washington was prohibitively high, so she expanded her search out to the suburbs. Eventually she rented a huge split-level house with five bedrooms in Reston, Virginia, a planned community about 30 miles west of the city, with a rent lower than the city apartment. I was not pleased, as it meant a long commute for me to work. It was a gorgeous house, however, and I could see why she wanted it. There was plenty of room. This house became the office and the center of all the business activities. By this point we had let Adrian go, so Susan and I were the only staff.

I was not interested in moving to Reston, since I had developed a life in the Maryland suburbs. But I also needed to save money, so I moved to a much less expensive apartment in Silver Spring. Instead of walking down the hall, I now drove 40 minutes to work every day. This business adventure was getting harder and harder.

29 Channeling Cyrus

For the first time in many years, I was geographically close to my family—family being my father and his wife Ruth, and my brother Frank and his wife Jean. We didn't see each other often, and kept in touch only sporadically, but I always knew they were there. One Sunday afternoon I was standing in the middle of my living room when I suddenly realized I was not lonely anymore. All my life, since leaving home the first time to get married at age twenty-one and then moving away, I had always had a slight empty feeling in the pit of my stomach, feeling lonely and yearning for something, not knowing what. Suddenly, I knew I was *home*. I had roots in the area, deep in the very ground, and it was comforting. I had never identified that feeling until it went away. I was born in Washington, even though it had not been my home for many years, and I *belonged* there as I had never belonged anywhere else. That empty feeling has never returned, even though I have moved many times, to different cities in different states. Something about connecting with my roots filled that empty space in a way that didn't depend upon my being there physically anymore.

The lack of frequent contact with my father was mostly because I was avoiding Ruth. I had known her all my life and never liked her. She was loud and brash and critical, with a voice that grated like fingernails on a blackboard. I did not attend their wedding because they married when I was in the midst of leaving George, and I just couldn't handle a wedding and couldn't pay for the trip anyway. I think Ruth always believed that I stayed away because I disapproved of the marriage, and nothing I said could change her mind.

Than and Ruth at their 10th wedding anniversary dinner, 1988.

One evening in late October 1988 Daddy called me, which was surprising in itself, but it was even more surprising that he had nothing in particular to say.

"Hi. How're you doin'?" he asked.

"Um, okay. How are you?"

"Fair to middlin'. Worked in the garden today. Pulled some carrots before winter sets in."

It went on like that for a few minutes, while I waited for him to get to the point. He surely didn't call just to chat. He didn't do that. But after a few minutes, he said, "Well, guess I'll watch some tv. Bye."

"Goodbye," I responded, puzzled and pleased that he just wanted to make contact.

Three days later, about nine in the evening, my phone rang. It was my brother Frank.

"Maya, I have some bad news. Daddy died a little while ago," he said, in a shaky voice. "We're at the hospital. He donated his body to research and they have to come get it right away. Do you want to see him before they go?"

Stunned, I took in the news. Did I need to see his body? It would take me almost an hour to get to the hospital in the suburbs.

"No," I replied, "let them go. I don't need to see him."

"Okay, we'll go back to the house as soon as they get here."

"I'll get dressed and meet you there," I told him.

By 11 o'clock we had gathered back at Daddy's house, the house of my childhood. Ruth was in shock, barely able to talk, so Frank explained what had happened.

Daddy had worked in the garden in the afternoon. Later, after eating a good dinner, he went into the living room to relax. He sat down in his favorite chair, took off his shoes, settled back, and died. He was gone in seconds of a massive heart attack.

Later it occurred to me that when he called me, he had some inkling, maybe subconsciously, that he was going to die soon, and wanted to make contact with me one last time.

It felt strange now to be the oldest generation, with both of my parents gone. I was fifty-five; I was only forty-four when Mother died. "Orphan" doesn't seem like quite the right word, not being a child, but that's what it felt like. Even though I had never turned to my father for help, it was always in the back of my mind that I could. Now that option was gone.

When that first unfriendly Unitarian church didn't work out, I expanded my search to the suburbs, and found one in Silver Spring, a sprawling suburb of Maryland, adjacent to Washington, where I moved in 1989. In contrast to the other church, the first Sunday I attended, I was surrounded by people at the coffee hour, wanting to know all about me. I felt wonderfully welcomed.

The church became my home again, as it had been for most of my adult life. The Silver Spring UU church was big enough to have many activities and small enough to be friendly and accessible. I joined several committees, and my social life revolved around the congregation.

At about the time we finished the book in late 1988, I had started dating a man I met at the church. "Jim," a high school English teacher, was a good-looking, mild-mannered man whom I half expected to duck into a phone booth any minute and emerge as Superman. He had recently separated from his wife, and his two nearly grown daughters lived with him. This was a new experience for me, as both of his daughters were black. Jim and his wife had adopted them when they were babies, as many liberal white couples did in the early Seventies. His wife was severely emotionally disturbed, and Jim was planning to divorce her. However, she developed lung cancer soon after they separated, and he dropped his plans. Both of us helped her when she needed it until she died a year later. Jim was eleven years younger than I, and although we got along well, deep down we both sensed it would not be a permanent relationship. He was a grounding influence for me during this turbulent time with Kate and our businesses.

With Kate's move to Reston and mine to Silver Spring, she and I spent far less time together than before. As it became more and more apparent that our business ventures were not succeeding, Kate seemed to lose interest in marketing the book or the software and instead was investigating an import business from Russia. In addition, I was getting tired of the long commute to her house.

As I reflected on working with Kate, I realized it was time for me to quit. With neither the book nor the Matrix selling, Kate branching out into other interests, and the businesses nearly broke, it was time for me to go. I had found a couple more editing clients and decided I could support myself editing, so I told Kate I was quitting. She was okay with it, perhaps relieved that she wouldn't have to pay me anymore.

Much to my surprise, I found that I could collect unemployment compensation by filing in Washington, even though I had been self-employed and for several months had neither worked there nor lived there. I've always suspected that it was granted in error, as Washington was notoriously incompetent at paper work in those days, but I didn't ask.

So I was able to collect a check while I started my new career, much as I had done in Peoria when working with the Freeze. I went through the routine of applying for jobs to keep the unemployment comp coming, but meanwhile worked hard at building up an editing clientele. Not much money was coming in, and I was barely getting by. In early 1991, when Christie got married in Chicago, it was all I could do to pull together the $600 for a plane ticket to go there. I borrowed a dress from a friend, since I had nothing appropriate to wear and no money to buy anything. Christie made her gorgeous wedding dress herself, and I finished fitting it the morning of the wedding.

Christie at her wedding to Ralph, Chicago, 1991. (She made her wedding dress.)

Ralph and Maya with baby Veronica, in Chicago, November 1991.

In November 1991, Christie gave birth to my granddaughter Veronica. I flew out to Chicago a week before the due date, and was there in the hospital when the baby arrived. I cherish the memory of holding her in my arms when she was just ten minutes old. She has brightened my life ever since.

❖ ❖ ❖

Developing an editing business was hard. I got a few small jobs from the Washington Independent Writers, and the man writing the book that Walt had given me kept me going for a while. I soon put together a book proposal for him and sent him on his way. Walt was right; the man's writing was atrocious. I was relieved to be finished with him, although I was sorry to lose the money. Fortunately, unemployment comp was almost enough to live on.

One day a friend called me and said that his friend Sue Mehrtens in California wanted to move to the Washington area and asked if she could stay with me while she looked for a place to live. I said of course, and prepared my second bedroom for her. When she arrived, we hit it off immediately. Sue is one of the most interesting people I know, a true "Renaissance woman." She was a gourmet cook, made her own clothes, wallpapered her own house, built a sail boat by herself, was licensed by the Coast Guard as a ship pilot, and was a university professor and academic researcher. There apparently wasn't anything she couldn't do, and do superbly. I was somewhat in awe of her. Sue soon found a house and moved to a town about ten minutes away.

Her most significant talent for me was that she had become a channeler. She had just taken a course to learn to channel spirit entities, and wanted to practice. I eagerly became her guinea pig.

She channeled an entity who called himself Cyrus. Actually, the voice that came through said that "he" was a crowd of entities, but they spoke through one voice. His voice was deep and sort of gravelly, very different from Sue's, so I could tell when he began to speak. He would always start with, "Hail, and greetings."

I had ten 1-hour sessions with Cyrus, about once a week, tape recording all of the sessions. We would settle onto the sofa at either my house or hers, and Sue would go into a light trance and begin to speak in the voice of Cyrus. "He" seemed to be a high-level entity, one who had never incarnated on earth. He was delighted to make contact with us and was available to answer questions. I felt somewhat intimidated by him and the process, and was hesitant about asking about trivial matters. He emphasized that he was not a fortune teller, that he didn't make prophecies. I learned later that if I pressured him to tell me the future anyway, he would do it, but his prophecies were always wrong.

He apologized for being hard to understand, saying that it was difficult to tailor his communication to our way on earth, that he didn't

Maya and Sue Merhtens at Gettysburg, Md., 1990.

"speak" in any language. He sounded stilted, like the way people wrote centuries ago.

My sessions with Cyrus convinced me of the reality of reincarnation. I had never quite believed in it, but as our sessions progressed, it became undeniable. Of course we had many lives! He told me about some of mine and how they were related to this life, and it all made sense.

Cyrus told me much about myself, about my spiritual makeup and where I needed to grow and develop. I wish I could find the recordings of all of the sessions, but I've found only two of the later ones. He described in detail what some of my previous lives had been like, and how I had progressed in my spiritual life at this point this time around. The most important thing he told me is my purpose in this lifetime—not people's purpose of life in general, but mine in particular. My purpose in this lifetime is simple: *to help raise the consciousness of the planet*. Simple, but not all that easy. That sounded right to me, and it has motivated me ever since. I mark the beginning of my serious, conscious spiritual development from this time. I had always been religious, since my late teens, but now I understood more what it meant to be "awake."

I had started a meditation group, and we held a group session with Cyrus on February 10, 1991, which I recorded and later transcribed. We were curious about who "Cyrus" was, and how the process worked. There were five of us present, and I introduced us and asked most of the questions. Following is just a short excerpt of the transcription. Cyrus' voice is coming through Sue, in a trance. Sarah, a Catholic nun, was one of the group.

****

Maya: Who are you? What's going on in this process?

Cyrus: To understand this process, you have to be open to the realization that you know all things, for you have a part of yourselves that is both eternal and continuously connected to the higher realms, the realms of higher frequencies and vibrations. And you live in the sea of wisdom but your conscious mind tends to cover this reality and block your easy access to this wisdom, this energy. And the process is simply a process of moving aside your consciousness to let this wisdom pass. We are speaking through an entity [Sue] who has simply learned the procedure. But each of you is capable.

Maya: When you say "we," who do you mean?

Cyrus: We represent the entities, multiple energies that each of you can access as you develop spiritually and attain sensitivity to these finer vibrations. But each of you has many guides. You are on the path to contacting these guides yourselves.

As you pose a question, you are directing a flow of energy through this sea of vibrations that you live in, and that activates the vocal cords of this entity. But you are asking a question in essence of yourself, and accessing your own higher wisdom. This, in certain cases, comes to you in forms you are able to access. And as you grow and change, these forms also change. And so your level of wisdom evolves and the information you obtain also evolves. You might think of this process rather like a radio, that there are waves and vibrations you cannot see, but the radio picks up and transforms into waves that you can hear. And this is a similar parallel process. You will feel the flow of energy as this entity does when you yourself learn this process. And you will be surprised at how simple it is. You need only two things: the desire and the conviction that you can indeed do it.

Maya: You have talked earlier about yourself, Cyrus, being an entity on the astral plane who has not incarnated. Are you an entity yourself?

Cyrus: In your terms, we call ourselves entities. These clusters of energy are energy vibrations of frequency, rather as you might think of a radio station. But on our plane, there is nothing quite comparable to what you think of as entities. There are essences of energy, but not something substantial as you think of a body. There are levels of energy, and the levels above the energy that I, as Cyrus, represent are much higher.

Sarah: What is the point of this spiritual development? Toward what?

Cyrus: Ultimately, it is the process of creation. That the souls are the result of the cosmos wishing to realize itself and to experience itself, and to create itself. And as you undertake incarnations, you are providing a creative process, an experience, on the physical plane, even as there are non-physical entities doing similar things on higher, non-physical planes. But the ultimate process is an open-ended process of creation. We would like you to understand that this is a very expansive and joyful and gratifying process and as you grow and learn, the cosmos lives and laughs and loves through you.

Sarah: Why does the cosmos need to create itself if it already exists?

Cyrus: It is not something static. It is dynamic. it is the original *Dymanis*—the Greek word for the powerful one. It is the original force, or life wishing to become more alive, and its existence is to grow, to create. Think of your own lives, and think of the moment when you felt most alive. Was it not a moment of creativity? This is what the living principle in you represents, the creative spark, and this is what has ignited the universe. The concept you have of God is rather overlain with much frivolous speculation and many erroneous theories that suggest an anthropomorphic deity, some very static or hierarchical figure or some image of rigid perfection and this is not indeed what the cosmic whole is in essence. You are in your essence God, God is self, God himself, God herself, and as you live most fully in the moment of creation, so indeed does the universe as a whole.

****

There was much more, including thoughts about karma and whether life begins at conception and its implications for abortion (Sarah, the nun, pressed this issue). He talked at some length about the events in the Middle East. The United States had just started bombing the Iraqi air forces in an operation called Desert Storm not long before this recording. He said that we would enter a "time of troubles" that would last from 2002 to 2011, when "the global hardship and chaos and anxiety level will be extremely intense and many people around the world will choose to leave the physical state. ... People will separate one from another and there will come to be a tremendous level of social, economic, and physical chaos. It will be your task as spiritual beings, as workers in the light, to help those you can help and to smooth this process."

Looking back now in 2018, I think he seriously misjudged the end date.

30 Struggling in Silver Spring

Many of the events of my life have resulted from networking. People know people who know people who somehow get connected with me and bring me work. It happened again.

Soon after Sue arrived in town, she connected me with Herman, a mid-level DuPont executive in Wilmington. Herman often had business in Washington and would visit with Sue and me. Herman was an unusual business executive in that he was very interested in consciousness in the workplace. He and Sue developed an idea for a book about the future of business and signed a contract with Berrett-Koehler Publishers in San Francisco to write it. They wanted me to edit it as they wrote, and we worked out an arrangement that Herman would pay me an hourly fee to edit, and I would get 20% of the royalties. Once the royalties came in, I would repay Herman the amount he had paid me to edit. This arrangement allowed me to be paid while I worked without waiting for royalties, but Herman would not be out of what he paid me. Of course he would get repaid only if the book actually sold, and he was willing to take that risk.

The book, called *The Fourth Wave: Business in the 21st Century*, was written surprisingly quickly, partly because much of it was material channeled from Cyrus. Cyrus would tell them what should be in the book, then Sue and Herman would write it, going back and forth between them, and then I would edit what they wrote. The book came out in 1993, and actually sold enough copies for me to pay Herman back. I still get a few dollars from sales every year. I doubt that Berrett-Koehler would have contracted for the book if they had known of

Howard and Sue Rees, at BSU reunion in Silver Spring, 1991. Rees was the adult leader of the student group at the University of Maryland where George and Maya met.

Cyrus's involvement. Several years later when I was in a meeting with B-K staff in San Francisco about another book, I unthinkingly let slip that the material for *The Fourth Wave* was channeled, and there was a shocked silence around the table.

Herman and his wife, a physician in private practice, lived in an 11,000-square-foot house with an indoor swimming pool near Wilmington, Delaware. One day in December I became acutely aware of the difference in our standard of living. When Herman came to my apartment to work that day, he was in an unusually sour mood.

"I'm pissed," he said. "The company cut my Christmas bonus this year. I'm only getting $20,000." I just stared at him, speechless. I grossed less than $10,000 that year.

Herman always meant well, but sometimes he didn't think how his comments would affect me. One day when he came to work and we hadn't seen each other for a while, he said, "You look great! Your face isn't as blotchy as usual!" I just smiled and said thanks. He meant it as a compliment.

Herman had an idea for another book, about his experiences introducing consciousness into his work at DuPont, and asked me to edit it. This provided me with more income, once *The Fourth Wave* was finished. We worked on it for several months, but eventually it seemed to me that it was not a viable book, and I suggested we drop it. I soon regretted doing so, because I had no more work.

These were extremely lean years. I did everything I could to find editing clients, but not very successfully. I got the occasional small job and made barely enough to pay the bills each month. I never knew how I was going to pay the next month's rent. One night I went to a meeting with a friend who wanted to drive his new car, so I drove to his house and parked in his driveway. It was night, and in the dark he didn't see my car as he backed out, and he smashed into the side of my car. He didn't want to file a claim on his insurance so paid me the $600 repair estimate, which was exactly what I needed to pay the rent. The damage to my car was only cosmetic, and I never got it fixed.

It went like that month after month, something coming in just in time to keep me going. After a few months of this I decided I couldn't make it freelancing and sent out more than fifty résumés to find a job. I got no responses, not even an acknowledgment that my résumé had been received.

Eventually, as my bank account approached zero, I went to my stepmother Ruth, whom I had stayed in touch with out of a sense of duty, and asked for a loan.

"I'm sorry to have to ask you, but I really need some help. Could you lend me $800 to get through the next month?"

"Well… I don't know. I need my money. I have to get a new water heater."

After a long pause, she reluctantly wrote me a check. I got a glimpse of her checkbook and saw that she had more than $40,000 in her account. At the time I was resentful, but now that I'm the age she was then, I understand how important it is to feel secure with enough money in the bank.

That $800 got me through another month. Then I had to replace my old daisy wheel printer, and my brother Frank lent me $2,000 to buy a laser printer. That's what they cost then; today you can get a good one for less than $300. I needed a good quality printer for my editing business.

This period is when my faith in the goodness of the Universe helped me through. On one level, I was scared and worried, but underneath, on a basic level, I knew that I had nothing to worry about, that everything was being taken care of. I've always had this deep-down knowledge that the Universe is taking care of me, and everything will work out okay. Without that grounding, this time would have been terrifying. I was in my late fifties and always had to push away the image of becoming a bag lady. I heard from other single women about my age that they all had this fear on some level. But even at the lowest times, I never once regretted leaving George. I was better off poor and free. Somehow I made it through another year.

Jim and I had been together for almost two years. I have fond memories of that time, trips we took, events we attended, our nights together. It had been good for both of us, but the relationship was waning, and we were seeing each other less often. It ended suddenly when I discovered that he was seeing someone else. I reacted very badly, I'm sorry to say, and made a terrible scene. I'm too embarrassed to recount it here. I was surprised at how upset I was. I knew we would not be together long term so it was not unexpected, but for some reason it hit me really hard.

I realized just how upset I was the next day. One of my regular freelance jobs was for ASHA, an association for audiologists and speech therapists, working onsite. They had an editing department with four editors and published several publications. That day I was in a cubicle editing an article for the house magazine, when Barbara, the editing manager, approached my desk.

"Maya, would you be interested in working full time here on the staff?" she asked.

"What do you mean?"

"Well, we just hired an editor who was supposed to start today and she decided this morning not to take it. We really need someone in that slot right away. Do you want it?"

I thought about a nanosecond, and said, "Sure!"

"We know your work, since you've been freelancing for us, but we still need to do an interview. Come in my office and let's talk."

Jim and I had broken up the night before and I was still hurting, and as soon as I sat down in Barbara's office I burst into tears. She waited for me to calm down, and started the interview. I started crying again. Barbara was a tough little woman from Brooklyn, with an abrupt manner. She waited again, and I blurted out, "I just broke up with my boyfriend."

"Oh," she replied. "I know how that is. Men are such scumbags. Go back and get to work. You're hired."

That job was my salvation, not only economically but emotionally. I was a wreck. The stress of trying to make it freelancing had affected me more than I knew. With this job, the regular hours and a regular paycheck gave me the stability I needed to get myself back together.

However, I soon realized that the pay, while more than I made free-lancing, was not quite enough to live on, so I took on extra jobs when I could get them. Some of the staff at ASHA had personal work they wanted edited, and I still had a network that sent me occasional jobs.

Wondering how I could get more money, I remembered how I had brought in extra money altering soldiers' uniforms long ago when George was in the army in Alabama, and it occurred to me that I could develop a sewing business now. The ASHA staff provided the perfect opportunity; I could alter clothes for my coworkers. Most of the staff were women, young professionals who had neither time nor skill to alter or repair their own clothes. They all knew me as an editor, so I put up a sign in the lunch room saying, "Let Me Edit Your Clothes!" and business came in quickly. I would meet a customer in the women's restroom where she would try on what she wanted altered, I would mark it up, take it home, do the sewing, bring it back to work, return it, and get paid. I made enough to buy my groceries, and it was gratifying to see women so happy to have their suits and dresses wearable again. One woman in particular was delighted. She had two expensive, lined wool business suits that she could no longer wear because she had lost forty pounds. I couldn't just take in the jackets enough to make them fit, so I redesigned them, taking out the extra material. She was very happy with the result.

One day I received a phone call from Sue Mehrtens, who had moved to Delaware.

"Maya, I'm setting up a session with something called the All Game. A man from Virginia is coming to facilitate it and we need a few more people. Would you like to come for it? You could stay overnight with me. Maybe you could get some others to come with you."

"Well, maybe. Tell me more."

Sue explained that the All Game was a board game designed to develop higher consciousness. It was facilitated by Vitae Bergman, a man who lived in the Virginia suburbs of Washington. It sounded interesting, and I recruited two other friends to drive up with me.

The game proved to be as interesting as it sounded. There were about ten of us around a big table, each taking turns throwing the dice to see how far we would move on a circle on the board. Each square on the board called for the player to draw a card, which gave directions of what to do next. The actions involved some aspect of spiritual growth. The game is hard to explain, but we all enjoyed it and learned from it.

Vitae and I kept in touch when we returned to our homes, and we became good friends. He was of medium height, a somewhat chubby man in his sixties, nearly bald, with a couple of degrees in medieval literature and a devilish sense of humor.

We soon discovered that we had a sad connection—his 19-year-old son had been killed in a car accident not long before. Vitae was still grieving, and the All Game helped. We bonded immediately, and stayed friends for many years.

Vitae was looking for someone to work with him facilitating All Games, and I volunteered to do it. We set up several games in my apartment, inviting my friends and some people he knew. We charged for each game, and ran several, but not many people wanted to continue. The game was designed to be experienced over a period of time, to allow growth development, but it required more time commitment than many people wanted to make.

Even though our effort was not successful long term, I will always be grateful to have Vitae as a friend. He was a spiritual mentor for me during this time when I was experimenting with different paths. His wife, Margot, was as interesting as Vitae, and I visited them several times years later on their farm in Virginia. They were both highly conscious people and probably deserve a whole chapter just for themselves, but this will have to do.

About this time, a friend introduced me to Gordon Davidson and Corrine McLaughlin. This couple taught classes on spirituality based on the Alice Bailey material, which in turn is based largely on Helene Blavatsky's writings and the Theosophical Society. It is sometimes referred to as "the perennial wisdom."

I was impressed with both Gordon and Corrine, with how grounded and sensible they were while also being deeply spiritual. In their classes I found a system of belief that answered many of my questions. It's odd that I have forgotten much of it now, considering how important it was to me at the time and for many years. The system is based on a spiritual hierarchy, with an entity something like God at the top, although the word God was never used. The hierarchy was so complicated that I never understood it all, but I got enough to be able to fit my own experiences into it. It is a philosophy, not a religion.

One of its basic tenets is that everything has electrical vibrations, creating consciousness, including apparently inert material like rocks. Rocks' vibrations are so slow that we can't detect them, but they are there. All evolution consists of increasing rates of vibrations, thereby increasing consciousness. Cyrus also could fit into this system, since neither he nor the Bailey material required nor excluded any particular religion.

The sessions with Cyrus and the classes with Gordon and Corinne opened me to new spiritual experiences, and consequently the Unitarian Church began to seem more and more intellectual and less and less meaningful. I had become extremely active in the church, being the chair of several committees, singing in the choir, and serving on the board of directors. The church gave the minister a Sunday off once a month and that Sunday the Worship Committee provided the morning worship service. I was the chair of that committee for a couple of years and loved helping to create services. I continued to create other ceremonies, including the New Year's Eve ceremony that I had conducted in Peoria. I had one highly successful Christmas party in my little apartment. I kept the door propped open, and people circulated in and out all evening. Several people stayed after midnight, sitting around in the living room chatting. I loved the intimacy.

Gradually, I stopped going to church. I was grateful to the Unitarians for providing a spiritual refuge and a social life for me for several years, but it just wasn't satisfying anymore.

It had been a long time since I had any of the paranormal, or intuitive, experiences that I used to have, but now that I was paying more attention to the spiritual, they began occurring again. I think I had been so focused on the material things for several years, with the Freeze movement and publishing *Beyond IBM*, that the spiritual just couldn't get through.

With both Christie and Gary living in the Chicago area, I made a point of flying out there at least once a year to see them. On one visit, in about 1992, on the return trip, I had to change planes once, and something happened to my ticket for the second leg of the trip. I think the person taking the tickets must have taken that ticket instead of my boarding pass at the first plane, but I'll never know. I handed what I thought was my ticket to the attendant at the counter to get my boarding pass, and she looked at it and said, "Where's your ticket?"

"Isn't that it?" I asked, puzzled.

"No. I need your ticket."

"I don't know what happened to it. I have my itinerary here, showing that I'm supposed to get on this plane."

"But I need your ticket," she insisted.

I didn't know what I could do. I didn't have the money for a replacement ticket. Silently, I said firmly, "God, you have to take care of this. I can't. *You* have to!"

And then I stood there quietly and waited. The clerk paused a moment, and then without a word, she reached into her pocket and took out a little brass key. Moving slowly, as if in a trance, she inserted the key into the lock in the drawer under the counter, pulled out a ticket, filled it out, and still without a word, handed it to me. I said, "Thank you," and hurried to the plane.

On another trip, I arrived back at BWI airport and took the shuttle bus to the parking lot. It was late, 11 o'clock or so, on a rainy, cold December night. The parking lot was huge, as big as several football fields. My little red Hyundai was the only car on the lot. The shuttle bus dropped me off and drove away. Glad to be on the last part of the trip, I tossed my suitcase into the back, inserted the key in the ignition, and turned it. Nothing. I tried again. Again nothing. The car wouldn't start. I didn't know what I could do. The shuttle wouldn't be back that night, and there was no place to walk to. Of course this was before cell phones.

As a result of my work with Cyrus and the courses with Gordon and Corinne, I had become more aware of the role of consciousness and its power. What some people call prayer I now called "focused consciousness." I had learned that focusing consciousness intentionally could affect the physical world. For example, the incident with the plane ticket may have been a case of God responding to my plea, or it may have been my consciousness affecting the clerk's consciousness, which may be the same thing. In any case, I focused my consciousness intensely on the car's engine, turned the key, and the engine started right up. Saying, "Thank you, thank you, thank you," I sped home.

This intensely focused consciousness served me well in another incident. I still don't know how to explain this one. It seems too impossible to be true, and I don't have a rational explanation except that somehow I was simply mistaken.

I was still living in the apartment in Silver Spring. One night I was headed to the gas station on the corner of a nearby intersection. I was driving out of the side entrance to the shopping mall on the corner to cross the street into the driveway to the gas station. I looked both ways, thought the way clear, and started across the street. But somehow I had not seen a car coming from the right, on the outside lane. I saw the car's headlights approaching fast, and it was obviously going to crash into the passenger side of my car in a few seconds. It was too late for me to stop to avoid a collision.

I yelled out loud, *"DON'T HIT ME!"*—a command, not a request, as intensely focused as I have ever been before or since—and the oncoming car did not hit me. I crossed the street into the driveway of the gas station, shaken but unhurt. I quickly looked back to see what happened to the other car, and it was gone.

The next day I went back there and saw that the driveway into the gas station was not directly across from the shopping center entrance, but was a few yards farther away. It was impossible for me to cross directly into it, and it was impossible for that oncoming car to avoid hitting me. It was only a few yards away when I saw its headlights. I like to think of this incident as what Carlos Castenada calls "stopping the world." I had been reading his books at the time.

I'm convinced that our thoughts are far more powerful than most of us realize. Thought creates the world, and thought changes it. We are co-creators with God. Since I think of "God" as "the primary creative force," my being a co-creator makes sense. I've been working with that concept ever since. I don't know what happened that night, but I like to believe that my intense concentration actually changed the physical world. I have never been in such a situation again, so haven't been able to test it in just that way.

I turned fifty-nine that year, and on my birthday on April 6, I answered the door to find a FedEx man holding a long, narrow box for me. I saw that it was from Christie in Chicago and couldn't imagine what it was. I was shocked to open it and find a huge bunch of long-stemmed red roses! I counted fifty-nine of them. I had never seen that many roses together before. I was delighted but then realized I didn't know what to do with them. They were slightly wilted, and I knew I had to get them into water right away. But how? They were too long to put in the sink and I had no vases big enough. So in desperation I dashed into the bathroom and plunged them into the toilet. But they couldn't stay there long, it was my only bathroom. I went to the maintenance man and got a 5-gallon paint bucket, filled it with water, wrapped a piece of fabric around it, and put the flowers in it in the living room. It was spectacular.

Maya with the 60 red roses Christie sent her
for her birthday.

I counted them again and realized there were actually 60 blossoms. I think Christie thought I was turning 60, which was a big enough occasion to warrant such extravagance. She was as poor as I was, so it really was a grand gesture. I loved it.

Through the classes with Gordon and Corinne, I met Margaret, a young woman who was a development director for a local nonprofit. She mentioned that she needed a cheaper place to live and was interested in sharing a house. Remembering my experience earlier with a group house, I suggested that we find another person and rent a house together.

Eventually, a friend of Margaret's connected us with Jeremy, a young man who needed a place to live, and we interviewed him. The friend recommended him as an intensely spiritual person, and we decided to include him in the house. In November of 1992, we found a four-bedroom house in Potomac, an upscale neighborhood near Silver Spring. The rent was high, but with three of us paying, it was doable. The house was on the eastern edge of Potomac, not in the western area with the huge mansions, but our address gave people the impression that we were rich, which we found very amusing.

Maya with friends Pam Dinkle (l) and Sarah Fahy (r), Silver Spring, Md., 1992.

The group house on Smoketree Road in Potomac, 1993.

Everything in the house started off well. We met for meditation sessions in the early morning, and I started a meditation/discussion group that met twice a month. Similar to the situation in Peoria, I was the oldest and had the highest-paying job (I was working for ASHA then), so I took the master bedroom with bath and paid the most rent. Margaret made a good income, but she was saving money for a particular reason and took

Vitae Bergman and Christie with baby Veronica on Vitae's sailboat on the Potomac River, 1992.

The housemates in Potomac: Margaret, Maya, and Jeremy, Christmas, 1993.

the smallest room with the lowest rent. Jeremy took the middle room, leaving one for guests. The basement was fully finished with carpeting, and we put my TV down there.

We didn't see a lot of Jeremy, as he liked to go hiking on weekends and spent his evenings in the basement with the TV, but eventually we noticed that he was smoking on the porch. We frowned, as he had told us he didn't smoke, but we didn't say anything. Then he began coming in later and later at night, and was acting strangely. One morning I noticed that the lamp on the table by the back door had been knocked over. The back door opened into the room that I used for my office, and Jeremy came in through that door at night. Gradually it dawned on us that Jeremy was coming home drunk.

We confronted him, and he admitted that he had been drinking heavily, but said he would stop. We let it go. His drinking was not causing any serious problems for us, and we didn't want to put him out. Our lives in the house settled into a comfortable rhythm.

31 My 60th Birthday

I turned sixty years old in April of 1993, and remembering the ceremony we held when I changed my name on my fiftieth birthday in Peoria, I decided to create another ceremony for my sixtieth. I sent out invitations, and about thirty people came.

The evening began with a social time while the guests gathered. When everyone was there, I called them together in the living room. We began with Paula Hirschoff reading an adaptation of the myth of Psyche, dealing just with Psyche's fourth task.

After the reading, we sang the chant "We All Come from the Goddess," and I then spoke to the group about the meaning of this birthday.

> "I want to say a bit about what it means to me to be entering my sixties.
>
> Looking back, it seems that my 50s was a time for gathering myself, for pulling my external life together. In these past ten years I have learned much about who I am and how to be in the world. Externally, my house is in order. I have finally grown up! It has taken me sixty years to get here, but I no longer have that little scared girl living deep inside me. I enjoyed her when she was jumping up and down, clapping her hands in glee, and I think I can still call on her for that childlike joy when I want to. But she isn't afraid any more.
>
> In my fifties I discovered something important and rather surprising. I discovered that I had to spend all those decades working through a lot of stuff, so I could get to the point that what I needed to learn I no longer needed to know.

Maya at her 60th birthday celebration in Potomac, 1993.

I needed to learn how to be angry and to express my anger, so I could learn not to need to be angry.

I needed to learn to be intimate, so I could learn not to need intimacy.

I needed to learn to grieve deeply, so I could reach that place where there is nothing to lose and therefore nothing to grieve.

I had to develop confidence in myself, so I could discover confidence in the Universe, which makes confidence in myself redundant.

I needed to learn who I am, so I could let go of the need to know who I am.

This next decade is the time for inner work, for solitude, for going within, for connecting with that inner self that some people call God. The external life is far less relevant now. I've done that.

On New Year's Eve, I asked the runes to tell me the outlook for me in 1993. The runes are small ceramic tiles marked with symbols drawn from Norse mythology, accompanied by a book that explains the meaning of the symbols. I drew the rune called Dagaz. This is what the *Book of Runes* says about Dagaz:

Here is the final rune belonging to the Cycle of Initiation. Drawing Dagaz marks a major shift or breakthrough in the process of self-change, a complete transformation in attitude. …

Because the timing is right, the outcome is assured, although not, at this point, predictable. Rely, therefore, on radical trust, even though the moment may call for you to leap, empty-handed, into the void.

That's what my sixties is all about—soul growth. The past couple of years I have been working on Psyche's fourth task. It's time now to make a total commitment to spiritual growth. It's time to learn, as Carlos Castaneda says, to "stop the world." Time to leap into the void. I'm grateful to you who have been my friends, who have helped to give me a base of love and acceptance from which to leap.

Blessed be."

When I finished, my friend Vitae led us in a guided meditation. We then adjourned to the basement, where Pam led us in an Angel Walk.

Our large basement was a comfortable, attractive space, with paneled walls and light blue carpeting. Pam asked the guests to line up in two rows, with the rows facing each other, and for me to stand at one end of the rows. She instructed me to close my eyes, and walk slowly between the rows. As I passed through, each person leaned in close to me and whispered in my ear something they wanted me to know, such as "you are loved," or "you are beautiful," or "walk in light," or "peace." It was an incredibly moving experience. With my eyes closed I couldn't know who said what, and the whispering seemed to come from everywhere and nowhere, as if it really were angels talking to me. When I finished the walk, I felt totally cared for and validated. I can still feel it, all these years later.

We then returned upstairs for food and conversation. A lovely, meaningful celebration.

That Christmas, I decided to visit friends in Virginia, about two hours away, and invited Pam to go with me. We had a good visit and dinner

Vitae and Margot Bergman at Maya's 60th birthday celebration.

Maya's 60th birthday in group house in Potomac.

with Vitae and his wife Margot, and as we were preparing to leave in the mid-afternoon, fluffy flakes of snow began drifting down.

"Think you'd better spend the night?" Vitae asked.

"Oh, it's just a light snow, we'll be all right," I said.

We set off about 2 o'clock for the easy drive home to the Maryland suburbs, but the farther north we went, the harder it snowed. About halfway home, we were in the midst of a blizzard. The roadway was completely covered in snow, hiding a sheet of ice. It was treacherous, but we were on an interstate highway, and there was no place to stop. Traffic was inching along and many cars were in the ditch along the way. We were in my car, but Pam was driving.

"Pam, you're going too fast. *Slow down!*" I said.

"Oh, it's okay, I can handle it," she replied, confidently.

Suddenly we saw that a car had stopped in the road right in front of us. Pam hit the brakes, but it was too late and we couldn't stop. We slid slightly sideways, and crashed hard into the right rear of the stopped car. We saw then that the driver had stopped to help push another car out of the ditch. What was he thinking! Not only was his wife sitting in the car but a little baby was in a car seat in the back. I couldn't believe this man had stopped right in traffic with his kid in the back. Fortunately, no one was hurt, and our car was drivable, so we maneuvered around them and drove on. But we were both shaken. My car was damaged, and I couldn't tell how badly.

The way was becoming more and more difficult. Finally a rest stop appeared, and Pam drove into the parking lot. We went into the women's restroom and considered what to do next. The restroom was warm and safe and we considered staying there for the night, hoping the road would be cleared by morning, but it was a pretty dismal place, and we didn't relish spending the night on the concrete floor.

We decided to push on. I took the wheel, and we proceeded very slowly toward home. When it got dark, it was even more difficult to tell where the road was, since everything was white in every direction. We lost count of the cars and trucks in the ditch. When we came to the exit for the Beltway, we saw that it was closed because the highway was impassable. There was nothing to do but to continue on into Washington and hope we could get to the road to my house in Potomac. But street after street was closed off. Eventually we realized that it would be impossible to get to my house that night. We could get to the road to Pam's place in Silver Spring, so we headed there, and arrived about 10 o'clock. I wrapped up in a blanket on her couch for the night, grateful for arriving safely.

In the morning we learned how bad the storm was. Streets everywhere were closed from the ice and snow, and it was noon before I could get home.

The insurance company totaled my car and gave me $3,000 for it. The claims adjuster looked only at the accident damage and couldn't see everything else that was wrong with it. It was a lemon when I bought it and was not worth $3,000. I took the money and bought another car.

That experience, like many in my life, was actually a blessing. No one was hurt, and I found a good used car that I could afford, a Toyota this time. I would have continued to deal with that broken-down Hyundai indefinitely if I had not been forced to get rid of it, and I could not have sold it for nearly what the insurance paid me. As usual, the Universe knew what was good for me.

Earlier in the fall, I decided I couldn't stand a staff job any longer, and quit my editing job at ASHA. It had been a good place for me until I got myself together, but it had become stifling, and I was ready to get back into the fray as a freelancer.

That fall my daughter Christie, having left her husband, needed a place to live temporarily and asked if she and Veronica could come stay with me. My housemates were not enthusiastic about having a toddler in the house, but they couldn't really refuse since we had room, so Christie arrived in October of 1994, just before Veronica turned three. I was now supporting all three of us on what freelance work I could find.

Fortunately, about that time a client referred his friend to me to edit a book. This friend, the senior partner in a huge law firm in Dallas, had been working on a book for a long time and wanted help in shaping the manuscript into a publishable book. This job, in addition to freelancing for a senior staff person at ASHA, was barely enough to support us all. Christie was going through a traumatic divorce and custody battle for Veronica, and we were all on edge.

Complicating the situation was our housemate Jeremy's continued drinking and obnoxious behavior. Eventually we told him he had to leave. When he left, Christie moved into his room, found a part-time job, and helped pay the rent.

While working at ASHA, I had met Don, a management consultant who had a contract with the organization to do some staff development, and we began dating. He was separated from his wife and was in the midst of a long, drawn-out divorce. Don had access to some personal development tools as part of his work, and he gave me one that measured a person's developmental level. I was surprised and puzzled when the result showed that I was at level seven, which was the "most highly developed," meaning my consciousness was on the global level. I thought it had to be a mistake, since I had no connection to anything global and had no idea how I ever would—not knowing how global my next work would be.

Christie had to fly back to Chicago for a custody hearing, leaving Veronica with me. There was a strong possibility that she could lose custody, and Veronica would have to go live with her father in Chicago, a frightening prospect. The hearing took place on Veronica's third birthday. On the day of the hearing, I was rocking Veronica to sleep in the house in Potomac, worried and scared about what was happening in the courtroom in Chicago, when it suddenly occurred to me, "Right now, right here, I'm fine." At that moment, nothing bad was happening to me or to my little granddaughter. I was able to be present in the moment, and I relaxed. The worry and fear disappeared.

Being able to do that has served me well in the years since then, whenever I'm tempted to get worried or stressed over what might happen. "Right now, right here, I'm fine" has become my mantra in stressful times. There has never been a time when that was not true, regardless of what possible disaster seemed imminent. Learning to stay in the present has helped me to develop a sense of equanimity ever since.

As a result of the hearing, not only was Christie granted custody, she was allowed to take Veronica out of state to live with me in Maryland. She had to take her back to Chicago and leave her to stay with her father one week a month, which was a serious financial hardship, but at least she kept full custody. Until she was five years old, this little girl had to be accompanied by an adult on every flight, which meant six plane tickets. Eventually the visits changed to holidays and summers, and once she turned five, she could fly unaccompanied, which she did, regularly, for fifteen years.

Christie found a part-time job, leaving Veronica home with me to take care of while I worked on my editing jobs. Veronica was an extremely insecure child and demanded constant attention, so I was continually struggling to find something for her to do, keeping toys at my feet for her to play with while I typed on the computer. Occasionally I had to take a conference call with a client, and I had to figure out how to keep her busy and quiet while I took the call. It was all very stressful. We soon found a

Granddaughter Veronica in the park in Potomac, 1994

preschool that we could barely afford a half-hour drive away, so my early morning was spent driving, and then in the early afternoon I had to pick her up, but at least I had a few hours of time to work uninterrupted.

The backyard of our house in Potomac was surrounded by a small grove of trees, with an open space that sloped toward the house. Sometimes when I looked out there, I saw a vision of a Native American man standing in the clearing, watching me. He was wearing a small feathered headdress and light-colored clothing. I couldn't see him clearly or for very long at a time, but I got a strong impression that this land was once his home, and for some reason he was lingering here. He was a friendly presence, and I welcomed him. I felt that we were being watched over and protected.

One day when we were sitting at the kitchen table, Veronica looked out the window and suddenly said, "Who's that?" I looked, and seeing no one, said, "I don't know." I didn't ask her what the person looked like. I wish I had, but she quickly turned her attention back to the room, and the moment passed.

Don and I continued to date for about a year. We decided to go to Baltimore one weekend, and when we were unpacking at the hotel, I saw him pull a flask out of his suitcase.

"Look at this," he said. "Isn't it beautiful? It was my father's." It *was* beautiful, sterling silver with intricate engraving, but I was more dismayed than impressed.

"Why did you pack that?" I asked, knowing it was full of liquor.

"Well, you never know when you might be someplace where you can't get a drink!" he replied, as if it should have been obvious.

When we went to dinner, he drank several vodkas on the rocks. As he drove us back to the hotel, he was swerving back and forth in our lane, narrowly missing other cars. I held my breath until we got safely back. At that point I realized I could no longer deny that he was an alcoholic. There had been indications all along, but it was easy to overlook them. I had made excuses, not wanting to recognize the signs.

I broke up with him soon after that, and felt more relieved than sad. Don was the last in a series of men in my life who had a problem with alcohol. I don't know why I was so often attracted to alcoholics. I do know that such men are often bright, interesting, and funny, and are often attracted to me. Life with an alcoholic can be exciting and unpredictable, and for a time that was what I wanted. Don cured me.

An unfortunate result of our breakup was that the meditation group that met in our house disbanded. Don had been part of the group, and I asked him to stop attending. The others in the group were uncomfortable with that, as they had no problem with him, and gradually they drifted away. I learned something about not trying to control a group to suit my own preferences. Another lesson.

32 Crozet Retreat

Having left the Unitarian church because it was too intellectual, I looked around for something else. Someone told me a about a spiritualist church in Washington, and I checked it out. It met in a small, nicely furnished building off MacArthur Boulevard. (I later learned it was only a few blocks from a house where my parents lived before I was born.) The church had two ministers, both gay men. I attended a winter solstice ceremony there that was the most moving I have ever witnessed. The younger of the two ministers, dressed in a flowing white robe, stood in front of a large table draped in white at the front of the sanctuary. He had placed many items on the table, such as candles, a bell, a goblet, and small bowls of incense. The table edges were covered in greenery. There were other items, like sprigs of holly and a small statue.

The minister intoned several long chants, waving his hands gracefully over the objects on the table. As I watched , I saw him change form, becoming someone else entirely, and the atmosphere became mysterious and other-worldly. Suddenly all the lights went out. We sat for some minutes in total darkness and silence. When the lights came back on, he lit the candles and gave a short homily about the light returning to the world. At that point he became himself again. I don't know how he managed to change like that. It was magical. It was one of those times when I realized that the world is sometimes not as we think it is, that this physical world can shift and change in strange ways. I don't know whether he actually changed or if he managed to influence me to see him differently, but either way, it impressed me so that I can still see him in my mind.

I took a class on intuition offered there. In one of the exercises, we were given sealed envelopes with something inside and were told to hold them and intuit what they contained. We took turns describing to the class what we thought was in our envelopes, and then opened them to see how accurate we were. I got the image of two tall dark objects side by side with another spiky kind of object off to one side. When I opened the envelope, I found a photo of two people standing next to each other, with a large pine tree beside them. It was very similar to what I had seen.

I noticed that of the twelve people in the class, nine were severely overweight. When I commented on it later to a friend, she told me that this is often the case with very spiritual people—they need the extra physical weight to keep them grounded. I don't know if that's true.

I attended that church for about a year during 1994 and 1995, and then decided it really didn't suit me. There was a bit too much spiritualism, and I stopped going. I was without a church community again, and wondered if I would ever find a church where I was comfortable.

However, this was a time of more spiritual exploration than I had ever done before. I read many books on meditation, and attended conferences and workshops on various aspects of prayer and healing. I took an eight-week energy healing class that met one evening a week. It was taught by Mietek Wirkus, a healer famous in Poland who spoke very little English. His wife's English was more fluent, and as Mietek gave us instructions, she translated.

I was disappointed that with all that teaching, I was never able to feel energy moving in anyone's body. At one point I felt it faintly when waving the back of my left hand down one person's back, but the sensation was fleeting and I couldn't repeat it. One evening, when we were standing in a circle and working on visualizing something, Mrs. Wietek stopped in front of me and said sternly, "Maya, *you think too much!*" She was right. I couldn't shut down my thinking, couldn't "empty my mind."

I also took Reiki classes, a healing method using energy transfer that was brought to the United States from Japan. It is administered by placing one's hands in certain ways on the client's body, and is based on the idea that an unseen life force energy flows through us and can be increased by the practitioner. I took both Reiki I and II, supposedly becoming a Reiki master, but I never felt like I really was. The second class was not well run and seemed like a waste of time and money. One of the attenders appeared to be mentally disturbed and continually disrupted the class.

I was disappointed that the teacher didn't stop the disruption. I thought about asking for my money back, but didn't.

Since then, I have been told that my energy is strong and healing, and others can see it and feel it even though I can't. I have learned to accept that the energy is there, whether I am aware of it or not, but I sometimes feel cheated, that I'm missing something important.

I also attended classes at the Shalem Institute for Spiritual Formation, located in Washington. I thought about taking the spiritual director course they offered, but it cost several thousand dollars and so was out of the question for me. But the courses I took exposed me to a more contemplative form of spirituality than I had encountered before. The Institute was directed by Tilden Edwards, an Episcopal priest, and had a loose connection with that church. It was a peaceful, nurturing place.

I had one experience there that was probably not directly connected with the Institute, but may have been. It still puzzles me.

One day I had gone to visit a friend, Donna, and while there I met her young housemate, Jill. I met her just long enough to be introduced, as she was on her way out. Later, when I attended an event at the Institute, I saw that Jill was there. We approached each other to say hello, and I heard a clear strong voice in my head saying, "She is a very sick woman."

Where did that come from? I was shocked, as Jill appeared to be perfectly healthy. We exchanged a few sentences, and then went our separate ways. A week or two later, Donna called me.

"Do you know anyone who is looking for a place to live?" she asked.

"Um, no, not off hand. Why?"

"Well, Jill's in the hospital and will be there a long time. I need to find someone to rent her room."

I learned that Jill had developed pneumonia, and Donna had taken her to the emergency room. Jill was admitted and after a few days was diagnosed with multiple personality disorder and was sent to the psychiatric ward for long-term treatment.

How did I know she was sick? I have no idea. I don't know where that voice came from. It has never happened like that again.

Without really intending to, I was moving in the direction of spiritual healing. My friend Pam, whom I've mentioned earlier, taught me a way to use the body's energy that has been helpful to me ever since. She showed me how to use muscle response testing, using my fingers. It's hard to describe in words. A person makes a circle with the thumb and middle finger of their left hand touching firmly and then take their right hand and make a circle with the thumb and middle finger, but with the circle inside the left hand. Then, while asking a yes or no question, you pull on the right hand fingers, trying to pull the left hand circle apart. If they come apart, the answer is no; if they stay locked together, the answer is yes. There's much more to it than that, but I can't explain it here. This sounds like magic and at first I didn't believe it was effective, but after using it for a while I discovered that it was amazingly accurate. Pam used it mostly for emotional issues, but I found it most helpful for medical questions.

Pam also told me about Perelandra and the Medical Assistance Program, or MAP. The Perelandra Center for Nature Research is a farm in Virginia, not far from Washington, a kind of small-scale Findhorn. The director, Michaelle Small Wright, established the center as a farm where she grows plants with the help of the nature devas. She actively asks the devas for help in planting and maintaining the gardens and prepares flower essences for healing. I visited there several times and bought a poster that shows one of the gardens with the caption "Only those who can see the Invisible can do the Impossible."

MAP is a method of meditation that invokes various spiritual entities for healing. It could be considered praying, except that it doesn't specify a God or gods. I used MAP, along with muscle response testing, as my main health program for all the years I didn't have insurance, and still use it in conjunction with allopathic medicine. I lost my medical insurance when I left ASHA in 1993, and this system became my way of learning what was going on with my health and what to do about it. I didn't get insurance again for several years, and seldom saw a doctor all that time. Experience with MAP helped me to develop an awareness of the invisible worlds and entities who are available and willing to help us.

Another step in my spiritual development at that time came out of a friendship with Sarah, a Catholic nun. She told me about a place for retreats in Crozet, Virginia, about an hour and a half away. A monastery occupied by cloistered nuns rather than monks, it had two log cabins on its grounds that they let people use for retreats, for free. It was intended primarily for priests and nuns, but was available for anyone. I arranged to go there for several retreats over the next couple of years.

I loved that place. The cabins were located at the end of a long gravel driveway off a winding county road in the foothills of the Blue Ridge Mountains, about 10 miles west of Charlottesville. The cabin where I usually stayed was a log cabin built in about 1862, to which the nuns had

The retreat cabin at Our Lady of the Angels monastery, Crozet, Virginia, 1993.

added a modern kitchen and bathroom. The original stone fireplace that had been the outdoor kitchen for the old cabin formed part of one wall of the new kitchen. I always imagined I could smell the remains of a fire where people cooked dinner more than a hundred years before. I often wondered if this might have been a slave cabin.

I wandered around in the woods one day and came upon an old graveyard that was overgrown with vines and bushes. The gravestones were deteriorating, and the writing on some was no longer legible, but I found one with a date of 1882 and the inscription "Faithful to the end." I wondered, faithful to what? Or whom? There were about a dozen small graves with just a small stone standing erect over each one, indicating a child's grave. So many children dying. It was a sad, poignant place.

The nuns at the monastery were cloistered, meaning they could have no contact with the public. Sr. Barbara, who made the arrangements for the cabins, was a petite woman with short grey hair and a sweet smile. I felt a strong connection with her, and was eager to get to know her.

One day I hiked through the woods to the big brick building and pulled the heavy wood door open. A sign said the place was open all the time and visitors were welcome to walk in. There was a little window over a counter in the hallway. I rang a bell that sat on the counter.

The pond at the cabin in Crozet.

The window slid up, and Sr. Barbara looked out at me, smiling.

"Can I help you?" she asked.

"I was wondering if you could spend a little time with me. I'd like to ask some questions and learn more about this place. I love the cabin I'm in!"

"Oh, we're not supposed to visit with the people retreating."

"That's a shame. I really would like to learn more about you and the monastery."

"Well……" she hesitated. "We *are* supposed to be available to anyone who asks for counseling… I suppose maybe….. The Mother Superior is away. I guess I could give you a few minutes. If you'll just take a seat over there I'll be right out." Smiling to herself, she closed the window.

I sat in the little foyer and waited. Sr. Barbara soon appeared carrying a tray with a teapot and two dainty cups. She was both eager and a bit shy. I got the impression that she felt she was getting away with being a naughty girl. We drank our tea and chatted for about half an hour. She had entered a Cistercian convent fifty years ago when she was eighteen and moved here to help open this monastery when it started. She was among the six women who came here several years ago and lived in the cabin I was staying in, but at that time it had no improvements, no kitchen or bathroom. They lived there while the present building was being constructed. I thought about how hard it must have been.

"Well, I had better get back to my duties," she said. "I have enjoyed visiting with you. I hope you have a rewarding retreat." And she gathered up the tray and walked away. I was honored that she shared that time with me. I left feeling that we both had benefitted from bending the rules.

The cabin was surrounded by forest. One day I walked out onto the back porch to look around, and out of the corner of my eye I saw a large brown bear ambling out of the woods into the cabin's clearing, followed closely by a good-sized cub. I saw the bear and the bear saw me at the same instant. We both jerked to a stop and stared at each other. She quickly swirled around, nudged her cub, and disappeared back into the woods. I don't know who was more surprised, mother bear or me.

When I checked out to go home, I turned in my key to Sr. Barbara at the little window in the monastery hallway. I told her about seeing the mother bear and her cub.

"Oh, how lovely," she exclaimed, clapping her hands. "She brought her baby down from the mountain to meet you!"

Well, that's one interpretation, I thought. *I like it.*

On two occasions I was able to stay for a week. I was alone there for the whole time and loved it. No visitors, no commitments, no phones—there was one telephone for emergencies that connected only to the monastery itself, half a mile away through the woods.

The most meaningful retreat there was the second time I stayed for a week. In deep meditation I was finally reconciled with my mother. She had died almost twenty years before, but I was able to connect with her on a soul level. I told her how sorry I was that I had mistreated her all those years and asked for her forgiveness. I had been so angry with her all my life, and I realized how unfair I had been and how unnecessary our estrangement was. It was not solely my fault, but I could have resolved it if I had only been able to own up to my own part in the gulf between us. It had taken me more than sixty years to resolve the hurt and anger, but I left there feeling at peace with Mother, and felt loved by her for the first time since I was a little girl.

As I was driving away, a bluebird swooped down in front of my car and flew a few feet in front of me all the way out to the main road before turning away.

33 *Perspectives*

Back in 1987, when I was working with Kate, I met Jacqui, the owner of an international chemical supply company. One day in December 1994, she called me. After the usual greeting, she said, "I have an editing job you might be interested in."

I was surprised, as I didn't think she had any need of editing. "Well, maybe. What is it?"

"I'm on the board of the World Business Academy, and we need an editor to put out our journal. Our editor quit, and we need someone right away to get out the next issue."

At that time my major freelance job was with a company that edited reports for government agencies, and the current job was a big one. I was committed to finishing it.

"I don't think I can do that, Jacqui. I don't have time now."

"Well… couldn't you farm out part of it?"

Remembering my friend Kathleen who was also a freelance editor and needed work, I replied, "I guess I could do that. Tell me more."

As a result of that phone call, I became the editor of *Perspectives on Business and Global Change* for the World Business Academy, the most satisfying and interesting job I've ever had.

Perspectives was a 96-page quarterly journal published by Berrett-Koehler in San Francisco, where the WBA offices were also. The WBA was created to further spirituality in business. Willis Harman, the president of the Institute of Noetic Sciences, was its co-founder and became my mentor.

The Willis Harman memorial issue of *Perspectives on Business and Global Change*, June 1997.

Since I was so new to both business and global issues, I had no idea how to get the articles to fill the journal. Fortunately, the previous editor had a stack of manuscripts waiting to be edited to fill the next issue. I recruited my editor friend Kathleen, and between us we did it all very quickly and put out an issue—late, but not by much.

I actually had a few articles left over, so I had a head start on the following issue due three months later. Willis knew so many people in many countries that he was able to find more articles for me. I would have been lost without his help for the first year or so. He would find something somewhere and send me a copy with a note "I think this might be good to use. What do you think?" I always agreed. He had amazing contacts with progressive businesspeople and read widely.

Since I was living in a Maryland suburb of Washington, my frequent communication with Willis in California had to be by telephone and email, and I quickly learned what an evolved person he was. He had the least ego of anyone I've ever known. He never pushed, never criticized, just gently suggested. With his store of knowledge and contacts, not to mention his many years of seniority in the organization, he could have simply said, "Here's a good article I want you to publish." But he never did. He always treated me as an equal.

The basic tenet of the World Business Academy was that the real business of business is to create a better world, not to make a profit. Making money is a byproduct, not the main goal. The articles were written by highly conscious people, some of them well known, such as Jean Houston, Margaret Wheatley, Peter Russell, Riane Eisler, David Korten, and even Vaclav Havel, president of the Czech Republic. I got to know many amazing people, mostly by phone or email, sometimes in person.

As the first year passed, people began to know me and sent me their articles themselves. Editing people who were already well published was a bit daunting, but they always treated me well. Probably the hardest part of the job was writing rejection letters. Some consultants sent me articles that were really just slightly disguised advertising for their companies, and I wouldn't publish them. With all the letters, I did my best to be kind while explaining that the article was not suitable, for whatever reason. Writing rejection letters may be as hard as receiving them.

Editing *Perspectives* stretched me. I was challenged to see the world from a global perspective, from a consciousness worldview. I began to see business not as a money-making endeavor, but as a way to incorporate higher consciousness into commerce. Corporate responsibility, stated as taking responsibility for the whole, was a watchword of the World Business Academy. The slogan on the front of the journal was "A Better World Through Business." I often remembered that personality test I took that said I had a global consciousness. I didn't at the time, but I was gradually acquiring one.

Getting a regular paycheck for *Perspectives* was helpful, but the pay was fairly low, and I still had to have other work. One of the WBA directors, a very well-to-do lawyer in Dallas, asked me to edit a book he was writing. Bill sent me a boxful of notes and pieces of manuscripts, and called to ask if I could make a book out of it.

"Umm….." I thought how I could say no tactfully. "It's interesting material. …."

"What do you think of its potential as a book?"

"Do you plan to work on it more?" I asked, tentatively. "I don't quite see how I could make a book out of it as it is."

"Well, I'm sorry you think so. I've worked hard on it and other people think it's great. Never mind!" he replied angrily, and hung up on me. I had no sooner put the phone down than it rang, and it was Bill calling back.

"I'm sorry," he said. "I shouldn't have reacted that way. Let's talk about it some more." He insisted he wanted me to work on the material, regardless of my evaluation. He was so nice about it I just couldn't refuse, and I relented. For months, we went back and forth with revisions, and he even paid for me to fly to Dallas to work on the final version. I did the best I could with it, but I don't think he ever published it. That job paid me enough to cover my bills for a year or so.

The journal job required some travel, including attending the annual meetings of the WBA. That year the meeting was held on Vancouver Island in British Columbia. On a sunny morning on my way to one meeting, I drove to Dulles Airport and approached the ticket counter.

The woman behind the counter asked, "Where's your passport?"

"Passport?" It hadn't occurred to me that Vancouver Island is in Canada. "Uh oh. It's at home, and I don't have time to go get it. I don't know what to do. I have to get on that plane!"

"Could someone bring it to you?" she asked. "Or could they fax it to you here?"

I used the airline phone to call Christie, hoping she was home. I was in luck! She answered the phone.

"Christie, go into my office and look in the third drawer in the file cabinet and get my passport." Fortunately, I had both a copy machine and a fax machine in my office. She opened the passport, made a copy, and faxed it to the number at the airline counter.

"Are you sure this copy is good enough?" I asked the clerk, nervously.

"It should be. It'll be fine getting out of the country, but customs in Canada will have to accept it to let you back in."

"Could there be a problem? Could they refuse to let me through?"

"Um …well, they could… but it'll probably be okay."

I decided probably had to be good enough, and boarded the plane.

Vancouver Island is a lush, beautiful place, and the annual meeting was excellent. I enjoyed a week of wonderful people and good food.

On the way home, I cautiously approached customs at the Canadian airport and laid my faxed passport copy onto the counter through the opening in the glass. The clerk barely looked at it, just stamped it, shoved it back to me, and waved me on. I don't think he even looked at me. Airplane security was different in 1995.

This trip coincided with one of granddaughter Veronica's visits with her father in Chicago, so Christie had arranged for me to get her there on my way home. Her father managed to find me at O'Hare Airport and handed her to me over a railing. She slept soundly all the way home. When we arrived at Dulles, we had to board the shuttle that takes passengers from the plane to the terminal. I couldn't wake her. I shook her and shook her and called her name, but she was so deeply asleep she wouldn't wake up. I had two suitcases to carry and couldn't manage to carry her too; she *had* to walk. The shuttle was about to pull away, and I was feeling desperate when a man leaned over and said, "Let me."

He picked her up gently and walked away with her, me struggling behind with the suitcases. By the time we got into the terminal, she was awake enough to walk to the car. I thanked my benefactor, and thought about Blanche DuBois always depending on the kindness of strangers.

Having a three- and then four-year-old in the house was delightful. I loved taking her to the park and watching her do her best to navigate the equipment that was designed for bigger kids. She was so proud of herself when she conquered something! She gradually gained confidence in herself and became more spontaneous. We often went to Glen Echo park on the edge of Washington. Our favorite ride was the very old, 52-horse carousel. At first Veronica was afraid of it and wouldn't get on it by herself, so I rode it with her, loving the excuse to ride it myself. Eventually she rode it alone, waving to me waiting at the railing every time her prancing horse came around. I remember those days fondly.

Editing *Perspectives* took most of my energy, but of course my personal life continued also. My son Gary and his wife had a baby, another boy, named Howard Raymond, after Gary's brother who died. They were living in Joliet, Illinois, and I didn't see them often. Howie was a "surprise baby," appearing twelve years after his brother Matt. By the time Howie was six, Matt had left home, so Howie grew up almost as an only child. I wish I had been able to see him more often in his childhood, but I couldn't afford the trip, and neither could his parents.

Even more personally, my health continued to be excellent, although I was beginning to get some pain in my right knee. It had bothered me for several years, but now at age sixty-three, it began to hurt enough to pay attention to. Having no health insurance, I didn't see a doctor, but tried whatever natural healing I could find. Acupuncture and chiropractic helped some, but I couldn't afford many treatments, and several painkilling supplements took the edge off. The pain was annoying, but tolerable. At the time I didn't suspect how painful it would become eventually.

In May of 1996 I attended the 45-year reunion of my class at Greenbelt High School, nearby in Maryland. I had attended a few of these reunions over the decades, and was surprised to discover as the years went by that my fellow students were not so bad after all. If I had been more secure, less self-centered, perhaps my high school years would not have been so awful. Or perhaps the other students had become more interesting people as they grew up, or I had become more tolerant. I have often wished I could go back and do high school over again.

At this time I met a woman who attended a school in Oklahoma called Sancta Sophia Seminary, and the more she talked about it, the more interested I became. She was working on a degree, meaning she read books and wrote papers at home but had to spend a certain amount of time on the campus in Tahlequah. Eventually she bought a house in the seminary community, moved there, and became one of their teachers. Meanwhile, I enrolled and started taking classes.

The curriculum was based on a combination of Christian, Buddhist, and Jewish teachings; the Christian part leaned strongly toward Roman Catholicism, the Jewish part consisted of classes on the Kabbalah, and the Buddhist part appeared mostly in some lovely statues of the Buddha. There was no actual religious tradition promoted at all, which was part of its attraction for me.

The teachings were based mostly on the writings of Alice Bailey. She developed her ideas largely on the work of the mystic Helena Blavatsky, who co-founded the Theosophical Society in the late 1800s. Bailey's works were written in the first half of the twentieth century. She is credited with being one of the first to use the term "New Age."

I read some of the books, wrote a couple of papers, and attended some classes in Tahlequah, but it didn't take long for my enthusiasm to wane. The curriculum was very strict and they required that I start as a beginner, and I felt that I was being required to spend a couple of years on material I already knew. I also lost interest in the intricacies of their theory of spiritual hierarchy. The theory was elaborate, detailing the energy levels of the world, from stones to archangels. It all seemed a bit much, and unnecessary. I hung in for a couple of years and then dropped out.

However, I was deeply impressed with Carole Parrish, the founder and president of the seminary. She was an incredible teacher. I was mesmerized by her. When I took her classes, I was so intent on every word I was never able to take notes. I went back to take classes and workshops from her occasionally for many years.

One of my favorite things to do during this time, 1995 and 1996, was to attend the Taizé services at the National Cathedral in Washington. Taizé is a small community in the south of France where during WW II, a monk, Brother Roger, established a place for people from many countries and faiths to gather and be safe and worship together. Gradually many people came there, especially young people. During the war they were forced to leave for a couple of years, but returned in 1944. The worship activities included chanting, and that part has been adopted in many places around the world.

In the Cathedral, about fifty people gathered in the crypt in the building's lowest level, a kind of subbasement. It was enclosed completely in grey stone—the floors, the walls, the ceiling. After a brief Bible reading, we would sing simple Gregorian-type chants, over and over and over. The sound of all those voices reverberating in that space, singing the same few lines over and over for five or ten minutes, was amazing. The chanting resulted in an altered state of consciousness and a melding of the individuals into a seamless whole. I joined the group two Sunday evenings a month for several years. I loved it, and miss it still.

One Sunday when I was taking care of Veronica, I didn't want to miss Taizé so decided to take her with me. I thought it might be her only chance to experience it. She sat beside me very still while we sang, but I didn't want to expect too much of her so we left early. As we crept out silently, she held my hand and whispered sweetly, "That was nice." I wonder if she remembers it after all these years. She was four years old.

34 Willis

In early May of 1996, Christie moved out of our house on Smoketree Road into a duplex with a friend her own age. The friend, Michelle, also had a four-year-old daughter, and it seemed like a good place for them. That left just Margaret and me in the house, and Margaret was spending most of her time at her boyfriend's place. We looked for another housemate, but couldn't find anyone suitable.

We went to visit with one woman who answered our ad in the newspaper, and during our conversation, I mentioned the advantages of living with other people and having access to more resources, like their books.

She shouted immediately, "Don't you *touch* my books! If you touch my books, *I'll kill you!*"

We left as soon as we could.

We didn't find another housemate, so Margaret and I were splitting the $1,400 a month rent, and then Margaret and Kevin decided to get married, and I would be the only one left in the house. I soon found an apartment in a complex nearby in Rockville called The Forest, but I couldn't get in until a month after Margaret left, so I paid one month's rent by myself, a considerable hardship. I moved in July 1996.

Surrounded by an actual forest, this light, spacious, two-bedroom apartment is one of my favorite places I've ever lived. I slept in the smaller bedroom and used the larger one as my office. This room was unusually large and included a nook where I put a twin bed, making it a guest room as well. Every window looked out at nothing but trees. The walk from the parking lot took me over a wooden bridge that spanned a small creek. It was a lovely place.

Unfortunately, however, I really couldn't afford it. The rent was $1,015 a month, plus utilities—more than half my income. At this point I began putting more expenses on credit cards than I should have, but I didn't see any alternative. My income didn't increase as much as I expected it to. I fell into the trap of thinking I wasn't really spending money when it wasn't cash, and the balance on two credit cards kept mounting.

For a while it was great. I saw Christie and Veronica often, sometimes having Veronica stay overnight with me. Christie was working for a non-profit and was dating a young man where she worked. My work with *Perspectives* continued to be fun and rewarding.

That summer, Willis Harman and I came up with the idea for a book, an anthology of articles from the journal. Willis pitched the concept to Berrett-Koehler, the journal's publisher, and got approval. Together we went back through several year's issues and selected the articles we thought were the best. Then we sorted them into sections, and wrote text to introduce each section. Willis wrote most of the interstitial material; I edited it and made revisions, and then we combined our ideas. It was wonderfully collaborative and fun.

We eventually had 278 pages in six sections, including an introduction and a conclusion, with the title *The New Business of Business: Sharing Responsibility for a Positive Global Future*. The sections had titles such as A Call for Systemic Change; Understanding Our Changing World; The Challenge of Long-Term Sustainability; and Discovering the Spiritual Dimension of Business. It was my job to put it all together, to get author permissions, assemble the sections, and so on. There was no extra pay for this, but I enjoyed doing it anyway. Willis and I would share the royalties.

Most of the book was finished except for one of the texts we were writing, when one Saturday morning I got a call. It was Charlene, Willis's wife.

"I'm sorry to tell you this, but Willis insisted I call you before anybody else. We just got back from the doctor. Willis was diagnosed with brain cancer. He's sorry he can't finish the book with you."

I was shocked. Willis was seventy-eight, but he was so vital and vigorous, I couldn't imagine him sick. When he was in Washington for a conference earlier that year, I walked with him to a restaurant for dinner and I could barely keep up with him. Now he was terminally ill. I would miss him terribly.

And what about our book? I would have to finish it by myself.

I set about writing the last material. I knew what it needed to say, so it wasn't too hard, but I was nervous about it. I called Willis's office to ask

The New Business of Business, edited by Willis Harman and Maya Porter, 1997.

him about what I was writing, but his secretary wouldn't put me through. "He isn't taking any calls," she said, emphatically.

The next day Willis called me, and we discussed the book.

"Violet won't let me take any calls, but I can make them, so I'll check in with you every few days to see how you're doing," he assured me. "She's being very protective, but she can't keep me from calling out!"

His cancer progressed rapidly. By the time I finished writing the text, he was having difficulty talking. One day when he called, he could barely speak. He would start a sentence, and then would pause for a long time between words. He could think clearly and knew what he wanted to say, but he couldn't find the right words. After a few minutes of this, I said, "This must be so frustrating for you."

"Oh, no," he replied. "It's *fascinating!*" For many years he had been dedicated to exploring consciousness, and now he was his own laboratory.

That was our last phone call. It was also the most meaningful. Those long pauses communicated more than words could. I felt more connected to him, closer to him, than I ever had. Sometimes words get in the way.

Willis died on January 30, 1997. The memorial service, held in Grace Cathedral in San Francisco, was attended by hundreds of people from around the world. I wasn't able to go, but later received an audio recording of the service. He was eulogized by some well-known people (whose names I can't remember now), from not only business but science and religion. Afterward, his young grandchild was heard to say, somewhat awestruck, "I didn't know he was so important. I thought he was just Grandpa."

In the next *Perspectives* issue, I printed three dreams that Willis had written for another publication. I'm including one here, because it speaks to me as well as it did to Willis.

Willis Harman, 1918–1997.

"In this dream I am in a solo space ship which has somehow become a derelict, destined to travel around the Earth for centuries. There is no way to deflect its orbit and manage a return to Earth. It is clear that I have two choices: I can stay alive as long as possible, eventually run out of air, food, and water, and die a slow death, or I can open the hatch and let the remaining air rush out, the cold come in, and have it all over in seconds. It is an agonizing decision, but I finally decide on the latter. I open the hatch and feel the air rushing past, and immediately find myself in a space that is not cold and black, but wonderfully illuminated and somehow "loving." I seem to be everywhere in the space, but nowhere in particular. I had never given the idea of heaven much thought, but this seems to fit. I feel intensely alive, supported in every sense, and totally content to stay here forever."

I finished the book, and it came out in late 1997. I think Willis would have been pleased.

The next issue of *Perspectives* was a memorial issue for Willis. I asked several people to write articles especially for that issue, including Harlan Cleveland, a friend of Willis'. I had published Harlan before, and was always a bit intimidated by him. He was seventy-nine years old at the time, and had a CV as long as my arm. Among many other positions, he had been an ambassador, a university president, editor of a national journal, and author of fourteen books. Who was I to be editing him?

When I asked him for an article, he said yes, he had something already written that he could send me. But when he sent it, I was dismayed. It wasn't good enough. The writing was okay, but it didn't fit this issue of the journal as a memorial for Willis. What was I going to do? I couldn't see myself calling Harlan and telling him I couldn't print his article. I stewed over it for a couple of days, and finally decided that my integrity as an editor was at stake. I had to tell him.

So I called him. After the usual greetings, I said, "Harlan, I'm not sure how to tell you this, but I don't think I can use the piece you sent me. It doesn't quite fit this issue. I'm sorry."

"Well. (long pause) … You're the editor, and that's your job…. I'll see if I can find something else. Give me a few days."

I should have known he would be gracious about it. I didn't know him at all at that time, but later I got to know him and his wife pretty

Maya's author photo in the New Business book, 1997.

well, spending time in their house in Virginia, and learned what a special person he was.

When he called me back, he said he found something he thought was appropriate, but it was much too long. "You'll have to shorten it," he said.

He was right. The piece was what I needed, but I had to shorten it by at least a third, which I set about doing. When it was done, I called him.

"I did it, and I want to send it to you for your approval."

"Fine. I'll be in New York for meetings. You can fax it to my hotel. I'll read it this evening and call you back."

That evening, I sat nervously waiting for the phone to ring. When he called, I grabbed the phone and waited for his verdict.

"I've read what you did," he said. Long pause. "You did a *masterful* job! It's seamless. I can't tell where you cut it. I couldn't have done that myself!"

What a relief! After that, I was much more confident of my judgment when dealing with difficult editorial decisions. I continued to edit *Perspectives* for six years, and I always missed Willis.

35 North Carolina Mountains

In the fall of 1996, my daughter Christie woke up one morning and said to herself, "I'm Grace!" And that was that; her name from then on was Grace. It wasn't easy for me to make the switch. I could hardly complain, since I had also changed my name, but I had chosen "Christina" for her and didn't want to give it up. It took several years for me to get comfortable calling her by her new name. I still occasionally slip.

Then in the spring of 1997, she flew to Hawaii to attend a conference. While there, she met John, who was in the Coast Guard, and started a relationship with him. She stayed in Hawaii an extra couple of weeks, and when she returned, she announced she was moving there to live with him. It was a whirlwind move; in two weeks she and Veronica were gone.

I missed them terribly. Hawaii is far away, and none of us had money for visits. At that time even long-distance phone calls were expensive, so our communication was mostly by email, which meant not much real connection with Veronica, as she was too young to use the computer. I felt isolated from them. It seemed like the lights had gone out.

I soon realized two things: There was no longer any reason for me to stay in the Washington area, and I couldn't afford to stay anyway. I was far in debt on those two credit cards, and it got worse every month. I felt such an emptiness with both daughter and granddaughter gone that it was easy to think of moving.

Sarah, the friend who had told me about the retreat cabin in Virginia, had moved with her friend Cita to North Carolina a couple of years before, and I had visited them there several times. She lived near a tiny town called Burnsville in the mountains thirty miles north of Asheville. She had used an inheritance to buy several houses there. I liked the area, and when she told me that one of her houses was going to be empty soon and I could rent it, I took the chance to move.

I drove to North Carolina and rented the house, and in October I packed up everything and moved to Burnsville. Actually, it was eight miles from Burnsville, in a little wide spot in the road called Bald Creek. Sarah lived in Celo, an area twenty miles away beyond Burnsville over twisting mountain roads.

The house was a 75-year-old wood frame bungalow on a mountainside, with a view out over a valley toward the west. Bald Creek consisted of about ten houses, a stone school, and a white Methodist church with a steeple. One street wound through it in a square, and my house was on the upper side of the square on what was one of the few level spots in the entire mountainous county.

As long as I had an Internet connection and FedEx, I could edit *Perspectives* from anywhere, so I continued in the job. Consequently, I was earning the same income but had a much lower cost of living and was able to start paying off those credit cards. For example, my rent went from $1,015 down to $365 a month. Food was cheaper, as well as utilities, and I was able to put at least $500 a month toward debt. In two years I was nearly debt free, and have stayed that way since. I learned my lesson.

I soon decided it was time to get a cat to keep me company. I went to the local shelter to find a kitten, but while I was looking at the many cats in the big room, one black, long-haired adult cat wandered over to me and pushed her head up against my hand, as if to say, "Well, here I am. Take me home." I did. I named her Toby; I've named all my cats Toby. This was Toby II. She was a magnificent animal, and she kept me company for ten years.

That Christmas was bleak. I had lived there only a couple of months and knew almost no one. My friends Sarah and Cita left town for the holidays, so I was more alone than I had ever been. To make it even worse, neither of the kids called me on Christmas day. I stewed over that for days until I thought, why didn't I call them? The phone works both ways! I soon got over my pity party and vowed never again to let my emotional well-being depend on someone else making a phone call.

The house had a huge area in the back that had been used by a neighboring farmer for at least fifty years. Sarah, my landlord, gave me permission to put in a garden there. I had never lived where I could have a

Maya's house in Bald Creek, North Carolina.

A side view of the house in Bald Creek, with Maya's huge garden behind it.

garden and was excited at the possibility, but I had no idea what to do. My father always planted a big garden next to our house, but I had not paid any attention to how he did it. I just enjoyed tomatoes and fresh corn in midsummer.

I knew I wanted it to be organic. By spring I had I made friends with the Websters, a couple who lived on the mountain across the valley who were such avid gardeners that they raised almost all their own food. They bought a few necessities like salt and coffee, but otherwise they grew what they ate. They were so committed to eating organic that they even bought organic wheat and had it ground into flour at a mill somewhere. They heated their house with a wood stove, and had gravity-fed water piped in from a spring uphill from the house. They were excited at the prospect of a convert, and were eager to help me.

Martin Webster, a short, wiry man with a bushy black beard, was an environmentalist and a sculptor. His wife, Barbara, was also slim with graying hair pulled back in a pony tail. I soon learned that she had two graduate degrees, one in music and another in math. She also crafted internationally award-wining quilts, which she sold for thousands of dollars, and was an excellent graphic designer. I hired her to do the composition of *Perspectives*, so I could send a disc for each issue to Berrett-Koehler, the publisher, ready to print. B-K paid her directly, as a contractor, like me. It was an excellent arrangement for all of us.

In February, I started planning my garden. The space was about 40 by 60 feet, on slightly sloped ground, in full sun—ideal for growing almost anything With a plot that big, I couldn't just plant things willy-nilly. On a big piece of graph paper, I figured out the dimensions to scale, and began sketching in sections for different plants. I needed to be able to reach everything, and with my short arms, that meant no more than two feet in from every side. I needed paths to get to all the sections and to bring in materials. It was fun figuring it all out. I made plans for tomatoes, beans, squash, zucchini, peas, cucumbers (and I don't even like cucumbers), a 40x20 patch for sweet corn, and several herbs. The idea of potatoes came later.

The peas went in first, being an early crop. They went into the raised bed that Martin built for me. He also bought the soil amendments I needed and delivered them to me. He showed me everything I needed to know to grow my own food. I got so much produce out of that garden I couldn't give it all away.

My neighbor Pauline kept warning me that I wouldn't have any corn to eat, as the deer and raccoons would get it all first. I was willing to share, and put out thoughts to the animals that they could have the ends of the rows, but to leave the rest for me—and that's just what happened. I could see where ears had been stripped off some rows at the ends, but there was plenty more for me.

I planted several rows of potatoes, and discovered when I dug them up that it's a hard, tedious job to get them clean. Dirt clung to the potatoes so tightly that scrubbing them with a stiff brush in a tub of water removed only part of it. I would never be able to eat those potato skins! I cleaned a bushel basket of potatoes and stored them in the basement, but unfortunately did not realize that they were too close to the furnace, and they all spoiled. But I canned many pints of tomatoes and tomato juice to enjoy all winter.

I spent a lot of evenings with my 86-year-old neighbor, Pauline, who lived in another white frame house across the street. She was a short, stocky woman, who got around with a walker. She had a big freezer in

Pauline Hensley, Maya's 86-year-old neighbor across the street.

Toby II, Maya's beloved cat for 10 years.

her basement where she kept enough food so she didn't have to shop often. However, her basement was basically a hole in the ground and the "stairway" down to it was not much more than a ladder. I don't know how she managed to get up and down, especially carrying food back up to the kitchen. Many years ago her husband had a stroke and spent years in a nursing home in Asheville. She never learned to drive, so she took the bus to see him 30 miles each way every day for seven years until he died.

I admired her for her independence and sense of humor. She had been a high school home ec teacher for 30 years, and knew about sewing and gardening. She must have been a popular teacher, because after all the years since she retired, former students still came to visit her when they were in town. At eighty-six, she knew all the old ways of doing things and was eager to teach me. I still use some recipes she gave me.

Often on a warm evening I would walk across the road to her house and we would sit in the big white rocking chairs on her porch and watch the sunset and chat. We were both lonely, and we kept each other company. For an elderly "mountain woman," she was surprisingly open minded and liked to hear about my life and work. She still had some of the old attitudes, however. One day when she was telling me about a young woman in the neighborhood who often drove her into town, she leaned over to me and whispered, as if it were a dark secret, "She has the *sugar*, you know." That was her way of saying the neighbor had diabetes.

As always, I wanted a church community, and started attending the little Methodist church around the corner in Bald Creek. Its minister was a woman, and she preached excellent sermons. The people were friendly enough and I was fairly comfortable there for a while, but one Sunday we sang two hymns about being saved by the blood of the lamb, and I couldn't stand it. I didn't go back.

I heard about a spiritualist church in Asheville and went there a few times, but it was thirty miles away and I felt a little uncomfortable with them, although I couldn't place just why, until the second Sunday I was there. They always ended the service with a message session, when intuitives, or psychics, would stand in the front and tell people what they saw or heard about them. On that Sunday, one of the psychics said to a woman in the room, "Martha, go home and tell your mother to see her doctor. I see a mass in her lung." Martha ran from the room in tears.

I was shocked. That was totally unethical! No real psychic would ever give such a message, especially in public. If he in fact saw such a mass, he at most should have said that Martha should talk to him later, or simply that her mother may have a health problem. I knew then that this group was not authentic, and I didn't go back.

Eventually I remembered that Sarah had mentioned there were Quakers in Celo, and I thought, well, why not check them out too. The "church" consisted of about fifteen people who met in a converted goat barn in the midst of a forest. It was twenty miles away, over two-lane roads that twisted and turned over the mountains.

That first February Sunday I walked into the little frame building and saw two rows of dark wooden church pews facing each other across a concrete floor. At one end was a huge stone fireplace, with a roaring fire. At the other end was an iron stove, also with a fire burning. The room was warm and cozy.

I had arrived early, and the only other people there were an elderly couple, who greeted me graciously but quietly. Other people soon trickled in, and I noticed that people smiled and nodded at each other, but there was no conversation. They all sat down silently and settled in.

I saw hymn books on the pews, and at that point the elderly woman announced a song number. Someone started singing, and we all joined in. We sang several songs, some of which I knew, and then with no signal from anyone, everyone put down their books and closed their eyes. No one seemed to be in charge. I knew there would be a period of silence, and having been a meditator for years, I was content to sit and wait.

After about half an hour, however, I was getting restless. I glanced at my watch and wondered how much longer this would go on. After another half hour, suddenly everyone was shaking hands with the person beside them. I wondered how they knew when to do that, but no one seemed surprised. One man started asking for announcements, and I realized the service was over. *Well, that was strange!*

As we were putting on our coats, people greeted me and introduced themselves. I was invited to join them for bread and soup in another little building next door. I did, and enjoyed myself enough to know that I would go back.

I made that trip around the mountain many times in the next few years. More than once I barely missed an oncoming car around a sharp bend, halfway in my lane. In the winter the roads were treacherous. I became fairly active in the Meeting (they didn't call it a church), but only what I could do on Sundays. It was just too far to go back during the week often.

Celo was a land grant community, established in the late 1940s, and most of the people in the Meeting lived there. They were back-to-the land folks, heating their homes with wood stoves and eating organic food from a huge community garden. The Friends, as they were called, were mostly professional people, many retired, who had come to live there to be as much off the grid as they could. Some succeeded in doing that, using solar power and water from a spring. There were many rustic little homes nestled in the woods here and there, including at least one straw bale house.

I fit right in with the Quakers. I gradually learned about what they believed and how they lived, and it didn't require any adaptation on my part. I had found my church. I discovered I had always been a Quaker and didn't know it. They didn't have a creed or a dogma, but followed what they called "the testimonies." Basically they believed in simplicity, equality, integrity, and peace, and I was fine with all of it. I also loved the silent worship. No one talked *at* me, no one told me to stand up or sit down or follow someone else's prayers. I was on my own.

Sometimes I almost wished someone *would* take me aside and tell me what I was supposed to be doing during the silence, but it never happened. It took me a long time to get comfortable with sitting quietly

Sarah Fahy and Cita Lamb, the friends in Maryland who moved to North Carolina. Maya rented the house in Bald Creek from Sarah.

for an hour, but eventually the time went quickly. As much as I liked the Meeting and the people, however, I didn't make any close friends, because I lived too far away to socialize except on Sunday.

Sitting in that silence an hour every Sunday, and being alone most of the rest of the time, gave me plenty of time to meditate and go deeper into my spiritual life. The teachings at the seminary provided a grounding I hadn't had before, even though I didn't buy all of their theories. Looking out my office window across the valley to the western mountains brought me a deep sense of peace. My confidence that the Universe was looking out for me was stronger than ever.

Remembering that my purpose in life is to raise consciousness on the planet, I felt good about my work. The articles in *Perspectives* were all about using spiritual principles in business, some more subtly than others, and with its worldwide audience, it surely was furthering my goal. And I was being paid for it! I was content with my life.

But one day I woke up with a strange feeling I couldn't at first identify. Something was missing, and suddenly I knew what it was—that presence I call the Universe was gone! I never really thought of its presence; it was always just there. Until it wasn't.

The Universe had abandoned me! It was the strangest thing—one day all was fine, and suddenly there was a huge emptiness where my spiritual ground had been. My usual confidence was replaced with a general, low-level fear, and I had no idea what brought it on or what to do about it. The best analogy I can think of is an old abandoned house around the corner. One day I decided to explore it, out of curiosity. But when I stepped on the porch, I realized the boards were old and decayed. I didn't know how rotten they were and if they would hold me. I stepped carefully on each board, testing it first to see how strong it was. That's how I got through the next few days—gingerly taking each step as if the ground might give way under me, as if it might be undependable.

I barely managed to get through each day, with a sense of dread that I was without support, without anything or anyone protecting me. "Abandoned" is not a strong enough word, but I can't think of a better one. "Deserted," maybe.

Then one morning three days later I woke up and the Universe was back! Just like that, the ground was solid under my feet again.

Whew! What was that all about? I wondered. Later I told my friend Peggy about it and she replied, "Oh, Maya, don't you know? Many people live like that all the time."

I was shocked. How do they stand it? I couldn't do it. I began to see how some people could kill themselves. All of my life I have had a strong feeling that I live in a benign world, that all is well, no matter how dire circumstances may seem at the time. I don't know where this faith comes from. It was not originally a religious belief, as I felt it long before I ever discovered any religion. I suppose it's just *grace,* and I don't need to know how or why. It's fundamental to my life and has only increased as I've gotten older.

That one intense experience of anxiety brought me a lasting appreciation of what the theologian Paul Tillich called "the ground of being." My ground of being had disappeared and then miraculously returned. It has never left me again.

36 Good Enough

In the summer of 1998, I drove from Bald Creek to Maryland to visit my brother and some friends in Washington. I had been thinking a lot about my mother and decided to visit her grave, but suddenly realized I didn't know where it was. I vaguely remembered traveling through neighboring suburbs on the day of her funeral twenty years earlier, but that was all. I asked my brother Frank where it was. He had never been back to her grave either, but he remembered the name of the cemetery. I found its address in the phone book.

When I arrived at the cemetery, I went to the office and learned the coordinates of Mother's burial place. The place is huge, and I had to drive to the location and search a while to find it. I saw many gravestones, some elaborate and some plain. But Mother's wasn't there! I went back to the office and asked again. Again I was given the same numbers, shown the place on the cemetery map, and assured that it was right there. Again I looked, and found nothing.

A third time I asked at the office, on the verge of tears, and finally someone explained that there was no gravestone, only a small metal plate nestled in the grass. So again I looked, and there it was—a plate with the section and row numbers, but no name. No one had ever put up a gravestone! I was stunned.

I needed to know why. I couldn't ask my father, as he had died in 1987, so I asked Frank why there was no grave marker. He said he didn't know, that he had never talked to anyone about it. Our father was an extremely thrifty and unsentimental man, so he probably considered a tombstone a waste of money. He was not buried there, as he had donated his body to a medical school.

I was upset, and insisted that Frank and I must put up a gravestone. But when I found out how much it would cost, I was heartsick. I couldn't afford even half the cost. Frank thought of a solution—we could donate some money for a plaque with both of our parents' names on a memorial wall at his church. More people would see that than would ever see a gravestone in the cemetery, and it wouldn't cost much. That seemed like a good idea, so I agreed.

But I wasn't satisfied. I needed to do something to acknowledge my reconciliation with Mother on that retreat several years earlier. It occurred to me that I needed to have a ceremony by myself at her graveside.

I drove to a florist where I bought a big bouquet of yellow roses, my favorite flower. I don't know if Mother had a favorite flower, so chose my own. I surprised myself by dissolving into tears during the whole transaction, while the clerk pretended not to notice. I asked her to tie up the bouquet with raffia instead of the usual garish satin ribbon, and drove to the cemetery in the late afternoon, hoping no one else would be there. I was in luck; the place was deserted. It was a warm but cloudy October day.

The cemetery was like a park, with rows of trees marking the boundaries, lending a sense of privacy. Grateful to be alone, I sat down on the grass by Mother's grave and talked to her. I told her I loved her, and knew that she loved me, although she had never told me so. After a while, I lay the flowers down on her grave. Just as I did so, the clouds suddenly parted and the sun burst through brightly, and then the clouds closed again. I felt heard, and knew that all was well. I said goodbye, and walked away, leaving the flowers there.

In early 1999, through the World Business Academy, I learned about a project called Peace Building for the 21st Century, usually called PB21. It was a gathering of about twenty people who met for a weekend every three months at the Fetzer Institute in Kalamazoo, Michigan. Composed of a cross-section of people from several countries, the group explored ways to create peace in the coming century. I asked if I could join, and when the facilitator learned that I had worked with Willis Harman, she said yes immediately. Willis was one of the co-founders of the group.

One of the members was a high-level government official in Mexico— I forget his title, but it was something like our Secretary of the Interior—

The plaques for Than and Frankie Porter at the memorial walk, Colesville Presbyterian Church, Silver Spring, Maryland. Placed on August 2, 1998.

and that spring, he invited us to hold our next meeting in Mexico, staying for a week, at his expense. He was obviously wealthy, and I don't know whether he paid for it out of his pocket or if his government paid, but we were treated very well. Once we arrived in Mexico City, everything was paid for.

I was nervous about going, because I had never traveled abroad and do not speak Spanish, and I didn't know how I would manage to get through the airport in Mexico City. But I had to change planes in Dallas, and as I got in line to get my boarding pass, I saw I was standing behind one of the women from PB21!

"Hi, Sara, I'm glad to see someone I know. Maybe between us we can find our way through the Mexico City airport."

"Oh, that's no problem," she replied. "I speak Spanish. Just stick with me." As usually happens in my life, what I needed had appeared when I needed it.

When we landed I followed her through customs. We were met at the airport by our Mexican hosts and driven to a restaurant with the rest of the group. I didn't need to speak the language at all.

It was a fantastic week. The first two days were at a Club Med resort, and from there we were taken in a couple of vans to another resort that was our headquarters the rest of the week. We had the whole place to ourselves, with a staff to serve just us. Every day we piled into the vans and were driven to some place our host wanted us to see. One day we saw the thousands of monarch butterflies that were swarming on the trees, another day we went to Teotihuacan, a pre-Aztec archeological site near Mexico City, another day we visited a cooperative enterprise run by *campesinos*, or peasants, where they grew acres of flowers to sell in the United States.

I don't remember what was going on nationally in Mexico in the spring of 1999, and was pretty oblivious to larger issues at that time anyway. On the first day we were in Mexico City, as we returned to the hotel from dinner, Sharif, a young black man, remarked about the occasional soldier standing on street corners with guns.

"Really? I didn't see them," I replied.

"If you were a black man, you would see them," he said, with a wry grin.

The same thing happened at the resort later. Sharif commented on the security patrol stationed in the woods surrounding the site. I didn't see them either, but he did. Apparently there was also a van accompanying us as we drove around the countryside. It hadn't occurred to me that our host was important enough in his country to warrant constant security. I also realized how fortunate I am that I don't need to think about watching for soldiers with guns in the bushes.

The last day's lunch was the time for our host, the government minister, to meet with the significant people in our group whom he wanted to consult about some government business, which was apparently the point of the trip. I wasn't included at his table, so I don't know what the topic was. At the dinner on the last day at the resort, our host presented each of us with a hand-carved "fantastical creature," created by a local artist. Mine, which faintly resembles a purple unicorn, still sits on the bookcase in my living room.

We were all driven back to Mexico City to a hotel to spend our last night in the country. That night, we had dinner in a the hotel. The conversation turned to a discussion of our family backgrounds. Many of the other people's parents had been doctors, lawyers, university professors, and such. Suddenly one of the most distinguished men turned to me and said, "And how about you, Maya? What did your father do?"

I panicked. What could I say? My father was a garage mechanic and carpenter with a high school education. We were a working-class family. I stammered a bit, managed to deflect the question, and changed the subject. I was embarrassed that my father wasn't good enough.

As I lay in bed later that night, I felt ashamed, not of my father, but of myself. I had been embarrassed by who and what I was, where I had come from. I wished I could go back and say, "My father worked with his hands. He built the buildings where your fathers had their offices, and he repaired the cars your fathers drove. His hands got dirty every day, doing hard, honest work. All through the Depression, he was never without a job. He kept the five of us fed and housed and clothed."

My father was a rough man, but he modeled how to be kind, generous, faithful, and tolerant. I remembered how active he was in the community, holding many volunteer jobs. He would give anyone anything he had if they needed it. I never heard him swear or say anything malicious about anyone. He showed me how to be responsible, to enjoy productive work. He showed me integrity and authenticity. He never pretended to be anything he wasn't. And he was *good enough*, good enough for me to be proud of him. And I was sorry, so sorry, that I betrayed him. I vowed that night to never again feel apologetic about my roots. I am who I am, and my history is what it is. And it's *good enough*.

I look back on my time in North Carolina with nostalgia, but not all of it was good. My right knee had been bothering me for years, but now it became more than a bother; walking had become very painful. In addition, my back began to hurt. In 1998, my second year in Bald Creek, I turned sixty-five and was eligible for Medicare—finally, after five years, I had medical insurance! The first thing I did was get my knee examined. Medicare paid for an MRI, and the verdict was that I needed a replacement, but I was adamant about not having surgery, so I tried every natural healing method I could find. I had acupuncture, chiropractic, exercises, energy healing, and supplements. Insurance didn't pay for any of that, but did pay for a complicated brace that was molded to fit my leg. Nothing worked. It was hard to maintain the garden the second year, and I was getting more and more restricted in what I could do. I started walking with a cane.

I began to think that I needed to move to be near my kids, as it looked like I was going to need help, with so much pain from both my knee and my back. Remembering the snow and ice in the winters in Illinois, I didn't seriously think of moving there to be near Gary, so Grace was my only option. She and her family had left Hawaii and moved back to the mainland. In April 1998, Grace and John had a baby, a boy they named Luke, and the year before, John's 8-year-old daughter Simone from his previous marriage had come to live with them, so they were now a family of five. John had left the Coast Guard and they had moved to Arkansas, where John had grown up. Maybe Arkansas would be okay.

The clincher came one day when I was working at my computer. I was gazing out the office window over the valley when out of the blue it dawned on me that my grandchildren were growing up without me.

They don't even know who I am! Why am I doing this? I can live anywhere.

It was time to leave my little cottage in the mountains and start over in Arkansas.

PART 3

Coming Home

37 Arkansas

"Okay, Toby-girl, in you go," I said, as I pushed my fluffy black cat into the wire crate that filled up half of the back seat of the Subaru. "We have a long ride ahead of us."

We were on our way to Springdale, Arkansas. I wondered how much Toby would miss the fields and barns where she caught her daily mouse. She would have a huge fenced yard at the new house and a shed, but no barns. Toby complained loudly for a couple of hours and then settled down quietly for the rest of the two-day trip.

The movers had arrived and unloaded before us, and I busied myself with unpacking. I was relieved that Grace had found me a big three-bedroom ranch for a reasonable rent in a good neighborhood less than ten minutes from her house. Couldn't have been better.

I had been somewhat apprehensive about moving to Arkansas, considering its reputation as a haven for "redneck hillbillies," but I knew there was a Quaker meeting nearby.

It can't be too bad, if there are Quakers there," I thought. *"It'll be okay."*

I arrived the first week of May in 2000, and on the second Sunday I attended the Quaker meeting in Fayetteville. I found a cozy group of about eight people sitting in a circle in the chapel of a building next to the University of Arkansas campus. It was all wood and stone, with many floor-to-ceiling windows that looked out on trees, even though it was in the city. I immediately fell in love with that building.

The makeup of the meeting was similar to the one I had left in Celo, although smaller—mostly middle-aged, well-educated, liberal white

The house on Ellen Street, Springdale, Arkansas, 2000–2003.

folks. The silent worship was almost exactly like the one in Celo. Again, no one seemed to be in charge, but everything proceeded smoothly. *These people seem to be of one mind*, I thought, *like a flock of birds that swoop around with no leader. It's amazing.*

The people were warm and welcoming, so that I instantly felt at home. After Meeting we all went out for coffee. When we were leaving, I pulled out my wallet to pay for my coffee. "Put that away," one woman said. "Your money's no good here." At first I was puzzled, thinking, *Am I really in a foreign country?* but then she laughed and I understood she was paying for me. I had to get used to LaDeana's quirky sense of humor.

That summer my knee was hurting more than ever. I put in a garden only 20 feet square, but even that much was hard to manage. High doses of ibuprofen helped only a little. Finally, I went to my new doctor and asked him what else I could do.

"Well," he said, "you know you need a knee replacement."

I had been told that before, of course, but this time it clicked. The resistance of all those years melted away. *Yes, it's time.* I asked him for a referral, and he sent me to Dr. James Arnold, who set me up for surgery. Having finally made the decision, I was eager to get it done.

So I spent the middle of three hot weeks in August in the air conditioned hospital and rehab. The surgery went well, and in three weeks I was driving and feeling good. I used a cane for a while and endured long weeks of painful, boring therapy, but once the pain receded, the relief was amazing. I could walk again! I soon forgot that it was not my natural knee.

I should have done this years ago, I thought. *Why was I so stubborn?*

At that time my medical insurance was the best I have ever had. The hospital mailed me a computer printout of the itemized cost of the surgery, and I was shocked to see that it came to about $50,000. It didn't cost me anything. Not one penny.

With the knee pain gone, my only pain now was in my back. I went to several different chiropractors, and they all helped, but only temporarily. It took two years, but I did eventually find a chiropractor who not only corrected it but taught me how to keep it well myself with exercises. It has been mostly pain free ever since, as long as I'm careful.

✳✳✳✳

"Mom, can you come over here and put Luke to bed? He just won't stop crying!"

"Okay, I'll be there in a few minutes." I replied. Luke, Grace's two-year-old son, routinely refused to go to sleep. He would cry and cry and cry, both for naps and for bedtime, but for some reason he would settle down with me. So I drove over there, lay down with him, read to him for a while, and when he had fallen asleep, crept out quietly and went back home. We never figured out why he resisted sleep so much or why he calmed down with me, and he eventually grew out of it.

I had moved to Arkansas because I anticipated I was going to need help from the family, but it turned out they needed me more than I needed them, such as lending them my car when they needed it and helping with finances when times were hard. Grace had found a good job when they first arrived in Springdale the year before, and John stayed home with Luke. But when Grace's job ended, she had trouble finding another good one.

But most of my help was taking care of the children. Sometimes I stayed overnight when Grace and John went away, but mostly I filled in when there were gaps in their schedules, or picking the kids up or taking them somewhere. Simone was ten years old, Veronica was eight, and Luke had just turned two. I have pictures of him inspecting the lettuce patch in my back yard, with his long red curls hanging down his back. His hair, the same copper color as his uncle Gary's at that age, had never been cut. It was gorgeous. It made him look like a little girl, but he was definitely all boy—rambunctious, eager, bright, and into everything. I loved the way Luke always greeted me—he would run to me yelling,

Grandsons Matt, 13, and Howie, 18 months, in Joliet, Illinois.

*"Grammieeeeee!"*and and throw his arms around my knees, which was as high as he could reach. They were good kids and easy to take care of.

November came, and I had visions of a Rockwellian "Thanksgiving at Gramma's" around the new table that could seat at least ten in my big kitchen/family room. I hadn't cooked a family dinner since I left my husband twenty-two years before. I invited Grace's family and a couple of friends, to make eight of us. I cooked most of the traditional turkey meal myself, with Grace bringing a dish.

It was a real treat to have family and friends around me for a holiday dinner, after all those years of being alone, and the dinner turned out well. But I had forgotten how much work it would be! I was exhausted for two weeks afterwards. That was the last holiday meal at my house; I happily let the kids do it thereafter.

That year was my first white Christmas in many years. It had snowed for several days, leaving three inches of snow on top of solid ice. I was determined that I was not spending Christmas alone after moving so far to be with the family, so I drove over treacherous streets to Grace's house for Christmas day. It was white knuckle time, gripping the wheel tightly the entire way. It was only a ten-minute drive and there was no other traffic, but it was dangerous, and I was immensely relieved to get there safely. Driving back home later was no easier.

The drive was worth it. A huge, beautifully decorated tree sparkled in the living room, and John and Grace together cooked a delicious dinner. I played with the kids with their new toys and had a delightful day.

It was good to be with family. I knew I had done the right thing moving to Arkansas.

About this time I met Barbara Bronstrup, a recent widow about my age who lived in Bella Vista, 30 miles north of Springdale. I had heard about a Theosophical Society in Fayetteville and decided to check it out. After the meeting, Barbara and I stopped in the parking lot to chat. We talked for a long time, and soon realized how much we had in common. We exchanged phone numbers and began a friendship that still affects my life all these years later.

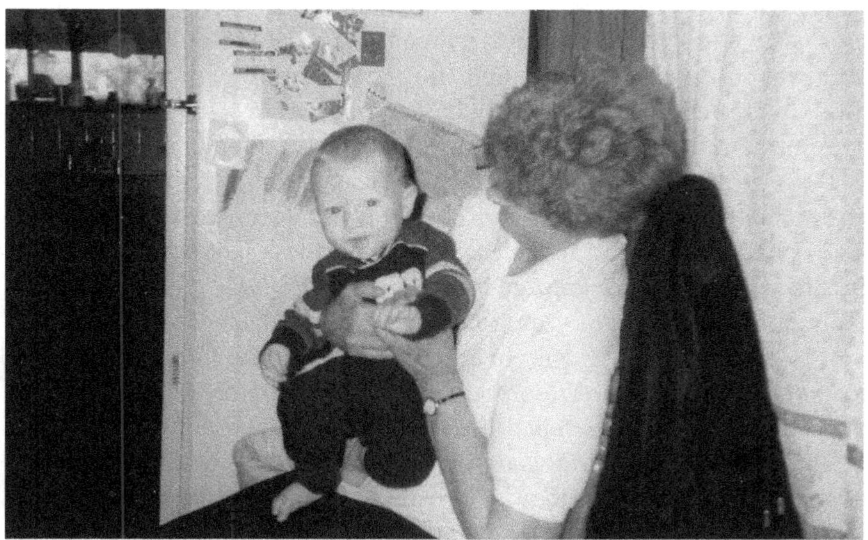

Maya holding Grandson Luke Dunn, in Springdale, 1998

Granddaughters Simone (left) and Veronica, in Springdale, 2000.

As we spent time together, Barbara would often say, "Laurie said I should take this," or "Laurie told me to do that," and I became curious about who Laurie was. Barbara explained that Laurie Frew was a naturopath, who advised her how to stay healthy using natural methods. Barbara was in excellent health, and the more she mentioned Laurie, the more interested I became. Finally I asked her for a referral, and made an appointment for myself.

I was surprised to discover that Laurie used the same muscle response testing method for diagnosis that I had learned from Pam back in Maryland. I had never met anyone else who used the finger testing method. Laurie was amazingly accurate at knowing what was going on in my body. She was good! For years I had been using what I knew about natural healing, but she taught me so much more. I saw her regularly and followed her suggestions, especially for supplements, even though none of it was covered by insurance. It was worth the expense.

That fall I drove to Illinois to see Gary and his family, including their 8-year-old son Howie, who was born when his brother Matt was twelve. Matt had joined the Air Force at seventeen, and Howie was growing up virtually as an only child. Visits there were always stressful, as Gary's wife

Mary and I struggled to get along with each other, but I went anyway, as otherwise I would never see my son.

I regret that I never got as close to Gary's children as I did to Grace's, and I don't know just how much blame for that is mine. The geographical distance was one factor, of course, though not insurmountable, but Mary was determined to keep Gary as far away from his family as possible, and neither he nor I made enough effort to get past her hostility. We had occasional brief phone calls, and once every year or so I made a strained visit. Consequently, his sons grew up barely knowing me.

One visit I remember fondly was when Matt was about eleven. They were living in a farmhouse in Illinois surrounded by soybean fields. It was late fall when the soybeans had been harvested and the plants were dead and dry. One day I invited Matt to go for a walk with me. We walked around a huge field, and when it was time to return, I decided we would take a shortcut cross the field. We soon discovered that the waist-high soybean plants were tough and scratchy, and it was a struggle to push our way through them.

Matt surprised me by saying, "Take my hand, Grammie. I'll help you."

"Okay. Thanks!"

Taking his hand to help me was a poignant reversal of my grandmother role. It pleased me that he saw the need and wanted to be the "grown up." That incident is one of the happy memories I have of my visits with Gary's family in those years.

****

I continued to edit *Perspectives*, finding a local graphic designer to create the files on disc to send to the publisher. I set up one bedroom in my house as an office, with plenty of room to spread out, and with three bedrooms, I still had a guest room. This house gave me more room than I had ever had since my divorce.

But by late in 2000, it was becoming apparent that *Perspectives* was not doing well. The World Business Academy had gone through a recent reorganization with some resulting bad feelings and greatly reduced membership, and the readership of the journal had dwindled. Its circulation was widespread, scattered over many countries, but it was now smaller than ever, and some of those people who received it did not read it. I was discouraged to discover that even some of the WBA board members never read it. The people who read it raved about it, but so few

Fayetteville Quaker meeting, August 2000, in United Campus Ministries building. (l-r) Emmet McCracken, Karen Takemoto, Anita Shekinah, Maya Porter, (unidentified), Scott Holloway, Judy Fowler, Kathleen Johnson, LaDeana Mullinix.

readers didn't justify the expense, and Berrett-Koehler, the publisher, was reluctant to continue subsidizing it.

At the same time the board considered ending publication, I decided I no longer wanted to edit it. The reorganization had eliminated the "little people," the consultants and small business owners and academics, which took the heart out of the organization and nullified the whole purpose of the journal. The annual meeting in San Francisco that year demonstrated the change. One of the attenders, who had traveled from South Africa at great personal expense, wrote to me, "I'm disappointed that this organization is nothing like what I expected. From reading *Perspectives*, I thought it would be very different. This group is so old paradigm—nothing like what I read in the pages of the journal."

I sent my resignation letter on October 10, and followed with a long letter to the board expressing my thoughts about the direction the organization had taken and how it might be changed. I did not receive a reply.

After six years of a challenging and rewarding experience, I was now no longer a journal editor. There was talk of changing the format and

Luke and Veronica in the sandbox at Maya's Ellen St. house, 2001.

putting *Perspectives* online, but I don't know if it actually happened. I soon lost touch with the WBA.

Just as I was wondering what I would do next to pay the bills, I received a call asking me to create and edit a newsletter for the Chaordic Commons of Terra Civitas, a new group organized by Dee Hock, the originator of the Visa credit card system. I had published Dee in *Perspectives*, and knowing my work, he thought I could do a good job with the newsletter.

One definition of *chaordic* is "a system governed by combining elements of both *chaos* and *order*." It refers to "the balance point between the two extremes in which the benefits of both can exist together." The concept is difficult to grasp, but enough people got it to create an organization, headquartered in Half Moon Bay, California.

I loved the concepts, which are based on the idea of a flat, horizontal hierarchy, with leadership shared among all of its members. Actions arise organically, out of common concern and interest. The structure is very much like Quakerism, although I doubt the Commons recognized the similarity.

I took the job, working with the group's director, so in early 2001, I was editing a regular publication again. We put out a 28-page newsletter three times a year. As with *Perspectives*, I was in one part of the country and all of the staff were in another, but it worked. The pay was not very good, but along with my Social Security check, I made enough to get by, and it was interesting work. In my mind, the Chaordic Commons was the organization the World Business Academy should have been.

38 A Crowded Summer

One day in May 2001, I received a disturbing phone call from Grace.

"Mom, our landlord just told us he is going to renovate our house and we have to move out, right away. We don't have any place to go. Could we come stay with you until we find something?"

What could I say? I didn't like the idea, but I how could I refuse?

"Uh.... I guess so. How soon?"

"By the first. In two weeks."

This meant the five of them moving into my house. I had three bedrooms, and all of the rooms in the house were large, so I figured they could squeeze in somehow. I needed to keep my office and my bedroom, but they could use the rest of the house.

They moved in over Memorial Day weekend. They disposed of much of their stuff at a yard sale, and crammed the rest into my house or stacked it in my two-car garage. It was crowded, but not as much as it could have been, because both of the girls spent most of the summer away with their noncustodial parents. Most of the time it was just the two adults and three-year-old Luke.

Grace had a part-time job and was gone most of the day. John was doing some day-trading so we set up his computer in the small bedroom. I was working almost full time, and between us we took care of Luke.

With all the work I had and the crowded feeling in the house, I spent most of that summer shut in my bedroom or office. Grace and John cooked meals, and I often made something for myself later. We had to schedule the use of the one shower. John and I have always had trouble

Maya's apartment in Spring Meadows, Springdale, 2003–2009.

communicating, with John's slow methodical style clashing with my impatience, and that summer was more difficult than usual. We got along with each other, but it was with great effort and clenched jaws. The tension in the house was hard to deal with. I took long walks in the evenings.

Midway in the summer, John rented a small office in Fayetteville, which got him out of the house during the day. Grace managed to get Luke into a Montessori school by doing some computer work in exchange for part of the tuition, giving me time to for my editing work.

Somehow, we managed.

Soon after the girls returned from visiting their other parents, Grace rented a house in Springdale near their previous one. They moved out on Labor Day weekend. Finally, after three very long months, I had my house back.

Also that summer, Ron Nahser, one of the WBA board members, approached me for an editing project. He wanted to publish a monograph of Willis Harman's writings related to spirituality in business, to be used to recruit new members to the WBA. Willis had been a prolific writer, producing many articles and papers and several books over his career, and compiling his thoughts into one document was a daunting project. I accepted the challenge eagerly.

Not knowing how big a job it would be, I asked Ron for a monthly fee. He agreed to $1,000 a month for four months. Grace was paying something toward the utilities, but no rent, and I was buying the groceries, so Ron's check in addition to the Chaordic Commons newsletter and Social Security would keep the bills paid for a while longer.

First I had to figure out how to accomplish the task. I had copies of Willis's books and of course the articles published in *Perspectives*, but I had to find the rest. The logical place to search was in the files of the Institute for Noetic Sciences (IONS) in California, where Willis had been president for almost twenty years.

I asked IONS if I could search their files, and when they heard why, they agreed to make all their files available to me. Ron paid for me to fly out to Petaluma for a couple of days. The IONS staff welcomed me graciously, putting me up on their beautiful new campus and giving me free use of their copy machine.

The office had several file cabinets full of Willis's works, including many letters. It took me all day to go through the files, pull what was relevant, make copies, and put everything back. The staff then searched their computer files to find what they had electronically of the papers I had pulled. They promised to email me everything they could.

Combined with all the papers already in my office, I now had an enormous amount of material. How could I make sense of it all? At first it seemed like an impossible task, but I remembered how I have tackled big jobs before.

Take it one chunk at a time, I thought. *What's the first step?*

Willis' writings covered more than just business, so first I had to determine what was generally on the topic. I made copies of all of the relevant pages in his books, and went through the material on my computer and the paper files and highlighted all the passages that dealt with business in general. That was a start, but I still had pages and pages of text.

I typed in what I didn't have in the computer, and then puzzled for hours over what to do next. How can I assemble this? It was like putting together a jigsaw puzzle without the picture on the box. Finally I figured out I could go through all of the documents, hard copy and onscreen, and number every paragraph. One document's paragraphs became A1, A2, A3, and so on; the next document's paragraphs were numbered B1, B2, B3, and so forth, through all of the documents.

I then set up my sewing cutting table in my bedroom. It was big enough that I could spread out most of the documents so I could skim them all at once and pick out what belonged with what. With scissors and Scotch tape, I did a physical cut and paste to put together the paragraphs in an order that made sense to develop the ideas. Since I had numbered the paragraphs, I could then go into the computer and cut and paste those paragraphs into one continuous document.

If I put his paragraph with that one… no, that won't work. This whole page could go here because it completes the thoughts on that page.… But that can't go before this! Darn, this is hard.…"

I spent days, weeks, figuring it all out. Eventually, after much printing, revising, and reprinting, I had a monograph that provided all of Willis' thoughts about the spiritual aspects of business in one coherent paper. It was all in Willis' words, verbatim, no paraphrasing and no rewriting. I sent it to Ron with a big sigh of relief and satisfaction. Ron was pleased with it.

However, by the time I finished it, the idea seemed to have lost steam, and I don't know if anything was ever done with it. It may still be sitting on a shelf somewhere.

****

One afternoon in June 2001, my brother Frank had called with sad news.

"David just called. Ruth died last night."

Ruth was my step-mother, whom Daddy married soon after Mother died in 1978. Daddy died in 1987, and Ruth moved into a nursing home in about 1996. David was her son, my step-brother.

As I explained in an earlier chapter, I had never liked Ruth very much, but I stayed in touch with her and visited her when I was in town. When she was still in her house and I lived in the area, I sometimes helped her with things like taking her to the grocery store. Once she asked me to change the sheets on her bed, which I thought was a strange request at the time, but later came to see what a difficult chore that is for a frail, elderly person.

I flew to Maryland for her memorial service. The arrangements were marred by one incident. Ruth had lived close to the border of Northeast Washington, a black part of the city, and when David called a funeral home to take her body, he just picked one nearby out of the phone book. When he looked at the death certificate he found that they had listed her race as black! Obviously the director had not seen the body. I thought it was funny, but David was livid. It took some persistent phone calls to get the form changed.

The memorial service was appalling. Ruth's grandson was a Pentecostal minister, and they asked him to conduct the service. He turned it into an evangelizing opportunity, with a hellfire-and-brimstone sermon, ending with an altar call. I was especially disturbed when he proclaimed enthusiastically that the most important day in Ruth's life was recently when she accepted Jesus as her savior. He said he had visited Ruth in the nursing home, and when he asked her if she accepted Jesus, she said yes, and he claimed that was when she was "saved"—"the most important day of her life."

Ruth's daughter Susan and I looked at each other across the pew and rolled our eyes. We knew better. Ruth was a life-long Methodist, playing the organ for her church services every Sunday for many years. For the past couple of years, advanced dementia had made Ruth unresponsive and completely unable to carry on a conversation. It was impossible for her to understand and respond to questions. I resented the preacher's high-jacking Ruth's service for his own purposes.

Later, there was the matter of the will. The estate was to be divided evenly between the heirs, and I had no idea how much money was in the estate. I was actually surprised there would be any inheritance at all. I always thought we would be lucky not to have to pay off debts!

Back in 1989, a year after Daddy died, Ruth asked his children if we would mind if she sold the house, the house we grew up in. This was the house Daddy paid $1,000 for in 1934 and had lived in for fifty-four years. We replied that we would not mind at all, that it made sense for her to move closer to her son. She sold the house and the lot next door for something like $140,000, but she bought another house and had been paying for her care in the nursing home for several years, so I had no idea if there was any money left. The will named David the executor. I knew it would be some time before I received a check and I would have to be patient.

When the work with Ron ended, other work dribbled in. A couple of local graphic designers paid me to proofread several books. One was *Letters from the Dust Bowl,* published by the Oklahoma University Press, containing letters spanning from 1908 to 1966 from a housewife who lived through the devastating drought of the 1930s in Oklahoma. Years later I recognized quotes from the book in one of Ken Burns' TV documentaries.

"Wait! I remember that letter! I know that woman!" I exclaimed to the TV screen. The program was narrated in the voice of Caroline

Henderson, the woman who wrote the letters. I felt a strange connection with the program, as if I were listening to an old friend.

That summer, 2001, I attended my 50-year high school reunion in Maryland. These reunions had become more interesting over the years, as I began to get to know my former classmates as adults and discovered that they were nicer people than I remembered. It surprised me every time how little people had changed. Hair had turned gray, of course, and a few pounds had been added, but facial features and voices didn't change that much. Mannerisms and personalities were recognizable. It may not have been so much that they were nicer but that I was. At least I was more tolerant.

I think this was the last reunion we had. I don't know why they ended, but we were all in our seventies, and perhaps as we got older, fewer of us were willing to make the trip. And fifty seemed like a good number to end with.

✳✳✳✳

I continued to produce the newsletter for the Chaordic Commons, and in July of 2002, the organization's first annual meeting was held in Charlottesville, on the beautiful campus of the University of Virginia. The people in this group were so pleasant, friendly, and cheerful that I enjoyed every minute. As a staff person, I was kept busy handling details and making sure everyone had what they needed. The atmosphere was upbeat and encouraging about the future of the organization.

The business part of the meeting was on Sunday, the final day of the meeting. When the director presented the financial report, it was accepted with no changes and little discussion. However, I noticed that the heading on the page was incorrect—it said that it was for the six months ending the previous December 31st— and this was July.

"Hmm… He used the last report and forgot to change the heading. I won't mention it now and embarrass him during the meeting," I thought.

When the meeting adjourned, I approached him and said, "Good report, but I see you forgot to change the heading."

"Uh…No, actually, I didn't forget," he replied. "Those are last year's numbers. I didn't use this year's numbers because I don't want the members to see how bad they are."

I was stunned. He actually fudged the report because the finances were bad? I didn't say anything, but I kept thinking what a sham the meeting had been. All that excitement about how well we were doing was fake!

I supposed he thought he could turn it around before he had to make another report.

But in December, the director resigned, and by early 2003 the organization was in tatters. It continued for a while in a simpler version, but not for long. It simply ran out of money. I wasn't surprised, but was disappointed that it fizzled out after so much promise. I had realized earlier that a major fault in its organization was that with all their grandiose vision, the founders had not planned for a revenue stream. They started with a huge donation—I've heard both a million dollars and half a million—and when that ran out there was not a sufficient source of income. I've never understood how those brilliant businessmen could make such a fundamental mistake.

Other work from various sources trickled in. The two graphic designers gave me more work, and a couple of organizations found me and sent me books and articles. It was enough.

39 Inheritance

Losing the Chaordic Commons newsletter meant less income for me, but I wasn't concerned, because in early December my step-brother David called.

"Well, it's all done, finally. I'm ready to disburse Mom's estate. Watch for a certified letter in the next week."

David had been working on closing the estate for a year and a half, and all that time I had no idea how much my share would be or when I would get it. David refused to communicate with either Frank or me and resented any questions about what he was doing. I never knew why he was so hostile, but perhaps he assumed that our questions implied that we thought either he would cheat us or he couldn't do the job well, neither of which was true. Frank and I talked about whether we should be concerned and decided that we trusted David and would just let it go. Eventually David told us that he had spent most of that time repairing and updating Ruth's house so it would bring a better price. We would have thanked him for it if we had known what he was doing.

Several days later I received a notice in the mail to come get a certified letter. I raced to the post office and signed for the letter. I waited until I got home to tear open the envelope. Inside was a check for $41,163.90—more money than I had ever handled in my life. I immediately deposited most of it into my savings account and put a few thousand into the checking account, vowing to use some of it to splurge on something frivolous. For a while I just let it sit there, and let myself relax into the security of having money in the bank.

As inheritances go, it wasn't much, but for me, it was huge. With a sigh of relief, I finally banished that nagging dread of becoming a bag lady.

I soon discovered a good use for some of that money. I had been seeing Laurie, the naturopath, for more than a year and was still impressed with how effective she was and how much I preferred natural healing methods over allopathic medicine. One day when I was at the receptionist's desk writing a check to pay for an office visit, I had a sudden epiphany.

I could do this!

I stopped with my pen poised above my checkbook. I raced back into Laurie's office and said excitedly, "I want to be a naturopath! Can I do that?"

"Of course you can. I'll get you the information for the school I went to."

I asked myself seriously whether I could do this at my age. In a few months I would be seventy years old. But I was confident that I could, that my mind was still sharp enough to learn new material, and I was strongly motivated. And I had Laurie to help me.

So in January 2003 I registered with the Trinity College of Natural Health. It would cost about $4,000 with books and weekend workshops, but with my inheritance, I could afford it.

First I wanted to cut my expenses. I was determined not to use the inheritance for living expenses, but to save as much of it as possible for as long as possible. I was sure I would have more need for it later in life.

A year earlier, I had been thinking about moving into a cheaper place and found Spring Meadows, an apartment complex nearby for older people with low incomes. I had applied for an apartment, and I received notice that one was coming available in early February. The timing was perfect.

I was moving from a large, three-bedroom house into a tiny, one-bedroom apartment of about 500 square feet. What would I do with all my stuff?

I expected to stay in the apartment for two or three years while I earned my diploma and started a naturopath practice. I asked my daughter Grace to store what she could in her house temporarily. She took some of my living room and office furniture and yard equipment. I sold my big dining room table and chairs and donated nine boxes of books to Farmington's new library. I measured the apartment, made paper cutouts of my furniture, and placed them on the floor in the apartment to figure what I could squeeze in. I made it work, fitting it all together like a life-sized jigsaw puzzle.

I moved on a bitterly cold day in February 2003.

Spring Meadows was a complex of about 15 one-story brick buildings in a cul-de-sac on the west side of Springdale, less than a mile from my house at the time. It was well kept, with many tall long-needled pines shading most of the buildings. It felt homey and safe. The apartments were situated side by side, four to a building, each with both a front door and a back door. With front and back windows as well, they were light-filled and airy. My apartment was on the back edge of the complex, with a six-foot wooden fence behind me, so I had some privacy in my back yard. There was even space for a very small garden.

The main advantage was that it was subsidized by the U.S. government under Section 8, which meant my rent was determined as a percentage of my income, and my rent the first year came to $157 a month, with all utilities paid. Definitely manageable.

One disadvantage was the lack of appliances, such as dishwasher, garbage disposal, and washer and dryer. The first two I didn't miss, but carrying my clothes to the laundry in the community building half a block away soon became an annoying chore. Another disadvantage, which bothered me more and more the longer I lived there, was that the management treated the tenants like kindergarteners. We were watched constantly to see that we didn't violate the many rules, and in order to stay, we had to submit all our financial records to them once a year to show that we still qualified. I resented the intrusion, but it was unavoidable.

When I came in to look at the apartment that was available, the manager told me frankly that I needed to know that the next-door neighbor was known for being very difficult, and I should consider that before I took the apartment.

"Oh, I can deal with that," I said. "I can get along with anybody. I'll take it."

As I strode eagerly down the sidewalk to my new apartment, keys in hand, I saw a woman sprawled in a lawn chair in front of the apartment next to mine. She was obese, her flesh spilling out of shorts and a tank top, even though it was a cold day. Her long hair was stringy and she was wearing slippers. She was talking loudly on her cordless phone, so I didn't speak to her.

I hope that isn't my neighbor, I thought. It was.

Once I moved in, I discovered what a mistake I had made, but it was too late. Elsie was truly obnoxious, the neighbor no one liked. She seemed to enjoy seeing how much she could annoy me. For instance, she had a little dog that she let roam, which was against the rules, and let it poop in my yard. Her daughter visited often, and the two of them sat on her patio and smoked for hours, so I couldn't enjoy my patio, as their smoke drifted over from ten feet way. One day she walked into another apartment, flopped down, and said, "Make me a sandwich!" The tenants believed Elsie had some special connection with the apartment management, as she broke all the rules with impunity, and often bragged about being close friends with the city mayor.

She was generally annoying to everyone, but with our front doors less than twenty feet apart, it was easy for her to focus on me. I soon cut a path across the grass to avoid passing her front door on the sidewalk to the parking lot.

Living in Spring Meadows, I was presented with several aspects of my personality that I might not have encountered otherwise. I grew up in a working-class home, but when I married an engineer, I moved into the professional, white-collar class. As a couple, we associated with other professional people, and I watched and learned how to be comfortable in that culture, so that it had come to feel like my own. Without realizing it, I had adopted an attitude of smug superiority over people "beneath me." That attitude surfaced clearly in Spring Meadows. I tried not to let it show, monitoring myself not to talk down to my neighbors and to listen to them uncritically, but I'm not sure how well I succeeded. I suspect that Elsie picked on me particularly because she resented my attitude.

I was different from the other tenants, not only being educated—actually going to school for another degree at the time—but I was much healthier, more active in the community, and most important of all, I was there temporarily. For most of the other tenants, this was the last stop. Their next move was to the nursing home or the cemetery.

Occasionally, I felt resentful that I had been "reduced" to living in such poor circumstances, but I reminded myself that it would end, and that I had chosen it deliberately, for a purpose. My neighbors did not have that knowledge.

Looking back, I think one of the reasons Elsie bothered me so much was that I could not control her behavior. Trying to control my circumstances has always been an issue for me, and it was unusual for me to be subjected to such an annoyance that I could not make go away. I have been gradually learning to deal with that issue, and I wonder if I would react differently to Elsie today. Perhaps, perhaps not.

Fortunately, the other neighbors were pleasant and friendly. Most of them were Arkansas natives, uneducated women who had lived on farms all their lives or worked in factory jobs, such as canning factories. Only a very few had computers or cell phones, and many did not drive. Being elderly, some in their nineties, they had many doctors' appointments, and got there by bus or taxi, using the free coupons the city gave out.

I enjoyed visiting with them and hearing stories about the early days on the farm. Eighty-year-old Bernice, my next-door neighbor on the other side, told me about a trip her family took when she was a child in about 1933.

"We went out west to Washington to pick apples. All ten of us piled into the old Ford Model T and took off. At night we stopped aside the road and slept in our clothes. We stayed a couple weeks and then came back the same way. Made a lot of money.

"In the summer I picked strawberries 'n spinach all day long. We all did. We worked hard."

Lovena, a 74-year-old in the next building, had owned a business selling Native American objects when she was younger. She and her friend traveled the southwest buying items like paintings and pottery, bringing them home to sell in Springdale. When she sold the business she kept many of the objects and decorated her apartment with them. She was one of the more interesting neighbors, and I visited with her often. One Christmas she gave me a delicate little dream catcher she made out of string and beads and feathers. It still hangs on my kitchen wall.

One difficulty I had with the neighbors was their racism. Most of it was directed at the Hispanics, whom they resented for "taking over their town." I learned to avoid the subject, as I couldn't find a way to get past their deeply ingrained prejudices.

Even with the disadvantages, it was a good place for me while I worked on my naturopath course. The course was by correspondence. I bought the required books online, and started receiving the lessons. I read the material, answered the questions on the tests, and mailed them in. There was no required time schedule, so I could do the lessons as time allowed while I still had some editing work. The school expected a student who was doing it part time to take several years to complete the course. I hoped to do it faster than that.

The books were interesting and not very hard. Being a words person, I especially enjoyed the class on medical terminology. Once I learned the basic components, I could decipher what any many-syllabled medical term meant. Human anatomy was fascinating, as I learned where all the parts of the body are and how they connect to all the other parts.

I drove to Tulsa for weekend workshops on herbology, aromatherapy, and other subjects.

The material became even easier when I started an internship with Laurie. I went to her office two days a week and sat in on her appointments. At the end of the day, she sat with me and quizzed me on what she had done and why. Depending on the client, she would sometimes actually confer with me in the client's presence, so I could get feedback on the spot. I learned more from these sessions than I did from the written materials. It was very close to on-the-job training, which is more instructive than book study.

A naturopath does not deal with symptoms, but with causes, and recommends herb and vitamins or certain foods, not drugs. If the client has high blood pressure, for example, the naturopath looks at what is going on in the person's life—what their diet is like, how much exercise they get, and so on, and then recommends lifestyle changes in addition to herbs or other supplements. If a person has an unexplained skin rash, the cause is likely a compromised liver. The liver filters all the blood in the body, and if it is not able to filter all the impurities, it tries to push them out of the body, which takes them as far as the skin. Taking milk thistle will often heal the liver, and the rash will disappear. I saw this happen more than once.

Laurie had a large practice, many whole families who had been coming to her for years. Her office was located in a health food store, so her clients could buy their supplements while they were there. Most of them did, although they could get them elsewhere if they preferred.

This was a good time, with steady editing work, interesting studies, and no worries about paying the bills.

40 France

I still wanted to do something fun with some of that cash in the bank. One day in January when I was talking on the phone with my friend Paula, I said, "I want to do something special for my seventieth birthday in April. I'd love to go to France. I have a standing invitation to visit some American friends living in Grenoble. I've got the money now, but there's no way I could go by myself."

"Do you really want to go? I'll go with you!" she said. "I lived in Paris for three months when I was in college thirty years ago and I'd love to go back. I want to see my old apartment again!"

"Are you serious? Would you really go with me?" I was ecstatic. Paula speaks French, and she knows Paris. She would be a great traveling companion. Could I actually do it?

Once she assured me she was serious, we worked out where we wanted to go, so we could each visit our friends and then see Paris together. Paula's friend Erica worked for the UN in Geneva and lived in Bretigny, a small town in France close to the Swiss border. We would stay with her a few days, then I would go on to Grenoble to see Mike and Lisa, then we would meet up to go to Paris for five days.

We agreed to go in May, when the weather was likely to be pleasant, and bought our plane tickets. I couldn't believe it! I was actually going to Europe!

When May came, I had no idea how to pack for two weeks in a foreign country. Paula, being a world traveler, gave me some tips, but I still kept dithering over what to take and of course ended up taking too much.

Maya relaxing in front of Paula's friend Erica's old stone house in France, 2003.

I found a place to board my cat Toby, arranged for a ride to the airport, and flew to Washington to meet Paula. I stayed there that night and the next day her husband drove us to Dulles airport.

It was a seven-hour flight overnight, landing in Frankfurt, Germany. Paula fell asleep and so did everyone else except me and my seat mate on the aisle. She was a large elderly woman who spoke no English. She had the foulest breath I've ever encountered, and insisted on talking to me, although I did my best to explain that I did not speak whatever it was she was speaking. I said, "Don't understand," shaking my head and gesturing every way I could think of, but she didn't get it. Eventually, she gave up, but occasionally she would mutter loudly something like "WAWAWA!"

As we were standing in the aisle waiting to disembark at Frankfurt, the attendant announced over the intercom, "Does anyone on board speak Russian?"

A man replied yes, and made his way to the front. We soon learned that the woman was carrying a note that said, *"This is my mother. She is handicapped. She does not speak English. Please help her get to St. Petersburg."*

I was floored. Someone thought it made sense to put their elderly, disabled mother on a plane with just a note to get her halfway around the world. It suddenly dawned on me that the word she had been saying over and over was "WATER!" She had been sitting there for seven hours needing water. I was so sorry that I hadn't understood her.

From Frankfurt we flew to Geneva, where Erica picked us up. We stayed for three days in her century-old gray stone house with white trim and red roses growing up the front. It looked so European and picturesque. The second day we went to see Mont Blanc, taking the funicular up to the viewing area at the top, where I had my first experience making myself understood in French.

I didn't want to join Paula exploring the mountain's glacier, so I stayed at the little café and waited for her. I decided to get a snack, and pointed to what I wanted on the menu on the wall for the counter clerk. When I sat down, I looked at the money in my hand and thought, *This isn't right. She shortchanged me.* Could I make myself understood to get it fixed? *I can do this*, I thought, *at least I should try.*

I approached the counter, and using what French words I could remember and gesturing to the menu on the wall and to the money in my hand, I got the point across. She said, "Oooh, oui," and handed me two euros.

Feeling triumphant, I enjoyed my snack and waited for Paula.

Paula was staying a few more days with Erica while I was going to Grenoble to see my friends. I had to take the train there from Geneva, and I was nervous about getting on the right train.

"Oh, don't worry, we'll go into the station with you and be sure you get the right one," Paula said. But when we got to the station, we realized just

Maya with Mike Kelly. Mike and his wife Lisa were her hosts in Grenoble, France, 2003.

as we were about to walk in that I was going to another country—from Switzerland to France—and had to go through customs. They couldn't go with me.

I was scared. In my extensive travels all over the United States, often alone and far from home, I had never been afraid of getting lost. But here, I didn't know the language! How would I know where to go? How would I find the right train? What if I got on the wrong one? How could I ask for directions?

There was no choice. I entered the station, went through customs, and looked around for signs or something to tell me where to go. I found a platform but didn't see anything to tell me where the train would be going. I saw a friendly looking woman standing there, and asked, "Excuse me. Grenoble?"

Smiling, she said, "I speak English. You are going to Grenoble?"

"Yes. Can you tell me where to get the train?"

"Come with me. I'm going there."

Of course she was. Whatever I need always appears when I need it.

We shared a compartment and had a pleasant trip as she practiced her English, telling me about her grandchildren.

Mike met me at the Grenoble stop and took me to their apartment. Mike had taken a leave from his job, and he and his wife Lisa and their two little boys were spending a year in France just for the experience. Mike explained that he and Lisa had an appointment that afternoon that they couldn't cancel, and the boys were in school, so I would have the afternoon to myself. I was glad for the time to be alone and rest.

I took a shower and washed my hair, and needed both a dryer and a curling iron. I found Lisa's hair dryer and used it, leaving my hair sticking out all over my head. But when I tried to use my curling iron, I discovered that the converter I brought with me didn't work, and I couldn't find a curling iron anywhere.

I can't leave my hair like this. What can I do? I'll have to go out and buy a curling iron.

The experience with money at the café on Mont Blanc had emboldened me. Surely I could find a place to buy an iron. I smoothed my hair down with my fingers as best I could, dressed, and left the apartment. I remembered that Mike had pointed out a shopping area just a block or so away. I headed to a sign that looked like it was a drug store. But in Europe, drug stores are just that—where you get your prescriptions filled, nothing else, so they didn't have what I wanted. I continued on around the corner, watching very carefully where I was so I could find my way back.

There's a department store! They'll have curling irons.

I approached the first counter I saw and gestured to my head, miming curling my hair. The clerk understood and pointed upstairs. I picked out an iron, paid for it, and found my way back to the apartment. *I did it!*

This was a simple incident, but it boosted my feelings of competence. Traveling abroad has many benefits, and one of them for me was learning that I can manage when I don't speak the local language. I would never have learned that at home.

Grenoble is a charming city, and my hosts' apartment was large and airy. They went to a boulangerie across the street for croissants every

Maya at a street market in Grenoble.

morning. They bought their groceries daily at a sidewalk market down the street. It was very quaint and lovely.

Mike and I had worked closely together on the Freeze Campaign back in Illinois in the 1980s and had kept in touch over the years, but we still had much catching up to do, so the next day he and I went for a long walk. We walked and talked for hours, stopping at cafés for coffee and taking a funicular to a museum up a steep hill. Amazingly, I didn't get tired.

The next day we met Paula at the train station and she and I continued on to Paris. We soon discovered that what might have been a disaster turned out to be a benefit. The day we arrived was the first day of one of France's frequent strikes. This time it was the transportation workers, and nothing was running. No subway, no buses. Taxis were available, but the lines at the taxi stands were a block long. So we walked. And walked. And walked. Fortunately, we were both in good shape; Paula is eleven years younger than I and a lifelong hiker, and I had all that warming up in Grenoble.

It was a benefit because we got to experience Paris at the sidewalk level. We stopped in shops along the way, taking breaks at sidewalk cafés, and enjoyed the sights and smells and sounds that we would not have

Paula and Maya at dinner in Paris, 2003.

known on the subway or even on a bus. The strike necessitated alternative ways of getting around; I saw a gray-haired woman in a business suit and high heels pedaling a bicycle down the street in heavy traffic, and a young man, also in a business suit, zipping down the sidewalk on rollerblades, zigzagging between pedestrians while looking at his cell phone.

Taking a cab one day, we went up the Eiffel tower, saw the Rodin museum, and strolled along the Seine. We almost got caught in a demonstration march, but realized what it was just in time to get out of the way. The third day I was exhausted so Paula went out by herself, letting me take a long nap.

One of the most memorable sights for me was Sainte Chapelle, the church constructed in the fourteenth century to hold Louis IXs' religious relics. The chapel walls consist of fifteen stained glass windows almost 50 feet tall. The sight is breathtaking.

I had packed a pair of pants one size larger than I needed, assuming that with all the famous French food, I would gain weight. I was wrong. With the lack of a kitchen for snacking, the small portions at restaurants, and all that walking, I actually lost weight. Another benefit of the strike.

Finally, it was time to go home. It had been a glorious twelve days.

We left France on May 17, just in time to miss a lethal heat wave that hit Western Europe that summer. My friends left Grenoble in June and missed the worst of it. More than 15,000 people died in France from the blistering heat, mostly elderly people who had been left at home when their families went to the beaches for their traditional long vacations. Throughout Europe, deaths may have been as high as 70,000. We had timed our visit well.

41 Opening My Practice

When I finished the course work, to get my diploma I had to either take a series of weekend seminars or write a dissertation. The seminars, being held in various parts of the country at staggered times, would take months to finish and would cost hundreds of dollars each; the dissertation would be quick and cheap. It was a no-brainer—I would write a dissertation.

I chose a topic that to my knowledge had not been covered before: muscle response testing, or MRT. As I mentioned earlier, I first learned the technique from my friend Pam in Maryland many years before, but had not known how to use it with other people until Laurie showed me. It was not taught at all in the course materials, and Laurie was the only one I knew who used it in her practice. I decided to explain its use for my paper.

For research I read all I could find about applied kinesiology, which is the study of the mechanics of body movements, usually in reference to treatment of injuries such as in sports medicine. Not surprisingly, I could find nothing online about MRT the way I was using it, so I was starting from scratch. Today there is much information about it online, some of it skeptical and some helpful, but I couldn't find any in 2004.

I wrote a description of how I used MRT in my practice, what little theory I knew about how it worked, and what results I had obtained with it. I also wrote a booklet with instructions and photo illustrations. The paper was light on references since there weren't many available, but I loaded it up with examples.

Maya in her naturopath office, 2004.[

The paper was accepted, and in mid-April 2004, I received my diploma as a Doctor of Naturopathy. I had it framed, ready to hang on my office wall.

But what office wall? I needed a space with access to a large variety of supplements for testing people, and clients needed a place to buy them when they came to see me. Laurie offered to set me up with a beginning inventory at a cost of about $4,500, but I would also have to rent office space and get furniture. It was daunting.

I declined her offer, as I didn't want to be in the business of selling supplements. It seemed too much like doctors sending patients to a pharmacy they own. I think that's illegal, and if not, it should be. I would have to go where the supplements were.

After a few refusals at other places, I went to the Avalon Nutrition store in Fayetteville and talked to Betty, the proprietor. I knew her because I had been buying some of my herbs there.

Betty Morris, owner of Avalon, where Maya had her naturopath practice

"Betty, I'm ready to open a practice as a naturopath. Can I set up in your store and see clients here?"

"Oh… I don't know. Where would you do it?"

"I could set off that back corner if I could find some screens or something. My clients could buy their herbs and stuff from you, and you could tell your customers about me. It would benefit both of us. What do you think?"

"Well… I guess so. Sounds like a good deal, if you can make the space work. Let's try it and see how it goes."

"Could I just give you a percentage of my fees for rent at first? I have no idea how much that will be, but it will take a while to get any business."

"Oh, you don't need to pay rent. It won't cost me anything for you to be here and I'll make money on the business you bring me."

So it was decided. I bought a small used desk, a chair, a bookcase, and some tall wooden screens to partition off the corner. It worked! Now to get some clients.

I printed a flyer, ordered business cards, and started looking for places I could give workshops or talks to let people know I was in business. I spent hours every day in the store, just so Betty's customers could see me and talk to me. Gradually people started seeking me out.

Appointments came in slowly, but in time I was spending a couple of hours a day several days a week in the office seeing people. I loved helping them improve their health, without drugs or surgery.

My "poster client" was Adelia, a 91-year-old woman who had multiple complaints. She had extreme edema (swelling) and was in much pain. I forget what her original problem was, but she had seen a doctor who diagnosed her and gave her prescriptions. The drugs had side effects, and the doctor gave her another prescription to counter them. That in turn had more side effects, which brought another prescription. She was taking half a dozen drugs and was miserable.

Together we figured out what her problem was and over a couple of months, with herbs and diet, she got off all the drugs and felt fine. One day she came in and waved her hand at me, saying, "Look! The swelling is gone! I can get my rings on! And I took a shower by myself this morning!" She was thrilled, and so was I.

Some people I couldn't help, either because they weren't willing to make changes, or I just couldn't figure out what they needed, but in most cases, it was gratifying to see clients get better.

The biggest benefactor of my naturopath practice was myself, and not from the income. I learned from my clients about what worked and what didn't and how to get healthy and stay that way, for my own use as much as for theirs. I learned from their experiences and applied what I learned to myself. I spent considerable money on supplements, but it was worth it, as my health was better than it had been in many years. I still had to take thyroid medication, but at seventy-two, I didn't need any other prescription drugs. I used muscle response testing on myself to determine what was going on in my body at any given time, and how much of what I needed to deal with any problems. It was very effective.

For example, whenever I began to develop signs of a cold, I knew what to take to fend it off. If I got a bruise, I stopped it quickly with arnica gel. I drove to Tulsa for a weekend workshop on aromatherapy, and learned of an essential oil blend that always stopped a cough for me. One of my clients was studying homeopathy and we traded treatments, which added even more to my tool chest.

Maya Porter is available for consultations at Avalon Nutrition Center in the Evelyn Hills Shopping Center, 1388 N. College Ave., in Fayetteville. Call **479-872-8460** for an appointment. The initial consultation takes about an hour and costs $40; follow-up sessions last half an hour and cost $20.

Hours: 9:30 to 6, Monday, Tuesday, Wednesday, Friday, and Saturday. Open until 7 on Thursdays.

Maya Porter
phone: 479-872-8460
e-mail: Maya8460@sbcglobal.net

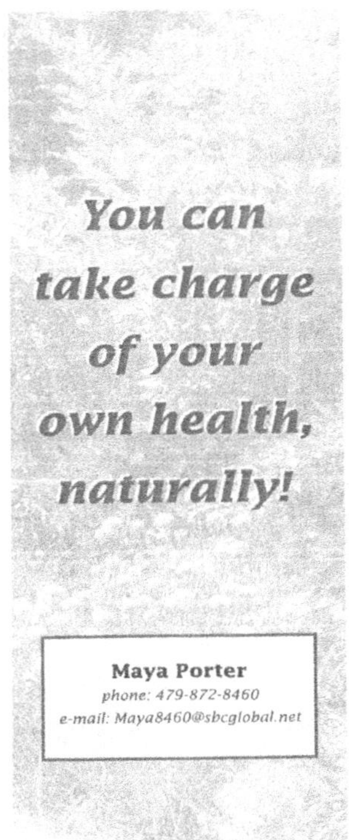

Be Healthy,
Naturally !

Maya Porter, M.A.
NATURAL HEALTH CONSULTANT

Maya Porter, a Natural Health Consultant, is now available to help you get healthy again, *naturally*. She has earned a diploma in naturopathy from Trinity College of Natural Health and also has a Master's Degree from Governor's State University. Maya's training included studies of anatomy and physiology, diet and nutrition, herbology, essential oils, and much more. She has also explored alternative health care on her own for 15 years.

The brochure advertising Maya's naturopath practice.

Probably the most helpful remedy I discovered is oregano. Not the spice in our kitchen cabinets, but a different variety, *Origanum vulgare*. It is antibiotic, antiviral, and antifungal. Once muscle response testing tells me what the problem is, I know whether oregano will treat it and how much to use. It works as well as many prescription antibiotics to stop different infections and has saved me many trips to the doctor and the drug store.

For example, one day I experienced an intense ache in my lower left abdomen. I poked around and decided it was in my left ovary, either a cyst or an infection. I tested myself with MRT and found that yes, it was an infection. I asked whether oregano would heal it, and received a yes.

Hmm. I think I'll treat this with oregano and see what happens. Either it'll get better or it won't, and if it doesn't, I'll call the doctor.

I tested and learned that I should take three oregano capsules three times a day, so I did. The pain decreased immediately. After three days I lowered the dose to two capsules twice a day, and then one capsule three times a day, for a total of seven days. The pain disappeared completely and has never returned. Over the years I've successfully treated urinary infections the same way.

I also continued my editing business. I was hired to edit two journals by Lyceum, a small publisher in Chicago. One was the *Journal of Baccalaureate Social Work,* which came out twice a year, and the other was *Social Development Issues,* which came out three times a year. They emailed me the articles, and I edited everything and sent it all back on a disc ready to print, with a hard copy, by FedEx.

This was one of the most difficult jobs I've ever had, not because the work was hard, although it was, but because the man I worked for was so hard to communicate with. He always spoke in cryptic sentences and got angry when I asked for explanations, so I had to guess what he wanted. He never gave me any feedback as to whether I had guessed right. When I asked for a contract, he was evasive and never would agree to one. But the checks came in and the work was interesting, especially the social issues journal. It printed articles on a wide variety of complicated issues in developing countries, increasing my already expanded awareness of global conditions.

My Social Security check had increased over several years, and with the work with Lyceum and earnings from my practice, my rent was also raised, and I started using some of my savings for special purchases, like patio furniture. I was careful not to take much, remembering my trouble with using credit cards for living expenses in the past.

I continued to attend the Quaker meeting, becoming a member and serving as the recording clerk, as they called their secretary. I had not made many friends, mostly Barbara and a few of her friends in Bella Vista, and the Quakers provided me with a social group. It takes time to get to know people well, and seeing them only on Sunday mornings didn't allow much interaction. I joined a couple of committees and got to know them better.

In 2005, I had a Christmas open house in my tiny apartment. About thirty people came, not all at once, fortunately, and it was fun. I provided all of the food, cooking for days ahead of time. About twenty people were there at a time, and it was really crowded, but I've found that makes for the best parties. One man brought his toddler who enjoyed playing with the food on the coffee table. It was a lot of work. I was glad I did it, but future parties would be potluck.

One of the Friends, as Quakers call themselves, was on the board of a midwifery school in Fayetteville. She asked me to join the board, and as I had not yet become as active in the community as I did later, I not only agreed, but recruited my daughter Grace as well. Grace, a strong believer in breast feeding, actually had a business renting breast pumps back in Maryland. The midwife school was struggling financially and eventually had to close, but we helped as much as we could in the meantime.

I was settling into a satisfying routine, living in one town for more than five years, a long time for me. Perhaps Arkansas would be my permanent home.

42 Death and Dying

In 2006, I became a hospice volunteer. People go into hospice when they are expected to die in six months or less and receive palliative care, not treatment. The training to become a volunteer was extensive, with classes meeting for several hours on Tuesday nights for eight weeks. As a volunteer, I would be assigned a patient who could be in any stage of that six months. I was to be available for whatever nonmedical tasks the patient or the family needed, such as light housekeeping, taking the patient to appointments, or even just sitting with the patient to keep them company. However, almost all of the people I was assigned to were admitted so late in their illness that I saw them only once, if at all. Unfortunately, many people don't know the benefits of hospice, and wait until the last minute to make the call. Consequently, many patients have only a few days or weeks of hospice care. That was the case with most of my patients. I was able to spend time with only one, and she is the only one I remember.

Martha, as I will call her, was in an assisted living facility. She was a bitter, brusque, down-to-earth woman in her late seventies with advanced cancer. I sat and talked with her for an hour every week or so. She was dressed and sitting up in her recliner when I arrived. It was hard to find much to talk about, and one day for conversation she wanted to show me her jewelry. I was concerned that she might offer me some, and I knew I couldn't accept it and didn't know if she would be offended.

"Bring me that box in the dresser drawer," she said, pointing across the room.

She opened the box for me to look at her necklaces and brooches. Fortunately, she didn't offer me any, and I was doubly relieved because I didn't like any of it. Another day I helped her walk around inside the building with her walker. We passed the dining hall, and next to it was a smaller room where patients could eat privately with visiting family. As we walked by, Martha said, "I had dinner there with my brother."

"I thought you told me your brother died years ago."

"Yes, he did," she replied. I didn't say anything. *Don't question her hallucinations if they make her happy.*

In one conversation, we talked about religion, and she said she didn't believe any of it. Earlier she had told me she was Jewish. But in a later conversation, she volunteered that she was afraid of dying. I asked her why, and she said, "I'm afraid God will send me to hell because I don't believe in him." I didn't point out the contradiction.

A couple of months later she moved to a nursing home, and when I visited, she was clearly near death. She was lying in bed, barely conscious. I held her hand in silence for a while, and after a little conversation, I asked if she was still afraid of dying. She shook her head, smiled, and said softly, "No." She died the next day.

In early 2005, I noticed that my cat Toby didn't seem well. She gradually got worse so I took her to the vet, who diagnosed her with diabetes. I went home with prescriptions for hypodermic needles and insulin. For a year or so I gave her an insulin shot once a day, and she seemed okay. But in November of 2006, she started sleeping more than usual, curled up in a closet all day. She was clearly very sick.

I took her back to the vet.

"Her diabetes has progressed to the point that insulin won't help any more. There's another treatment we can do that might extend her life for a couple of months. Shall we try it?"

I thought about it. "I don't think so. I can't see treating her more just to extend her life for a short while. She's twelve years old. I think it's time to let her go."

"Are you sure? You can take her home and think about it a few days."

"I don't need to think about it. I'm sure. What will happen with her body?"

"We can cremate her if you want us to."

I thought about how I might bury her. John, my son-in-law, would bury her in their back yard, but they were out of town for a week. There was no place I could dig a grave even for a small animal.

"Yes, cremate her. Just give me a few minutes."

I held Toby in my lap, stroking her long silky fur and talking to her softly while the vet prepared the dose. Shortly after the needle was inserted in her leg, my beautiful friend Toby went to sleep for the last time. I held her until she stopped breathing, and then fled the clinic in tears. I cried for three days.

Toby stayed present with me for a long time. I would often see her out of the corner of my eye, strolling down the hall, or hear her at the door wanting in. It was hard to let her go.

One day in 2007 I received a call from Susan, the clerk of our Quaker meeting.

"I've just been contacted by a nursing home in Springdale. They have a resident who says she's a Quaker and wants a visit. Can you go?"

The patient was Ethelyn, a gentle woman in her late seventies who had been a Quaker in California where she grew up but had not attended a meeting since moving to Arkansas many years ago.

I asked David, a member of the meeting who played the guitar, to go with me to visit her. She was surprised to see us, not knowing there were any Quakers in the area. We learned that she had been a member of a programmed meeting, which meant it was similar to a Protestant church, with a minister and a sermon, unlike our unprogrammed meeting, where worship consists of sitting in silence for an hour. We tried sitting in silence with Ethelyn, but she simply fell asleep, so we decided to sing with her instead, as David accompanied us on his guitar. We chose the hymns from an old hymn book I had that she probably sang in her childhood. She didn't sing, but mouthed the words to all the verses of all the songs. She remembered them from those many years ago.

For two years, we met with Ethelyn twice a month, reading the Bible to her and singing. Occasionally another Quaker would join us. When David couldn't make it, I sat with her and we talked about her life, looking at the family pictures on her dresser. I came to know her and her family well.

Ethelyn gradually declined over the two years. One day I received a call from her daughter saying that her mother had died and asking if the Quakers would hold a graveside service for her. Six of us drove to Siloam Springs, and after the traditional open casket funeral, we convoyed to the cemetery. Susan led us in a short service of singing and silence before the casket was lowered into the grave. The other mourners knew nothing about Quakers and seemed a little puzzled by us, but the daughter was grateful.

I was glad we were able to give Ethelyn some spiritual comfort in her final years. I thought about her and my hospice patient. They had such different ways of approaching death.

Many people say they are not afraid of death but of the process of dying, especially if it includes a period of sickness and pain. As I get older, I think about that. My health is excellent, and I will probably die suddenly of a massive heart attack, as almost all of my family has done for three generations. I may be kidding myself, but that history leads me to think I won't experience a long illness.

But I'd rather not go suddenly, in the blink of an eye, as my father and so many of my relatives did. I'd rather have at least a short time of knowing the end is coming, to say goodbye and prepare myself. I think of my friend Vitae, who died a few years ago. He was seventy-eight when he had a heart attack that sent him to the hospital. He seemed to be recovering but had another severe attack, and was clearly dying. His wife, Margot, was at his bedside. He was in severe pain, and he asked for only enough morphine to make the pain bearable, but not enough to dull his awareness. He said, "I want to be conscious so I can experience the whole process as it happens." And he was. Margot said they had a deep, intimate communication while he was dying. She had to lean in close to hear him, as he had only enough breath to whisper, and at one point he said, "Don't hold my hand. If you hold my hand, I can't go."

I want to be there for the experience, too. I want to know what is happening and to be a participant, to leave my body with intention.

I see death as a continuation of life in another form, just leaving the physical body and moving on to a different plane. I don't believe in the traditional heaven and hell, but I think the form we take after death is determined largely by how we have lived—not as a punishment or reward, but as a natural extension of the condition of our soul in life. If I'm peaceful and loving when I die, I will move on to a nonphysical state of peace and love. I don't think it is a matter entirely of whether I do good or bad deeds, but the basic state of my soul. That state determines how I act in my lifetime, and that state also influences what my "life" will be after death.

I also believe that we determine when and how we die, not consciously, but on an unconscious level. I think we have a plan when we enter life, and when that plan is complete, it's time to go. I've had a similar belief for most of my life, which is one reason I wasn't more devastated when my son Howie died. Naturally, I grieved, but I'm convinced that he had finished what he had intended to do in that life and was ready to move on to another one, with another plan.

This belief system raises lots of questions, of course, and I don't have the answers, but I don't need them. Not knowing, even the possibility of being completely wrong, doesn't bother me. I'm confident that whatever death brings, it will be good, and I needn't be concerned about it. All I need to concern myself with is living in a way that if death is a continuation of the same, it will be just fine.

43 Berkeley

In 2005, I thought about buying a house. I had never considered it seriously before because I always wanted to be able to leave town on 30-days'
notice, which I did, several times. And no bank would give me a mortgage,
because I was self-employed with an unpredictable income. Being an older
single woman didn't help, either.

But with the housing bubble of the early 2000s, it was possible to get a
"no-doc" loan, meaning with a large down payment, no documents were
required proving my income. I could probably get a mortgage! I started
looking at houses but didn't find anything I liked. I remember one house
in particular, a three-bedroom ranch. As soon as I walked in the door
with the Realtor, I felt such bad energy I couldn't get out fast enough. I
learned that the house was on the market as a result of a bitter, vicious
divorce, and the residual negative energy was overwhelming. I couldn't
possibly live there.

It would have been a gamble anyway, since I didn't know how well my
practice was going to do, or when I would be earning a living with it. It
was just as well I didn't find anything I wanted.

I thought I ought put some of my money somewhere besides a savings
account and bought some shares in Whole Foods. The company was just
becoming well known and I liked the idea of organic food. I put $2,000
into it, knowing that I really didn't know what I was doing and didn't
want to risk much. I later got cold feet and sold it all at a loss. The stock
market is not the place for me.

One good use of my inheritance was to replace my car. I sold my old Subaru to a student for $2,600, took $8,000 out of the savings account, and bought a 1999 Camry. I was able to buy the new car, paying cash, before I sold the old one, and I've been able to avoid having a car payment ever since, a significant benefit.

Another withdrawal from savings was for hearing aids. I had bought some really cheap ones several years earlier, but when I dropped one on the parking lot and it was run over and crushed, I had to get a replacement. I went back to where I bought them, but the store was gone. I realized later that it was one of those outfits that comes into town, sets up a storefront, sends out a mass mailing, sells cheap aids to unsuspecting customers, and quickly moves on to the next town. I found a reputable place and bought new ones. They were not the high-end model, but were still expensive, something like $2,500. I had been slightly hard of hearing since my forties, and it had worsened as I got older. Hearing aids made a big difference in my quality of life.

My Quaker meeting rented meeting space in a building that was owned by a coalition of religious groups, the United Campus Ministries. We were entitled to a representative on their board of directors, and I filled that position. When the board decided to renovate the building, I chaired the committee. About $60,000 was available for the work.

I recruited committee members from the other organizations that also rented parts of the building, thinking they had an interest in how well the building functioned. We met often, and explored what needed to be done and who would do it. I had never been responsible for a project like this before, let alone one with a budget that size, and I wasn't sure I was up to it. It was daunting.

The committee met with contractors, getting estimates and choosing among them, and picking out equipment and lighting fixtures, among other things.

I decided to use the Quaker method of making decisions with the committee, not just coming to consensus but really discerning "the sense of the meeting"—what everyone really wanted. It was surprisingly easy. I started and closed all the meetings with a short period of silence. One obstinate older man often argued, but he couldn't get anyone else to agree with him and always came around eventually.

We replaced the entire heating and air conditioning systems and all the lighting in the two-story building, and repaired a badly cracked stone sidewalk at the entrance. The sidewalk had not only cracked, one whole section had sunk several inches. The stone mason we hired managed to jack up that section and added new stones so that it looked as good as new.

I paid particular attention to the new lighting fixtures. I'm very conscious of how much lighting affects us and how often we don't realize it. I wanted the new lights to be bright enough but not garish, and to be esthetically pleasing. Much institutional lighting is neither. The committee spent a lot of time looking at specifications and samples and talking with the contractor, but it was worth every minute. We succeeded in getting just what we wanted.

We spent the whole $60,000, but the first few months saw payback, as the building's utility bills decreased drastically. It was both a challenging and satisfying experience.

In the spring of 2007 I stumbled upon a website for a group called the Quaker Institute for the Future, or QIF, a Quaker think tank. It was started by some academics who wanted to foster research into how Friends can influence the future of our secular society. In the previous two years, it had sponsored month-long research seminars at the College of the Atlantic, in Bar Harbor, Maine. This year it was not possible to have it there, so rather than miss it altogether, it was decided to hold it for one week in Berkeley.

I emailed the contact person for more information, and as a result, flew to Berkeley for a week-long seminar in July.

Each of the attenders had a project they brought with them to work on during the week. Mine was the effort to establish a sustainability program at my Quaker Meeting. I had received the Meeting's blessing to work on it and was planning to develop my thoughts about it at the seminar.

Spending a week in Berkeley was a treat by itself. We met at a seminary next to the UC Berkeley campus, and used the campus library. We had lunches at excellent but inexpensive restaurants with menus like I never saw in Arkansas.

I was presented with a couple of unexpected challenges, however. I was given lodging with a woman who lived far from the meeting place and used a wheelchair. I was expected to help her get around, wrestling her wheelchair into her car and driving us to the meetings. After doing this twice, she decided not to attend any more. It took every ounce of my strength to get her heavy chair into the car and out again, and I was relieved to stop doing it. I think when the arrangement was made, no one knew how little I am and how difficult it would be for me.

The schedule called for each of us to present our projects in the morning on different days and get input from the others about them, then in the afternoons go off and work on developing them. I was chosen to go first. I was a bit nervous to speak in front of about twenty strangers, but once I got started it went easily. They responded enthusiastically to my presentation and were very encouraging about my project.

The second challenge arose when I discovered that the computers I was told I could use were not usable for me. Everyone else in the seminar brought a laptop; I didn't have one and was told one would be provided, but my host's computer was a Mac, which I didn't know to use and could not figure out, and the ones at the library were not connected to the Internet. They were intended for their students to use just for connecting within the library system. Consequently, I couldn't work on my project while I was there, which kind of negated the whole purpose of the seminar.

My response was to join a group from the Strawberry Creek meeting in Berkeley, who were working on a project very similar to mine, establishing sustainability practices at their meeting house. They were very welcoming and we had some interesting discussions. It was probably more instructive for me than if I had worked on my own.

Every night we met at a different local attender's house for dinner, which we each took a turn preparing, two people each night. My turn was the night before we left, and I had no idea what to do. I was beginning to panic, wondering what I would do for dinner, when one of the men turned to me and said, "I'll bring pizza for everyone if you'll bring a salad."

"You're on," I replied, greatly relieved. Salad I could do.

One of the local women took me to a grocery store and helped me decide what to buy and how much ingredients for salad for twenty. It came out just right. There was one piece of pizza left over after dinner and the salad bowl had one stray piece of romaine in it.

I think everyone knew I was the poor person in their midst and didn't mind that I had to pay for only a bunch of greens. Dinner for twenty would have been beyond my ability either to pay for or to cook.

It was all in all a wonderful week. I got to know some good Quakers who came from around the country from Alaska to Florida and learned about their interests and projects. I enjoyed the gorgeous flowers and fruit of sunny California, including picking figs from my host's tree to have with crème fraiche for dessert, and obtained support for my project at home.

When I returned to Fayetteville, I established an Earthcare Witness Committee in the Quaker Meeting, which embarked on a plan to educate our members and encourage them to act sustainably. We engaged in many efforts, including holding a potluck and discussions on sustainability once a month for nine months, using the workbook *Voluntary Simplicity*. We even made a field trip to Pea Ridge to a farm to get organic fertilizer from their guinea pigs for our gardens. The farmer need the manure pile moved and we wanted the manure. I wish I had a picture of the six of us standing ankle deep in guinea pig poop, shoveling it into boxes to put in our cars and trucks. It was smelly but fun.

One of our big projects was exploring how Fayetteville could establish a local currency, and we brought Paul Glover from Ithaca, NY, to speak at a public meeting. Paul was the originator of a very successful local currency called Ithaca Hours. We were not able to get our city organized, but we created our own Quaker Hours to use among ourselves. We discovered that while the idea has merit, it was more difficult to establish a currency than we thought. But we learned much about how currency systems work.

In other projects, we held a metal drive, donated a bicycle to a the university's Razorbikes for students to use on campus, arranged for us to buy paper supplies in bulk, created a series of Green Tips for cleaning products, held a seed swap for gardeners, and calculated our carbon footprints. We also wrote a statement about the need for stopping climate change called a Climate Change Minute, which our Meeting adopted. We then sent it on to our Quarterly Meeting, which adopted it and in turn sent it to our Yearly Meeting, where it was also adopted and became an official position of Quakers in five states.

That week in Berkeley was a good investment.

44 75th Birthday Trip

In April of 2008 I would be seventy-five years old. I didn't need a celebration as extravagant as my trip to France for my seventieth in 2003, and perhaps the next best thing was a long trip in this country. My friend Sue had invited me to visit her in Vermont and I wanted to see my friends and brother in the Washington area, so decided to make an extended trip to see them all. And why not go by North Carolina and see my friends there too? It wasn't that much out of the way.

I needed to pick a time when the weather would be good in Vermont. Sue said that the snow and ice would be gone in April but then everything turned to mud, so not to come before May. I wanted a weekend in Burnsville in North Carolina, a few days with my brother and another few days with Paula in Washington, and some time with my cousin Val in New York. And of course I had to stop to see Vitae and Margot in Virginia. I could do it all in three weeks.

It was an ambitious itinerary, and arranging visits with all these people on one trip was a challenge, requiring a lot of detailed coordination. I drove much of the trip but took the train for the longest leg, from Washington to Vermont, stopping over in New York on the way north.

I've always loved long-distance driving, taking many trips around the country alone over the years, so "hitting the road" again was a treat. I took out many books on CDs from the library to make the miles go by faster. I packed enough food for lunches at rest stops and for munching while behind the wheel. I devised a system of keeping the CDs in a box beside me in the right order so I could change them without taking my eyes off the road.

Driving from Arkansas to visit Denise in North Carolina took two days, with an overnight stay in a motel in Jackson, Tennessee.

Denise is a statuesque young woman with long red hair and a generous spirit. She lived with her husband and little son in the small house she grew up in. She drove me around Burnsville to revisit all the places I knew, including my old house and Pauline's house across the street. Pauline had died a few years earlier at age 91, and I was sad to see her house still empty. She lived alone in that little house on the mountainside until one day she felt sick, went to the hospital, and died four days later, independent until the end.

I went to the Celo Quaker meeting Sunday morning. It happened to be the last day they met in the old meeting house, the converted goat barn, before moving to the new building the next Sunday. I realized again how similar their meeting is to mine in Fayetteville. I was greeted warmly by the Friends I knew from eight years earlier, making me feel right at home.

On Monday I drove to Maryland to stay with my brother Frank and his wife Jean. They lived in a two-bedroom condo in a large retirement village. Frank had been diagnosed with MS in his fifties, and it had progressed in the past couple of years, enough that he now used a scooter to get around when he left the house. Jean was in the early stages of dementia, which I didn't realize until I noticed we were having a conversation a second time in five minutes. Frank had endless patience with her, seeming not to mind, acting as if every conversation was new. They had an obvious deep love for each other.

We decided to take a drive around Berwyn Heights where we grew up. The old cement block building where we went to grade school had been converted to a family home. It looked so small! I remembered it being much bigger, but of course then I was seeing it through a child's eyes. We also drove by our old house, which didn't look much different. I was a little surprised that I had no emotional reaction to it at all.

One small incident marred my visit a little. Frank smiled broadly as he proudly showed me how he had attached a manual pencil sharpener to the end of a bookcase, after building a small shelf to hold it. I said, "Why didn't you just screw it onto the upright at the end?"

I immediately regretted my words when I saw his face fall. "Oh," he said. "I didn't think of that." Frank had always been the "slow" one in the family, and once again I had shown how much "smarter" I was. My words reinforced his feelings of being inferior, and I felt ashamed of myself. If only I had thought before I had spoken.

Early Thursday morning Frank took me to the Amtrak station to get the train to New York. Once in New York, I had to change trains at Pennsylvania Station to get to Dover Plains to visit cousin Val. Such a huge place, with so many people! Bewildered, I couldn't find where to get my next train, even after asking at several information counters. Finally, I found someone who understood what I needed and directed me to the escalator up to another level to the right concourse. A huge screen stretched across the main waiting area, and I had to stand and watch it scroll to see where my train would be. I got tired standing there, but the only seating area was around a corner where the screen was out of sight, and I didn't dare go there and risk missing my train. Eventually I found the right train and settled gratefully into my seat.

I had packed only one small bag for the whole trip so I could manage it by myself, knowing that I could do laundry at my hosts' houses as I went, but it was still a struggle to drag it around the station. Hauling it into the train was also difficult.

Valerie and I didn't really didn't know each other at all, having met only once briefly many years earlier at a family reunion. She is fifteen years younger than I, her father being my father's younger brother. She had been divorced for many years, and was living with her youngest son, who was in his early twenties. They lived in a large split-level house in a wooded area out of town. Val insisted on giving me her bedroom, which took up one whole level of the house, while she slept on the couch in the living room. She said she often slept there when she was too tired to go upstairs, and was perfectly comfortable there. I gave up arguing with her.

For years, Val had been a project manager for large construction projects like shopping malls, but the construction business vanished in the Recession and she had been out of work for a couple of years. The house was in disrepair, and she didn't have the resources to fix it. She was fighting the bank over foreclosure. Her good nature came through, however, and we caught up on family news. Her hobby was genealogy and she told me far more about seven generations of our family history than I could possibly remember.

One day Lukas, another cousin, came up from New York City with his partner and took us all out to dinner in a very nice restaurant. We laughed a lot. All of my father's family has an irrepressible sense of humor.

My next stop was Vermont, and getting the train in the little Dover Plains station was easy. It was not a long ride to Watertown where Sue met me at the station.

Cousins Val LaRobardier, Maya, and Lukas Porter, in Dover Plains, New York, 2008

Sue, a short woman in her late sixties, has short dark hair and a dry wit. Extremely bright and competent, she does not suffer fools gladly. She is a former college professor and researcher, author of several books, a gourmet cook, and founder of a university based on Jungian studies. She is the first person I knew to install solar panels to power her whole house.

Sue drove us all around Vermont, and we visited the Tom and Jerry's ice cream factory and the von Trapp family lodge in Stowe. I was a bit disappointed that I didn't get to enjoy Sue's delicious meals, as her 92-year-old aunt was living with her and did all the cooking. The food was okay, but a let-down. Sue had to do some work while I was there, so I had down time just to rest and read some of her interesting books. I stayed until Friday, when it was time for another train ride.

I love trains, but the ride straight through from Vermont to Washington was exhausting. Thirteen hours is too long, even in the relative comfort of a train with its wide seats and room to move around. I ran out of the food I had packed, and the café food was barely edible. A couple of my seat mates were interesting, but much of the time I had the whole row to myself.

Someone had left a *New York Times* on the seat. Browsing it, I was surprised to see Harlan Cleveland's picture looking out at me from the obituary page. I had edited Harlan in *Perspectives* and visited him and his wife in their home in Virginia. I recognized the picture as his favorite, the one I used in the journal. He was wearing a heavy white sweater with Norwegian decoration all over it—very casual, like Harlan. His obituary took up a fourth of a page, which in the *Times* is extensive. He had a very distinguished life of ninety years. I was sad to learn that he was gone.

The train was an hour late, arriving after ten-thirty, and Frank's son Chris met me at the station. He got lost on the way to Frank's house, but he soon figured it out, and got us there by midnight.

I had left my car at Frank's so I could drive the next day to Paula's in the city. It was good to see her again. Short like Sue, also in her sixties but blond and slender, she and her husband Chuck have a beautiful three-story house in upper Northwest, a lovely part of Washington, with two guest bedrooms and a full bath on the third floor. It's very pleasant, but each visit it gets harder for me to manage the stairs. Paula has been a freelance editor and photographer, and we always have much to talk about.

They live near the Washington Cathedral, where I attended the Taizé chanting when I lived there, and I had a sweet meditation in the sanctuary on this trip. In the gift shop I found a funny little statue of a gargoyle like the ones on the Cathedral roof to take home. As always, we visited art galleries, and I discovered that I tired sooner than I used to. I also discovered that I was no longer comfortable driving in the city. It was good to get on the highway again to drive to Vitae's in Virginia.

Vitae and Margot lived in a brick pre-Civil War plantation house close to the Shenandoah River. Margot is an artist, exhibiting in galleries and teaching at a university. The house was pretty rundown and ramshackle, and they had a comfortable, laid-back lifestyle. Several years earlier when the river flooded, the water reached the house. The walls in every room were hung with Margot's artwork, and they spent several frantic hours taking all the paintings off the walls and carrying them up to the second floor. Margot's mother lived with them then, and being bedbound, she also had to be carried upstairs. Fortunately, the water stopped rising before it reached the second floor, but most of the first floor was under water. On a previous visit I had helped them clean the mud out of the kitchen. Until then I had never really thought about what a mess a flood leaves behind.

Vitae is hard to describe in a few words, deserving a whole book himself. In fact, his wife has written one. As I mentioned in an earlier chapter, he died about two years after this visit. Vitae decided early in life that his mission was to become as conscious as possible, and devoted his energy to doing that. He was a kind of spiritual advisor for me in the first few years I knew him. Of medium build with a stomach that revealed his love for food, almost bald and with a bulbous nose, he was not physically attractive to me, which made it easier to avoid any romantic involvement. As time went by, I relied on him less but always enjoyed sharing our adventures. To Vitae, life was a cosmic joke, and from his larger point of view, everything was funny. I laughed more with him than anyone. We were deeply connected on a spiritual level. One day years before, when we were sitting in my living room in meditation, my mind began to wander. Suddenly he looked at me and said, "You went away."

I also felt close to Margot, although I didn't know her nearly as well. On this visit, one morning she and I were sitting at the kitchen table talking, when I looked up and saw Vitae outside, mowing the lawn. I said to Margot, "I love your husband."

"I know," she replied, smiling. "So do I." She knew exactly what I meant.

The last day of my visit, I woke up feeling sick—sick enough that my breakfast came up just as I was about to leave. I debated whether to stay another day, but decided I felt better and left. Bad decision—I got sicker as I drove south. The nausea gradually faded and I thought I would be okay but after a couple of hours diarrhea started. There was nothing I could do but keep going.

I made it to Nashville where I stopped at a motel. I spent the night running to the bathroom. In the morning I considered whether to stay there another day or to drive on. I couldn't face a whole day and night sick in that room, so left for home. I got to know every restroom between Nashville and Springdale, including the one in a MacDonald's where I rinsed out my shorts.

At last, on June 21, I was home. It had been a wonderful trip, the last two days notwithstanding. A lovely birthday observance. I still smile when I think about it.

45 Closing My Practice

Then the recession hit.

It started in 2008, but I didn't really notice the effects until early 2009, when my clients began to disappear. They had always paid me out of their pockets because no insurance plans covered me, and now they couldn't afford me. My practice gradually fell away.

At first I didn't make the connection with the recession, but when Betty's store also began to lose customers, we both realized that people everywhere had less money to spend on nonessentials, and our businesses were in trouble. When people had to choose between food and supplements, food won.

When it became apparent that the downturn was not ending soon, I decided to close my office. It was a surprisingly easy decision. I had learned some interesting facts about myself and health care in the past four years, and I realized I was not seriously invested in continuing to be a naturopath. The recession provided a good excuse to quit.

I had noticed when I was interning with Laurie, my own naturopath, that I was vaguely uncomfortable with her practice. It took me a while to identify what bothered me: It was her total confidence that she knew exactly what she was doing, that she knew the answers and was always right.

Consequently, her clients had total confidence in her, and this was key to her success as a practitioner. Confidence in the doctor is the most important factor in the success of treatment. Complete faith in the practitioner no matter how competent he or she is or what the problem or treatment, believing that the doctor will make you better leads you to get better results. Trust is key. And my problem was that I could not present myself as an absolute authority, that I was certain that I was right either in my diagnosis or treatment.

I presented my thoughts to the client as possibilities, not certainties, leaving it to them to try my suggestions and see if they were effective. I could never be absolutely certain about what I was doing and was not willing to pretend I did.

Most of my clients did get better, and I believe that enlisting them as collaborators in their health rather than dictating to them was the better way. But it doesn't seem to work that way for successful health practitioners. The God-like doctor is not the norm anymore, but patients want answers from authority figures who have complete self-confidence.

I also didn't want to do the necessary PR in the community to get more business. When I signed up for the course, I thought my age would not be a problem, and in some ways it wasn't, but now at seventy-five, I didn't have the drive to put myself out there to do workshops and seminars and classes. I did some the first couple of years, and then I just didn't want to do it anymore. Thus, I didn't get enough clients for the practice to be self-sustaining from referrals from current clients, as Laurie had done. Her practice relied entirely on client referrals, and she was constantly busy. I couldn't get to that point, even before the recession.

In addition, I had become increasingly uncomfortable being responsible for other people's health. Every patient signed a disclaimer that they knew I was not a medical doctor, that they were responsible for their own health, and that I made suggestions for them but they decided what to do. But this did not negate the fact that they were counting on me to know what was going on in their bodies and giving them good ideas of what to do about it. In that sense, I *was* taking responsibility for their well-being, and it felt like too much. I don't know how medical doctors do it, knowing that patients are counting on them to know everything and to always be right and to keep them alive and well. I would sometimes lie awake at night wondering whether I had gotten something right and if my suggestions with a specific client would help. There was always the possibility that I had missed something and my recommendation might even be harmful. As far as I know, that never happened, but the possibility weighed heavily on me.

And finally, I wasn't making any money. Even before the recession, the income was small and sporadic, and I had to keep some of my editing business to pay the bills.

Considering all of these factors, I was relieved that it was time to call it quits. Of course I couldn't just close the office suddenly, as I had a few ongoing clients. I alerted them that I would be available a few more weeks and referred them to the only other naturopath in Fayetteville. Laurie was still available, but she had moved her office to Bella Vista, 30 miles away.

I finally went to the store owner, and said, "Betty, I've decided to close my practice. I just don't have enough clients to be worth it."

"Oh, Maya, I'm sorry to hear that, but I understand. I just hope my store survives. Things are really tight."

The bookcase and the desk chair went to my home office. One of my clients wanted the room dividers, and I left the little desk for Betty to use as a display surface. I carried the philodendron out to the car, and my office was gone.

I missed my clients, the interactions with them, the intimacy while determining what was going on in their bodies and in their lives. And I have to admit I enjoyed their gratitude.

It was easy to blame the recession rather than see myself as a failure, but I didn't really need a scapegoat. I had lasted four years and had the satisfaction of knowing there were people out there who not only were healthier because of me, but were able to take better care of themselves into the future because of what I had taught them. That was a comforting thought.

And best of all, I could keep myself healthy. I had learned so much by working with the wide range of illnesses and conditions of my clients. I knew how to evaluate material I read in publications and online, to know what was reasonable and what was nonsense. I was comfortable disagreeing with my doctors when they wanted me to do certain tests or procedures. When I considered doing something for my health, I could use muscle response testing to learn if it was a good idea or not. In many ways, I could take charge of my own health, and it has paid off in good health ever since.

✳✳✳✳

The recession of 2008 affected my children far more than it did me. Both my daughter and son and their spouses were out of work for months. When I learned that both of them were about to lose their houses to foreclosure, I lent them each thousands of dollars from my inheritance. I was confident that I wouldn't need the money any time soon, and they would pay me back when they could. They're still paying it off, and I haven't needed it yet. It felt really good to be able to help them. I could imagine my father smiling approval, since it was originally his money and he was such a generous man. If he were still alive, he would have lent it in a heartbeat.

I also financed a car for my granddaughter Veronica. She got her driver's license on her sixteenth birthday, in November 2007, and immediately found a part-time job. Her parents and I took turns driving her to work and back for a few months, but obviously she needed her own transportation. At sixteen, she couldn't get a bank loan, so I bought the car and she paid me back over four years, at zero interest. She made the payments faithfully, working while finishing high school and attending the University of Arkansas. It was an old car and barely lasted the four years of the loan.

I also used some of the money to help the older granddaughter, Simone, to go to Japan as an exchange student right after high school. I am still impressed at how brave she was at age seventeen to fly halfway around the world for a year to a new culture where she didn't speak the language. She was there for ten months, and loved it. It was hard at first, especially the first night. Her host family took her upstairs to her room and left her. She looked around and, panicked, called her father on her cell phone: "Dad, there's no bed!" No one had told her that the bed was a mat rolled up in the closet. She did well, and majored in international relations in college with a minor in Japanese when she returned.

My savings account was dwindling, but I knew it would all come back eventually and wasn't concerned. But I did need to increase my income. How could I get more editing clients quickly?

The question suddenly took on more urgency. The two social work journals I had been editing for several years provided most of my income. The publisher had been sending the materials every few months, on schedule. I realized one day that I had not received the next issue. I waited another week and then called the publisher.

"Oh," he said, "I gave that to someone else." He said it casually, as if it were unimportant. I was stunned.

"You mean I'm not going to edit it anymore?"

"That's right."

"Both of them?" I asked, incredulous.

"Yeah, both of them."

This was the publisher I had so much difficulty with before, the one who was so hard to communicate with. I didn't know what to say. He was

Three generations of the Leas family at Gary's wedding reception, 2015. (l-r) Joyce Leas, George Leas, Veronica Lapetina, Cindy Leas, Gary Leas, Matthew Leas, Grace Dunn, Maya Porter, Luke Dunn, John Dunn. Seated: Susan Frederickson, Matt's fiancé.

obviously unconcerned that he had simply taken away my work without even telling me.

I hung up the phone in shock. My rent was only $150 a month, and I still had money in the bank so I didn't panic yet. But now I really needed to figure out how to get more clients soon.

I had belonged to an online editing Listserv for many years, and found another editor there who had an excellent marketing plan. She graciously explained to me how she did it. She found university professors online and sent them a postcard about herself and her services. This method had been working effectively for her for years, and I thought about how I could adapt it to my business.

Editing in the social work field had been my specialty for several years. All social work departments at universities in the United States have to be certified, and the certifying organization has a website. Every university with a certified social work department is listed, and the school's website lists their faculty with contact information. I designed a marketing postcard and ordered a hundred of them from an online printing company. Then I found the names and addresses of professors online, hand-addressed the postcards, stamped them, and mailed them.

Fortunately, it worked, and clients began to respond. I was soon making enough money that I gradually built up my checking account. I realized I needed a website and got a friend to build a simple one for me, so prospective clients could check me out.

46 Grace Moves

In the late summer of 2009, Grace and John decided to buy a house. Grace was doing the searching, and I went with her on some of the appointments with the realtor. We looked at one house that she really liked, but it was out on the eastern edge of Rogers, far from Springdale. I thought the house would be a poor choice, mostly because of the location, and said so.

We looked at several other houses, including some that were lovely but out of their price range, and I thought they were still looking , when one day I stopped in to see them.

"Well, we bought a house!" Grace said.

"Oh? Which one?' I asked.

"That one with all the rooms in Rogers."

I was shocked. That was the one I did not want them to buy. I turned away quickly so she wouldn't see my tears.

We talked about a moving date, and I left as soon as I could. I felt abandoned and hurt. My needs apparently didn't matter. She hadn't even discussed it with me, probably because she knew I would try to talk her out of it. In my gut I felt it was the wrong choice, and not only for my sake, but because I didn't think they would be happy there. But it was done. The contract was signed.

I went home and had a good cry. I moved to Arkansas in 2000 to be near them, because I thought as the years went by I would need them. It turned out that over the past nine years they had needed me much more than I needed them, but that could easily change. I was in good health, but I was seventy-six years old. How soon might I need their help?

They would be only thirty minutes away, I reminded myself. *That really isn't so far, and if I have a real emergency, I'll call 911, not Grace. I have good neighbors who help me with things like getting my car fixed. Maybe it isn't going to matter much.*

I would not have been seeing them as much even if they stayed in their house in Springdale. Our time together had been mostly as a result of taking care of the children—picking them up, taking them home, staying with them overnight when their parents went out of town. With Luke now twelve years old and the girls in their late teens, they didn't need babysitting anymore.

But it mattered. As a result of the move, I seldom saw Luke, since spending time with him meant making plans for something specific. I wasn't picking him up at school, taking him to Scout meetings, or helping him with homework. Consequently, I didn't spend nearly as much time with him when he was a teenager as I had with his sisters. I arranged outings with him when I could, but I couldn't think of many things to do with a teenage boy that I could afford, so we didn't forge the relationship like I had with the granddaughters. Perhaps I wouldn't have anyway, just because he's a boy. We maintained a loving relationship, just not as close a bond as I would have liked. He was always an affectionate, considerate child, and stayed that way throughout his teens.

Grace and I have a different relationship than most of my friends seem to have with their daughters. We have a strong connection and love each other deeply, but we don't need to communicate a lot. We may go several weeks without even a phone call, and that's okay. Some of my friends talk to their daughters every day, maybe for an hour at a time, and I can't imagine what they talk about. Grace and I don't need to know the trivia of each other's lives. We talk when we have something we want to talk about, not just to chat. When they lived only a few minutes away, I would occasionally drop in to visit and catch up on what was going on in their lives. That wouldn't happen now, so without phone calls either, we would have much less contact than before.

The effect of the move on me was more emotional than practical. I didn't realize how much I was aware of their presence less than ten minutes away, until they weren't there. I felt disconnected, family-less. Not that I really was, it just felt that way, and perception is sometimes as important as reality.

Grace and John tried to convince me that I should move to Rogers also. I had been mistaken about the house not being good for them; they loved it, and thought the solution to the distance was for me to move near them. They just couldn't seem to understand that all of my life was centered in Fayetteville, in the opposite direction. They also apparently didn't recognize the difference in the cultures of the two cities, how different they were. Fayetteville is very progressive, sometimes called "funky." Some say it is full of aging hippies, and that's about right. Rogers is more conservative, solidly Republican, and more business oriented. Sam Walton founded Walmart there and the company still dominates the city. I would not feel at home in Rogers, and didn't even consider moving there.

I would need to rely on my friends and neighbors more than ever. Fortunately, I had gotten to know the people in the Quaker meeting well enough to feel that I could count on them almost like family.

****

In contrast, during that time, 2009–2010, my relationship with my son moved in the other direction—we became closer than we had been since he was young. As I have indicated earlier, his wife was a difficult person who was determined to keep Gary away from his family. She succeeded most of the time, and I saw him infrequently for thirty years. But when they divorced, Gary and I were able to re-establish our relationship. We had long phone conversations, and he and his son Howie drove from their home in Illinois to Arkansas for Thanksgiving in 2009. We gathered for a wonderful turkey dinner at Grace's house, the first time all of us had been together.

The next year I flew to Illinois for Thanksgiving with Gary. His son Howie was staying with his mother in Arizona then. I was pleased that with his wife gone, Gary was able to make many friends. People had not wanted to hang out with them when he was married, but now he invited a group of friends to come for Thanksgiving dinner. Gary is a good cook and he put on a delicious dinner. Half a dozen friends sat down with us to eat and another half dozen or so came by as the day went on.

This was the first time I really experienced Gary's life and was somewhat surprised to discover how different it was from mine. He was a pipefitter, and had a typical working-class lifestyle. He was a smoker, a drinker, and a conservative Republican, and so were all his friends. None of them had more than a high school education, and had no interests in common with mine. They were all good-hearted, hard-working people, "salt of the earth" types, and obviously cared about Gary. He was very popular. Having friends was a treat for him, after all those years of isolation, and he reveled in their company. I was happy to have time with him with his friends, even though I had to retire to my room from time to time to escape the cigarette smoke.

It was a great visit. Gary and I sat on the porch swing and talked and talked. We drove to the cemetery to visit his brother's grave. We explored what it was like growing up with their critical father. We laughed at some good memories. It was such a relief to be able to spend time with him and to see him happy for the first time in many years.

✴✴✴✴

The late 2010s brought many changes to our family. The granddaughters each graduated from college and moved away. Simone, the older girl, married Josh, a Delta airlines pilot, and moved to St. Paul, Minnesota, and Veronica went straight from graduation to an excellent job in Chicago. Luke, in high school, was the only grandchild still in town. He would go on to become an Eagle Scout and graduate from high school. What a change from when I moved to Arkansas in 2000! The grandchildren were all little kids then. I was deeply grateful to have been here for their childhoods.

In 2013 my son Gary met Cindy, and in 2015 they married in an informal wedding in their back yard in Joliet, Illinois, which turned out to be a fun family reunion. Many of the grandchildren and grandnephews and nieces were there and met for the first time. We took a picture of the three generations, including my ex-husband George and his wife Joyce, the only photo ever taken of all of us. It was delightful to see Gary and Cindy together. Gary was happier than I had seen him since he was a kid. Cindy is the best thing that ever happened to him.

Gary's son Matt was doing very well with a high-level job in the government in Washington, and his other son, Howie, was living with his mother in Arizona and was doing well also. The family was growing up and moving on.

✴✴✴✴

For a couple of years I had thought about finding another place to live. With Grace and her family moving to Rogers, I had no family connection in Springdale any more. Spring Meadows was satisfactory, but just barely. The restrictions were annoying, and I was tired of driving into Fayetteville for everything, but I kept dismissing the thought. I had lived there for seven years. I didn't think I could afford market rates for a house or

Maya's duplex on Mary Drive in Johnson, Arkansas, 2018

even an apartment. Inertia is hard to break, and it was so much easier just to stay put.

Then on Thursday, November 12, 2009, I had a dream that lit a fire under me. It was one of the few dreams I've had in my life with a clear message: "Get out of Spring Meadows. *Now*! Not later—*right now!*" The message couldn't have been clearer: It was absolutely necessary that I find another place to live as quickly as possible.

The next morning, Friday, I looked in the want ads for houses and apartments and found a likely place in Johnson, a little town tucked between Fayetteville and Springdale. When I arrived to meet the landlord, I saw that it was a brick duplex in what looked like an okay neighborhood, not expensive but not low-income either.

When I entered the front door and looked around, I was not impressed.

"Oh, …I don't know.…" I said.

Seeing my hesitation, she said, "Well, I have another one next door. Let's go look."

We walked next door and she let us in. The large living room was bright with sunlight and I knew instantly it was the right place for me. She showed me around, and I said I would take it.

"I like it, but I want storm doors put on. Can you do that?"

"Okay," she replied. "No problem. My husband will meet you here with a lease to sign tomorrow."

"I'll be here with my checkbook," I said. And that was that.

On Saturday morning I signed the lease, and on Monday I gave my 30-day notice to Spring Meadows. I would move into the new place on December 15.

Several people had moved out recently, and when I told Leila, the manager, that I was leaving, she said, "Oh, Maya, not *you!*" She actually had tears in her eyes. For some reason she had taken a liking to me, and was sorry I was leaving.

"I'm scheduled for my annual recertification for subsidized housing next week," I said. "Will we still do it since I'm leaving?"

"No, I'll cancel it. No need to do it now."

The dream had to do with the recertification and avoiding that session was critical, thus the hurry. I clearly still qualified for the apartment, so I don't know what would have happened if I had stayed, but I was content not to find out.

That is the only time I have ever made such a sudden, drastic change in my life based simply on a dream. I've never had such an instructive dream before, either, and this one was so clear and so compelling I couldn't ignore it.

My rent in Spring Meadows had increased as my editing business increased, but the new place still cost more than twice as much, at $595 a month, plus all utilities. It would be a stretch, but as always, I counted on the Universe providing what I needed. I asked myself why I hadn't done this sooner and didn't have a good answer, except that I had gotten comfortable and liked the low rent. I had never intended to stay there for seven years.

Moving into a bigger place is a lot easier than into a smaller one. The duplex had two bedrooms, and I could take everything, plus the furniture Grace had been storing for me in her house. My Quaker friends Karen and Garin helped me pack and move all the small stuff in their pickups, so all I paid for was moving the large furniture. LaDeana, one of the Quaker women, planted daffodil bulbs in my new front yard during the move when I wasn't looking. They came up in the spring and have bloomed every year since. I think of her every time I see those little green shoots peeking up out of the ground.

Now I had a place with a back yard where I could actually garden! As soon as the ground thawed, I put in a large garden all along one side of the back yard. I planted tomatoes, beans, lettuce, peas, peppers, and several herbs. There's nothing like putting seeds in the ground and watching plants emerge that will produce food, and there's not much so rewarding as stepping out your back door, picking that food, and eating it for dinner. It was not the huge garden I had in North Carolina, but was very satisfying, nevertheless.

For the first time in years, I had neighbors with children. They were all ages, from toddlers to teenagers, and got along surprisingly well. There was a lot of noise, but it was playing noise, happy noise. I never heard crying or fighting. The adults were friendly and helpful. It was a safe neighborhood.

I had found a good home.

47 New Meeting Space

After I moved to Johnson and Grace moved to Rogers, time with the family was limited mostly to special occasion dinners, like birthdays and holidays. These events gradually became more and more difficult for me, because I couldn't hear. Since the conversation around the table was always very spirited and rapid and the girls had soft voices, much of what was said went right by me. There was a limit to how often I wanted to ask "What?" over and over, so I got used to sitting there smiling a lot and wondering what was going on. I could hear enough that I could sometimes join in, so I could still enjoy being there. New hearing aids helped, but no aids take the place of normal hearing.

Deafness is a hard disability to deal with. There are worse ones, of course, but deafness is difficult because it is invisible. When people appear to be normal, it is easy to forget that they can't hear well. I sometimes think I should wear a button that says, "Speak up! I'm hard of hearing." It's an isolating condition, because it is often preferable to stay home than to be in uncomfortable situations. I soon discovered that I couldn't understand the dialogue at plays unless I could see the actors' mouths. It was impossible to understand song lyrics on the radio or in videos, and I couldn't understand speech over loudspeakers, especially in airports. I began avoiding large gatherings, because in order to hear the person near me, I had to turn the aids up and then the surrounding noise was too loud and exhausting.

Eventually I discovered closed captioning on television. I learned to position myself so I could see a speaker's mouth, and arranged more one-to-one meetings with friends. I found the few restaurants that were relatively quiet, and discovered that most of the others will turn their music down if asked. I just kept finding more and more ways to get by, refusing to isolate myself more than absolutely necessary. I knew that avoidance was a bad road to go down, as being isolated is a problem in itself that often leads to a decline in other faculties. I discovered that occasionally I missed something I was told, or heard it incorrectly. But I adapted, and over the years it has been more of a constant nuisance than a serious problem.

Adapting for disabilities in general became an issue for the Quaker meeting. We had wanted to find a new meeting space for a long time, because our building was not accessible for people with mobility problems. It had two floors with a mezzanine between, and the restrooms were on the mezzanine. No matter where we met, upstairs or down, we had to climb stairs, and several of our people used either a cane or a walker. We had appointed a Meeting Space Committee to find another place to meet, and I served as its clerk.

For two years we looked for an appropriate space, but could find nothing that we could afford with our tiny budget. The committee looked at many spaces, but they all had features that made them unusable for us in one way or another. Then an organization called OMNI Center for Peace, Justice, and Ecology bought a building that had space suitable for us to rent. Many of the OMNI members were also Quakers, so it was a good fit. We talked to the OMNI board and learned that yes, they would be agreeable to us meeting there.

However, we had to decide whether it was a good move for us. It seemed to me an obvious yes, but in good Quaker process, we had to come to unity on the subject. We visited the building, had meetings about it, and I thought we had decided to do it, when one Friend, I'll call him Don, objected. His reasoning was that OMNI was known in the community as a progressive, liberal organization, and more conservative visitors to our meeting might get the impression that we are a liberal group and stay away. In our process, everyone has to be in unity to make a decision, and Don said no. That was the end of it. We weren't moving.

That was the way it stood until something unexpected happened.

Occasionally Daryl, a Quaker in Alabama, came to our meeting when he was in Fayetteville visiting his parents and sister. He came to town for the funeral when his mother died, and then again when his father Lyle was very ill. Daryl came to Meeting one Sunday morning and explained that he might have to leave early, as he was expecting news about his father any minute. Just as we ended our worship meeting, he received a phone call that his father had died. As Daryl was leaving for the nursing home, Don, the Quaker who had objected to our move, volunteered to go with him.

Later, we learned what happened there.

As Don stood at the bedside with Daryl looking down at the man lying on the bed, he had a change of heart about moving Meeting to the OMNI building. Lyle had attended our Meeting at some time in the past, but when he became older, the building was too difficult for him to manage so he had not been there for years. Don suddenly realized how important it was that we move to a location that was accessible for people who are disabled. If we had moved earlier, Lyle would have been able to continue to attend Meeting all those years. How many other people would be similarly affected if we didn't move?

With that epiphany, the obstacle to renting space in the new OMNI building disappeared. We arranged to move on the first Sunday in November of 2010.

The move occurred just in time. Peter, a member in his eighties, had a stroke in early November. When he recovered sufficiently to attend Meeting, a ramp at the new meeting place enabled him to attend with his walker and later a wheelchair. In addition, one of our members had extensive back surgery that month and would not have been able to manage the stairs at the old building either.

And that month I had a knee replacement.

One morning I woke up with so much pain in my left knee I could barely walk. I had been taking a supplement that was supposed to create new cartilage and it appeared to be working, so I was startled that the joint had suddenly given way completely, with no warning. But I soon learned that the pills were actually a painkiller, and the damage had been accumulating but I hadn't felt the pain. Now it was bone on bone, and I needed a knee replacement.

I managed to get through the move into my new house with high doses of ibuprofen, but in early October 2010 I gave up and called a knee doctor.

The surgery on this knee took place ten years after the other one, and I discovered how much harder it is to recover at seventy-seven than at sixty-seven. But I persevered with the tedious exercises and eventually recovered full use of the knee. I was grateful that we were meeting in the new building; getting up and down the stairs at the old meeting location would have been difficult for me also.

The new meeting space was not only easier to use, it had better parking and was quieter because it was not on a major street. Moving was a good decision for all of us.

48 Losing My Brothers

In February of 2011, I received a phone call from Frank's daughter, Barbara.

"Aunt Maya, I have some sad news. Dad died last night."

"Oh no! What happened?"

"He just collapsed in the hallway. Mom called security and they came right away but it was too late. They think he died instantly from a heart attack."

"Barbara, I'm so sorry. How are you doing?"

"I'm okay. But it's so sudden. I'm still kind of in shock."

****

My earliest memory of Frank is of the three of us playing in the dirt at the base of a big pin oak tree in the front yard. We had little toy cars, metal with rubber wheels, and we scraped roads in the dirt and made miniature garages out of sticks. I was probably about three years old, so he would have been about six or seven.

Frank was always slow—his thoughts, his movements, his speech. He was intelligent but not quick, unlike the rest of the Porters. Consequently, it was easy to underestimate his abilities. His high school counselors would be astonished to know that the student they thought unlikely to learn went on to college and earned a Ph.D. in plant pathology.

His speech was especially slow. He spoke in phrases, with long pauses between them. One day when we were talking on the phone and I was straining to be patient, he suddenly chuckled and said, "I like to talk to you. You let me finish my sentences!"

Betty Jean, 3; Bobby, 5; Frank, 6, in the backyard
of the house in Berwyn Heights.

When Frank graduated from the University of Maryland in 1952, the draft was very much on his mind, with the prospect of fighting in the Korean War. He began to question whether he could kill other human beings. After much thought and discussion with friends and counselors, he decided he was a conscientious objector who would not fight but was willing to serve in a noncombatant role.

When our parents received the letter telling of his decision, they were horrified. In their view, he was being unpatriotic and a coward. Daddy wanted to send him a scorching telegram immediately, but Mother talked him out of it. Mother, in her typical "what will people think" mode, wrote to him, "I hate to see you ruin your whole life. You will be all alone in the world!" I was somewhat puzzled by his decision, but I had so much confidence in him that I didn't question it. Eventually our parents made their peace with it and told him that they would support him. As far as I know, he never suffered any stigma from his decision.

The Baptists are not known as a peace church, so he had an uphill battle with his draft board. At first he was refused, but he appealed and endured an investigation by the FBI and a hearing. Apparently his sincerity came through, because he was granted CO status and entered the

Army the same month the Korean War ended, July 1953. After training, he was assigned to the medical corps at Camp Kilmer in New Jersey. When he was discharged in June 1955, he went back to school and earned his master's degree and then a doctorate. He worked for most of his career for the U.S. Department of Agriculture, in one capacity or another, as a plant scientist.

Frank met Jean Boyer when they both attended a group on campus at the University of Maryland. When Frank went to Wisconsin for the summer to work at a camp, he mentioned that he didn't expect to get mail that summer. She sent him a letter that said in its entirety, "This is mail." They began corresponding, and one day he wrote her a note saying, "If you still like pizza, and if you know where we can get it, and if our schedules should mesh, maybe we could go out for some pizza." Her reply was succinct. "Regarding pizza, all I can say is, *if* you get around to asking me, I would love to."

They soon realized they wanted to spend the rest of their lives together, but there was one hurdle they needed to consider: Jean was seven years older than Frank. They eventually decided that if it didn't matter to them, it didn't matter what other people thought. They were married in March 1955, and their ages never made a difference. They had a stable and remarkably happy marriage for the rest of their lives.

Frank may have been slow, but he had more financial savvy than any of us. He and Jean were extremely frugal; their policy was always to save enough money to buy whatever they wanted rather than going into debt. He also learned to invest in the stock market. He made some mistakes, but over the years they accumulated substantial assets. Consequently, he became the person the rest of us went to for help when things got tough.

I benefited greatly from his financial sense when in 1958, my husband and I asked Frank and Jean for a loan for the down payment to buy our first house. They lent us $1,200, about $10,000 in today's money, not a trivial amount. It amazes me that they had that much money available and were willing to lend it to us.

In his mid-fifties, Frank was diagnosed with multiple sclerosis. He continued to work for a few more years, but eventually the fatigue and weakness progressed so far that he very regretfully had to retire on disability.

He soon came to view MS as a blessing, however, because it gave him time to write. He had never been quite sure what his real calling was, and when he began writing, he knew—*he was a writer*. For the next twenty years he devoted most of his time to writing essays and letters. He wrote

Frank, at his seventh grade graduation, on the steps of Grammie's house next door.

about everyday experiences and what he learned from them. He joined writing groups and as time went by his writing improved. When he and Jean moved into a retirement complex, he was asked to read some of his essays on the facility's radio station. He loved it when other residents stopped him in the halls to tell him how much they enjoyed his broadcasts. He compiled some of the essays into a booklet and distributed them to friends and to people who attended his readings.

In 1987, I was just getting started in my copyediting business and Frank asked me to edit some of his early essays. In the process, he realized that my old daisy wheel printer wasn't professional enough to print jobs for clients. He lent me $2,000 to buy a Hewlett Packer laser printer, which is what they cost then. I was extremely poor at that point, and would have been hard pressed to succeed without that printer. I have always been grateful that he was both able and willing to help me out at critical times in my life.

Frank was healthier than most people, in spite of his MS, as the disease just weakened him and slowed him down. One day several years later, as I walked with him through a building, I was alarmed to watch him staggering down a hallway, touching the walls to keep from falling. That day I persuaded him to start using a cane. Eventually he progressed to a scooter, which he used at first only outdoors and then in the house as well. He called it his "horse."

By the time his grandson Tim was two years old, Frank was increasing his use of the scooter. One day in the backyard Frank got the idea to drive the scooter with one hand and pull Tim in his wagon with the other, both of them laughing in delight. Frank said with deep satisfaction, "I never thought I'd be able to run around the yard with my grandson." So typical of his attitude toward his condition: Don't complain, find ways to cope, move forward, and enjoy life.

Frank, date unknown, probably in his early 40s.

Frank never lost his good humor, staying constantly upbeat and cheerful. Even in later years when Jean began losing both her hearing and her memory, he dealt with it without complaint. Jean was well down the path of memory loss when Frank said to his daughter, "She's still a joy to live with. We'll stay together as long as we can." He just made adjustments as they were needed, and carried on.

Even though he was eighty-one, his death was a surprise, considering his good health. He had always been the rock, the dependable one.

In one of his essays, he recalled that after getting his bachelor's degree in general science, he couldn't decide what field to pursue for his master's. He took an aptitude test, and the counselor told him, "Go ahead and do whatever you want to do. You won't set the world on fire at anything, but you'll do all right."

Later, as he was standing on a street corner one day, he resolved, "Okay, so I won't set the world on fire, but I can keep my corner warm."

For the rest of his long life he kept his corner warm.

****

Six weeks after Frank died, our brother Bobby died.

I didn't learn about it until August, however. I received a letter from Nelia, Bobby's wife, that Bobby had died in March, at age eighty. She included the program from his service, with a photo of him. It was blurry, but I could see that he had changed so much I would not have recognized him. I had sent Bobby a note telling him that Frank had died, but did not hear back from him. Nelia said that she had just found my note in August with my return address and wanted to let me know that Bobby was gone.

Bobby was named Than Robinson Porter, but we always called him Bobby, short for Robinson, to distinguish him from Daddy, whose name was also Than. The names caused some confusion outside the family. For instance, when he graduated from high school, Bobby discovered that the name on his diploma was Robert Porter.

He is hard to write about because his life was so troubled. At least it seemed so to me; I can't know what it was it like for him. I just know our family's experience of him was difficult and painful.

Bobby was handsome, with dark brown hair and brown eyes. He was also extremely intelligent. He made straight A's in every class from the first grade through college, except for one C in one class at the University of Maryland. He was devastated by that one C and was furious with the professor, insisting that it was the professor's fault.

Bobby, 5 (left), and Frank, 6..

He was not only brilliant, he was also arrogant and intolerant of people who were not as smart as he, which was just about everyone. He was not close to either Frank or me.

I think Bobby got along pretty well with the family through his teens. At some point in the early 1950s, Bobby moved out of the house and lived in Washington. This is the period when he developed an interest in minorities, especially African Americans. Washington was becoming a largely black city at that time. He joined a black church.

From here on there are gaps in what I know of the chronology of his life. After graduating from the University of Maryland, he was drafted and sent to Japan. When he got out, he went to George Washington University to get his master's.

Later he went to New York University and earned a Ph.D. in physics. At some point during this time, he cut off contact with our family. I don't know how or when that happened, whether it was a sudden break or if he just gradually stopped communicating, but it isn't unusual for a young person who has already been away from home for years not to keep in frequent touch with the family.

Frank told me that one day Mother got a phone call from a woman named Luz. She said she was Bobby's wife, and asked if Bobby had been

Bobby, at his seventh grade graduation.

violent in childhood. Mother was taken completely by surprise by the call, as she did not know that Bobby had married, and she replied, "No, never." It's hard to believe that she had not been aware of it; more likely she did not want to admit that her son had always had a quick, fierce temper that sometimes erupted in violent outbursts. As children, we had learned to keep our distance from Bobby when he was angry.

After the call, our parents established occasional contact with Bobby and Luz. Luz was from the Philippines, and was studying for her Ph.D. in nursing, also at NYU. They received their degrees in the same graduation ceremony, and I have a charming photo from a New York newspaper showing the two of them in their graduation robes, smiling and adjusting each other's mortar board. The caption says, "Using Their Heads." Luz and Bobby had three children, but I don't know what Bobby was doing or where they were after graduation. I have a vague memory of all of us gathered at our parents' house one Thanksgiving, and I liked Luz.

At some point several years later, probably around 1975, Luz called Mother and Daddy and said that she had to leave Bobby, and asked for help. I probably learned the rest of the story from Frank. I don't know any details, and I may have some of it wrong.

Apparently Bobby had been violent either with Luz or the children, or both, and she had to get away, but did not have any money. Daddy lent her enough money to move and get established in another state, taking the children with her.

Bobby was furious that Daddy had helped Luz. He blamed our parents for the breakup of his marriage, and cut off all contact with any of us. From then on, I lost track of him. Apparently the folks had a mailing address for him for a while, as Mother sent him presents for his birthday and Christmas, year after year. They were all returned unopened.

Mother was broken-hearted. She had effectively lost another son, considering the baby boy she gave up before she was married. I was just angry. I thought he was an obnoxious jerk and was somewhat relieved to have him out of our lives. I think Frank may have been more ambivalent. At one point he told me that he wished he had had a brother, recognizing that Bobby had never really been a brother to either of us.

The years went by and we all went on with our lives. Mother and Daddy kept in touch with Luz, sporadically, for years.

When my father died in October 1988, Ruth, his second wife, received a letter from Nelia Porter, who had married Bobby, apologizing for Bobby not attending the memorial service, as he was sick. We didn't know that Bobby had married again and learned from the return address that they were living in a nearby town.

A couple of months later, Bobby and Nelia came to see me in my apartment in Washington, where I was living then. I was very surprised to hear from him, and was somewhat apprehensive to have him visit. When they arrived, I learned that Nelia, like Luz, was also from the Philippines. She had recently arrived here and spoke very little English. She appeared to be in her twenties; Bobby was fifty-eight.

Bobby looked old and thin. His hair was obviously dyed black. Our visit was strained, but pleasant enough. Nelia, a plump woman with a sweet face, sat on the couch and smiled a lot. I wondered how much she understood of the conversation.

I learned that Bobby had been living in that nearby town for many years. He was doing some kind of computer work, and they were living in an apartment in the house of a friend from his college years. He was angry that we thought no one knew where he was all this time, that we had not attempted to find him. He did not explain why he had not attempted to contact any of us, which would have been easy since Daddy had continued to live in the family home until his death. Bobby's main purpose in visiting me was to learn whether he would inherit any money from Daddy. He was disappointed but not surprised to learn that no, everything was left to Ruth, his widow.

Bobby said that at one time he had been teaching in a university in the Philippines, but that he had been fired, "for no reason." Then he was fired from another teaching position, and he said that the schools had all gotten together and prevented him from getting another job. In his view, he was being persecuted. The more he talked, the clearer it became that he was deeply paranoid. He blamed everyone else for all of his problems. "You know Daddy broke up my marriage to Luz, don't you?" he asked. As for the universities, "They all had it in for me." He recounted other incidents when "they were all against me."

Luz and Bobby Porter (Than R.), upon getting their Ph.D. degrees from NYU. The photo was in the *New York Times*, ca. 1960

I was relieved when they left, and hoped he would not contact me again. I was a little afraid of him.

During this visit I had learned much more about my brother, and when he left, I had to reassess a lot of my thinking of the previous thirty years or so. So much fell into place as a result of that visit. I realized that Bobby was not merely obnoxious; he was mentally ill, and probably had been since early adulthood. I felt guilty that I had just written him off, rather than trying to understand him or help him. Probably there was nothing I could have done, since he would not respond to any of us, but if I had known the situation, it would have at least changed how I thought about him all those years.

I had no more contact with Bobby or Nelia, but I had their address. When Frank died in 2011, I sent them a note with a copy of the obituary. I heard nothing back at the time.

Nelia's letter in August telling me of Bobby's death was astonishing. She described what a wonderful man Bobby had been, how kind and loving and generous, and how much she would miss him. She also said that none of the three children had responded to the news of his death or had attended his service. She was hurt and puzzled, and asked me if I knew why they would do that.

Nelia's question about why the children were estranged from their father put me in a quandary. I needed to respond, and I struggled with how to be both honest and kind. I was grateful that my brother had apparently found happiness and satisfaction in his life and certainly did not want to tarnish his memory for his widow, but I also owed it to his children to be truthful to what I knew—or at least true to what I had been told.

I wrote to Nelia, explaining as gently as I could that the story I heard was that Bobby "mistreated" his children when they were young. She wrote me a long letter in response.

Nelia said that Bobby was never violent with her, that all he needed was someone who understood him and his "depression." She added that he was a fine man, a good educator, and a very brilliant man. She said they had a good life together.

I doubt that Bobby ever had a professional diagnosis of mental illness or any treatment. Calling it depression may be accurate, but it is more likely a euphemism for paranoia, even schizophrenia. Of course I can't be sure of that. I can't be sure of any of this, except that he had twenty-five years of marriage with Nelia, and she says it was a happy time. That has to be enough.

49 Shift

Sometime in 2011, I began to feel an internal shift. I had always been an initiator: If I had an idea, I made it happen. Whatever opportunity came along, I grabbed it and ran with it. But I began to pull back a little, to put myself out there less often. It happened gradually, unintentionally. It was like somebody turned my dial back ever so slightly when I wasn't looking. I started wanting to take a back seat to everything.

I began to feel a distancing—not a wall exactly, but a veil between me and other people. It was not unpleasant, and didn't feel like a loss. Just different, and puzzling.

Is this what it means to get old? I wondered. I was seventy-eight that year. My health was still good, I was my usual cheerful self, and I wasn't depressed. I had plenty of energy—it was something else. I had no *drive*.

Does everyone experience this, whatever it is? I didn't know who to ask. I hadn't read about this and hadn't heard any of my friends talk about it. I wanted to know if this was a universal experience or something peculiar to me, and I didn't know many people my age well enough to ask such a deeply personal question.

This would make a good book, I thought. *Time for research.*

I started reading. I got books from the library by older people, mostly women, and each book sent me to another one. I read May Sarton's memoirs, Gail Sheehan's books, even some Jung, and other authors I hadn't heard of. Much of the writing dealt with the stage near the end of life, which wasn't surprising considering the age period being addressed. I found lots of thoughts about getting old, but nothing exactly like what I was experiencing. I went online and found blogs and essays. I read about thirty books and articles. They were all interesting, but didn't address what I was looking for.

My next thought was simply to ask people about their experiences. Who could I interview? I could start with a few neighbors. The first was Bernice, my former neighbor in Spring Meadows, who was eighty-eight years old then. I took a tape recorder and talked to her for almost two hours. I thought that if I started slowly, just asking her to reminisce about her life, I could lead up to asking about her inner life in her old age. It was harder than I expected. She was eager to talk about her life, but I struggled to find the right words to express just what I was looking for. Either she had no inner life, or she didn't want to share it with me, or she couldn't put it into words. She was comfortable talking about death and what it feels like to be old, but it didn't sound like what I was experiencing.

"Oh, I don't do the things I used to," she explained. "I just don't have the energy and my hip hurts and my hands are too jumbled up to crochet anymore. And I quit driving, so I don't go anywhere unless my daughter takes me. So I stay home a lot."

These were physical challenges, not mental or emotional. I could identify with them, although not at the level Bernice was experiencing, but physical challenges were not what I meant.

I interviewed more people—my neighbors Pat and Lovena, and then friends Sarah and Jane together. The three of us had a lively, fun conversation about getting old. I transcribed all of the interviews and looked for indications of any feelings like mine. I didn't find any. Finally, a friend offered to interview *me*, to see if talking about my own life would reveal clues about what was happening. It didn't.

Eventually I sat down at my computer and tried to write the beginnings of a book. I worked on an outline, and then on an introduction. But after hours of writing, I realized there was nothing there. It was all fluff; there was no meat in it. I had put hours and hours of effort into reading and interviewing and transcribing and had found nothing to use.

Meanwhile, life went on, and one day I realized the feeling was gone. *Well, how weird,* I thought. *What was that all about?*

Maybe the reason I couldn't find what I wanted in the interviews was because it wasn't a life stage at all, just a phase that I happened to go through. Maybe it was unique to me. Maybe I had just been over-stretched and needed some time off. I don't know why it happened or why it went away.

And then it dawned on me: I had been doing the very thing I thought I couldn't. I had jumped into finding an explanation for why I had lost initiative! Perhaps the effort itself was the antidote to whatever was going on.

And I felt better when I realized it wasn't all wasted effort. I had learned about other people's lives, especially how they were facing death, and collected material that may be useful eventually. Maybe the feeling will come back when I'm in my nineties, and the research will be more relevant and it will be time to write about it.

In April 2013 I turned eighty. At seventy I went to Europe for two weeks, and at seventy-five I took a three-week trip up and down the East coast, but this time I wasn't up for anything so demanding.

I decided to have a party and invited thirty people to an open house, expecting that they wouldn't all come at once as my living room wouldn't seat them all. Fortunately, people came at different times, and not more than twenty were there at a time so we could all squeeze in. It was interesting to get people together from different groups in my life who didn't know each other. I probably should have planned some activity to get them to mix, but I didn't, and it was a rather sedate party, unlike some I've hosted in the past. But I enjoyed having so many of my friends in my house.

Reaching eighty felt good. Such a solid number! Any more years would be a bonus.

Since my teens, I had always appeared younger than I was, and to some extent still did, even as my hair turned gray. I was fairly slim, energetic, and active. I found that my appearance worked against me sometimes, as people expected me to be more capable than I was. I felt like saying, "Give me a break. I'm an old woman! I can't do that!"

I had to recognize that I was getting old; denial was not helpful. Life was becoming a series of adaptations.

I wasn't as strong as I used to be and had less stamina. I couldn't walk much more than a mile at a time and couldn't stay out in the sun more than a few minutes without getting heat stroke. That was a new thing: I had no idea heat stroke came with old age. My doctor prescribed a handicapped placard for my car so I could park near buildings on hot, sunny days. It felt strange to be officially "handicapped." I could still mow the lawn, but I had to do it in stages, in the evening when it wasn't sunny.

I had gradually been adapting to less and less gardening, planting everything in large pots because I couldn't get down to the ground anymore. I wrote frequent notes to myself, because I was forgetting things. Nothing major, just enough to be annoying.

I started restricting my driving at night. I stuck to streets I was most familiar with, and stopped driving to outlying towns after dark. One day I realized that I was feeling somewhat incompetent behind the wheel, which was really disturbing as I had always been a confident driver. Suddenly I realized what the problem was: I was sitting too low! I already used a cushion, but I needed an additional one. I added another two-inch cushion, and I was fine again. What a relief! I knew I was shorter than I used to be, but didn't realize that it would affect my driving. I could see over the wheel, but the angle I was seeing the surroundings changed when I was an inch shorter. I wondered how many other elderly drivers, especially women, were losing their competence behind the wheel because they shrank as they aged. I had lost an inch and a half in the past ten years. I had always been short, and now I was barely five feet tall.

It was also time to think about end-of-life issues. Arkansas publishes a document called *Five Wishes* that details what people want and don't want for treatment if they become incapacitated. I changed it a lot, adding conditions and removing others, until I had a statement that satisfied me. The next time Gary and Cindy came for a visit, I sat them down in my living room with Grace and John and went over my statement with them. That's a hard conversation to have, but they responded positively. They all needed to be aware of my wishes and agree with me and with each other about when to "pull the plug." I opted for less treatment rather than more, since I'm comfortable with dying and don't want to prolong the process.

That out of the way, I next needed to look at the future of my finances. I was still editing to support myself, and expected to do so for some time yet, but probably not for many more years. How long could I keep up with technology? How much longer could my brain handle the details of editing? As long as I stayed with what I knew, editing was almost automatic after 28+ years, but if I had to learn new software I would be in trouble.

My Social Security check was too small to live on. My children assured me that they would help me financially when I needed it, but being dependent on them was absolutely my last choice. Could I possibly get my expenses so low that I could actually live on that check? I started looking at options.

The obvious first move was finding a cheaper place to live. I loved my two-bedroom duplex, but it was bigger than I needed, and the rent kept going up. The rent and the utilities already took up two thirds of my Social Security check.

The Fayetteville area is an expensive place to live. Even the smallest apartments cost more than I could afford. Then I remembered that my friend Jane had moved into a complex that was designed specifically for low-income seniors, and I checked it out. It was still more expensive than I wanted, but could possibly work, so I applied. The waiting list was two years long! That actually seemed about right, as I was confident I could work for that much longer. I was thinking long term.

How else could I get my expenses down? I had kept detailed records of my income and expenses for years, so went over them and noted where my money went. I could reduce many of the expenses, and if I were really frugal, I could almost live on my SS check. Asking Grace and Gary for a small amount monthly felt acceptable, and I began to relax that I had done all I could to prepare for the future. The Universe would take care of the rest, as always.

50 Politics

Meanwhile, I continued to be immersed in community activism. The Quaker meeting often had a book study group, and in 2014 we studied *The New Jim Crow*, by Michelle Alexander. The book explained how the criminal justice system methodically targets black men, incarcerating them at an alarmingly high rate. The result is a system very similar to the Jim Crow laws of the twentieth century. I had no idea how strongly I would be affected by that study.

As we discussed the book, we became more and more incensed. This was not justice! We were inspired to take action. I asked the Meeting to revive the Peace and Justice Committee that had been dormant for several years, and volunteered to clerk it. (In Quaker terminology, "clerk" means chair.) The Meeting agreed, and in February of 2015 the new P&J committee was established. That committee became the focus of my activism for the next few years.

We immediately realized that as law-abiding, middle-class citizens, most of us knew little about how the criminal justice system actually worked, so we set about educating ourselves. We invited various professionals in the system to join us individually at our monthly meetings, including the local police community spokesperson, a retired public defender, a district court judge, the county prosecuting attorney, a former parole officer, and a lawyer who was a former judge, among others. We lobbied the state legislature and joined a group in Little Rock who sent a letter to the Arkansas Supreme Court asking for action on reforming the fees and fines system. The Court replied that a statewide committee of judges had been appointed to study the issue. The chair of the committee was a judge in Fayetteville, and we arranged for her to join us to report on the committee's progress. Over the next few years we had many activities to educate the public for criminal justice reform. We were an extremely active committee, and it required much of my time and energy.

One evening I attended a staged reading of life stories written by women residents at the local correctional center and was moved by their words.

If I had suffered the kind of abuse they experienced, where would I be today?

I responded by joining a group from St. Paul's Episcopal Church in Fayetteville to create a halfway house for women being released from the center. After several years of planning, it opened as Magdalene Serenity House with eight women residents.

The Prison Story Project expanded further to working with men on death row to tell their stories, and I was asked to join its board of directors. Later, the Arkansas governor decided to execute eight of the men on death row within an 11-day period in April. Some of the men were participants in the Prison Story Project, and the people in the project had come to know them personally. We were all devastated that these men were going to be killed, all within a few days, virtually a mass execution.

Even though I had not met any of the inmates myself, I felt that I knew them from hearing their stories, and their impending deaths weighed heavily on me. I needed to do something, but didn't know what. Then I felt what the Quakers call a "leading," a strong impulse to a certain action. I was led to stand in a vigil in a public place to bear witness to the executions. I told my Meeting and some other people that I was going to stand on the sidewalk in front of the county courthouse in Fayetteville for half an hour at noon, every weekday, from then until the end of the executions, a three-week period. I didn't know if anyone would join me, and I didn't care. I was willing to stand there silently, every day, alone if necessary.

When I attended an event at St. Paul's, the pastor during his announcements asked me to speak about the vigil. I had not intended to make a public announcement and was taken by surprise, but I thought, *Oh well, why not?* and stood up and described what I planned to do. Unexpected tears rolled down my cheeks as I spoke. I had no idea that I felt so strongly about it. As a result, some people from that church joined the vigil, every day.

I was careful to state that this was a *vigil*, not a demonstration or a pro-test. No signs, no shouting. I did hold one sign that said "8 executions" so it would be clear why I was there. I was pleased that other people joined me, sometimes as many as fifteen, sometimes only three or four. Several days I was standing on busy College Avenue, facing traffic with my eyes closed, and then looked up and saw that people had approached qui-etly and were standing beside me in a line stretching down the sidewalk. Some passing motorists honked their horns or shouted support. I was surprised that a local TV station showed up for an interview.

Over the three weeks, four of the men were executed, and four others had a stay of some kind. We all grieved hard for the ones who died. It was a sad time.

I had never done anything like a vigil before and didn't know what it would be like. It was an odd feeling, just standing there, in public, silent, not moving. I soon realized that bearing silent public witness is a pow-erful statement. Many friends and acquaintances approached me and thanked me for doing it. The men on death row knew we were doing it and also thanked us.

****

And then came the November 2016 election.

I had rebelled at paying Cox any more money and disconnected my television months before, so was checking the returns from time to time on the computer. Eventually I clicked on CNN and saw the shocking news: PRESIDENT DONALD TRUMP!

I couldn't believe it. *No, it can't be!* I felt horror, disgust, and dread, and the following weeks and months proved Trump's presidency to be every bit as disastrous as I feared. President Trump appointed people to key cabinet positions who either had no expertise in their agencies' fields or were opposed to them and were clear in their intention to reduce the agencies' powers. He also signed many executive orders that repealed those signed by President Obama, such as the order to protect the "Dreamers," the young people who had been brought to this country by their undocumented parents and had grown up here. Many of his actions were efforts to remove regulations that had been put in place to protect the environment and consumers. Acts of racism and violence escalated throughout the country, especially against minorities and women.

As the Republican majority in the U.S. House and Senate began their attacks on bills passed by the Obama administration, the progressive voters started organizing. Protecting our democracy became a priority for me equally with reforming the criminal justice system.

I joined an Indivisible group, based on a manual put out by a group of former Congressional staffers. Our first aim was protecting the Affordable Care Act, which Congress was set on repealing. People all over the country were rising up in protest, calling out Senators and Representatives everywhere demanding they not repeal "Obamacare." In northwest Arkansas, people from Indivisible staged a raucous town hall meeting with one of our senators that made international news. It was even written up in a newspaper in a small town in southern France!

I joined protests at our senators' offices, wrote letters, and made phone calls. I began a campaign of writing letters to the editor of the statewide newspaper in support of progressive issues and organized a group to write letters regularly. I posted my published letters on my Facebook page to get wider exposure, far beyond Arkansas. Many people who had never been politically active before realized it was time to step up and make their voices heard, resulting in new candidates on ballots around the country in the 2018 mid-term elections.

All of these activities continued simultaneously, with the Peace and Justice Committee continuing to be active, meaning I was involved in about eight different groups of one kind or another. I loved it. The busier I was, the more time and energy I had. I certainly had my drive back!

I saw my friends becoming more and more disturbed and depressed by what was happening to the country. They were so angry! It was hard to see the goodness in what was happening, but I was convinced it was there. People were suffering, as services were cut and violence increased. Looking deeper, however, I could see benefits.

For several years, some people had been predicting that our society would be experiencing a major upheaval. It was becoming clear that our major institutions were in flux: The traditional nuclear family was no longer the norm, the public school system was deteriorating, the heath care system was dysfunctional, the U.S. Congress was broken.

Sometimes systems have to be dismantled so they can be rebuilt. I saw the Trump administration as an instrument for shattering the status quo, allowing new systems to emerge. It would be a painful time, much as surgery can be painful in the short term but brings long-term benefits. I wondered how readers in years to come would see this time, how history would treat the Trump years. It may be a long time before the effects can be assessed objectively.

One benefit that was quickly apparent was that the American public woke up. The people began to take back their power as they realized they had not been paying attention. As the federal government failed to respond to public opinion, the public began to act on the local level. City and county governments began passing their own regulations, for instance, some cities followed San Francisco's example and declared themselves a "sanctuary city," refusing to cooperate with federal officers in arresting immigrants, and some jurisdictions outlawed "fracking" in their borders when the federal government wouldn't act. Ordinary citizens who had never been politically active began running for local offices. Change was happening from the ground up, as the forces at the top refused to act in the people's interest.

I believe there are planetary forces at work that will eventually prevail to create a better society. Taking the long view, I could not join my friends in their anger and fear. My basic faith in the Universe reminded me that, contradictory to appearances, as Julian of Norwich said, "All will be well." Actually, I prefer the wording "All *is* well." Under the surface, and on the grand scale, all is working toward the benefit of humankind and the planet.

It's important that I do my part to bring that about, but fortunately, it doesn't depend on my efforts alone.

51 Subtle Energies

An even bigger issue than protecting our democracy that got my
attention at this time was climate change. It was not a new issue, but had
moved from the fringe to the mainstream, and people and organizations
were advocating many activities to curb it. I had always supported their
efforts, but I had become convinced that it was too late, that the damage
to our environment was irreversible and we were in for some unavoidable difficulties in the years ahead. We could take steps to mitigate the
results, but the ultimate effects were inescapable.

Simultaneously, I sensed a spiritual awakening, with thousands, perhaps millions, of people around the globe developing a higher spiritual
consciousness. These two trends inspired me to think about how I could
prepare myself for the coming changes.

I always had a strong sense of security, that whatever happened to
me externally would never hurt me internally. I even had a vague belief
that actually nothing would ever hurt me externally, although on one
level I knew that was magical thinking. It was comforting, nevertheless. I
thought that whatever happened with climate change, I could adapt to it
successfully. I was fairly confident that my inner security would sustain
me through any threats from climate change.

But I didn't want to go through it alone. I wanted to be with a group
of people who were aware of the coming changes and were spiritually
conscious enough to deal with them creatively. I wanted to connect with
people who would meet regularly to understand the deeper meanings
of the coming changes, and support each other with our inner resources

and resilience, whatever happened. But who could I get to join me? I thought of one person and asked her if she was interested. That conversation reminded me of another person, and that person suggested another, until we had six people who agreed to meet. We called ourselves a salon, and started meeting one afternoon a month. That group, combined with the Quaker meeting, has deepened my spiritual life in the years since.

The group included some world travelers who had connections with highly conscious people around the globe. One of them was personally connected with David Spangler, a spiritual teacher on the West Coast. I had heard of David, and now began to read his books and newsletter. He is not a "guru," but a teacher who shares insights from his experiences for others to learn from.

David's experience is with what he calls the "subtle world." He connects with "subtle entities," nonphysical beings who appear to him and tell him about their world. It might sound crazy, but he is well grounded with a background in science. It's not channeling, nor is he clairvoyant. He connects with the energies and understands communication from them nonverbally. His work with the subtle energies overlaps well with the MAP system that I had been using for many years.

The MAP (Medical Assistance Program) invokes nonphysical entities who come to help with healing whatever ailment the petitioner asks about. As I explain in an earlier chapter, I learned about it from material by Machaelle Small Wright, who established the Perelandra farm in Virginia. Perelandra is similar to Findhorn in Scotland, but on a much smaller scale. Machaelle invokes devas and nature spirits to help with the cultivation of the plants on her farm. I visited Perelandra a couple of times when I lived in Maryland.

I realized that the entities invoked in the MAP system are similar to the subtle beings David invokes. David's work encouraged me to accept the reality of nonphysical beings who connect with us. All the major religions record instances of supernatural or subtle beings appearing to people, such as the archangel Gabriel appearing to Mohammad and Jesus appearing to the disciples after his resurrection, and these appearances are accepted as valid by their followers. Was this different?

All those years I had been using MAP for my health, I had no evidence whether anything was actually happening. Were there really entities on my "team" who were healing my body? All I could be sure of was that I was relatively healthy. I didn't know how much to attribute that to the MAP system, but I wasn't about to stop using it to find out.

As I approached eighty-five, all these influences began to pull me farther and farther away from the mainstream. My lifestyle didn't seem extreme to me, but I was moving away from the way most people lived. I didn't have a TV, didn't listen to commercial radio, rarely went to movies, didn't eat processed food, bought my clothes at thrift stores, was a Quaker, read four or five books a week from the library. I even played solitaire with real cards on the kitchen table. Who does that in the twenty-first century?

Once, for some extra cash, I considered answering an ad to rate products, until I saw that I would never buy any of them—Hostess cup cakes, Fruit Loops, Hamburger Helper, Mountain Dew.

I fell farther and farther behind on current culture. I recognized only a few names of famous singers and actors, and had never seen most of the popular television programs. The material world was still important and I liked being comfortable, but the immaterial world was becoming equally important.

One evening I had an experience that brought that home to me. I had been living alone for many years, and most of the time I was fine with it, but once in a while I felt intensely lonely. This particular evening I was lying on the couch, wishing I had a partner and feeling very alone, when suddenly I was aware that my house was filling up with a warm, loving presence. It gradually filled the whole house, like rising dough or an expanding cloud. I couldn't actually see it, but I could feel it strongly. It felt golden and sparkling. It was clear to me that I had not ever been alone, I just hadn't been aware of the presence that was always there. And this presence would not die or leave me; it was permanent. I have not felt so lonely since.

The Universe has a way of bringing me what I need just when I need it. This time it was a book, *On Becoming an Alchemist,* by Catherine Mac-Coun, listed as recommended reading in one of David Spangler's books. I probably would not have looked at it if David had not recommended it. Other books about alchemy I'd seen were full of arcane symbolism and gibberish. This one was different.

MacCoun explains that alchemy is not merely metaphorical, but an actual physical reality. The book explains how one can learn to change the physical world by nonphysical means.

What an exciting thought! Could I learn to do that? Maybe my magical thinking isn't so outlandish after all. If the nonphysical beings that David and Machaelle interacted with were real and available to me, it wasn't such a stretch to think that I could become an alchemist.

MacCoun says that in alchemy, the change takes place in the "between," the relationship between you and what you want to change. She says you must first discover your true relationship with it, and then change it by changing yourself. She claims that alchemy never defies the laws of nature, but observes the workings of those laws at an earlier stage than is evident to the physical senses. Anything that manifests on the physical level begins with an idea or intention, and matter is too dense to be altered just by the mind, but ideas and intentions are the mind's natural medium. If you can perceive something at the formative stage, you can alter the intention that gives rise to it and thereby change the material outcome. That made sense to me.

She goes on to describe some exercises to help develop the necessary imagination to get started. One that fascinated me was to mentally picture chairs—all the different kinds of chairs you can think of, and then picture *chairness*—without a chair. I can do it for a split second, but no more.

I wanted to somehow combine alchemy with the other two systems, David's work with the subtle energies and the MAP system. I didn't know how I could do that and still function effectively in the physical world. I didn't want to become a hermit or a monk; I still felt compelled to be an activist and I enjoyed my creature comforts, simple though they were. Life in a cave or monastery didn't appeal to me—not yet, anyway.

How far could I go in withdrawing? What would have to change? How could I balance intense inner work and an active outer life? This was not a new dilemma. I thought about Brother Lawrence and his little book *Practicing the Presence,* and another book about fundamentalist Christians who pray to God constantly for answers to the most mundane things, like what shirt to wear for the day. There are models out there, if I wanted to look for them.

For now, with all my activities and working and writing, there wasn't going to be much time for long periods of meditation, or whatever it would take to become an alchemist. It would have to wait.

52 Turning Point

One evening in March 2018 as I was getting ready for bed I happened to notice a strange indentation in one of my breasts.

Well, that's weird. Guess I better get it checked out.

My primary care doctor sent me immediately for a mammogram. When the diagnosing doctor saw the result, she said, "There's definitely a mass there and I'm ninety percent sure it's cancer. But," she hastened to add, "it's treatable and it isn't going to kill you."

That was somewhat reassuring, but still a concern. *There's a ten percent chance it's benign,* I thought. *Not good odds, but better than none.*

The needle biopsy was scheduled on the Friday before Easter and I wouldn't get the results until Monday. On Sunday the family gathered at Grace and John's house for dinner to celebrate jointly Easter, my birthday, and grandson Luke's birthday, and I didn't say a word about my diagnosis. It would have been a downer on a festive occasion, especially with Luke home from college for the holiday. But it felt weird to keep quiet about such significant news.

Monday I got the call that the mass was malignant, as expected. Next came the MRI to determine exactly where and how big it was. For the MRI I had to lie face down in a machine with my arms extended straight out over my head and not move a muscle for thirty minutes. Not painful, just extremely uncomfortable. In fact, it was so stressful that as soon as they started to move me into the machine, I realized I couldn't do it. I said, "*Stop!* Let me up! I can't do this. I'm going home."

The technicians didn't know quite what to do. After some discussion, as I was getting dressed, one of them said, "We have another opening at 3 this afternoon. How about you come back then and we give you some Valium? Maybe that will relax you enough to get through it."

"Okay. I'll try." So that's what we did, and it worked. It was still unpleasant, but tolerable.

After the MRI I saw a doctor (interestingly named Dr. Harmes) who interpreted it for me.

"If you have to have cancer," he said, pointing to the images on the screen, "this is the best possible kind to have. It's slow growing, probably hasn't spread, can easily be removed, is estrogen receptive positive, and hardly ever comes back." He rattled off some numbers, all of them very good.

But I still didn't know for sure that it hadn't spread. Only examining tissue from lymph nodes during the surgery would determine that. It probably hadn't, but in life and death situations, *probably* isn't good enough.

For the next few weeks, I considered what might happen to me.

What if it has spread? What if....?

I could die. I might have to decide how much treatment I wanted. What about a mastectomy? A double mastectomy? Would I do multiple rounds of chemo? Radiation? At what point would I say, eighty-five years is enough, I'm done?

All my philosophizing about death needed re-examining. It wasn't just hypothetical anymore. I probed deeper into what I *really* thought and *really* felt. Was I actually okay with dying?

Yes, I thought. *I really am okay with dying. Maybe I won't see the grandchildren married and with their own kids. There's no end to the milestones I'd like to see, but I won't see them all. This is as good a stopping place as any. And I'm eager to see what's on the other side.*

That felt right.

On April 26, three weeks after my eighty-fifth birthday, I checked into the hospital for a lumpectomy. I had confidence in my surgeon, a grayhaired, grandfatherly man, who had been highly recommended by two of my nurse friends.

When I woke up in the recovery room, Dr. Eck approached my bed and said with a wide smile, "It hasn't spread. The lymph nodes are clear. You're fine. You won't need any further treatment. "

It was the easiest surgery I've ever had. Recovery was quick and almost painless, with no after effects besides a slightly mutilated breast—a small price to pay.

I can live with that, I thought, and then chuckled. *Yes, I really can* live *with that!*

****

They don't mess around with cancer. From the time I saw the indentation in my breast until I was cancer-free was exactly seven weeks: discovery, doctor, mammogram, biopsy, MRI, and surgery—just like that. Finished. No more treatment needed. I've had dental work that took longer.

The physical effects were minimal and brief, but the mental effects were more significant and long-lasting. One of my first reactions when I thought the cancer might have spread was *"Oh, no! I can't die! I haven't finished my book!"*

That was funny at first, and then I realized I was serious. I had to concentrate on writing and getting my memoirs done! I recalled that my brother Frank had been writing his book of essays for twenty years and died with it unfinished. The manuscript may languish in a box somewhere and never be published. I couldn't let that happen to me.

The whole episode led me to take stock of my life. Where was I putting my time and energy? What was priority?

While I was pondering all this, I learned that the senior apartment complex I had applied to live in had raised their rent, and living there wouldn't save me much money. Now it wouldn't make sense for me to move, which was actually a relief, as I had had misgivings all along. I didn't really want to live there, but I thought I had no alternative if I wanted to stop working. My rent was sure to go up, as property values in my area had risen sharply in the past two years.

I wanted to stay in my duplex, but to do that, I had to give up thoughts of retiring and do the opposite: increase my income by expanding my editing practice. Retiring was a fantasy; it was never going to happen. Fortunately I had work I could do, which not many women my age could say. I decided I needed to concentrate on two things: earning a living and finishing my book. Everything else had to take a back seat. I had spent more than fifty years saving the world, and now it was someone else's turn.

To free up time and energy, I set about withdrawing from most of the responsibilities I had taken on with all those organizations. One by one, I resigned from my leadership positions. I knew I needed to stay involved with people to avoid the isolation of living and working alone, so I would continue to attend some meetings but not be responsible for anything.

Withdrawing from community activism would also give me time for a social life. I could meet a friend for lunch or coffee, and go to an occasional movie. I would stop following up on emails from organizations or reading materials they sent me. I started automatically deleting emails from various groups, unread, although I couldn't quite bring myself to leave their email lists entirely. That seemed too drastic.

I decided this would be a six-month sabbatical from volunteering, which would allow me to finish the book and give copies to the family for Christmas presents. It could become permanent, but I wanted to keep the door open to returning. Could I really give up activism? Maybe it was an essential aspect of my personality. I would find out.

I would also have time and psychic energy to engage more with the subtle worlds. Working and writing would not require all of my attention; I would still have time to devote to meditation and connecting with subtle beings. Reaching that state of meditation takes time and commitment, more than I have been willing or able to devote to it in the past. Clearing my mind of distractions requires taking attention away from day-to-day tasks, and I wanted to discipline myself to maintain a dedicated schedule of listening and connecting.

This was no minor tweak in my life; it was a major change in direction—clearly a turning point.

* * * *

Perhaps it is also an ending point, a good place to end this story of my life. It has been an interesting journey, both living it and writing it.

Growing up, I was developing as an independent nonconformist, and then spent twenty-three years in a marriage suppressing that person, trying to be a "good wife." My independent self eventually broke free, and I left to create my own life.

All the adventures and episodes during the years between leaving my marriage in 1978 and arriving in Arkansas in 2000 tested my adaptability and developed my resourcefulness. Moving constantly, establishing new relationships, working new jobs, creating new networks, all challenged me to find my own way. Some spiritual exploration was always occurring, but it was often overshadowed by earning a living and establishing myself as a competent, successful individual.

Living in Arkansas, I was close to family again for the first time since my divorce all those years earlier, except for the brief period when Grace and Veronica lived with me in Maryland when Veronica was a toddler.

In Arkansas, grandmothering became a major focus of my life. Being a Quaker added a significant religious dimension, the years of silent meetings helping to temper my natural hyperactivity.

Much of my energy during those twenty-two years was devoted to helping my children and grandchildren through various difficulties, but now, in 2018, the kids are settled, the grandchildren are pretty well launched, and I can turn my attention elsewhere. My health is good, I have work I can do, my mind is still pretty sharp, and while I don't have the energy of my younger years, I have enough.

Many times I have been distracted from my inner life, but I always came back to it. Spirit did not give up on me. I'm ready for a period of withdrawing from such an active life and entering into a deeper exploration of the nonphysical world.

I estimate it will take me six months to extricate myself from all my responsibilities gracefully and to get this book into print. This will be a transition time, a time to acclimate myself to a more contemplative life.

But this is really not so much an ending as a beginning. Perhaps in ten years I will write Part 4, describing my adventures with the subtle worlds. Perhaps I will be an alchemist by then, although from reading MacCoun's book I suspect that will take longer than a decade to accomplish. Or I may find that this turn is temporary, a phase, and I will go back to saving the world.

Who knows what I will be doing when I'm ninety-five!

Granddaughter Veronica's graduation invitation picture at University of Arkansas, 2012.

Grandson Luke and his father, John Dunn, on Luke becoming an Eagle Scout, 2016

Grace Dunn, 2013.

Grandson Howie Leas, at his junior prom, 2012

Grandson Matt and Susan at their wedding with his daughter
Madeline, 2017

Simone and Josh Cantrell, at their wedding on July 14,
2015, in Belle Vista, Arkansas.

CPSIA information can be obtained
at www.ICGtesting.com
Printed in the USA
LVHW041917200120
644180LV00011B/502